THE CRISIS OF PHILOSOPHY

SUNY Series in Philosophy
Robert Cummings Neville, Editor

THE CRISIS
——OF——
PHILOSOPHY

Michael H. McCarthy

State University of New York Press

Published by
State University of New York Press, Albany

© 1990 State University of New York

Printed in the United States of America

For information, address State University of New York
Press, State University Plaza, Albany, N.Y., 12246

Library of Congress Cataloging-in-Publication Data

McCarthy, Michael H., 1942–
        The crisis of philosophy/ Michael H. McCarthy
                p.   cm.— (SUNY series in philosophy)
        Includes index.
        ISBN 0-7914-0152-9—ISBN 0-7914—0153-7 (pbk.)
        1. Philosophy, Modern—20th century. 2. Philosophy, Modern—19th
century. 3. Philosophy and civilization. 4. Civilization,
Modern—20th century. 5. Civilization, Modern—19th century.
6. Methodology.   I. Title.   II. Series
B804.M35 1989
                                                    190—dc19 89-30040

Contents

In constructing a ship or a philosophy one has to go the whole way; an effort that is in principle incomplete is equivalent to a failure.

Bernard Lonergan
Insight XIII

Preface

It has always been difficult for philosophy to define itself, to articulate its nature and purpose, and to state its distinctive relation to other cultural practices. At critical moments in its history, such self-definition has been required and partly achieved. When Socrates distinguished the philosopher from the sophist and cosmologist, when Aquinas clarified the contrast between philosophy and revealed theology, and when Kant differentiated transcendental and empirical inquiry, they were addressing deep cultural misgivings about their enterprise. The differences in cultural context required corresponding differences in philosophical response. In ancient Greece, Plato needed to distinguish Socratic dialectic from Homeric poetry and sophistic rhetoric and to demarcate Socrates' study of the soul from naturalistic speculations about the heavens. In medieval Europe, Aquinas needed to defend the power and legitimacy of natural reason against all who insisted that Scripture and tradition were the exclusive sources of truth. At a decisive moment in the history of the enlightenment, Kant needed to differentiate the method and purpose of philosophy from those of mathematics and the new science of nature.

The preceding examples suggest a significant interdependence between the history of philosophy and the history of culture. An important transformation in cultural context appears to require a parallel shift in philosophical self-understanding. During the past two hundred years, skepticism and uncertainty about the practice of philosophy have never been more acute. This enduring unease is traceable, in large measure, to the fact that philosophy again finds itself in the midst of a cultural transition. The classical culture shaped by Greek philosophy and medieval theology essentially has broken down; the distinctively modern culture that replaced it is still struggling for maturity. The extended crisis of philosophy through the last two centuries is the natural reflection of this ongoing crisis in modernity.

Modern culture differs from its classical antecedent in four significant respects: it is predominantly secular rather than religious; its scientific and cultural practices are independent of philosophical and ecclesiastical authority; it enjoys a heightened sensitivity to human historicity and change; and, its operative conception of human culture is empirical and pluralistic rather than normative (it no longer takes classical political and social arrangements as the measure of human order). Historical changes of this magnitude can properly be called critical. The Greek noun *krisis* (derived from the infinitive *krinein*, to decide) refers to a judgment or decision. Its Latin analogue, *discriminem temporis*, signifies a division in historical time, a turning point that disrupts the continuity between past and future. To speak of a crisis in philosophy, then, is to speak of a cultural turning point that requires philosophers to make a critical assessment of their common past and uncertain future.

It should not be assumed that a crisis in philosophy is only an occasion of peril. As the ancient, medieval and enlightenment contexts indicate, cultural turning points often precipitate historic philosophical development. In the contemporary context, momentous developments in the understanding of nature and history have required philosophers to rethink their conception of human rationality, their explicit ideal of knowledge, and their traditional view of philosophy's theoretical and cultural functions. The results of this reexamination have been uneven. It is generally agreed that classical theories of reason and science are no longer adequate and that the model of philosophic practice those theories supported no longer commands allegiance. But it remains a matter of the deepest dispute where philosophy is to go from here.

In earlier crises, the challenge to philosophy came from outside its own ranks: statesmen, theologians, or scientists put the practice of philosophy into question. In the present case, philosophers themselves are the severest critics of their own history. And these critics are thinkers of exceptional power and influence. Nietzsche, Dewey, Wittgenstein, Heidegger and Rorty, in their very different ways, have turned against the philosophical tradition in ethics, metaphysics and epistemology. They have tried to delegitimatize the traditional philosophical disciplines by dissolving their defining problems and by rejecting the vocabulary and distinctions required for their formulation. Richard Rorty, in particular, has made an explicit appeal for a postphilosophical culture, a culture in which the concerns of Socrates, Aquinas, and Kant are no longer taken seriously. To indicate the magnitude of the change he desires, Rorty draws an explicit parallel between his project and the modern process of secularization. Over the course of five centuries, European culture gradually abandoned its preoccupation with religious and theological questions. Theology ceased to occupy the central position in Western universities and became an optional or marginal region of the intellectual landscape. Rorty hopes that a historic transformation has begun in which the Socratic concern for the good, the Thomist absorption with God, and the Kantian attachment to rigorous science will become equally marginal and optional. If Rorty's expectations are fulfilled, the crisis of traditional philosophy will end with its gradual disappearance.

How has philosophy come to the point that some of its most original thinkers are calling for its abandonment or reconception? The remote origins of the present crisis are traceable to the scientific revolution of the seventeenth century. As the natural sciences matured and emancipated themselves from philosophical authority, philosophy began to lose its regulative theoretical function. With the emergence of mathematical logic and the empirical human sciences in the nineteenth century, the realignment of theoretical inquiry had reached a turning point. Revolutionary changes in the content of human knowledge had led to an even more fundamental change in the ideal of knowledge itself. Empirical science had become the paradigm of reliable cognition and the accepted measure of reality. In this empirical climate of opinion, philosophy's epistemic standing was compromised in two ways; first by its close association with metaphysical rationalism, and second by the conflation of its methodological practice to the exercise of speculative reason.

At the close of the eighteenth century, as the first stage of the enlightenment was culminating in the French Revolution, Kant appeared on the scene to assess the meaning of the Copernican legacy. Kant recognized the greatness of modern theoretical science, but he wanted to limit its scope and validity. He shared the empirical opposition to traditional metaphysics and theology, and he raised to the level of principle their critique of speculative reason. Yet, he argued that empirical knowledge rested on a deeper foundation of transcendental categories and principles; the recognition of these transcendental supports undercut natural science's claim to serve as the measure of being. The proper function of philosophy in an age of enlightened criticism is to submit reason itself to critique. Kant invented the discipline of transcendental epistemology and charged it with three related responsibilities: to protect the purity of pure reason, to preserve the rigor of theoretical knowledge, and to assess existing cultural practices against the requirements of reason and the criteria of science. Kant's transcendental strategy was intended explicitly to preserve the dignity of philosophy by assigning it a field of inquiry, a distinctive method, and a set of obligations more fundamental than those of its scientific rivals.

Kant was able to maintain the distinction between science and philosophy only by supporting a network of basic but controversial dualities. The most important of these Kantian dualisms were those between pure and empirical representations, transcendental and empirical methods of inquiry, and pure reason and nature as fields of existence and knowledge. In general, Kant assigned the investigation of the transcendental subject to philosophy and allocated the objects and relations of inner and outer sense to empirical science.

Two important traditions in nineteenth-century thought rebelled against Kant's dualistic scheme. Hegel and his disciples attempted to overcome duality in the direction of absolute idealism. Bluntly stated, they wanted to idealize nature by reconceiving it as the objective expression of absolute spirit. The idealization of nature led, almost predictably, to a countermovement committed to the naturalization of the mind. The naturalistic strategy received its strongest support from Darwin's evolutionary theory, which traced the causal origins of the human species back into the animal kingdom. Where Hegel had conceived the human spirit by analogy with divine Geist, the naturalists emphasized the continuity between rational human activity and the behavior of the higher primates. The nineteenth-century naturalists aimed at more than an ontological reversal of idealism. By bringing human reason and knowledge within the realm of nature, they hoped to naturalize philosophy itself. They accepted Kant's decision to make epistemology the foundational philosophic discipline. But they balked at his assertion that the theory of knowledge must be transcendental rather than empirical in character. The naturalistic strategy in epistemology was to make the theory of science an empirical scientific theory. The emerging discipline of experimental psychology was selected to undercut Kant's transcendental strategy by becoming the scientific theory of reason and knowledge.

The attempt to naturalize philosophy by transferring its epistemological functions to empirical psychology met stern and immediate opposition. Hostility to psychologism provided the critical bond between Frege, Husserl, and the early Wittgenstein. Although sensitive to philosophy's precarious situation, they rejected the solution offered by naturalistic psychology. Yet, they could not agree on a constructive program, providing philosophy with a theoretical project in complementary relation to empirical science. Frege restored rigor to philosophy through the practice of logical and semantical analysis; Husserl revitalized Cartesianism with his creation of transcendental phenomenology; in the *Tractatus* Wittgenstein identified philosophy with logic and metaphysics while sharply segregating both from empirical factual disciplines. Between 1879 and 1930, a concerted effort was made to reconceive philosophy as an authentic theoretical discipline and to recover its epistemic legitimacy. These programmatic exercises, of course, did not occur in isolation. The attempt to redefine philosophy provoked intense dialectical struggle among naturalists, neo-Kantians, phenomenologists, and adherents of linguistic and logical analysis.

If the first phase of modernity had been marked by the emancipation of science from ecclesiastical and philosophical authority, its second stage was shaped by a reconsideration of the arguments urged in support of scientific autonomy. In the seventeenth and eighteenth centuries, philosophy was attuned to the creation of a new science of nature. The dominant philosophical movements developed original accounts of reason and method to explain the unprecedented success of mathematical physics. In the nineteenth century the ideal of verifiable empirical knowledge was extended from natural into moral philosophy. The history of human ideas, institutions, and practices became the focus of the new empirical sciences of man. In this transition to a heightened historical consciousness, the influence of Hegel was prominently felt. Although Hegel's speculative idealism and his comprehensive philosophical synthesis were largely rejected by the empirical human sciences, many of the most important Hegelian themes were incorporated into their practice and outlook. Hegel's emphasis on concreteness and historical development, his stress on human sociality and culture, his attention to the multiple expressive embodiments of spirit, and his confidence in the immanent intelligibility of human history, gradually subverted the Cartesian and Kantian picture of human rationality and subjectivity. Hegel's emphatic historical consciousness initiated the second phase of the enlightenment and, in so doing, effectively challenged the original self-understanding of modernity.

The challenge of historical consciousness is apparent in three critical areas: the conception of human reason, the understanding of empirical science, and the reassessment of foundational epistemology. The dominant images of reason in the first stage of the enlightenment were fashioned by Descartes and Kant. Scientific reason had to be purified of all reliance on authority and tradition, liberated from all traces of history and all dependence on culture. This ideal of rational purity reached its culmination in Kant's transcendental ego, which, in its fundamental atemporality, was withdrawn from history altogether. As the naturalists had wanted to relocate human reason in nature, so the partisans of history wanted to relocate it in culture. In direct contrast to the Cartesian and Kantian pictures, historicized reason is situated in time, embedded in a social and linguistic community, and dependent for its ideas and beliefs on a process of cultural education. In the second stage of modernity, reason lost its purity.

The reconception of reason led inevitably to a new understanding of knowledge. The Cartesian picture of science is that of an axiomatic-deductive system of propositional truths resting on a foundation of self-evident principles. Knowledge in the strict sense is equivalent to science, and science is explicitly modeled on the Euclidean ideal. Although Kant alters some important features of Descartes's epistemological account, he preserves his insistence on apodictic certainty and stipulates the apriori character of scientific judgments. Kant's ideal of science is even more rigorous than that of Descartes. When historical reflection is brought to bear on the practice of science, however, a very different picture emerges. The self-evident axioms, the invariant logical structure, the required apodictic and a priori judgments, the Euclidean ideal itself, all become questionable. A new postclassical theory of science begins to emerge, in which scientific beliefs are treated as probable opinions rather than certain truths. The propositions of science signify verifiable facts rather than invariant necessities: they are regularly challenged by successive theoretical alternatives, and they rest on a nondemonstrative and historically variable evidential base. As reason loses its purity, science simultaneously loses its rigor.

But where do these important changes leave enlightenment philosophy as a whole? If the tasks of foundational epistemology were to protect the purity of reason, to preserve the rigor of science, and to test the compliance of cultural practices with the requirements of the epistemic ideal, then the entire project has been gutted by the new historical perspective. Since foundational epistemology was the heart and soul of modern philosophy, its decline as a credible enterprise leaves the future of philosophy in question. The first stage of modernity attempted to subvert the epistemic claims of theology and metaphysics. In the second historicist stage, the normative disciplines of ethics and epistemology were severely unsettled. Taken in its entirety, the modern age has left philosophy in crisis, with its past discredited and its future without prospect.

According to Richard Rorty (*Philosophy and the Mirror of Nature, The Consequences of Pragmatism*), this is precisely where *Philosophy* belongs. By *Philosophy* (upper case emphasized) Rorty refers to a historical tradition stretching from Plato to Husserl and Carnap, whose leading thinkers wanted to develop a rigorous science of being, goodness, and truth. From Rorty's perspective, the accepted distinctions in traditional histories of *Philosophy* between realists and idealists, rationalists and empiricists, actually conceal a deeper underlying unity. This is the fellowship of those who desperately tried to put philosophy on the sure path of science. Rorty opposes this fellowship even when it includes analytic philosophers to whom he is openly indebted. For Rorty, the enduring significance of analytic philosophy lies not in its aspiration to science, but in its demonstrated ability to put traditional *Philosophy* on the defensive.

The same can be said for Rorty's appreciation of the linguistic turn. He draws freely on Wittgenstein, Quine, and Sellars but he uses them for therapeutic rather than constructive ends. His purpose in adopting Quine's pragmatic holism, Sellars' principle of the ubiquity of language, and Wittgenstein's metaphoric therapy is not to make *Philosophy* finally respectable but to (finally) set it aside. Rorty acknowledges that the historic consequences of the end of *Philosophy* will parallel those of the end of theology. But in each case he expects Western culture to emerge from the change in a saner and sounder condition. The new *philosophy* (lower case emphasized) would model itself on literary criticism rather than science. It would be explicitly nonfoundational, nonrigorous, nonpure. The philosopher of the future would be an all-purpose intellectual, like Harold Bloom or Rorty himself, no longer judging the practices of culture from a standpoint beyond history, but willing to add his own variable voice to the ongoing conversation of humankind.

Rorty believes that if human historicity is taken seriously, the traditional philosophical disciplines of metaphysics and epistemology could not survive. The cultural shift from classical to historical consciousness marks a turning point in metaphilosophical reflection, a turn that Rorty contends should detach philosophy from its preoccupation with knowledge and engage it more fully with poetry and art. Rorty describes the shift he intends as a transition from epistemology to hermeneutics; if this transition occurs, cognitive practices and epistemic discourse would lose their special hold on the philosopher's attention. Human inquiry and cognition would be seen simply as one more way of coping with the environment that sustains human life. The most enduring consequence of Rorty's holistic pragmatism would be the end of traditional philosophy.

I am very reluctant to adopt Rorty's intoxicating story as the final word. He sees clearly that the cultural context of late modernity undermines the Cartesian and Kantian strategies that dominated the first stage of enlightenment thought. The postclassical theory of science is inconsistent with earlier forms of foundational epistemology; and the enlightenment absorption with scientific discourse to the exclusion of other forms of symbolic and linguistic meaning has unduly narrowed philosophy's range of attention. But the relentless emphasis on historicity tends to obscure the permanent human need for cognitive integration, a need Rorty's hermeneutic strategy leaves basically unmet. If philosophy has an enduring theoretical function that is challenged by a significantly new cultural context, then it needs to adopt a comprehensive strategy that is faithful to that function and responsive to its altered situation. Rorty's strategy is responsive to the cultural inclinations of late modernity, but it is not faithful to what is best in philosophy's past. As he has said, the self-image of a philosopher depends almost entirely on how he views the history of philosophy.[1] Where he seeks to overcome that history, to deconstruct and dissolve it, I seek to appropriate it critically, to make a patient and careful assessment of its achievements and limitations.

Philosophy's permanent theoretical function is the distinction and critical unification of the existing modes of human knowledge. The separation of modern science from common sense and the increasing specialization of the empirical disciplines have shattered the classical metaphysical synthesis based on Aristotelian principles. Specialized cognitive development since the seventeenth century has regularly outrun the effort of philosophers to integrate it. The human mind's native desire for unity has kept the yearning for philosophy alive, but the failure to design a plausible strategy of integration has made its traditional function seem quixotic. Is the aspiration to cognitive unity and wholeness still credible in the dynamic context of autonomous sciences that regularly revise their own theoretical principles? The answer is clearly negative if philosophers seek to achieve cognitive integration through the practice of logical inference. This reliance on logic, deductive, inductive, or transcendental was the underlying principle of unity in the different varieties of foundational epistemology. But modern science is an ongoing process of discovery, refinement, and revision, not a permanent propositional achievement; logical strategies of epistemic integration simply cannot keep pace with it.

The limitations of logic, however, should not divorce philosophy from its traditional synoptic intentions. The synoptic quest remains credible because the dynamic pluralism of contemporary science and scholarship is traceable to a unified intentional foundation. At the source of all cognitive development and revision is a normative pattern of recurrent and related intentional operations. There is a universal and invariant structure of cognition, a generalized empirical method, if you will, of which the methods of the empirical sciences and common sense are specialized determinations. This universal structure is not in opposition to historical change but the very condition of its possibility and meaning. To appropriate, to make epistemically one's own, this cognitive process, operative but not objectified in all human inquiry, is to achieve a foundational ground from which the critical integration of knowledge might proceed. The cognitive foundations in this strategy are not a fixed set of explanatory categories and principles or an invariant stratum of theoretical discourse but a matrix of intentional operations in which all categories and all discourse find their originating causal ground.

When science was conceived as a permanent propositional achievement, it was reasonable to attempt cognitive unification through logic. In the context of historical consciousness, when science is understood to be an ongoing, collective process of inquiry, the basis of unity becomes located in empirical method. This historic shift in heuristic strategy from logic to method has been actively developed by the Canadian philosopher Bernard Lonergan. Lonergan is as sensitive as Rorty to the philosophical significance of the cultural context of later modernity. But, unlike Rorty, he does not believe this requires philosophy to abandon its quest for cognitive unification. Rather, it requires of philosophy a new integrative strategy.

As Lonergan envisages this strategy in his most important work, *Insight*, it rests on the analysis and objectification of the invariant structure of human cognitional process. On the basis of an adequate cognitional theory, it is possible to develop a nuanced account of cognitive meaning, a normative theory of epistemic objectivity and truth, and a progressive and verifiable metaphysics. Rather than abandoning epistemology and metaphysics, Lonergan bases them critically and methodically on a theory of cognitional fact. Nor is he dismayed by the recurrent controversies that have made metaphysics and epistemology intellectually suspect. Recognizing that a critical philosophy must address the scandal of unresolved philosophical conflict, he develops a dialectical analysis of opposing accounts of knowledge, objectivity and being based on anterior theories of the structure of human cognition. Lonergan offers in *Insight* a comprehensive, critical, and methodical strategy of cognitive integration that fully respects the progressive and pluralistic character of contemporary science and common sense. Taken as a unified whole, Lonergan's work contains the firm outline and partial execution of a philosophical project continuous with philosophy's historic purposes and equal to the exigencies of the present. His is a notable theoretical achievement that should finally receive the critical attention it deserves.

In this Preface I have attempted to give the reader a preview of the philosophical narrative and dialectical strategy central to *The Crisis of Philosophy*. In its overall intention, this work bears a certain resemblance to Alasdair MacIntyre's *After Virtue*. Both works attempt to address philosophical crises through recovery and transformation of the Aristotelian tradition. MacIntyre was seeking a rational alternative to emotivism in practical philosophy. I am seeking a rational alternative to relativism and pragmatism in epistemology and metaphysics. In MacIntyre's philosophical narrative, the breakdown of the enlightenment moral project, best symbolized in the ethics of Kant, opened the door to emotivism. In my account, the shift from the first to the second stage of the enlightenment undermined confidence in the objectivity of knowledge. MacIntyre opposed the premodern moral tradition of the virtues to the Kantian emphasis on laws and rules. I oppose the premodern tradition of intellectualism in the philosophy of mind to the Cartesian and Kantian emphasis on ideas and concepts and to the later analytic emphasis on linguistic expressions. As MacIntyre tried to construct an objective contemporary morality around the central notion of virtue, I try to construct a comprehensive philosophy around the intentional operations of direct and reflective insight. In each case, core notions are borrowed from the Aristotelian tradition, even as that tradition itself is notably modified. MacIntyre's appropriation of Aristotle is explicitly selective. His theory of the virtues has a social rather than a metaphysical foundation and is attuned to tragedy and history in a way that Aristotle's *Ethics* was not. My appropriation of the Aristotelian tradition is equally critical. The core of that tradition, for my purpose, is Aristotle's epistemic realism, but I disengage that realism from Aristotle's theory of science and give it a critical foundation in cognitional theory that he did not. I share MacIntyre's conviction that the Aristotelian tradition requires a greater sensitivity to history, but an intellectualist understanding of human historicity does not require the rejection of foundational invariance. The classical tradition was not wrong to insist on something substantial and common to human nature and cognitive activity, but it failed to appreciate how that common ground was the basis for continuous historical development.[2] In a way that MacIntyre does not fully appreciate, the contemporary insight into history is consistent with the ancient concept of *physis*, as an immanent and universal principle of motion and rest.

At the beginning of a text as long and complex as this one, it is reasonable to ask what is really at stake in the crisis of philosophy. What difference will it make how the crisis is finally resolved? As I see it, the crisis of philosophy is inseparable from a more comprehensive crisis in modern Western culture. This crisis concerns the common meanings and values by which we live together, our working relation to the past, and our understanding of what it is to be human. This crisis has come about because our inherited religious and moral traditions have lost their authority. Modern philosophy attempted to replace religion as the source of cultural unity. But the progressive separation of cultural activity from the preoccupations of Cartesian and Kantian thought have opened the possibility that contemporary science and culture will be worked out in total independence of the philosophical tradition.

Since the beginning of the scientific revolution modernity has struggled with the fact of tradition. It could no longer accept tradition's authority as the great medieval theologians once did. The most influential modern thinkers viewed tradition as an inherited burden, as something from which to be liberated. But, in the course of the next two centuries, they gradually created an alternative tradition that Harold Rosenberg has called the tradition of the new.[3] In the second phase of the enlightenment with the recovery and expansion of historical sensitivity, the autonomous individualism of this new tradition has lost its credibility. Both the Cartesian and Kantian projects no longer command allegiance, but it is profoundly uncertain to what we should turn as we turn away from them. The hermeneutics of recollection typified by Gadamer calls us to recover the insights of traditional humanism. The hermeneutics of suspicion, represented by Nietzsche, Marx, and Freud, caution us of what is concealed beneath the masks humanism wears. We can neither simply belong to tradition nor disengage ourselves from it. And the same is true of our relation to culture and philosophy. What we seem to require is a form of critical belonging that makes the appropriation of cultural resources an occasion for independent individual thought. What we clearly require is a central core of thinkers who are at home in both the past and the present, and who are able to understand and appraise the achievements and limitations of each. The philosophers whom I most esteem are at the very center of that core, keeping the past alive, meeting the requirements of the present, and looking with common concern to the needs of the future. They represent what philosophy at its best has always represented, the human capacity for self-transcendence. It is this capacity that is defended or denied in philosophical quarrels about objective knowledge and the virtuous life. At the ultimate center of each cultural and philosophical crisis is the unending debate about our common humanity. What is it to be fully human? How shall we live together responsibly in freedom?

I want to conclude with a brief note on the critical standpoint and expository strategy of this text. The critical tradition to which I am most indebted is that of Aristotle. But like MacIntyre, I view that tradition as essentially dynamic and open to conflict. My deepest philosophical debt is clearly to Bernard Lonergan; his influence on my thinking is so pervasive I am really not sure where it begins and ends. I have drawn abundantly upon his extended contrast between classical and historical consciousness, his strategy of cognitive integration, and his foundational categories of analysis and criticism. But most of Lonergan's writing was directed to a very different audience from the one I envisage. His detailed exegetic work was on Thomistic and conciliar texts and his comments on the history of philosophy touch only marginally on the thinkers considered in this work. Thus, the interpretive reading of Frege, Husserl, Wittgenstein, Sellars, Dewey, Carnap, Quine, and Rorty is entirely my own. Where Lonergan was educated in the tradition of scholastic philosophy, my own specifically philosophical education began at Yale, where scholastic philosophy had very limited representation. Almost all that I know about philosophy, I have learned by nearly twenty years of teaching it at Vassar College. It was there, through numerous conversations with colleagues and students and long hours spent in the library, that my critical outlook has been shaped.

My expository strategy is fairly straightforward. In the opening chapter, I briefly outline the fundamental questions and themes that this work shall address. In the spirit of Aristotle, I use the next six chapters to compare and contrast the opinions of our predecessors insofar as they bear on the contemporary crisis in philosophy.[4] Unlike Aristotle, I make a deliberate effort to present their opposing views sympathetically. The intended result is a continuous dialectical narrative tracing the path of metaphilosophy from nineteenth-century naturalism to Rorty's linguistic and pragmatic holism. In the sixth chapter, the narrative strategy alters slightly, as I try to reconstruct the history of epistemology, as it appears from a critical standpoint synthesized from the writings of Dewey, Wittgenstein, and Rorty. I should make it clear that this epistemological narrative is not the one I would write if I were speaking for myself. I tried intellectually to pass over into their external perspective so that I could understand why Rorty drew such different conclusions from reflection on the same historical period. Chapter VII contains an exposition and partial defense of Lonergan's philosophical project in cognitional theory, epistemology, and metaphysics. The concluding chapter attempts a more extended defense of Lonergan's cognitional theory and the epistemic and metaphysical realism that it implies. This chapter outlines and then applies a set of dialectical principles conceived by Lonergan as a way of resolving enduring philosophical conflict. The theme of philosophical conflict brings the work full circle by returning us to the question of the philosophical tradition and its future role in the history of the West.

Let the last word of this preface be one of deep thanks: to my family, my colleagues, my students, and to those whose love of wisdom has sustained the practice of philosophy and made us care passionately about its future.

The Crisis of Philosophy

*The most difficult task of philosophy has always
been to define itself in meaningful ways.*[1]

A. Autonomous Science

A salient feature of the modern period of Western thought has been the narrowing of the province of philosophy and the reduction of its intellectual authority. This narrowing has been accomplished principally through the gradual but decisive emancipation of the empirical and formal sciences from traditional metaphysics and logic. In determining their own heuristic programs, methods of investigation, and theoretical principles, the new sciences have had to stake claim within what was originally philosophic territory. The reasons for this theoretical realignment have been complex, but the dominant note has been an erosion of confidence in the procedures and cognitive claims of philosophy coupled with a readiness to supplant them with the methods and theories of the emerging scientific disciplines.

The modern eclipse of philosophy finds its distant origin in the medieval period. In conceptually distinguishing theology from philosophy, Aquinas had invited human reason "to grow in consciousness of its departments of investigation, to determine its own methods, to operate on the basis of its own principles and precepts."[2] Aquinas' invitation was later accepted by the intellectual leaders of the scientific revolution and explicitly thematized in the philosophy of Descartes. Descartes' *Discourse on Method* proclaims the liberation of reason from the disciplining authority of the philosophical and religious tradition. He believed that reason is and ought to be autonomous in determining the truth about created existence. Although Descartes clearly separated reason from religious faith, he did not effectively distinguish metaphysics from empirical knowledge. This failure can be traced to his classical heritage and to his passion for theoretical unity. Descartes argued from the unity of the human mind to the unity of rational method and logical system: as human reason is essentially one, so its method and theoretical achievement should also be one in every province that it surveys. Although Descartes divided the universe of rational investigation into mind and body, this metaphysical dualism was paired with a monism of method and theory. The method for discovering scientific truth is the same whether we are examining God, the human soul, or the physical universe. He expected rational method consistently applied to result in a unified axiomatic system founded on intuitively evident truths. In Descartes' famous metaphor of the tree of science, philosophy serves as the roots of the tree because it establishes the indubitable axioms from which the mathematical laws of nature (the trunk) are to be deduced.[3] Philosophical axioms and physical theorems, though distinguished as logical ground and consequent, belong to a single deductive system embracing both metaphysics and mechanics. The logical continuity between philosophy and physics is apparent in Descartes' attempt to deduce the conservation of momentum in nature from the demonstrated immutability of God.

The result of the Cartesian theoretical project was unstable. Although he distinguished metaphysics from mechanics by supporting a real distinction between mind and body, this ontological division is effectively subordinated to the monism of method and theory. Descartes's successors were restless with his uneasy compromise. On the rationalist side, Spinoza refused to accept the ontological dualism; on the side of classical mechanics, Newton rejected Cartesian philosophical premises as the theoretical foundations of physics. As Galileo had struggled earlier to emancipate cosmology from Aristotle's metaphysical authority, Newton felt compelled to do the same against Descartes. With the advance of the scientific revolution from physics into biology and the empirical sciences of man (from natural to moral philosophy), a second and more subtle claim for autonomy was raised: that the liberation of reason from faith should be complemented by the liberation of empirical science from philosophy.

During the eighteenth and nineteenth centuries, this proposed emancipation was achieved. Philosophy surrendered its regulative control over science and suffered a crisis of identity and definition that it has not yet resolved. The low estate of philosophy, like that of religion, was due in part to their fighting unsuccessful rear guard actions against science. But there were other, deeper grounds for the malaise. Since the time of Plato and Aristotle the theoretical enterprise had been essentially coextensive with philosophy.

Philosophy symbolized the human effort to achieve systematic comprehensive knowledge about reality. With the advent of the scientific revolution and the gradual differentiation of the empirical sciences, this symbolism lost its force. Rather than representing the dynamic development of new knowledge, philosophy came to appear as the major obstacle to scientific progress. The modern sciences of nature, though in part a legacy of Greek speculative curiosity, were tied inseparably to considerations of power and productivity. The clear primacy accorded by the ancients to theory over practice was reversed in modern intellectual culture. Bacon's emphasis on fruits and works and Descartes's appeal to the flowering branches on the tree of science signaled a new alliance of scientific inquiry with the project of mastery and control over nature. The Greek identification of knowledge and virtue was transmuted by the moderns into a new indentity of knowledge with power.

The intellectual authority of Aristotle, against which the leading modern thinkers struggled, heightened the perceived opposition between philosophy and science. The original insights of Copernicus, Kepler, Galileo, Newton, and Darwin all faced resistance by central cosmological or metaphysical principles in Aristotle's thought. Although Aristotle in fact had been a deeply empirical thinker, he symbolized to the moderns the unhappy contrast between the speculative philosopher and the experimental scientist. This way of conceiving the contrast between Greek theory and modern physics was deeply misleading, emphasizing Aristotle's stress on logical demonstration to the exclusion of his empirical methods of discovery. But the moderns knew Aristotle through his supposedly finished system not through his practice of inquiry; and against that system, attributed to *the Philosopher*, they rebelled.[4]

Aristotle was an obstacle to the acceptance of modern scientific theories not because he was unempirical but because his heuristic principles and cosmological beliefs, invested with epistemic authority, were opposed to those of the leading moderns. The emphasis in classical mechanics on the measurement of physical variables, the correlation of those measurements through mathematical laws, the verification of those laws through observation and experimentation, and the potential utility of these results for prediction and control—for many these features became canonical indices of all authentic knowledge. As once physics had been required to satisfy the metaphysical and epistemic demands of philosophy, now the situation was reversed. The prestige of physics rose as that of philosophy declined, until the old representative of theory came to be judged by the standards of the new. The criterion of continuous intellectual progress was used with particular force to put philosophy on the defensive. A clear line of theoretical development could be traced from Copernicus to Newton, a line apparently without parallel in the history of metaphysics or epistemology. Neither the ancient concern with being nor the modern preoccupation with knowledge had established clear criteria by which conflicting philosophical claims might be adjudicated.

Philosophy lacked a decision procedure to bring its quarrels to a halt; it seemed to its critics to "revolve in a circle with mean and contemptible progress."[5]

Numerous interpreters of the crisis of philosophy have viewed its decline as the beginning of its disappearance. Positivism, philosophical naturalism and certain strains within pragmatism all foresee the eventual elimination of philosophy as the positive sciences become sovereign in the realm of inquiry. Once the theoretical enterprise was indistinguishable from philosophy; they believe it will soon be universally equated with the different branches of empirical science. Philosophy will have passed from the scene of knowledge, like royalty, never to return.

Historical communities find themselves in crisis when important developments or declines, both theoretical and practical, prevent their members from taking accepted judgments or practices for granted. Crises often reveal these uncritical acceptances to be prejudices or prejudgments; they force human beings to rethink the questions to which those judgments were originally answers or to confront new questions to which earlier answers are no longer relevant. It is now evident that the scientific revolution occasioned a crisis for philosophy and for the whole of Western culture.[6] The emancipation of empirical science from philosophical authority required philosophers to reconceive their intellectual purpose. Philosophy no longer controlled the sphere of theoretical inquiry. Did it any longer have a significant theoretical function? How was that function to be distinguished from the purposes of empirical science? Could philosophy be defined with a distinctive identity that made it a valued colleague rather than an archaic rival of the emerging scientific disciplines? One purpose of this book is to answer these questions as clearly and accurately as possible. But the answers I propose are informed by careful scrutiny of prior philosophical reflection on these issues. The unparalleled emphasis on metaphilosophy in the last one hundred years is the result of the intellectual dislocation just described. I do not consider this emphasis unjustified, nor do I think that contemporary philosophers should suspend their activity until they fully understand what they ought to be doing. In philosophy, as in other human pursuits, a crisis presents an opportunity for remembrance and for original reflection. Remembrance is needed to identify the sources of the present impasse; fresh thinking, if it is well aimed, may discover a new way for philosophy to go in the aporetic situation created by empirical science's achievement of autonomy.

It is important to recognize that the ongoing crisis of philosophy has resulted more from cognitive development than theoretical decline. Important distinctions were neglected by modern philosophers, earlier insights were often lost, and numerous errors were made; there was, I believe, a general decline in the level of philosophical understanding. But the emergence of modern natural science was a cognitive *advance* that produced a crisis precisely because it was a radical *development*. Earlier frameworks of integration supplied by traditional philosophy were not able to assimilate it successfully; nor, I would contend, were the new frameworks of integration proposed by the great modern philosophers. The intellectual culture of modernity still has not learned to understand and appraise its most influential achievement.

Every significant change requires adjustment by the environment that it affects; the depth of the required adjustment is proportionate to the depth of the corresponding change. The following sequence of epistemic categories is serially ordered to reflect progressively more important kinds of cognitive change. Note that in each case both identity and difference are required for an intelligible change to occur.[7]

1. *Change of belief*—a change in the truth-value of a proposition whose truth-conditions remain constant.
2. *Change of intension or sense*—a change in the truth-conditions of a proposition or the defining marks of an explanatory concept whose role in a system of theoretical explanation remains constant.
3. *Change in categorial framework*—a change in the truth-value of the set of propositional principles that define an existing horizon of inquiry or a change in the explanatory categories and vocabulary used to systematize knowledge in an ongoing specialized discipline.
4. *Change in heuristic structure*—the acceptance of a new model of intelligibility and explanation by a discipline that traditionally had been committed to an older one; when physics shifted from understanding nature in terms of Aristotle's four causes to understanding it in terms of empirically verified mathematical laws, a radical shift in its operative heuristic structure occurred.
5. *The emergence of new realms of meaning*—differences in realms of meaning have their source in novel developments of intentional consciousness. New realms emerge with the adoption of a specialized language and a distinctive mode of questioning, understanding and verification that constitutes a group as an intellectual community unintelligible to those not apprenticed in its ways of speaking, thinking, and acting. Different realms of meaning have different purposes and norms with reference to which they appraise internal success or failure. The purposes, exigencies, language, and mode of apprehension of common sense constitute a practical realm of meaning from which the theoretical realm of meaning has been progressively differentiated in Western culture. As common sense is a specialization of human intelligence in understanding the concrete and particular, so theoretical science is a complementary specialization in the abstract and universal on which the concrete converges or from which it diverges nonsystematically.[8]

6. *The historical evolution of a new stage of meaning*—cognitive development occurs through the specialization and differentiation of human inquiry. When common sense and theory were rudimentarily distinguished by Aristotle (as what is first for us and what is first in itself)[9] and more sharply divided later by Galileo in the first phase of the enlightenment, a new stage of meaning emerged based on the recognized distinction of complementary realms of meaning. At the outset of both classical and modern philosophy, no clear distinction was drawn between science and philosophy as forms of theoretical meaning. This presumed homogeneity was broken by the scientific revolution of the seventeenth century and fully destroyed in the nineteenth century by the development of numerous empirical sciences effectively independent of philosophical control. The emergence of the specialized sciences as autonomous theoretical disciplines is the first step in the evolution of a new stage of cognitive meaning, a step that has occasioned the present crisis in philosophy. But this historic transition is only the beginning of our story and only the first of the two major sources of the crisis. For, in the course of the scientific revolution, radical changes of belief, intension, categorial framework, and heuristic structure finally climaxed in a revised concept of scientific theory itself. This change in the *theory of science* is more important than any alteration in particular *scientific theories*. However, the two occurrences are not causally independent, for the emergence of historical consciousness in the human understanding of nature and knowledge precipitated the revised understanding of the theoretical enterprise and required a new definition of philosophy. The historical argument that I will be defending in this chapter can be put summarily: The crisis of philosophy since the nineteenth century is the joint result of the autonomous development of the empirical sciences within the theoretical realm of meaning and the transition from classical to historical consciousness in the understanding of scientific theory itself.[10] How is that second critical transition to be defined?

B. From Classical to Historical Consciousness

By *classical consciousness* I refer to a conception of theoretical science that dominated Western philosophy from Aristotle until Kant. It is a conception that originates in Greek geometry but was later extended to all the sciences of nature. As thematized by Aristotle in his *Posterior Analytics*, it holds that scientific knowledge is true, certain, knowledge of causal necessity reached by empirical methods of inquiry and systematized in an axiomatic deductive structure based upon self-evident definitions and principles. Science is conceived as the permanent achievement of truth attained through a disciplined but finite course of individual investigation. Theoretical invariance is to be found in the truths discovered by scientific inquiry, in their logical systematization, and in the objects whose intelligible structure the scientific propositions articulate. As the intelligible structure under investigation is permanent, so are the truths that give it scientific expression, mirroring in their logical progression the pattern of causal dependence within the order of being itself.

A clear distinction is required within this account of science between the order of inquiry and the order of demonstrated[11] knowledge. Science is the goal or *telos* of theoretical inquiry. It is the acquired epistemic power to demonstrate or deduce the essential truths about a subject matter, a power achieved through the successful completion of the process of discovery. As long as exploratory inquiry continues within a specific discipline, the ideal of science has not been achieved. According to Aristotelian principles, the nature of any reality is disclosed fully in its completed form (its *eidos* is revealed in its *telos*). A philosophical theory of science should articulate its constitutive essence; to do so it must be based on an examination of knowledge in its logically perfected state. To understand the oak tree you look to the mature specimen rather than the acorn; you look to the end or completion of the process not to its origin or stages of development.

Though Aristotle had a nuanced sense of empirical inquiry, the theory of science outlined in his logic focuses not on the ongoing process of discovery but on the permanent achievement to which it ideally leads. The impression given by the *Organon* as a whole is that scientific knowledge is a difficult but attainable objective, that it is an individual accomplishment admitting of closure and finality. Because of this expectation of closure, the acquisition of scientific knowledge brings certainty. Cognitive certitude and finality are necessary though not sufficient conditions of science. The truths of science, though discovered individually, can be taught to others as part of a timeless, permanent, public fund of knowledge. Because the conclusions of science are founded on the intuitively evident principles reached through inquiry, direct challenge to the truth of those principles puts the claim to science in jeopardy. The public dimension of science is compromised if the axiomatic principles of knowledge lose their compelling evidence. A central epistemic dilemma posed by this theory is the validation of axioms whose intuitively evident truth is denied. Whereas Aristotle recognizes that insight into first principles is the epistemic fruit of sustained investigation, he does not seem to anticipate the problem posed by alternative sets of explanatory axioms. His is an innocent confidence that foundational truths exist, that they admit of eventual discovery, and that their truth and explanatory priority will compel rational assent.

This confidence was shaken by the Copernican revolution in physics, which led in time to the repudiation of Aristotle's cosmology. Through the discoveries of Kepler, Galileo, and Newton, the axiomatic principles of Aristotle's physics were shown to be neither evident, certain, nor true. But the logical *ideal of science* first articulated by Aristotle retained its power even as his specific *scientific theories* were openly denied. The Cartesian quest for certainty, with its insistence on intuitively evident axioms, its conception of science as a permanent individual achievement, and its aspiration to true certain knowledge of causal necessity, retains the Aristotelian or classical legacy nearly unimpaired. It is true that Aristotle's concept of causality was abandoned by modern physics and replaced with a heuristic ideal based on invariant mathematical laws; and it is also true that the moderns subordinated theoretical understanding to practical power as the primary motive of science. But, with these important exceptions, the classical theory of science was faithfully preserved. The relentless search in modern rationalism and empiricism for indubitable foundations on which to erect the structure of science is unintelligible without the tacit acceptance of the classical ideal. *The problem of knowledge dominates modern philosophy insofar as it tried to fit modern scientific theories to the classical theory of science.* Kant's Copernican revolution in epistemology, despite its radical reconception of the metaphysical standing of the object of science, is still conservative in its endorsement of the classical position. For Kant, Euclidean geometry, Newtonian mechanics, and Aristotelian formal logic are all permanent theoretical achievements. Precritical philosophers had failed to uncover the full conditions of their possibility and thus had erred in their metaphysical interpretation, but they had not erred in upholding universality, strict necessity, and apodicticity as essential criteria of scientific knowledge.

As E. W. Beth has argued, there were dissenters from the Aristotelian canons of science in pre-Kantian thought but they were a distinct minority.[12] The classical conception of science survived the skeptical spirit of modernity. By its survival, it imposed on philosophy a distinctive conception of epistemology. Given that science must be a logically organized structure of truths founded on self-evident axiomatic principles, philosophy's task was to uncover those underlying principles, to establish their certainty, and to show, at least in principle, how the legitimate scientific disciplines could be reconstructed on this foundational base. Epistemic skeptics, like Hume, swim against the tide with their denial that this program can be executed. Hume's quarrel, however, is not with the definition of the project but with the power of human reason to complete it.

Despite significant changes in belief, intension, categorial framework, heuristic structure, and metaphysical conviction, the theoretical realm of meaning preserved its identity for two thousand years through constant adherence to the classical theory of science first outlined in Aristotle's logic.

That theory imposed on scientific inquiry a rigorous normative ideal, and it imposed on philosophy the task of monitoring scientific compliance with it. But in the nineteenth century, as the result of diverse cognitive pressures, the classical conception of science was subverted. By this I do not mean that philosophers universally abandoned it or that scientists explicitly repudiated it. Rather, it lost touch with the heuristic anticipations of actual scientific practice and eventually with the implicit meaning of the term *science* as used by those within and without the scientific community.[13] One way to describe the shift from classical to historical consciousness is to note that scientists surrendered the quest for epistemic certainty and adopted the ideal of complete explanatory understanding. Rather than perceiving the revision and replacement of scientific theories as a sign of defeat or failure, scientists came to view fundamental theoretical revisions as occasions of triumph.[14] These revisions, in turn, were not expected to be permanent achievements but relatively stable systemizations of understanding subject to further development and refinement. Classical consciousness defined science in terms of an allegedly finished propositional achievement; its successor, historical consciousness, defined it as an ongoing normative process of inquiry, unified by canons of method, resulting in a continuing succession of theoretical systems. No longer an affair of solitary individuals, science has become an essentially communal enterprise, marked by the specialization and division of labor, open to the collaborative sharing of controlled belief, and unified by the constant of empirical method. It no longer seeks theoretical invariance in permanent essences, unchanging natural laws, self-evident principles, or perfected categories of explanation but in the operative method by which laws are discovered and verified and categories and principles revised and refined. Bernard Lonergan's compact formulation effectively summarizes this most profound cognitive change:

> The Greek formulation as envisaged by Aristotle demands of science true certain knowledge of causal necessity. But: 1) Modern science is not true but only on the way to truth. 2) It is not certain; for its positive affirmations it claims no more than probability. 3) It is not knowledge, but hypothesis, system and theory, i.e. the best scientific opinion of the day. 4) It's object is not necessity but verified possibility. Natural laws aim at stating not what cannot possibly be otherwise but what in fact is so. 5) Finally, while modern science speaks of causes, still it is not concerned with Aristotle's four causes of end, agent, matter and form, but with verifiable patterns of explanatory intelligibility. For each of the five elements constitutive of the Greek ideal of science, the modern ideal substitutes something less arduous, more accessible, dynamic and effective.[15]

The transition from classical to historical consciousness had decisive implications for philosophy. At approximately the same time that philosophy lost its metaphysical authority over science, it lost its epistemic function of testing the compliance of actual scientific theories with the classical ideal of knowledge. Scientific practice proceeded without concern for philosophical direction and approval, while philosophy, deprived of its traditional theoretical functions, became divided and uncertain about its cognitive purpose.

The cumulative effect of these cultural and technical changes has been the creation of a climate in which human rationality and epistemic objectivity are in doubt. The demise of foundational epistemology has confronted philosophy with a new set of challenging questions:

1. What are the appropriate norms of rational consciousness, given that the Cartesian requirement of apodictic certainty no longer seems plausible?
2. Is the ideal of cognitive invariance and unity still credible in the face of conceptual pluralism and theoretical change; if it is viable, where might such foundational invariants be located?
3. What concept of semantic and epistemic objectivity is consistent with the essentially social and historical character of human inquiry?
4. What notion of truth and what kind of ontological import are still predicable of scientific theories, given the indirect nature of hypothetical verification and the lack of algorithmic decision procedures to resolve scientific disagreement?
5. What distinctive cultural contribution can philosophy make in an age of autonomous and specialized practices resistant to all forms of governing authority.

C. The Matrix of Cognitive Meaning—
An Orienting Map

By stressing the historical horizon of philosophy in the second half of the nineteenth century, I have not meant to imply that philosophy lacks a transhistorical purpose. A central argument of this text is that philosophy has a permanent integrative function to perform, but that reasonable strategies of integration will vary with the complexity of the materials to be integrated. Philosophic strategies of integration evolve as cognitive developments outside philosophy disrupt traditional frameworks of synthesis. The transition from classical to historical consciousness and the autonomous development of science which accelerated that transition have required contemporary philosophers to reconsider whether and how the integration of knowledge could now be achieved. As the succeeding chapters will confirm, there is no philosophical consensus about the strategy to follow in the project of cognitive synthesis. Some major philosophers in the contemporary period have resisted the transition to historical consciousness, fearful that it leads to epistemic relativism and the loss of theoretical objectivity. Others, like the positivists and philosophical naturalists, have proceeded boldly from the autonomy of science to the assertion of its exclusive theoretical legitimacy; they have sought either to eliminate the cognitive functions of traditional philosophy or to perform them with empirical replacements. Transcendental thinkers, like Cassirer, Husserl, and the early Wittgenstein, have opposed the reduction of philosophy to the level of factual knowledge while struggling to define the distinctive theoretical insight philosophy might continue to provide. There is no shared answer to the central question: What is the theoretical contribution of philosophy to be once the autonomous and historically developing sciences abandon the quest for certainty?

In the narrative that follows, I will explore and appraise opposing philosophic attempts to answer this basic question. To assist the reader's understanding of the narrative, I propose to outline a matrix of cognitive meaning. This matrix is meant to serve as a provisional map that will permit us to grasp the basic issues in the contemporary crisis and to chart realignments in the province of philosophy during the transition from classical to contemporary thought. The full significance of the matrix, its expository and critical power, should emerge with the gradual progression of the text. Distinctions asserted at this preliminary stage shall be defended as the argument of the work unfolds.

Let me begin with a brief introductory note on meaning. Animals live in an environment with which they enjoy both causal and intentional relations. But the limits of an animal's intentionality restrict the scope of its world. Animals clearly possess sensitive consciousness that they use effectively in adapting themselves to their immediate circumstances. They manage to survive both individually and collectively by orienting themselves within the world they experience directly. To the best of our knowledge the horizon of their consciousness is limited to this world of immediacy. The prelinguistic child is akin to the animals in the correlation between his or her consciousness and his or her world.* The infant also lives in a world of immediacy. With the acquisition of linguistic and symbolic powers, the child transcends its restricted environment and enters a larger world mediated by meaning. As the human person develops intellectually and morally, his horizon of meaning and responsibility continually expands. There is no fixed limit to the world of the human being because there is no fixed limit to human intentionality in its

---

*Terms such as "his" and "himself" should throughout the work be taken as abbreviations for "his or hers," "himself or herself," and so on. M.H.M.

intellectual and rational forms. Human perceptual consciousness, like that of the animals, is inherently limited, though it can be extended dramatically through the mediation of instruments devised by the mind and shaped by the hands. Intellectual and rational consciousness, however, are marked by an immanent tension. Although their actual achievement is always finite, their native orientation and tendency are inherently unrestricted. There is a restless dynamism characteristic of human intentionality that regularly goes beyond any finite achievement.

Because of intentionality, the human being's relation to the world is essentially mediated by meaning. The scope of our awareness and concern extends into the past and the future; the close-at-hand and the spatially remote; the possible, and obligatory as well as the actual. This many-dimensional world is open to us because of meaning. But human meaning is not a natural given like the sky above our heads or the earth beneath our feet. It has its source in intentional operations, both our own and that of the intersubjective communities to which we belong. This intentionality creates the meaning by which we understand the world and conduct ourselves within it. Purposive human transactions with the world are as complex as the patterns of intentional experience. We engage the world biologically, aesthetically, artistically, dramatically, practically, intellectually, and so forth. These different types of transaction are mediated by different functions of meaning. Intentional meaning is *effective* when it guides our productive and artistic relations to the world; it is *constitutive* when it gives identity and significance to our responsible decisions and actions; it is *communicative* when it regulates our intersubjective transactions through speech and writing; and it is *cognitive* when it mediates our efforts to know the world as it really is.

Animal knowing appears to be essentially intuitive in nature; but properly human knowing, although it has an intuitive component, is deeply discursive. It advances through asking and answering questions. Human beings know the world not through their immediate experience of it but through the intelligent generation and reasonable affirmation of intentional signs. The world of our knowledge is a world mediated by true propositions, by the justified answers we give to the questions we ask one another. In this way, we know not only the past and the spatially remote but potentially the entire universe of being and value. Once the discursive nature of human knowledge is recognized, a basic question confronts the philosopher. Shall we start our analysis of cognitive intentionality with these mediating signs or can we go behind them to their originating source and ground in the intentional subject? This is the critical issue dividing conceptualists and intellectualists in the philosophy of mind and the theory of knowledge. The following account of cognitive meaning is openly intellectualist in its underlying commitments.[16]

> 1. *The core of cognitive meaning* is the unrestricted human desire to
>   know: unlimited in scope, disinterested in nature, and detached in its

normative operation, it is the permanent ground or principle (*arche*) of all human inquiry.[17]

2. *The sources of cognitive meaning* are the conscious intentional operations that jointly constitute the process of human cognition.[18] When not obstructed by alien desires, the desire to know unfolds in a normative pattern of recurrent and related operations, yielding progressive and cumulative results. Cognitive meaning is generated, refined, systematized, and eventually revised through this recurrent intentional process.

3. *The acts of cognitive meaning* are the basic intentional operations that formulate or posit answers to the questions that initiate and guide human inquiry. Questions for intelligence—what, why, how often, and so on—are met by formal acts of meaning in which tentative and hypothetical answers are submitted for critical verification. The question that guides critical reflection—is the tentative answer true—is met by a full act of meaning, an assertion (yes), denial (no), or suspension of judgment (I don't know). Full acts of meaning affirm or deny the correctness and adequacy of the answers articulated in formal acts of meaning to the exploratory questions of intelligence.

4. *The terms of cognitive meaning* are the successive answers fashioned by human inquiry to its own questions for intelligence and reflection. Formal terms of meaning are the propositions provisionally hypothesized in formal acts of meaning and subjected to truth appraisal in critical reflection. Full terms of meaning are truth-bearing propositions whose truth value has been determined and asserted in full acts of meaning. All the acts and terms of meaning have their proximate intentional source in direct and reflective insights, the pivotal acts in the complex structure of cognitional process.[19]

5. *The norms of cognitive meaning* are the standards of appraisal by which the process of inquiry and its resultant acts and terms of meaning are reflectively evaluated. Canons of method articulate normative standards for the appropriate conduct of inquiry; the principles of logic express the standards of clarity, consistency, and rigor for formal terms of meaning; epistemology makes explicit the standards of objectivity and truth for full terms of meaning. The norms of cognitive meaning are the immanent critical exigencies regulative of the mind's intentional activity in the pursuit of knowledge. Logic, epistemology, and cognitional theory articulate and thematize standards of correctness already operative implicitly in the prereflexive exercise of human intelligence and reason.

6. The human desire to know normatively unfolds in cognitional process and climaxes in the assertion or denial of full terms of

meaning. *The objects of cognitive meaning* are the reality that is known through this self-correcting process of learning. Rationally affirmed propositional truth is the medium through which objective existence is humanly known. The core of cognitive meaning, the unrestricted desire to know, is fully united to the objects of cognitive meaning, the reality that is to be known, through the sources, acts, terms, and norms of meaning in which it normatively unfolds. A philosophical theory of knowledge is required to give a full account of these interdependent dimensions of cognition and the structure of being isomorphic with them.

7. *The linguistic expressions of cognitive meaning*: human beings conduct their inquiry and communicate and criticize its results in the medium of a common language. Questions for intelligence and reflection, formal and full terms of meaning, though they have their ground in intentional desires, operations, and norms, receive their full objectification in discourse. The complex network of theories, hypotheses, sentences, and sentence fragments in which partial, formal, and full terms of meaning are objectified and publicly communicated are the linguistic expressions of cognitive meaning.

8. *Realms of cognitive meaning*—cognitive development occurs through the differentiation and specialization of cognitional process. Distinct *exigencies* of the human spirit are met by specializations of inquiry that generate original realms of cognitive meaning while creating new and continually evolving linguistic communities. The members of a realm of meaning share a common tradition and a common intentional life, that is, a common field of experience, a common method of understanding data, conceptualizing questions and answers, and verifying results, a common estimate of importance and relevance. To paraphrase Wittgenstein, learning one of these languages is learning a new form of cognitive life.[20]

a. *The practical exigence* of human beings unfolds in the specialization of intelligence known as common sense. What is common to the numberless varieties of common sense is their intentional standpoint rather than their explicit cognitive content. The common sense of one region, time, or specialized group will differ from that of others, but the intentional pattern of questioning, understanding, and judgment will be essentially the same. Common sense is a collaborative intellectual mastery of the concrete and particular insofar as it is relevant to the practical purposes, desires, and fears of specific historical communities. The transactions of common sense are conducted in ordinary discourse through a mode of linguistic expression exempt from the strict logical requirements of clarity, coherence, and rigor. Common sense has no theoretical inclinations.

Its questions and answers are bounded by the interest and concerns of daily human living within the appropriate group; its canons of relevance restrict further questions to those that make an immediately palpable difference to particular problematic life situations in the community.

b. *The systematic theoretical exigence* has gradually developed, over two millennia, into the specialization of intelligence known as *empirical science*. Theoretical science seeks to understand things not in their descriptive relations to human perceivers but in their explanatory relations to one another. The theoretical realm of meaning is the fruit of the collective human aspiration to universally valid explanatory knowledge. Technical canons of method and statement are devised to control its terms of meaning whose linguistic expressions are subject to the exacting norms of logic and epistemology. Communities of scientific meaning train new members in their methods and logic, operate within a shared technical language and paradigm unintelligible to outsiders, and conduct their inquiry within a highly complex network of interlocking beliefs. The community of theoretical science is a family of interdependent, hierarchically organized, normative practices based on tradition and authority, which historically put their own traditions and authorities into question.[21]

c. The *reflexive methodological exigence* becomes prominent when common sense and theoretical science have become historically distinct and relatively autonomous realms of meaning. The increasing heterogeneity of consciousness and discourse prompts human beings to become reflexive about their cognitive activity, to seek understanding of what they are doing and achieving in the practice of mathematics, empirical science, historical inquiry, common sense, philosophy, theology, and so on. This exigence promotes a specifically *philosophical realm of meaning* distinct from the practical and the scientific realms it investigates. Its purpose is to distinguish, intentionally ground, critically analyze, and finally integrate the successive historical achievements of the sciences and common sense. Although the aspirations of reflexive philosophy remain theoretical, in the present context of philosophical crisis, it lacks the agreement on method, language, and inherited belief characteristic of empirical science. Philosophers today are implicitly united by a common synoptic goal, but they clearly do not possess a common program for achieving it.[22]

d. The *transcendent exigence* drives the human spirit to raise questions about the ultimate foundations of existence and value. Is there an absolute, intelligent, unconditional ground of contingent reality? Is this ground a personal center of moral responsibility and a proper subject for moral evaluation? These ancient questions about God and the answers and aspirations they evoke receive diverse linguistic expression in the different realms of cognitive meaning; for example, the ordinary religious discourse of common sense, theological doctrines modeled on the classical ideal of science as well as historically sensitive theologies, aware of the difference between transcendent and contingent being and sensitive to the need for functional specialization in theological inquiry.[23] Human discourse about God may be phrased in ordinary language as in the prayers, symbols, and homilies of pastoral common sense, or it may be technical and theoretical as in the formulations of systematic theology.

9. Successive differentiations of intentional consciousness in response to distinct exigencies of the human spirit have created three historically distinct *stages of cognitive meaning*.

a. *The pretheoretical* stage of practical common sense dominated the West until the advent of pre-Socratic philosophy and ended when Aristotle's logic systematized the classical ideal of scientific theory.

b. In the second stage of meaning, common sense and systematic theory became distinct forms of cognition but empirical science had not yet become independent of philosophy. Either metaphysics or epistemology functioned as the foundational discipline on which theoretical science rested. This stage of *classical consciousness* in the realm of theory extended roughly from Aristotle to Kant. The historical sensitivity of Hegel, the evolutionary interests of Lyell and Darwin, the emergence of non-Euclidean geometries and non-Aristotelian logics, the liberation of empirical science from philosophy all propelled cognitive meaning into a third stage.

c. In the third stage of *historical consciousness*, common sense, empirical science, and philosophy have become distinct, complementary, and independent realms of cognitive meaning; the classical ideal of scientific theory and the quest for certainty have been abandoned, but the undefined character of foundational analysis and the uncertain prospects for theoretical integration face philosophy with a serious crisis of identity and self-definition.

10. *The architecture of philosophy in the third stage of meaning.* The different dimensions of human knowledge that I have outlined in the matrix of meaning offer a specialized subject matter for distinct though related philosophical disciplines.

a. *Cognitional theory* distinguishes the core, sources, and acts of cognitive meaning and explores their intentional relations; through intentional analysis of the origin and process of human cognition, it proposes an explanatory account of what human beings are doing when engaged in the pursuit of knowledge.[24]

b. *Formal logic* studies the relations of presupposition, implication, and deducibility among formal terms of meaning (actual or potential); it articulates the normative standards of intelligibility that a truth-vehicle or deductively ordered system of truth-vehicles must satisfy.

c. *Epistemology* studies the necessary conditions under which the assertion or denial of full terms of meaning is rationally justified; it articulates the normative requirements and implications of objective knowledge and truth.

d. *Metaphysics* studies the basic intelligible structure of the objects of cognitive meaning (actually existing things and their properties); it also seeks to integrate the multiple realms of cognitive meaning without conflating their essential differences. Competing metaphysical strategies of integration are based on opposing estimates of the locus of theoretical invariance within the comprehensive matrix of cognition.

e. *Semiotic analysis* investigates the linguistic expressions of cognitive meaning in terms of their correlated sense and reference. Its task is to explicate the concepts (*Begriffe*) or thoughts (*Gedanke*) expressed by linguistic signs and to fix the objects, if any, to which those signs refer. Cognitive semiotic analysis broadly divides philosophers into those who explicate formal terms of meaning through the assignment of truth conditions and those who do it by specifying their conditions of knowledge and verification.[25]

f. The different *realms of cognitive meaning*, common sense, empirical science, philosophy, and theology, admit of analysis by each of these distinct philosophical disciplines. In successive historical periods, the leading philosophers have given priority to different disciplines, treating their basic questions and answers as foundational to the philosophic examination of knowledge as a whole. The central issue in this dispute over foundations is the most effective order of philosophical inquiry. Classical consciousness, with its anticipation of permanent theoretical meaning, emphasized the order of logical systematization. One discipline is systematically prior to another if its explanatory categories and principles are logically presupposed in the statement and solution of the other's problems.

In the comprehensive theoretical project of Aristotle the order of systematic exposition proceeded from *metaphysical* analysis of the objects of meaning (the theory of being) to *logical* analysis of the terms and norms of meaning (the theory of science) to *cognitional* analysis of the psychological sources of meaning (theory of sensitive and intellectual operations). The explanatory categories of metaphysics were used to define the central terms of logic and rational psychology. Metaphysics was treated as the foundational form of theoretical knowledge because its universal categories of potency, form, and actuality were presupposed in the systematic expression of the results of all human cognition.

Modern philosophy begins with the repudiation of Aristotelian metaphysics and the comprehensive cosmology it supports. Descartes established the heuristic program of modernity by making epistemology systematically prior to the theory of being. Epistemic analysis of the norms and terms of meaning (Cartesian ideas) became the primary philosophical task. Once indubitable axioms are discovered through clear and distinct intuitions, the system of scientific truths can be rationally reconstructed with deductive rigor. The existence, nature, and properties of the objects of meaning (formal reality) are determined by appeal to the deductively ordered true ideas of axiomatized science. For Descartes philosophy began with epistemology, proceeded to the logical reconstruction of science, and climaxed in a metaphysics of nature based on the conclusions of the prevailing mathematical physics.

Within the horizon of Cartesian epistemology, the terms of cognitive meaning were conceived of as ideas. Descartes's way of ideas was new because it displaced the Aristotelian priority on the causal analysis of sensible substances. According to representational theorists of consciousness like Descartes, the intentional awareness of mind-independent objects was mediated by a prior intuition of mind-dependent ideas. The subordination of metaphysics to epistemology in the Cartesian architectonic reflected this mediated dependence of things on ideas in the order of awareness. Deep confusions about the nature of ideas and doubts about their suitability as vehicles of intersubjective inquiry and objective truth encouraged modern analytic thinkers to give an unprecedented emphasis to the linguistic expressions of meaning. Though words replaced ideas as the focus of philosophical attention, the priority accorded to terms of meaning was preserved. The semiotic analysis of linguistic expressions thus became the critical philosophical project on which both epistemology and metaphysics were now dependent.

Followers of the linguistic turn, although committed to the priority of semiotic analysis in the architecture of philosophy, are themselves divided into partisans of classical and historical consciousness. Frege and the early Wittgenstein, as representatives of the classical ideal, anticipated theoretical invariance either at the object-linguistic level of scientific terms of meaning or at a level of transcendental logic (universal and invariant syntactical laws) underpinning all conceivable object languages. Quine, Sellars, Rorty, and the later Wittgenstein have abandoned the anticipation of theoretical permanence and of epistemically prior terms of meaning and have fallen back on various pragmatic strategies for choosing between competitive object languages and theories as a whole. These pragmatic canons of selection became the ultimate court of appeal in the adjudication of reputed theoretical conflict.

With the transition from classical to historical consciousness, philosophical emphasis had to shift from the unification of permanent theoretical systems to the need for integration of a regular succession of such theories. Cognitive invariance is no longer anticipated in objects, terms, or expressions of meaning, if at all, but in the intentional core and sources of meaning that generate and then eventually revise the evolving judgments of science and common sense. This major change in heuristic anticipation has suggested a new architectural model for philosophy. In the strategy recommended by Bernard Lonergan for the third stage of meaning, philosophy should begin with intentional analysis of the process of cognition, proceed to a logical and epistemological analysis of the terms of meaning generated through that process, and conclude with a metaphysical investigation of the objects known though those terms. The basic philosophical principles and categories are drawn from cognitional theory which thus emerges as the primary philosophical discipline. One enduring function of philosophy remains the integration of cognitive meaning, but the critical base from which to execute that function becomes the self-appropriation by the intentional subject of the core, sources, and norms of cognitive development and revision that he discovers in his own intentional experience. Moreover, the model of synthesis ceases to be the logical systematization of diverse terms of meaning drawn from the sciences and common sense and becomes instead the methodological coordination of complementary heuristic structures. Cognitive integration in the natural and human sciences is no longer considered to be a permanent accomplishment founded on self-evident and certain truths but an ongoing and collaborative theoretical process to be conducted from a strategic and invariant critical standpoint. The elaboration and defense of this concept of philosophy will be given in Chapters VII and VIII.

In introducing this matrix of cognitive meeting, I have hoped to do several things at one time: to articulate the structural complexity of human cognition; to outline a possible division of philosophical labor in the territory of knowledge; to survey historical realignments in the architecture of philosophy while suggesting their epistemic causes; to situate and define the existing crisis of philosophy, and to outline competing strategies for resolving it; and to indicate how philosophy could be historically minded without abandoning its permanent theoretical purpose of cognitive integration. My objective has been to prepare the reader for the ensuing philosophical narrative rather than to persuade him of my own beliefs. I have tried to lay the conceptual groundwork for a sustained investigation of the sources and shifts of metaphilosophical controversy during the last two centuries.

D. Pure Mathematics and the New Logic

The seventeenth -century revolution in physics led to the liberation of natural science from philosophy. The nineteenth-century revolution in logical theory had a parallel effect on the formal sciences, since its major innovations were equally subversive of accepted philosophical principles. The novel developments in this movement were the axiomatization of mathematics, the radical formalization of arithmetic, and the algebraicizing of logic.

The dominant influence with which axiomatization had to contend was the Kantian philosophy of mathematics.[26] In the transcendental aesthetic of the *Critique of Pure Reason*, Kant developed a theory of mathematics designed to account for the instantiation of mathematical structures in the physical universe. Reduced to its essential structure, the Kantian argument had this form. Euclidean geometry is the a priori science of physical space and first order arithmetic the a priori science of physical time. Though mathematical knowledge applies directly to the objects of perceptual experience, it is not derived from the empirical examination of these objects nor justified by recourse to them. The unified structures of geometry and arithmetic are constitutive of the empirical world, not abstractions from it; they are necessary conditions of the world's intelligibility. But space and time, though empirically real, (that is, verifiable features of perceptual experience), are understood by Kant to be transcendentally ideal, since they are pure forms of human sensibility and not mind-independent properties of things in themselves. According to Kant, the truths of mathematics are synthetic a priori judgments; a priori because they apply with strict necessity to all possible experience, synthetic because their truth value cannot be determined on purely logical grounds or by means of purely logical operations.

Kant based his philosophy of mathematics on a specific account of the heuristic procedures required to discover and verify mathematical truths. According to this account, pure intuition plays the central role in the acquisition and justification of mathematical knowledge. The fundamental reliance on pure intuition for the discovery and verification of arithmetic and geometrical truths ensures their synthetic a priori character. "Arithmetical propositions are therefore always synthetic. This is still more evident if we take larger numbers, for it is there obvious that, however we might twist and turn our concepts, we could never by the mere analysis of them, and without the aid of intuition, discover what the number is that is the sum."[27] Kant's strategy stresses the contribution of pure intuition to mathematical understanding, but it does not encourage a rigorous examination of the logical structure of mathematical theories. Three major developments in nineteenth-century mathematics radically reverse his order of priorities. These were the construction of non-Euclidean geometries, the acceptance of a positive theory of transfinite cardinals, and the renewed emphasis on argumentative rigor advocated by Karl Weierstrass.[28] The possibility of consistent non-Euclidean theories implied that Kant was mistaken in confining geometry to a study of the space of external sensible intuition. Cantor's positive theory of infinite sets explicitly contradicted Kant's claim that the existential use of the concept of actual infinity led directly to the antinomies of reason. Weierstrass's work in the foundations of analysis effected a shift from intuitive to rigorous deductive procedures as the dominant method of mathematical verification. Each of these developments cast doubt on the reliability of intuition as a source or test of mathematical knowledge.

A corollary to the disengagement of pure mathematics from reliance on intuition was the separation of mathematical theories from the domain of their empirical applications. This separation, known as formalization, was of immense importance for the philosophy of mathematics. Since Aristotle, many philosophers had contended that mathematics was the science of measurable quantity. The ground for this claim was the realization that mathematical truths could be used to express quantitative relations observed to obtain in nature and art. The willingness to view mathematical structures apart from their application to perceptual experience promoted an abstract and formal conception of this science. Although Aristotle had supported he axiomatization of mathematics, he did not foresee the prospect of complete formalization. For him, mathematics was the abstract study of quantitative relations holding between the perceptual dimensions of natural objects and artifacts. Under its new conception, mathematics was understood to be a universal science of ordering relations whose range of instantiating terms was not confined to measurable quantities. The demand for the intuitive applicability of mathematical truths was replaced by the requirement that well-ordered axiom sets be internally consistent. With the adoption of logical consistency as the criterion of mathematical validity, it became imperative to display mathematical theories in their most perspicuous logical form, to exhibit clearly their deductive structure and principles of inference.

This revised assessment of the nature of mathematics was supported by the new mathematical methodology. Whatever heuristic importance intuition may have in the stage of original discovery, under the formalized approach it was not essential to mathematical demonstration and proof. Proof structures could be given rigorous symbolic expression in a formalized language. The validity of these structures was not dependent on the intuitive meaning assigned to the symbols, but solely upon the prescribed laws that govern their combination and transformation. These formalized symbolic structures admitted a variety of legitimate interpretations. Quantitative, spatial, and temporal interpretations could lay no claim to special privilege. By bracketing the question of a unique or privileged interpretation, mathematics became a more thoroughly abstract discipline based on postulation and formal deduction. Axiomatization had represented a return to an original Euclidean ideal; but formalization was a novel and distinctive contribution of the nineteenth century. With respect to symbolic interpretation, it is important to distinguish between the operational constants and the variables of a formalized system. Although the constants are not uninterpreted, their interpretation is not assigned intuitively. The rules of a system implicitly define its operational constants and prescribe the range of arguments and values they functionally connect. But the syntactical rules do not prescribe particular substituends for the variables. Any substitution of values for the uninterpreted variables that satisfies the constraints on the operational constants is a legitimate interpretation.

The gradual recognition of the formal character of pure mathematics prepared the ground for a new philosophy of logic as well. The Dutch philosopher of mathematics E. W. Beth has observed that when mathematics became disjoined from the notion of quantity, the close analogy between logical operations and variables and those of algebra was disclosed.[29] Beth cites Boole's work, *The Mathematical Analysis of Logic*, for providing the first clear recognition of this analogy. Both Boole and DeMorgan, relaying upon this insight, developed a new conception of logic as a species of nonquantitative algebra. To understand this novel approach to logic, let us first examine the precise relationship between arithmetic and algebra. The operational constants in both disciplines are the same, but the numerical constants of arithmetic have been replaced by numerical variables in algebra. Algebra studies the invariant lawful properties of numerical operations. Since these properties hold for all arithmetic truths, the shift from numerical constants to variables signals a shift in the scope and level of generalization. What are the supporting parallels that apply to logic? If we use sentential logic as our example, how can we effect a shift in generality from our customary propositional discourse to propositional logic? The logical constants at the two levels are in this case not the same, as Strawson has forcefully reminded us.[30] But the constants of propositional logic are a regimented version of their ordinary language counterparts, regimented for purposes of algorithmic simplicity. These constants are not defined by intuitive appeal to ordinary usage but through the technique of implicit definition by truth-tables. The truth-tables of propositional logic define its logical constants just as the rules of algebra implicitly define its central operations. The actual sentences formulated in natural language become sentential variables in propositional logic. The intent again is to express the shift in level of generalization effected by the implicit definitions. Once this level of formalization has been reached, we are free to develop propositional logic as a syntactically regulated calculus. A calculus is a method of symbolic operation resting on a precise notation and explicit rules of formation and transformation. The rules determine which operations on the symbols are permissible and which are not. The only general restriction on a calculus is that its pattern of notational results admit of consistent interpretations.

Boole did not adopt a fully conventionalist attitude toward his proposed algebra of logic. He accepted the transformation of propositions into propositional variables, but he argued that the rules for combining those variables must be based on the laws of the mind. The rules of any calculus that could be interpreted as offering a formal analysis of *logical relations* must correspond to the laws of thought.[31] We are not at liberty in constructing a *logical* calculus. The predicate *logical* predetermines the range of rules governing the operations with the propositional variables. Boole's colleagues in the movement to algebraicize logic frequently adopted a less normative position. Venn, for example, admitted alternative sets of combinatory rules that implicitly defined an equal number of alternative calculi. This historic controversy between Venn and Boole has not yet been resolved: it persists in the continuing argument between those who adopt formalization as a method of algorithmic computation and rigor and those who see in it the basis for a complete philosophy of logic and mathematics.

The movement to develop the science of logic in the form of a calculus using algorithmic methods originated in England. It first received expression in a calculus of class logic and later in a calculus of relations. The supreme development of this tendency occurred in the work of Schroder in Germany, whose *Lectures on the Algebra* of Logic argued for a thorough reform of traditional systems of deduction.[32] According to Schroder a consistent application of the algebraic method should permit a synoptic grasp of the entire field of deductive inference. When surveyed from this perspective, Aristotle's syllogistic logic was seen to be but a single region in a comprehensive science of valid inference. In addition to systematizing the method of logic and extending its range, Schroder argued that the algebraic approach finally clarified the essence of logic as a formal science. In becoming mathematicized, logic would benefit from the axiomatic and formalized approaches reaching maturity in arithmetic. Just as the alliance with physics and physiology had emancipated philosophical psychology from the dominant influence of Descartes, so the reform of logic hoped to emancipate it from the presuppositions and authority of Aristotle. "Until the nineteenth century logic remained philosophical just as psychology remained introspective, and the first became mathematical at the same time the second became experimental."[33] In both cases, there was a parallel desire to assert independence of traditional philosophical positions and to refuse the demand for a philosophic justification of these major innovations in method. The claim by mathematical logic and experimental psychology to complete theoretical self-sufficiency soon became intensely contested as our study of Frege, Brentano, and Husserl will show.

Recognition of the parallels between logic and mathematics inspired movement in two directions. Boole and Schroder assumed the analogical priority of algebra and interpreted logic as a nonquantitative algebraic discipline. The opposite tack was taken by Frege, the great German mathematician and philosopher. Frege stressed the systematic priority of logical concepts and principles over those of arithmetic. Spurred by his belief that the conceptual foundations of arithmetic were vague and uncertain, he chose to illumine them through a detailed criticism of the prevailing philosophies of mathematics and through the construction of a new symbolic notation, the *Begriffschrift*, which could be used to demonstrate the totality of arithmetic truths.[34] Frege's ruling conviction was that arithmetical concepts could he adequately defined in logical terms and that arithmetic theorems could be rigorously deduced from logical premises and laws of inference. Given Frege's normative concept of rigorous science, the foundations of mathematics would not be secure until the truth of its premises and the truth-preserving character of its laws of inference were known to be indubitable.

As the most important philosopher of mathematics in the nineteenth century, Frege raised foundational questions to a new level of prominence. He promulgated the view that arithmetic was theoretically unsound until its elementary concepts and axioms were identified and clarified and its methods of definition and demonstration rendered fully explicit. Starting from his initial concern with the conceptual foundations of arithmetic, he began gradually to investigate the general presuppositions of theoretical science. Because he took the classical ideal of theory with uncommon seriousness, he highlighted elementary issues at both the intra and extratheoretic levels. Over time, he placed a broad range of foundational concerns on the agenda of epistemology. He restored philosophy to serious dialogue with a developing science and reopened the question of their proper interdependence.

E. Foundational Inquiry

No image suggests the terminal goal of philosophical analysis better than the metaphor of foundations. Since its origin in pre-Socratic thought, philosophy has been a foundational inquiry. In its earliest recorded period it sought to discover the *arche*, the original principle of cosmic genesis. Later, in Plato and Aristotle, the ultimate ground of existence and value was conceived in less naturalistic terms as the absolute principle of perfection (the Good) or the unmoved mover (the *noesis noeseos*) that moves natural substances by its power of attraction.[35] Metaphysical foundations, the first principles and causes of being, dominated the philosophical horizon during the classical and medieval eras. But in modern philosophy, beginning with Descartes, epistemic foundations, axiomatic principles or the evidential grounds of knowledge, became the primary concern. The attention of philosophers became riveted on logical rather than ontological principles, on clear and distinct ideas rather than on primary substances or intelligible forms. In all of these periods, the foundational metaphor was used to refer to that which underlies or gives support to another entity without being in need of further support itself. There is an asymmetric relation of dependence between that which is founded and that upon which the founded rests. This dependence is literally conceived in terms of physical support, but the point of the metaphor is to suggest numerous kinds of presupposition and dependence: causal, logical, epistemic, semantic, and intentional. Technically speaking, a foundation or principle is what is first in an ordered series. In mathematics, for example, to grasp the principle of a series and its rule of genesis is to command an ordering perspective from which the whole of the series can be surveyed intelligibly. Depending on the type of serial ordering, the foundational principle could be a first cause (causal priority), an axiomatic truth (logical priority), a starting place for inquiry (methodological priority), an originating intellectual operation (intentional priority), a basic level of knowledge (epistemic priority), or a transcendental condition supporting the possibility of some problematic human attainment. Each of these modes of serial ordering corresponds to a different type of investigative analysis, to a different sort of philosophical foundation.

Our concern in this chapter, like that of the moderns, shall be with the foundations of cognition. We shall discover that the complexity of human cognition, particularly in the theoretical realm of meaning, permits importantly different concepts of foundational research. The existence of the common metaphor conceals divergent, even contradictory, interpretations of the properties and functions of an epistemic foundation and of the methods by which to discover them. This conflict bears directly on the crisis in contemporary philosophy, for the different models of foundational inquiry tend to correlate with opposing strategies for the integration of knowledge and with the acceptance or rejection of the classical theory of science.

What circumstances motivate the search for foundations in the theoretical realm of meaning? If general criteria of theoretical objectivity are widely accepted, then foundational issues tend to be localized to a particular discipline. If the discipline is in its embryonic stage, then the major concern is to determine its distinctive heuristic program: to identify the type of data, the range of questions, the basic explanatory categories, the relevant kinds of evidence, and the method of verification that could define it as a collaborative form of specialized inquiry. For a developed science in a state of epistemic consensus and maturity, the quest for foundations has a primarily intra-theoretic character; the motivation is largely logical and aesthetic. What selection of axioms, undefined terms, and rules of inference will permit systematization of the discipline's secure theoretical results? Logical ideals of clarity, coherence, rigor, and elegance regulate this level of foundational research. Specialized disciplines enter a stage of theoretical crisis with radical changes in their categorial framework, with the emergence and adoption of novel heuristic structures or with a shift in paradigms and research programs. The Copernican and Galilean revolutions constitute such a crisis for classical physics, as did Darwin's evolutionary perspective in traditional biology. The emancipation of the empirical and formal sciences from philosophy's epistemic regulation and the transition from classical to historical consciousness constitute an equivalent crisis for modern philosophy. Changes of this magnitude create new horizons for collaborative inquiry and require those mature enough to be at home in both the old and the new frameworks patiently to work through the numerous transitions that are demanded. Such crises tend to be unnecessarily protracted when superficial opinions backed by passion dominate the discussion and debate.

Judgments about the existence and location of invariance within the matrix of cognitive meaning tend to dictate philosophic strategies in epistemology. Philosophers committed to the classical theory of science anticipate invariance at the level of full terms of meaning, the level of propositional truth. Since they think of theoretical science as a permanent achievement, their foundational quest is for the primitive terms and axioms that shall serve as the logical ground of an axiomatized theoretical system. Their foundational research has two correlative moments; they seek to eradicate all obscurity and uncertainty about the foundational terms of meaning, the quest for clarity and apodicticity, and then they logically reconstruct the remainder of the theory on this absolute and evident epistemic base. Historically sensitive epistemologists, by contrast, acknowledge a succession of competing theoretical systems in the history of science and, thus, treat presently accepted terms of meaning as provisional rather than invariant. They do not refuse the logical demand for clarity and rigor in the systematization of knowledge, but they recognize that logical operations are insufficient to generate higher theoretical viewpoints and to resolve fundamental heuristic disagreements. Logic consolidates and refines existing theoretical achievement but by itself it cannot be the source of new levels of categorial and heuristic development. What, then, is the ground of continuity and consistency within an historically evolving scientific discipline? The intratheoretic constant is the methodological and heuristic structure of the discipline that serves as the thread of identity through systematic categorial change; at a deeper level, the regulative theoretical ideal provides a basis for continuity during revolutionary changes in both method and heuristic structure. When the ideal of science itself changes, as it has in the third stage of cognitive meaning, the philosophical understanding of human knowledge is profoundly disrupted. This is our situation today in the domain of epistemology.

Epistemic analysis of particular theoretical disciplines has an exclusively *logical cast* when the anticipated invariance is at the level of propositional truth, whether the propositions in questions are axiomatic principles or observation sentences. It tends to include both *logical and intentional analysis* when invariance is expected in the core, norms, and sources of cognitive meaning rather than in the partial, formal, or full terms of meaning. A dramatic example of these different strategies will surface when we examine the contrasting approach to the foundations of mathematics taken by Frege and Husserl.

Epistemic analysis is not restricted to specialized theoretical disciplines. More serious foundational issues arise when the theoretical realm as a whole is submitted to skeptical doubt and interrogation. Are epistemic objectivity and truth really possible, not just in physics or mathematics but in the theoretical enterprise as such? Recent proponents of relativism, skepticism, and historicism have given an urgency to this question that it lacked prior to the advent of modern science and a deeper familiarity by philosophers with its history. As I remarked in an earlier context, many defenders of the classical theory of science refuse to abandon it precisely because they consider it the exclusive alternative to relativism. They defend the objectivity of theoretical knowledge by articulating the regulative norms for full term of meaning, by showing that existing theories do or could satisfy those norms, and by arguing that skeptical positions presuppose these regulative criteria even as they deny their validity or satisfiability. Historically minded epistemologists need not deny that there are invariant norms that formal and full terms of meaning must satisfy. They can accept the classical principles of logic as necessary conditions of propositional intelligibility and also accept explicit epistemic criteria for the objectivity and truth of propositions that are give unconditional assent. But they should transcend the self imposed restrictions of the classical theorist by searching out the transcategorial basis of all theoretical change and development in the core and sources of cognitive meaning. The basic form of foundational method in philosophy is the intentional analysis of the process of cognition through which formal and full terms of meaning emerge and are verified and through which the objects of scientific inquiry are known. Through the intentional analysis of cognitional structure, philosophers can discover a level of invariance deeper than any propositional or categorial term of meaning because it is the ground for the emergence, revision, and replacement of all such terms. The model of foundational analysis adopted in Cartesian epistemology depended on the quest for scientific certainty.[36] The abandonment of that quest in the third stage of meaning has led numerous contemporary epistemologists to contend that knowledge has no foundation.[37] They base this denial on the absence of certain and evident truths that could serve as the axiomatic or evidential ground for the validation of scientific theories. Like their classical predecessors, they seek epistemic foundations at the level of unrevisable propositional truths; but unlike their classical forebears, they contend that no truths of this sort actually exist. A major argument of this text is that they have located the foundations of cognition in the wrong place. The shift from classical to historical consciousness demands the reconception and not the abandonment of the foundational metaphor.[38]

Whether the foundations of knowledge are sought in propositional truths or in the originating intentional operations that generate and appraise terms of meaning, any foundational candidate must possess certain properties and perform certain functions. Foundational principles are expected to be culturally universal and historically invariant. They are intended to provide the basis for a transhistorical, transcultural community of inquiry and knowledge. Although the foundations of cognition need not themselves be instances of knowledge, in principle they must be accessible to discovery and verification by an unrestricted community of investigators. If they are located in a set of justificatory propositions, they must preserve their truth value and their epistemic priority over time. If, as I shall claim, they are a normatively patterned set of intentional operations, they must provide the common recurrent structure within which cognitive development and revision occur. They must be the base or ground, whether causal, logical, semantical, or intentional, on which the changing edifice of knowledge rests. There are numerous legitimate ways in which to order the complex field of human knowledge: orders of discovery and inquiry, of demonstration and systematization, of transcendental presupposition and intentional genesis. What is foundationally prior in one ordering may clearly be posterior in another; as Aristotle repeatedly argued, what is first in the order of inquiry is often last in the order of demonstration and science.[39] Depending on the depth of the epistemological issue, different orders become relevant and different strata of foundations come into play. This fact may explain why alternative epistemological strategies can legitimately preserve the metaphor of foundations, even as they seek to find them in contrasting regions of the matrix of cognition.

In the nineteenth century, the quest for the foundations of knowledge precipitated a major heuristic disagreement. Darwin's success in biology had made the evolutionary model of causal explanation seem universally compelling, particularly to those with naturalistic allegiances in metaphysics. As these philosophical naturalists saw it, all explainable phenomena were to be understood by a reconstruction of their causal genesis. Existing organic structures, historical artifacts, even forms of knowledge like scientific theories could be made fully intelligible through the discovery and articulation of their temporal history. According to this model, the foundations of any reality, whether naturally or humanly produced, were identical with its causal origins in nature. The philosophical search for foundations was reduced by the naturalists to the discovery of the causal sequence of events through which the phenomenon to be explained had come into being. In the concerted effort to naturalize all the dimensions of knowledge, this heuristic principle was rigorously applied to the causal explanation of scientific terms of meaning. The foundations of knowledge thus were removed from the intentional matrix of cognition and relocated in noncognitive and nonintentional natural causes operating in accordance with natural laws.

Those who espoused a logical rather than causal ordering of scientific theory resisted this genetic conception of first principles. They saw clearly that logical priority in the theoretic realm belonged to primitive concepts and explanatory axioms, not to temporally prior natural causes. On their account, epistemology was a second-order rational science concerned with the logical analysis and reconstruction of theoretical systems; it was not a first-order theory of spatiotemporal causes and effects. Now, in principle, genetic and logical analyses of science are not in conflict, provided that the concept of causal genesis is sufficiently rich to include the intentional causation of propositional terms of meaning. But the naturalists' use of the principle of evolution as a heuristic norm eroded the distinction between spatiotemporal objects and abstract propositions, between the genesis and the perishing of biological species, and the intelligent discovery and adoption of scientific theories. For these nineteenth-century naturalists, all things relevant to the understanding of knowledge were presumed to evolve through a process of physical causation and change.

The dogmatic heuristic assumptions of naturalism had little relevance for foundational research in the science of mathematics as it historically developed. Foundational concerns in mathematics really stemmed from the rejection of inherited assumptions and the resultant loss of secure theoretical orientation. The construction of non-Euclidean geometries undermined faith in the classical theory of science, which had taken Euclid's *Elements* as the paradigm expression of authentic *episteme*. The dependence on selfauthenticating intuition was undercut by developments in set theory and mathematical analysis. Both movements resulted from and gave support to a nonexperientially oriented concept of mathematical knowledge. The method of formalization permitted an extensive technical expansion of mathematics into the new theories of real and complex numbers. The resultant freedom from intuitive grounding raised questions about the meaning of the new mathematical symbols and about the relation of their referents to the natural numbers. The arithmetization of analysis attempted to prove that the different levels of unintuitable numerical objects could be understood as the result of complex set formation procedures that took the natural numbers as their basic elements. As Kronecker remarked, "God gave us the natural numbers; the rest we have made on our own."[40]

The project of arithmetization presumed the conceptual dependence of higher level mathematical theories upon first-order arithmetic. The intelligibility of the new mathematics rested on the evidential clarity of the basic number theoretic concepts and operations. In pursuing this derivative intelligibility to its allegedly ultimate ground in arithmetic, Frege uncovered a profound irony. Even though traditionally arithmetic had been regarded as a paradigm instance of rigorous science, philosophers of mathematics could not agree about the meaning and reference of its basic terms or about the method of justification for its truth claims. Frege's dismay at this theoretical chaos motivated his research in the *Foundations of Arithmetic*, research devoted to the semantical clarification of arithmetical language.[41] His concern was not with the symbols of arithmetic, as such, but with the proper understanding of their meaning and reference. Frege's intellectual quest took him on a path of foundational discovery from higher mathematics to arithmetic, from arithmetic to logic, and from logic to basic issues in epistemology, philosophical semantics, and ontology. In order to secure the objectivity of mathematics, he devised a complex ontological system based upon general epistemic and semantical principles concordant with the classical ideal of science. In the philosophical order, the metaphysical scheme supported the semantic interpretation of theoretical language and the epistemic justification of theoretical knowledge. In the mathematical order, the science of logic supported arithmetic, which in turn supported the upper levels of classical mathematics.

Frege often defended his foundational conclusions through destructive polemical criticism of rival theories. He was especially severe with formalistic and psychologistic philosophies of arithmetic; the first because it failed to distinguish numbers from numerals, and the second because it corrupted mathematics with irrelevant psychological concerns about mental operations and contents. At the decisive historical juncture, when mathematicians required the clearest conceptual understanding of arithmetic, popular philosophies prevailed that completely misrepresented the sense of arithmetical propositions. In the *Foundations of Arithmetic*, Frege tried to restore the needed clarity by the reduction of arithmetic to logic. Elementary arithmetic concepts and axioms are redefined in logical categories; the thesis is advanced that the theorems of arithmetic can be rigorously deduced from a theoretical base of exclusively logical axioms. By including set theory within the province of logic, Frege could plausibly claim that the science of logic provided the complete theoretical foundation of all higher mathematics outside geometry. Thus, he originated the project of logicism that Russell and Whitehead attempted to complete in the *Principia Mathematica*. In the period separating Frege's *Grundgesetze* and the publication of the *Principia*, important paradoxes were discovered in Cantor's set-theory. These paradoxes intensified concern with the theoretical foundations of mathematics because set-theory had been expected to play a critical role in the justification of mathematical knowledge. Logicism, in all of its variations, was subjected to severe criticism and the dominant competitive schools in the twentieth-century philosophy of mathematics began to emerge. The famous "crisis of foundations," a crisis traceable to weakened confidence in the consistency of set-theory and to doubts about its privileged role in the axiomatization of mathematics, therefore had no connection with naturalistic concerns about genetic priority or causal precedence. Logicists and naturalists, though using the same foundational metaphor, were committed to fundamentally divergent heuristic strategies. When they searched for the foundations of knowledge, they were not looking for the same things nor even for things of the same kind. Naturalism was intent on explaining the causal genesis of knowledge as a special case of human evolution; the mathematical foundationalists were absorbed in questions of epistemic justification and conceptual clarity. What was ultimately at stake, though this was rarely acknowledged, were the precise relations and differences between the causal and logical orders.

F. Philosophy Naturalized

There is, perhaps, in all modern life no more
powerfully, more irresistibly progressive idea than
that of science.[42]

Aristotle spoke of metaphysics as the most difficult, rare, and excellent of the theoretical sciences. He gave it pride of place because of the perfection of its subject matter, the first principles and causes of being. The excellence of its object made metaphysics the supreme form of knowledge, even though the most difficult to obtain. In the hierarchical ranking of the *episteme theoretike*, the likelihood of certainty was subordinated to the dignity of subject matter. Implicitly, Aristotle elevated the quest for understanding over the quest for certainty. These epistemic priorities were preserved in the medieval era by Aquinas who slightly modified Aristotle's hierarchy in raising sacred theology to the rank of highest science. For sincere believers, infused with the virtue of faith, revealed theology combined both the epistemic virtues of ontological excellence with a supernaturally grounded certitude.

In modernity, the classical and medieval criteria were reversed. Rationally achieved certainty became the essential feature of authentic knowledge, the hallmark of genuine science. In Descartes's philosophy the metaphysical certainty of the rational ego that has endured the rigors of hyperbolic doubt is a necessary and sufficient condition for reaching scientific truth.[43] By the mid-nineteenth century, science had become a collective rather than individual enterprise; the solitary individual's certitude was supplanted by collective agreement among an international community of trained investigators. Community of method, language,and inherited belief became the basic condition of scientific progress, the source of its expanding fund of secure results.

In the course of the enlightenment, the prestige of the natural sciences had clearly eclipsed both metaphysics and theology. According to the positivists, the superior "sciences" of the ancients were primitive forms of belief incapable of commanding rational assent in an enlightened age. The ideal of empirical science became the norm against which all candidates for knowledge were measured. The traditional regulative function of philosophy was jeopardized by this epistemic revolution. Not only had the empirical sciences become emancipated from philosophy, but their very success had disclosed philosophy's nonscientific character, its lack of consensual agreement and historical progress, and its incapacity to adjudicate conflict. Until the nineteenth century, the scientific revolution had been confined largely to the investigation of nature. Moral science, the study of man, continued to provide philosophy with a respectable theoretical task. But the achievement of Darwin in biology and the conversion of Hegel's historical concerns into empirical disciplines put philosophy severely on the defensive. If empirical science had the exclusive investigatory rights for both humanity and nature, what cognitive responsibility could philosophy possibly claim? The crisis of philosophy experienced in the nineteenth century turned on the following question: How could philosophy become scientific, and thus intellectually reputable, without becoming an empirical science?

The great philosophers at the turn of the century—Frege, Husserl, Meinong, Russell, and Wittgenstein—devoted their exceptional energies to the resolution of this question. They sought to define a subject matter, method, and cultural function for philosophy that would preserve its theoretical standing without interfering with or submitting to empirical science. In defense of their metaphilosophical programs, they rejected the thesis of philosophical naturalism that only an empirical discipline modeled on natural science could be properly scientific. The naturalists had wanted to abolish the numerous dualisms characteristic of modern thought: Descartes's ontological dualism of mind and matter, Kant's methodological dualism of transcendental and empirical inquiry, the pervading epistemic dualism between philosophy and science in which philosophy claimed for itself epistemic privilege.[44] Their antidualist strategy rested on the following contention. If the reputedly higher human cognitive processes were relocated in a matrix of physical events subject to empirically discoverable causal laws, then the Cartesian dichotomy between first philosophy and science would lose its credibility. Support for that distinction had rested on the alleged irreducibility of the mind to the natural order. But, once the mind had been naturalized, metaphysically and methodologically, empirical science would emerge as the sovereign measure of reality and truth, and philosophy would disappear as an independent theoretical discipline. All metaphysical questions then would be subject to the regulative authority of empirical science. All epistemic issues would be decided by appeal to publicly observable evidence. There would be one world to investigate, one method for explaining it, one cognitive authority embedded in the international community of science.

The elimination of philosophy as a cognitive discipline required the transfer of its remaining theoretical functions to science. The naturalization of philosophy would remain incomplete until successor empirical disciplines had replaced the philosophy of mind and epistemology. Nineteenth century naturalism selected a recently developed science, empirical psychology, to perform both of these inherited functions. The causal explanation of mental states and events conceivably could serve as a theory of knowledge *if* knowledge were defined as an ordered complex of mental particulars functionally dependent on physical causes. In fact, this was the precise view of knowledge and mind assumed by the nineteenth-century discipline of psychophysics.[45] On the psychophysical model of cognition, physically defined causes operate on the nervous system of sentient organisms producing knowledge in the organism as an effect. According to the strict materialists, knowledge consisted of brain states in the body's cerebral cortex, but the more common view was epiphenomenalist. Two sets of empirical laws were needed to explain the genesis of knowledge. Physical events stimulating the nervous system produced atomic ideas, irreducible mental states, in the knower. These basic ideas were then subject to distinctively psychological laws that organized them into clusters of complex ideas. As the laws of nature regulated the behavior of physical particles and systems, so the laws of association regulated the behavior of the ideas they produced. Since human knowledge was identified with a complex pattern of these very ideas, the purpose of epistemology was causally to reconstruct the genesis of knowledge through the lawful association of the basic epistemic particles.

This heuristic strategy gained its limited plausibility through a battery of assumptions widely shared by the early naturalists:

1. Human knowledge consists in a complex of ideas in the brain or mind of a person.
2. Its genesis can be explained through nonintentional physical and psychological laws operating on irreducible eidetic elements.
3. The theory of knowledge, like very empirical theory, is concerned exclusively with the causal explanation of externally or internally observable phenomena.

    4. Having an idea as a conscious mental state is equivalent to possessing knowledge of some kind.

    5. All the ideas of which knowledge allegedly consists are analogous to sensations, nonintentional states of consciousness directly caused by physical stimulation of the nervous system.

    6. The causal explanation of an epistemic *episode* is equivalent to its justification as an *epistemic* episode.

Although philosophical naturalism had wanted to overcome the Cartesian bifurcation of the mind and nature, it adopted uncritically the ambiguous terminology of *ideas* that Descartes had bequeathed to modern philosophy.[46] The different types of entity to which Descartes refers under the rubric of *ideas* serve an extraordinary range of dissimilar functions. Some are the conscious effects of physical causes operating on the human body (ideas as conscious sensations like pains); some are propositional terms of meaning, truth-vehicles, involved in logical relations of implication and deducibility (ideas as bearers of truth-value); some are the immediate objects of the mind's intentional awareness (ideas as the immanent intentional contents of mental acts); some are epistemic representations of formal reality, the world external to the mind, whose truth-value consists in their resemblance or lack of resemblance to what they represent (ideas as copies of the external world); finally, sometimes, *ideas* refer to the mental acts of the ego, that is, to episodes of intentional consciousness. What is common to these very different kinds of Cartesian ideas is their essential ontological privacy. They are all mind-dependent particulars whose *esse est experii* by the individual ego to whom they belong.

    Cartesian ideas, like their naturalistic counterparts, include both intentional and nonintentional states of consciousness. No sharp and clear distinction is drawn between conscious sensations like pains that cannot bear a truth-value and propositional terms of meaning that do. This diverse array of mind-dependent particulars creates a dangerous ambiguity when scientific knowledge is identified with an organized complex of psychological ideas. Given the elasticity of the Cartesian idiom, this could mean that human knowledge consists in a logically ordered structure of truth-bearing propositions judged to be true by a community of intelligent subjects. But it could just as easily mean that knowledge consists in the conscious experience of nonintentional sensations causally produced through interactive physical stimulation. The critical difference between *rationally assenting* to a proposition's truth and *having the experience of* a conscious sensation is irremediably blurred in both Cartesian epistemology and the naturalistic discipline created to replace it.

    The attempted naturalization of epistemology, modeled on the transfer of Newtonian atomism into the realm of ideas, was a colossal blunder. It treated the domain of human knowledge as the mental equivalent of the Newtonian concept of nature, as an assemblage of epistemic particles, ideas, subject to psychological laws. It systematically neglected the basic distinctions that differentiate philosophy from natural science. I am referring to the distinctions between intentional and nonintentional fields of investigation, between logical and psychological laws, between normative and descriptive categories, between causal explanation and epistemic justification. To override any of these central distinctions is to commit a specific version of the naturalistic fallacy. As Brentano and Husserl later argued, the fatal error of naturalism was not its desire to make philosophy scientific,[47] but its failure to conceive correctly the appropriate subject matter of philosophy. The philosophic investigation of knowledge is concerned with the different intentional factors within the comprehensive matrix of cognitive meaning. The core, sources, acts, terms, and norms of cognition are all inherently intentional. The empirical psychology advanced by the naturalists as a comprehensive epistemology was not an intentional discipline. The favored idiom of ideas obscured this decisive principle, permitting the confusion of propositional terms of meaning with nonintentional states of consciousness and the further confusion of logical and epistemic norms with laws of association. The immediate result of this critical obscurity was *psychologism*, the attempted reduction of authentic philosophical disciplines to the nonintentional psychology of sensation. The irony of the proposed reduction is striking. In their effort to make philosophy scientific, the naturalists embraced a theory of knowledge that rejected the essential conditions under which the conduct of science is possible.

G. Psychologism and its Critics

The revolutions decisive for philosophy are those in which the claims of former philosophies to be scientific are discredited by a critique of their "scientific" procedure.[48]

Philosophical Naturalism presented itself as a plausible solution to the crisis of philosophy. It would make philosophy scientific by transforming the theory of knowledge into empirical psychology. It would complete the inexorable process begun by Galileo in which autonomous scientific disciplines displaced their philosophical predecessors. The crisis of philosophy would be resolved by its eventual elimination as a rival or complement to science.

The psychological theory substituted for epistemology was empiricistic rather than empirical.[49] It took as its point of departure the Humean conception of the mind. In his psychology, Hume treated the intentional subject and its operations like quasi-objects. He reduced intentional consciousness to a temporal succession of one-dimensional psychic states, which he called *perceptions*.[50] These unit states of awareness were isolated from any structural reference to an object beyond themselves; they were simply nonintentional occurrences occupying a temporal position within a single stream of consciousness. The unity of the intentional subject was dissolved into the pure flow of these psychic elements. Because the units of awareness lacked intentional reference, Hume's theory implied that the objects of empirical consciousness were confined to a single psychological subject. His analysis precluded the possibility of individually different subjects intending a common objective world through numerically distinct intentional acts. It thus precluded epistemic objectivity, for on its premises no object of awareness could be experienced as identical by different subjects or even by the same subject at different times in its history. The elusive terminology of ideas allowed Hume and the naturalists, as it had earlier allowed Descartes, to treat a single objective entity, the idea, with remarkable latitude. In different expository contexts, Humean ideas are required to serve as objects of knowledge, as bearers of truth-value, as acts of awareness, and even as constitutive ingredients in the perceptual bundle comprising the intentional agent. The outcome of this unresolved and unacknowledged ambiguity was extreme intellectual disorder. The new empiricist epistemology effaced nearly every important distinction in the matrix of cognitive meaning.

Husserl and Frege led the philosophical opposition to the ambitious naturalistic project. They joined in accusing naturalistic epistemology of psychologism; they insisted that the theory of knowledge could not be reduced to empirical psychology without violating essential conditions of scientific objectivity. Following Aristotle, Husserl identified the theory of science with logic and logic with the comprehensive theory of propositional truth. On his analysis, S is a science if and only if S is an axiomatic deductive system of true propositions. He believed that systematic knowledge consists of true, deductively ordered, propositional terms of meaning, not of psychologically patterned ideas lacking in intentional reference. Thus, causal explanation of the genesis of nonintentional ideas cannot replace any of the legitimate philosophical disciplines. According to Husserl, a valid theory of science must distinguish, as naturalism did not, among (1) the real objects investigated by scientific inquiry (metaphysics);(2) the ideal propositional content asserted about these objects (logic and epistemology); (3) the intentional operations of investigation, confirmation, and assertion (eidetic phenomenology);[51] and (4) the linguistic expressions referring to those objects and expressing that ideal content (semiotic analysis). None of these legitimate philosophical disciplines is replaceable by naturalistic pscyhology.

The conflict initially crystallized around the psychologistic treatment of logic and mathematics. The naturalists wanted to clarify and justify these disciplines in the light of established or anticipated psychological theories. Empirical psychology could be established as the foundational form of knowledge if the following claims were effectively sustained: that natural science depends on logic for the axiomatization of its discoveries and that the science of logic depends on psychology, on the causal analysis of the origin and behavior of ideas. The second dependence rests on the assumption that logical laws hold between ideas, that they are generalized descriptions of the interaction between these basic mental contents. The following outline suggests the typical pattern of naturalistic argument. The laws of logic have been traditionally conceived as laws of thought. But human thought consists in the temporal succession of ideas in the conscious lives of individual persons. The antecedents and successors of these psychological thought atoms are other ideas mutually connected by laws of association. Thus, the laws of logic on which the practice of science universally depends, in fact, are laws of descriptive psychology, justified by appeal to inner observation. The sciences invariably depend upon logic, logic upon empirical psychology, and psychology on the individual's immediate acquaintance with the contents of his own stream of consciousness; in that immediate acquaintance with ideas, we reach the alleged foundation of all knowledge.

Husserl's first objection to psychologism attacked its circularity. As an empirical science, psychology must conform to logical principles in its theoretical structure. Thus, its practice presupposes the validity of logic which it cannot then be invoked to justify. The attempt to ground logic epistemically in any empirical discipline must fail, for these disciplines invariably presuppose the logical laws they are introduced to explain. Either logical laws need no epistemic foundation or they must be justified by a discipline at a different epistemic level from empirical science.[52]

Husserl also rejected the psychologistic account of logical objects, the ideal terms of propositional meaning. To paraphrase his argument: the ancient description of logical laws as laws of thought had been misconstrued by the naturalists. Propositions are not real temporal particulars exclusively confined to an individual stream of consciousness. Nor are they nonintentional mental states subject to laws of association and natural causation. The psychological analysis of Humean ideas is irrelevant to the logical analysis of a science's theoretical content. Logic is a science of truth, of intersubjective terms of propositional meaning. Unlike ideas, propositions are not unrepeatable occurrences in either the physical or the psychical realm but the publicly accessible content of an unlimited set of intentional operations and the common objective meaning expressible by synonymous declarative sentences. Unless intersubjective propositions are distinguished from private ideas and logical laws from laws of association, science must surrender its claim to objectivity. For, without publicly accessible propositions, there is nothing for scientists to argue about together nor anything epistemically shared for them to affirm as true.

Husserl's original refutation of psychologism in the *Logical Investigations* had been inspired by Frege's passionate attempt to protect the theory of logic against incursions from psychology. Whereas Husserl traced the roots of psychologism back to the "naturalization of consciousness,"[53] Frege viewed it as the offspring of uncritical empiricism: "Not everything is an idea. Otherwise psychology would contain all the sciences within it or least it would be the highest judge over all the sciences."[54] Once we carefully distinguish, as British empiricism did not, among the three distinct ontological realms of ideas, thoughts, and things, he continued, the foundational status of psychology becomes completely implausible. The place to begin this deconstruction is with an investigation of truth-vehicles, the proper objects of logical inquiry.[55]

Frege contends that the purpose of every science is to discover truths about its distinctive subject matter. This claim is not initially controversial: controversy arises, however, when we attempt to identify the logical subjects of which 'true' and 'false' are properly predicated. As we have seen, psychologism treated ideas as the bearers of truth-value. Frege believed that this disqualified psychologism as a theory of science because ideas, *Vorstellungen*, are never candidates for truth; only thoughts (*Gedanke*) are true or false.[56] What does Frege mean by a thought? Thoughts serve two interrelated functions in his theory: semantically, they are the sense or meaning expressed by indicative sentences; epistemically, they are the intentional content apprehended or grasped in acts of understanding and judgment. According to Frege, the ultimate bearers of truth are not sentences but the timeless thoughts they express.

As abstract and atemporal entities, thoughts belong to a third ontological realm, carefully distinguished by Frege from the outer world of perceptual objects and the inner world of subjective ideas. How does Frege demarcate these three realms of existence? Let us approach his distinction with illustrative examples taken from the three worlds. Sensible objects in the public realm of space and time, (for example, trees, planets, and human artifacts) belong to the outer world. The inner world of ideas includes sensations, emotions, images, and other ontologically private states of consciousness. The abstract realm of thoughts, the distinctive domain of logical inquiry, consists of propositional terms of meaning, such as the Pythagorean theorem, the second law of thermodynamics, or the principle of excluded middle. The entities belonging to each of these realms are related differently to human consciousness. *Objects* in the outer world are sensibly perceivable by an unlimited number of cognitive subjects. Each *idea* belongs to a single, private inner world such that two subjects can never be the bearers of the same idea. *Thoughts*, although sensibly imperceptible, like ideas, resemble sensible objects in their semantic and epistemic publicity.

By what criteria does Frege technically distinguish these three realms of being? He views ideas as ontologically private states of consciousness, uniquely attributable to the single psychological subject who bears them. They are nontransferable psychological states or events experienced by their bearers but neither perceived nor perceivable by them. Ideas exist only as long as they are consciously experienced, and they never exist apart from a conscious subject who is numerically and specifically distinct from them. Together with the intentional acts of the subject they constitute the subject matter of empirical psychology.

Perceptual objects to Frege are concrete physical things existing in a public world of space and time. Such objects exist independent of their being perceived, and they enter into a limitless variety of mind-independent relations with other objects in the outer world. Perceptual objects are subject to temporal genesis and perishing, but their life spans are generally much greater than those of ideas. Although we can discover truths about perceptual objects, they are not themselves bearers of truth. They are *objective* or mind-independent entities in contrast to the *subjective* mind-dependent ideas.

Frege views thoughts as abstract, immaterial realities, expressible in indicative sentences and apprehended and affirmed in intentional acts. They are ontologically and intentionally public like perceptual objects, but they have neither spatial location nor temporal duration. They are the only legitimate carriers of truth value, yet unlike ideas they have no bearer to whom they belong. They resemble perceptual objects in their ontological independence of the mind, but they cannot be sensibly perceived like their objective worldly counterparts. Thoughts provide the appropriate subject matter of logic, whose scientific purpose is to discover the invariant laws of implication and deducibility that obtain among them. Logical laws are laws of thought not laws of thinking; they apply to the objective order of propositional truths not to the subjective order of evanescent ideas and acts. Psychology can tell us nothing about their existence, essential properties, or intelligible relations. The postulated primacy of psychology is easily refuted once basic semantic and ontological principles are recognized and honored.

Frege's initial campaign to prevent the reduction of logic to psychology later developed into a general defense of philosophy against the strategies of naturalism and empiricism. The way to make philosophy scientific, he believed, was not to neglect or deny the essential conditions of science. The crisis of philosophy could only be deepened by its transformation into empirical psychology. However, if the structural limits of naturalism were identified, a way could be found to preserve both the autonomy of science and the theoretical functions of philosophy. Perhaps, through a systematic critique of psychologism and of the prejudices that sustain its plausibility, the proper relation between philosophy and the empirical sciences could be discovered. In that case, the crisis of philosophy could become the occasion for its authentic renewal.

2

The Primacy of Logic—A Case Study in Foundational Inquiry

*Casting Frege himself in his chosen type of role,
we would best regard him as a Columbus.
Discover he did but he didn't discover what he
thought he did.*[1]

A. The Logician's Perspective

Frege was first and foremost a logician. He made novel and important contributions to the science of logic and used those insights in investigating the foundations of arithmetic. When he turned to philosophy, he brought the distinctive perspective of the logician to bear on the examination of knowledge and language. "In logic we are concerned with the truth in the strictest sense of the word."[2] Language interested Frege because it is the human vehicle for the expression and communication of truth; science interested Frege because it achieved the discovery and systematization of truth.

Within the comprehensive matrix of cognition, the terms and norms of theoretical meaning held Frege's attention. Frege called formal and full terms of meaning *thoughts* (*Gedanke*), and he identified them as the legitimate bearers of truth value. As a logician he studied the nature and internal structure of thoughts and their relations of implication and deducibility. The purpose of logical analysis, as he saw it, was to articulate the internal organization of truths, to show how different logical elements combined to constitute the unity of a thought. Each thought by virtue of its internal structure stood in lawful relations to other thoughts. The logician's function was to discover these lawful truth connections and to articulate them in a rigorous axiomatic system. Human beings have access to the realm of truth through intentional acts of understanding and judgment and through the expressive power of language. Fregean thoughts serve as the intentional content of cognitive operations and the semantical content of indicative sentences. "The thought, in itself immaterial, clothes itself in the material garment of the sentence and thereby becomes comprehensible to us."[3] He saw language and mind as of interest to the logician only insofar as they make possible the apprehension and communication of truth.

According to Frege, the realm of thoughts is timeless and invariant. Its constituents have a perfect definiteness of nature and fixity of relation. There is nothing murky, vague, or ambiguous in the territory of logic. The logician demands that language respect this exactness when it is used to articulate truth. The normative ideals of clarity, coherence, rigor, and perspicuity are requirements imposed by logic on language in its theoretical employment. They are the standards Frege used to criticize natural languages and the regulative criteria guiding his construction of a new symbolic notation intended for the systematic expression of mathematical truth.[4]

The logician's interest in knowledge similarly is restricted to the clarification and justification of truth. The science of mathematics provided Frege with his original epistemic concern. The source of that concern was the widespread confusion in the nineteenth century about the conceptual content of mathematical truths and the appropriate method of their verification. Frege sought to resolve epistemic confusion through the techniques of logical analysis and reconstruction. He believed that truth claims are justified when they are deduced from epistemically evident axioms; concepts are clarified when they are defined in the logically simplest terms. Fregean epistemology is a species of applied logic.

The goal of every theoretical science is the discovery of truths about its proper objects. The particular goal of logic is the discovery of the laws of truth that hold between thoughts. These timeless laws can safely be called laws of thought, if a firm distinction is observed between acts of thinking and their assertible contents. The objects of logic are not mind-dependent acts or states but imperceptible and invariant truth vehicles. It is these immaterial thoughts which are, strictly speaking, true or false, rather than the sentences that express them, the acts of judgment that affirm them, or the speech acts in which their truth-value is publicly asserted. Human thinking, according to Frege, does not produce thoughts; it apprehends them, very much as acts of sense perceive their sensible objects. Neither the thoughts grasped in thinking nor the perceived spatial objects depend for their existence or essential properties on the mind's awareness of them. The truth-value of a thought is as timeless and mind-independent as its bearer. The objects of logic are unaltered by the process of their discovery or expression. None of their essential properties is made more intelligible through increased understanding of any temporal process whatsoever. Logic, therefore, is the most fundamental theoretical science. Whereas all the other disciplines presuppose logic's laws of truth, their discoveries contribute nothing to clarifying or verifying these laws.

The logician's restricted theoretical concern is most evident in Frege's treatment of natural language. His semantical theory is confined to those aspects of language essential to reference and truth. Linguistic expressions are analyzed by citing their functional contribution to the truth conditions of the sentences to which they belong. Frege constructs ideal requirements for a logically perfect language in which the principles of classical logic have unrestricted validity. Measured against this standard, existing natural languages are found wanting; they are imperfect instruments for the systematic expression of true thoughts. Three deficiencies in particular are emphasized: failure of reference for proper names, ambiguity of sense for referring expressions, and general lack of perspicuity. In a perspicuous language the syntactical structure of the sentence is an accurate guide to the semantical structure of the thought it expresses. In a logically perfect language, the syntactical laws regulating the construction of sentences mirror the logical laws governing the constitution of thoughts. The timeless precision of the world of truth should find its visible model in the articulated structure of the sentences that express truth. The reader of an ideal language could discern the logical structure of thought in the grammatical structure of language. The thought, in itself immaterial, thus clothes itself in the material garment of the perspicuous sentences.

Frege took pains throughout his career to distinguish the world of the logician from that of the linguist and psychologist. In the realm of logic thoughts are neither mental nor linguistic. However, he repeatedly relied on language to clarify the important logical distinctions between functions and objects, sense and reference, and thoughts and their internal constituents. Because the world of thoughts has a perspicuous model in the world of sentences, it is imperative that the model be made as accurate as possible. This principle justifies the construction of an ideal language and explains Frege's frequent appeals to language in support of extralinguistic claims. The frequent use of semantic ascent can, however, be misleading. "I am compelled to occupy myself with language although it is not my proper concern here."[5] For Frege the decisive distinctions are logical not linguistic. Priority in the order of exposition should not be confused with priority in the order of justification. The critical linguistic distinctions and laws are founded deep in the nature of things, particularly in the nature of truth. The world of language is made by human beings; the logician's world admits of human discovery but is exempt from human alteration. It is the foundational realm on which theoretical language and science rest.

B. The Locus of Epistemic Invariance

Frege's convictions about truth were shaped in a philosophical climate dominated by the theory of evolution. He opposed universal application of the genetic perspective because it threatened the necessary conditions of epistemic objectivity. Unless there were timelessly true thoughts immune from historical change, there could not be a transhistorical community of science. Frege never doubted that such a community did exist. Instead, he raised to explicitness the requirements it presupposed, in particular the requirement of invariant truth. The historically evolving community of science rests on a foundation of epistemic invariance.

Frege located the required invariance in the field of logical inquiry, the abstract realm of thoughts from which change was permanently excluded. Epistemic objectivity demands that we recognize a third ontological realm, distinct from the outer world of material objects and the inner world of ideas and intentional acts. There must exist a third realm of truths that are imperceptible like ideas but independent of the mind like natural objects. Time effects no alteration in the logician's world of immaterial truths. The principle of evolution finds no purchase here. Invariance is achieved through the postulation of timeless thoughts, whose discovery is the task of science and whose articulation the essential purpose of language.

Thoughts, though they are real (*wirklich*), are importantly different from other entities whose reality we recognize. Unlike temporal entities that exist in reciprocal causal relations, thoughts are immune from essential change and ordinary patterns of causality. They acquire indirect causal power through the mind's ability to think, understand, judge, and express them. It is vital to remember Frege's belief that the mind exercises no causal power over thoughts. In their being, truth-value, and logical relations, thoughts, he insisted, are completely independent of mind. However, their causal independence did not preclude psychological or linguistic accessibility. Thoughts could not play their required epistemic function unless scientific investigators could grasp their truth-conditions, rationally assent to their truth-value, and epistemically debate them with fellow theorists in a common language. Science is the transcultural, transhistorical enterprise in which invariant truths are discovered individually, expressed and defended publicly and affirmed collectively. There can be no science unless human beings have equal access to the common realm of truth; there can be no science unless that common realm is unaffected by the human discovery and communication of it. The laws of truth are boundary stones set in an eternal foundation that thinking cannot displace.[6] They provide the constant, universal frame of reference for human inquiry.

It is useful to distinguish the two levels of foundational inquiry in which Frege engaged. The first, or transcendental, level explores the necessary conditions of scientific objectivity. What conditions must obtain if the scientific enterprise is to achieve eternally valid results? Frege argued that there must exist an invariant realm of truths, universally accessible across time, capable of guaranteeing epistemic, semantic, and intentional objectivity. However strange such a realm might seem to those with empirical or naturalistic prejudices, its acceptance is necessary if the validity of science is to be upheld. For anyone who accepts the intelligibility of common discourse, there is no rational alternative to recognizing this abstract logician's world.

The transcendental discovery of the invariance of truth should not be confused with the logical analysis of particular thoughts. To grant Frege the necessity of a foundational realm is not , at the same time, to grant him a particular analysis of its contents. We should distinguish between the epistemic priority *of* the logical order and analytical priority *within* it. Foundational analysis, in Frege's general practice, is the decomposition of thoughts into their basic elements and relations and the reduction of arguments to their premises, inference rules, and conclusions. Transcendental analysis establishes the existence of a realm of truth for the logician to explore; logical analysis is the reduction of that realm to its primitive elements and axioms, the intratheoretic base for systematic definitions and demonstrations. On Frege's theory of knowledge, science, as a human enterprise,rests on a transcendental foundation of invariant truths; particular sciences rest on a logical foundation of indemonstrable axioms and undefinable concepts. Until a given discipline has uncovered these logical primitives and used them to reconstruct its truth-claims, it lacks the theoretical clarity and rigor authentic science demands. Like Aristotle before him, Frege modeled his theory of science on the example of "axiomatized mathematics."

C. The Specter of Psychologism

Frege's philosophic career began with his intensive study of the foundations of arithmetic. In the course of his research, he developed a complex of logical beliefs and analytic methods strongly divergent from those of his predecessors and contemporaries. He was driven to philosophical reflection because of his discontent with the theoretical foundations of arithmetic. The mathematicians of his day were more intent on developing techniques and proliferating theorems than with disclosing the underlying conceptual structure of their science. "If I compare arithmetic with a tree that unfolds upwards into a multitude of techniques and theorems while its roots drive into the depths, then it seems to me that the impetus of the root, at least in Germany, is rather weak."[7] When Frege spoke of the roots of arithmetic he referred to its primitive axioms, elementary concepts, and rules of inference, the logical ground on which axiomization might proceed. Disregard of foundational issues was scandalous, he believed, in a science expected to serve as a model of theoretical rigor. Mathematics was not entitled to its exemplary role until its basic theoretical content was clarified. "If mathematicians have divergent opinions about equality, this means nothing less than that mathematicians disagree as to the content of their science; and if we regard science as essentially consisting of *thoughts*, not of words and symbols, it means that there is no united science of mathematics at all, that mathematicians just do not understand one another."[8]

The absence of conceptual clarity in arithmetic was most apparent in the controversy over the concept of number. Without a clear understanding of this basic concept, no deeper insight into the intelligible content and justification of arithmetic was possible. But the prevailing philosophic theories of arithmetic failed to provide the required clarity. Without exception, they misunderstood the meaning of the simplest mathematical concepts and methods of justification. Frege focused his criticism on the most influential theories of his time: Mill's mathematical empiricism, Kant's arithmetical intuitionism, and the formalist theories of Heine and Thomae.[9] The burden of his criticism was simple: none of these philosophers offered a convincing semantical analysis of arithmetic sentences nor a plausible method for the justification of mathematical knowledge. They made the meaning of mathematics obscure and its rightful claim to knowledge uncertain.

Frege's polemics were intended as prolegomena to the execution of his major intellectual project, the defense of logicism.[10] According to the logicist thesis, arithmetic is reducible to the science of logic. All arithmetical concepts could be defined in purely logical terms and all arithmetical truths rigorously deduced from purely logical laws. Arithmetic and the higher forms of analysis based on it are analytic a priori disciplines, requiring neither pure nor empirical intuitions for their evidential support. For Frege, the foundations of arithmetic were dependent on logic in the double sense of science and technique. Through the *logical* operations of definition and deduction, derivative arithmetic concepts and theorems were reduced to set-theoretic concepts and axioms. By extending the scope of logic to include set-theory, Frege could claim that the theoretical content of arithmetic was wholly explicable in logical terms. Logical theories provide the axiomatic base and logical techniques the method for the clarification and justification of mathematics.

Frege's penetrating foundational research generally met with indifference or neglect. Mathematicians found it too philosophical, and philosophers found it too much like mathematics. But the major deterrent to serious consideration of the logicist project was the deep confusion in the late nineteenth century regarding the subject matter of logic. Frege entitled this confusion *psychologism*. In the course of his philosophic career he resisted many species of this general intellectual disorder. In its different forms, psychologism threatened the correct understanding of mathematics, logic, philosophical semantics, epistemology, and metaphysics. The common ground of these different psychologistic variations was a failure to recognize the nature and contents of the logical order. Without a proper understanding of abstract terms of meaning, neither language, thought, nor science could be conceived coherently.

Frege first encountered psychologism as a philosophy of logic. In that context it was a mistaken theory, rooted in empiricist prejudices, about the subject matter, method, and epistemic results of logical inquiry. Logical psychologism identified the objects of logic with mental acts or ideas, its methods of deduction with the heuristic procedures of an inductive discipline, and its a priori truths with empirical generalizations. It tried to substitute the empirical science of psychology for logic. Given the logicist thesis, this attempted substitution threatened both logic and mathematics with theoretical disorder. Given the general dependence of science on logical laws, it threatened the integrity of the entire theoretical enterprise. In the light of Frege's deepest intellectual loyalties, psychologism was a specter he needed to destroy.

What made this confusion of distinct disciplines plausible? According to Frege, the essential confusion stemmed from a recurrent ambiguity in the concept of law:[11] Theoretical laws can be either descriptive or prescriptive in nature. The traditional designation of logical laws as laws of thought stresses their descriptive aspect. If it is assumed that the laws of logic bear the same relation to thinking that the laws of grammar bear to language, then the psychologistic thesis becomes intelligible. Defenders of that thesis began with the received identity between the laws of logic and the laws of mind. The purpose of determining laws of thought is to make explicit factual patterns that recur in human thinking. These laws serve to single out that family of beings whose mental activity is described in a particular way. They are factual reports, inductively established, with no guarantee of invariance. Taken as general descriptions of psychological activity, such laws could define a norm for science only in the sense that they record the pattern of thinking most characteristic of a limited group of human beings at a given time. This would be a case of treating a comparative uniformity of behavior as a prescriptive standard or measure.

Since the factual patterns of human thinking are subject to change, the laws of logic, thus understood, lack eternal or unconditional validity. They will vary as the patterns of mental activity they describe vary. They cannot serve as a standard for evaluating that activity except as indicating deviations from normal psychological practice. This modified conception of logical laws has profound implications for the nature of truth. "For me what is true is something objective and independent of the judging subject; for psychological logicians it is not."[12] The psychologistic understanding of logic makes the truth of a judgment depend on its "general validity." Questions of truth or falsity are construed as questions of agreement or disagreement among prospective judges.[13] A judgment has general validity when its acceptance by a particular community of judging subjects is unanimous. Adherence to this principle undermines the possibility of a universal and invariant order of truth. Truth is neither constant nor epistemically binding but subject to variation with the individual judgments of the human beings who determine it. The psychologistic concept of truth compels us to include in our account of truth's essential features a reference to the subjects who assent to it. Frege's scorn for this analysis is unqualified. "One could scarcely falsify the sense of the word 'true' more mischievously than by including in it a reference to the subject who judges."[14]

Frege insisted that we distinguish, as the adherents of psychologism do not, between the truth-value of a thought and the human activity of taking that thought to be true or false.[15] He viewed logical laws as laws of truth not psychological reports about observed patterns of judgment. Laws of truth make no reference to the conduct or epistemic preferences of human beings. The truth-value of a thought is as independent of its own discovery or affirmation as the logical relation of implication among thoughts is independent of the actual performance of inference.

Because Frege rejected the descriptive interpretation of logical laws as psychological reports, it should not be assumed that he accepted a primarily prescriptive account of logic. To him, logical truths are descriptive of the invariant relations that obtain between independent *contents* of judgment (full terms of meaning). They are laws of thought (*Gedanke*), not laws of thinking. They express constant relations of deducibility among timeless propositional truths. However, these laws are prescriptive for the practice of inquiry. "One and the same logical law is first and foremost a law of to-be-true and only then has a normative function."[16] Logical principles are prescriptive because they determine what human beings should take to be true if they are to comply with the permanent realm of truth. "Anyone who has knowledge of a law of truth has by the same token acknowledged a law that prescribes the way in which one ought to judge, no matter where, or when, or by whom the judgment is made."[17] To misconceive the objects governed by logical laws invariably would lead to a misconstrual of their epistemic status and regulative function. This would threaten not only mathematics and logic but the entire realm of scientific theory.

Frege intended his criticism of psychologism to restore logic to its proper autonomy as the a priori science of true thoughts. Unless this were done, the logicist project stood no chance of a fair hearing. But the initial defense of logicism led him inexorably into general issues in semantics and epistemology. These philosophical concerns also were foundational but at a different level from the set-theoretic reductionist strategy of the *Grundgesetze*. In defense of logicism, Frege tried to axiomatize the science of arithmetic on a set-theoretic conceptual foundation. To support his project, he proposed a specific semantical interpretation of the sentences of arithmetic, intended to rebut both psychologistic and empiricist criticisms. He defended that interpretation by constructing a general semantics and ontology with implications for all of human knowledge. Unhappily, Frege's strategy was to merge these distinct levels of foundational argument for reasons that should become clearer as this chapter unfolds.

D. Principles of Philosophical Analysis

In the *Foundations of Arithmetic*, published in 1884, Frege criticized the dominant philosophical interpretations of mathematics. He ridiculed the formalists' confusion of numbers and numerals, the empiricist treatment of mathematical sentences as empirical generalizations, and the pervasive psychologistic orientation we just examined. To Frege these theories were not simply wrong, they were preposterous. They reflected an extreme degree of intellectual confusion, one that could be corrected only by the introduction of explicit methodological principles that would regulate further foundational research. These heuristic principles were needed to shape the philosophy of arithmetic into a theoretical enterprise with a future. They were meant to demarcate the elementary distinctions that an investigation of mathematics must observe. Their original purpose was to remove the conceptual disorder that hindered the appreciation of logicism. But they eventually became the basis for Frege's comprehensive semantical and ontological theories.

It is difficult to find a general rubic for these methodological principles. Two of them make explicit ontological claims and the third lays down a rule of procedure for semantical analysis. As a unit, however, they illustrate the tight interdependence between onotological and linguistic considerations in Frege's thought. Although Frege claimed that ontological distinctions always ground linguistic principles, much of his ontology is based upon a general theory of linguistic meaning. The linguistic theory is itself presented as the only philosophy of language consistent with scientific objectivity. In Frege's mature philosophy, epistemic, semantic, and metaphysical considerations were fully intermeshed.

The first principle states: "Always separate sharply the psychological from the logical, the subjective from the objective."[18] Its manifest purpose is to demarcate clearly the subject matters of logic and psychology. Logical entities are objective and public; the objects of psychology are subjective and private. What does this mean? Frege seems to have two criteria of objectivity, ontological independence *of* the mind and intentional accessibility *to* the mind. Those entities are objective whose existence and essential properties are causally independent of any mind's operations but completely accessible to every mind's discernment and awareness. By contrast, subjective entities depend on a particular mind for their reality but preclude direct sensible or intellectual awareness even by their bearers. Their ontological privacy consists in their nontransferable possession by the single consciousness to which they belong. Although this consciousness *has* them as episodes in its history, it cannot *perceive* them sensibly. Psychological realities are directly experienced by their bearers but they cannot be perceived or directly apprehended by anyone else. Although Frege includes both intentional acts and nonintentional conscious states in the field of psychology, his chief example of a subjective entity is an *idea*.[19] An idea in the subjective sense is governed by the psychological laws of association. Ideas are evanescent and indefinite mental states, evoked by experience, language, or reflection. They belong to the temporal stream of an individual's psychic life at a particular moment in its history. Different persons may have similar ideas in response to the same sentence or object, but there is no possibility of two persons having or experiencing the same idea.

Ideas, as subjective psychological entities, are explicitly contrasted with thoughts and concepts. Thoughts are the primary subject matter of logic; concepts are among their essential constituents. Both are equally public and objective. Fregean ideas, *Vorstellungen*, seem to be creatures of human sensibility, but concepts are properly the concern of intellect and reason. They cannot be *perceived* like sensible objects; they cannot be *had* like ideas; but the identical concept must be understood by anyone who hopes to understand the thoughts it partly composes. Fregean concepts are a distinct category of objective reality, belonging neither to the physical nor the mental realm of existence. Like the other abstract entities logic surveys, they are inhabitants of the third realm.

To Frege, the sphere of privacy and subjectivity belongs exclusively to psychology. Logic does not have this total claim to the sphere of objectivity. Both concrete and abstract entities share the causal independence of mind that makes psychological inquiry irrelevant to their comprehension. Neither physics nor logic is concerned with the nature and operations of the thinking subject, and the answer to any question whatsoever in psychology must be for mathematics (logic) a matter of complete indifference.[20] The first principle, if adopted, provides logic with a charter of complete independence from psychology.

The second principle states: "Never ask for the meaning of a term in isolation, but only in the context of a proposition." Frege required a comprehensive philosophy of mathematics to provide a coherent account of mathematical discourse. In the *Grundlagen*, he showed that the prevailing interpretations of mathematical symbols misrepresented their theoretical meanings. His new principle of semantical analysis initially was intended for the clarification of arithmetical language, but eventually it became the cornerstone of his general semantics. It supplemented the first principle's opposition to psychologism by radically distinguishing the *meaning* of a term from the play of *ideas* that accompany its use. There is a familiar tendency, reinforced by empiricist principles, to treat the meaning of linguistic symbols as the mental pictures or images they evoke (recall Hume's requirement that every meaningful expression correspond to a particular impression or idea).[21] When the sense of a sentence becomes dependent on individual feelings, reactions, or beliefs, it loses its ability to provide a framework of collaborative argument. If shared scientific inquiry is possible, there must be a common ground of objective linguistic meaning independent of the psychological reactions of the participants. The sense of language must be separated from the private impressions caused by its use.

To preserve the general possibility of intersubjective meaning and the specific intelligibility of arithmetic, Frege insisted that we treat the sentence as the basic unit of semantical analysis. The linguistic priority accorded to sentences rests on the logical priority of the thoughts they express. These thoughts provide sentences with sense or meaning, and their constituents provide sentence fragments with an equivalent objective correlate. In the order of *recognition*, sentence fragments are prior to sentences. You cannot understand the sense of a sentence unless you understand the sense of its parts. But in the order of *explication*, the priority is reversed. The sense of a sentence fragment consists in its functional contribution to the total sense of the sentences of which it is a part.

The crucial concept for understanding the meaning of language is truth. In Fregean semantics only that which is relevant to the truth or falsity of a sentence belongs to its sense. We can explicate the thought a sentence expresses by specifying its truth-conditions. This is the correct method of semantical interpretation, for the sense of the sentence is understood once we grasp under what conditions the sentence is true. To grasp the sense of a sentence does not require that we be able to determine its truth-value. Truth-conditions are not knowledge-conditions; the meaning of a sentence may be quite distinct from the evidential criteria by which its truth-value is determined.[22]

The symbols of mathematics should be interpreted by defining the sense of the most typical sentences in which they occur. In the case of arithmetic these are equations that state, in effect, that the same number is the common referent of distinct numerical expressions.[23] In this context of providing truth-conditions for equations, Frege explicates all of arithmetic discourse. The strategy of truth-conditions is contrasted with the empiricist attempt to find ideas for each of the arithmetic signs. "We can form no idea of the number either as a self-subsistent object or as a property in an external thing, because it is not in fact anything sensible or a property of an external thing."[24]

That we can form no idea of its content is therefore no reason for denying all meaning to a word, or excluding it from our vocabulary. We are indeed only imposed on by the opposite view because we will, when asking for the meaning of a word, consider it in isolation, which leads us to accept an idea as its meaning. Accordingly any word for which we can find no corresponding mental picture appears to have no content. But we ought always to keep before our eyes a complete proposition. Only in the proposition have the words really meaning. It may be that the mental picture floats before us all the while, but these need not correspond to the *logical elements* in the judgment. It is enough if the proposition as a whole has sense. It is this that confers on its parts also their content. The self subsistence which I am claiming for number is not to be taken to mean that a number word signifies something when removed from the context of a proposition, but only to preclude the use of such words as predicates or attributes which appreciably alters their meaning.[25]

By excluding psychologism from semantics, we help to prevent its spread into arithmetic. "Only by adhering to this (second principle) can we, as I believe, avoid a physical view of number without slipping into a psychological view of it."[26]

The third principle states: "Never lose sight of the distinction between concept and object." The first two principles are framed to preserve a clear separation between *subjective* and *objective* factors in ontology and semantics. Principle three insists on the objective ontological distinction between objects and concepts. The conceptual contrast between objectivity and objects is more apparent in German than in English. As Furth remarks, there is no etymological tie between *objectiv* and *Gegenstand*.[27] This etymological independence reflects the corresponding separation in Frege's ontology between the different sorts of objective reality.

Frege divided all of reality into functions and objects. This is the most basic of his ontological divisions, the one that parallels his systematic linguistic classification of referring expressions. Though both functions and objects are objective, they may never be substituted for one another, nor permit an exchange of predicates. "What is asserted about a concept [function] can never be asserted about an object: for a proper name can never be a predicative expression though it can be part of one. I do not want to say that it is false to assert about an object what is here asserted about a concept, I want to say it is impossible, senseless, to do so."[28]

In defending and clarifying the function-object division, Frege vacillated between the material and formal modes of speech. The syntactical and semantical differences between proper names and predicates were invoked repeatedly to clarify the ontological divide. He explained that proper names, the symbols denoting objects, are complete expressions; the predicate expressions that refer to concepts are incomplete.[29] To continue the parallel in the material mode, objects are described as saturated entities and functions as unsaturated.

Frege borrowed the category of function from mathematics and generalized it for ontological purposes. The logical categories of concepts and relations were then incorporated into the ontological framework by treating them as species of functions whose values for all arguments are truth-values. Concepts, technically defined, are one-place functions that take all objects and only objects as their arguments and the true or the false, two unique objects, as their values.[30] The category of function cannot be defined because it is logically primitive; but it can be illuminated by recourse to language. Concepts, for example, are the referents of grammatical predicates that differ from objects in their essentially predicative nature. "What I call the predicative nature of a concept is just a special case of the need for supplementation, the unsaturatedness that I give as an essential feature of the function."[31]

Functions are essential to the inner structure of thoughts. "Not all the parts of a thought can be complete; at least one must be unsaturated or predicative, otherwise they would not hold together."[32] This need for completion by objects constitutes the specific nature of all functions. "The essence of the function is to be found in the correlation which is established between the references of the introduced object names and the references of the object names which arise";[33] that is, between the argument objects and the value-objects that the function lawfully connects.

In Frege's ideal language the truth-value of each concept must be determined for all objects. This principle ensures a unique referent for every referring expression and unrestricted validity for the principle of the excluded middle. When the value of a concept for an argument is the truth-value, the true, the argument object is said to fall under the concept.[34] Complex concepts can be intensionally defined by stating the properties an object must have to fall under them. In general the properties of the subsumed object do not belong to the concept. The characteristic marks of a concept, as distinct from its properties, establish the concept's identity and coincide with the properties of the objects falling under it. Frege's is not a copy theory of concepts nor a picture theory of truth. The logical order does not resemble the order of nature. Thoughts are true when their truth-conditions are satisfied; concepts are instantiated when objects fall under them.

Taken as a block, Frege's three principles help to establish the central position of concepts in his philosophy. The first principle sharply separates concepts and ideas as a way of distinguishing logic from psychology. The second principle binds concepts to thoughts on the analogy of predicates and sentences. The third principle insists on the unsaturated nature of concepts and their need for completion by objects. It seems that in the theory of concepts a connective link has been found between language, meaning and being.

E. The Limits of Empiricism

Frege finds the solution to numerous philosophical problems in the acceptance of abstract entities. His semantic, epistemic, and ontological theories all depend on the third realm as a guarantee of required objectivity. His enduring opposition to empiricism is rooted chiefly in its restriction of existence to natural or mind-dependent objects. Frege first encountered philosophical empiricism in the mathematical theories of Mill, Heine, and Thomae. Although disagreeing in their interpretation of arithmetic sentences, these thinkers were committed to a common empiricist outlook. They tended to restrict what is real to what is sensible. "There is at present a very widespread tendency not to recognize as an object anything that cannot be perceived by means of the senses; this leads, here, to numerals being taken for numbers, the proper objects of our discussion."[35]

Mill's empiricism led him to claim that numbers are sensible properties of concrete collections of observable objects and that arithmetic sentences are empirical generalizations about such properties.[36] Heine's and Thomae's formalism identified numbers with meaningless inscriptions to which mathematicians arbitrarily assigned rules for purposes of calculation. By conceiving of arithmetic as a game played with empty signs, the formalists hoped either to dodge the question of numerical existence or to resolve it by reducing numbers to sensible marks. Both positions, though evidently problematic, were reinforced by the empiricist criterion of existence, which limits the real to that which can act directly or indirectly on the senses.[37]

Frege believed that implicit endorsement of this criterion was a contributing cause of psychologism. It explained the tendency to treat numbers, concepts, and thoughts as ideas. Since logical entities do not act upon the senses, the empiricist classifies them as ideas by default and thinks of ideas as objects of inner sense modeled on external objects of perception. If logical entities are not spatial objects, they must be ideas, for inner and outer objects of perception exhaust what there is. There is no third, ontological, realm imperceptible by sense but epistemically accessible to reason.

Neither empiricism, formalism nor psychologism achieved an adequate philosophy of mathematics. Frege demonstrated their failure by contrasting the properties of numbers with the attributes of written inscriptions, psychological ideas, and sensible properties.[38] The differences between numbers, numerals, and ideas, once noted, are undeniable. Numbers and sensible properties are harder to differentiate. "There does exist a certain similarity between number and color; it consists, however, not in our becoming acquainted with them both in external things through the senses, but in their being both objective."[39] When we say that numbers are objective, "outside of the mind," we do not mean to apply spatial predicates to them, but to deny their dependence on mind altogether.

According to Frege, the objective realm must not be limited to the sphere of the sensible, nor the class of objects to spatial objects, nor intentional awareness to sensible intuition, nor the bearers of truth-value to sentences or ideas. Empiricism, by its rejection or denial of abstract entities, misrepresents the logician's world and unduly narrows the scope of the mind. Its limits must be transcended to ensure a defensible theory of science and a credible philosophy of language. Again, Frege took insights achieved in defense of logicism and gave them a systematic prominence that transcends their context of origin.

F. A Common Stock of Thoughts

Frege designed his philosophy of language to satisfy the requirements of demonstrative science. The cognitive function of language dominates his account of linguistic meaning. Nonepistemic uses of language are acknowledged but the semiotic theory is not framed to accommodate them. The origin of the theory in the analysis of arithmetic discourse decisively orients its development.

Frege viewed science as the communal enterprise for the discovery and systematic assertion of truth. Its activity could be divided into the successive stages of inquiry and demonstration. Inquiry consists in the discovery, discussion, and epistemic appraisal of thoughts. When a class of true thoughts bearing on a common subject matter has been found, the task of science is to integrate those truths in an axiomatic-deductive system. The normal activity of the logician is to test these axiomatizations for clarity, coherence, economy, and rigor.

First-order sciences are concerned with the truth-value and logical priority of thoughts but they leave their specific nature unexamined. Theories of knowledge, however, cannot ignore the bearers of scientific truth. They are required to explain how a transsubjective, transhistorical community of science is possible. Frege rejected empiricist epistemology because it could not account for the objectivity of knowledge. He asserted that epistemic objectivity requires a common body of truths open to reasonable affirmation. It requires an identical assertible content equally accessible to all members of the scientific community. Neither empiricism nor psychologism could provide an analysis of truth that preserved the identity of epistemic content. "We must not fail to recognize that the same sense, the same thought, may be variably expressed. It is possible for one sentence to give no more and no less information than another; and for all the multiplicity of languages, mankind has a common stock of thoughts."[40] This common stock of thoughts makes science possible both as a form of shared inquiry and as a permanent fund of compelling truth.

The purpose of language, epistemically conceived, is to express and transmit the common stock of thoughts. This accounts for the primacy of sentences among linguistic expressions, for only they have thoughts as their senses. The thought, which serves as the sense of the sentence, also serves as the intentional content of the acts of understanding and judgment. As a plurality of subjective acts can have an identical intentional content, so a plurality of sentences across different languages can have an identical semantical content. Thoughts provide the nexus of intersection for mind and language. Semantical relations connect discourse with extralinguistic meaning; intentional relations connect minds with extramental truth vehicles.[41] At the level of thoughts, the semantical and intentional content are the same.

Frege's theory of linguistic meaning is explicitly relational. In the fundamental semantical rubric, E (in L) expresses its sense and stands for its reference, linguistic expressions are semantically related to extralinguistic entities. Sense and reference are the extralinguistic aspects of meaning essential to truth. Frege's analysis of mathematical equations led to the original distinction between *Sinn and Bedeutung*. He introduced it to explain how identity statements could be cognitively informative. Our knowledge is amplified when we discover that two expressions with different meanings have an identical referent. This shows that the meaning or sense of an expression cannot be identified with its referent. How then are sense and reference connected? We always refer to an entity under some limited aspect of its being. Through its sense, a sign gives us information about its referent, information that is always partial. Comprehensive knowledge of an entity would require us to know immediately whether any given sense held true of it, but we never attain such comprehensive knowledge. The sense of a referring expression intellectually presents its referent under a limited mode of its being.

In its introductory use, the sense-reference distinction was limited to expressions designating objects. As Frege generalized his semantical theory, he extended its application to all referring expressions. Functional expressions and sentences as well as singular terms were analyzed according to the common semantical rubric. The primacy of sentences, though partly weakened by their assimilation to proper names, was essentially preserved, for the semantical analysis of sentence fragments tied their sense and reference to that of the sentences that contained them. The truth-conditions (sense) and truth-value (reference) of a sentence are a function of the meaning and denotation of its constituents.

The semantical content of language is objective in the by now familiar Fregean sense. Both sense and reference are ontologically independent of the mind and intentionally accessible to it. Frege treated as subjective all aspects of linguistic meaning not essential to truth. The tone of a poem, the emotions evoked by a phrase, the beliefs associated with a sentence are explicitly segregated from language's objective content. The logician's perspective regulates the whole affair. The objective meaning of language is restricted to what bears directly on the truth-conditions and truth-value of indicative sentences.

In his theory of sense and reference, Frege tied the objectivity of knowledge to that of language and mind. All minds must have equal access to identical epistemic contents: all languages must have equal power to express the common stock of thoughts. The essence of objectivity, seen from this angle, is intersubjective accessibility to an identical set of thoughts whose truth-value and logical relations are independent of their discovery, affirmation, and expression. Neither thinking thoughts nor saying them makes them so. Frege believed that the only way to preserve such objectivity was to make thoughts completely independent of the mind's operations. As there is one common sensible world, so there must be one common intelligible world, the logician's domain. The independence of natural objects from the mind's causation is the model Frege used to explain the objectivity of truths. But it is not immediately clear that the intersubjective accessibility of thoughts requires such radical independence of thinking. Must we accept Frege's third realm ontology to preserve scientific objectivity?

G. Privacy, Objectivity, and Realism

In the course of his struggle with psychologism, Frege came to connect inseparably the notions of subjectivity, privacy, and idealism. By treating ideas and mental acts as exemplary instances of the subjective, he was able to claim that dependence on the mind precluded public accessibility. If the epistemic content of judgment and the semantical content of discourse were confined to a particular mind's inner states, then both knowledge and language would forfeit their objectivity.

Frege's reduction of subjectivity to privacy was possible because he modeled the subjective on the *ideas* of British empiricism. These subjective entities do depend for their existence on a particular mind's awareness of them; in addition, they are treated by the empiricists as the immediate objects of knowledge and the semantical correlates of language. Frege was not simply arbitrary, then, in his association of subjectivity with solipsism. "If man could not think, and could not take something of which he was not the bearer as the object of his thought, he would have an inner world but no outer world."[42] Frege called the solipsist with only an inner world of ideas to consider an *idealist*. Such a person could neither be aware of nor refer to anything other than his ontologically private states. The solipsist's metaphysics could only include entities that, like ideas, depended for their being on one's consciousness of them. If dependence on subjectivity is equivalent to privacy and privacy to solipsism and solipsism to this special form of idealism, then idealism surely is incompatible with objectivity. And if the only alternative to such idealism is a realistic ontology of thoughts and things, then we must accept Frege's metaphysics or abandon objective knowledge.

Frege made short shrift of idealism by coupling it inexorably to solipsism. He could do this because he confined his attention to the psychological idealism characteristic of classical British thought. But his argument neglects any reference to transcendental idealism, which explicitly tries to preserve epistemic and semantic objectivity. There is a parallel flaw in his defense of realism. Frege's metaphysical realism treats thoughts and things as equally independent of cognitive operations. But he ignored the version of epistemic realism that distinguishes the ontological standing of the objects and terms of cognitive meaning. Although equally intersubjective and public, they are not equally independent of intentional activity. Neither the critique of idealism nor the defense of Fregean realism can rest on the objectivity premise alone.

The precise function of realism in Frege's philosophy has been carefully explored by Rulon Wells. Wells outlined four theses of what he calls *common sense realism* in the course of explaining Frege's complex and original ontology.[43]

1) A belief that there is an objective reality, independent of, but accessible to human knowledge.
2) Though human error is abundant, we do in fact possess much genuine knowledge of this reality including the standard parts of mathematics.
3) All knowledge is a cognition of timeless objective truth.
4) Not only the natural sciences but logic and mathematics have objective truths as their subject matter.[44]

Wells contended that Frege took the truth of these particular theses for granted. Rather than submit them to critical evaluation, he inquired into the conditions of their possibility. The construction of Frege's ontology is construed on the model of a transcendental deduction. The theses of realism correspond to the *quid facti*; the detailed and abundant ontology corresponds to the *quid juris*. The strange feature of the deduction is that the presuppositions of "common sense" realism prove uncongenial to common sense. This oddness may be explained in either of two ways. Either Frege has erred by including more in his ontology than epistemic objectivity requires, or common sense is limited by its unreflective character. Failing to investigate its presuppositions, it finds them startling when brought to light.

Our study gives substantial support to Wells's claim that the theses of realism are presumed without criticism. It does this indirectly by emphasizing the distinctions to which Frege appeals in his critical and constructive arguments. A review of the arguments would disclose his constant reliance on assumptions embedded in Wells's reconstruction. These assumptions function as the pivot of Fregean criticism but they are not justified independently. It is possible to support objectivity and oppose psychologism without being a realist in Frege's sense. In the succeeding chapters, we will meet alternative arguments against psychologism and empiricism that do not rely on Frege's ontology.

Whether Frege would accept Wells's reconstruction is uncertain, for there is one section in the *Grundgesetze* where he appears to argue for realism rather than to presuppose it. The context is a critique of Erdmann's logic in which Frege claims that Erdmann's idealism leads directly to solipsism.[45] For Frege, solipsism is the philosophic dead end; it effaces every critical distinction and principle that Frege struggled to preserve. Any set of premises that imply solipsism must be philosophically unacceptable.[46] Yet, Frege insists, only metaphysical realism permits escape from the circle of subjectivity. "If we want to emerge from the subjective at all, from the realm of ideas, we *must* conceive of knowledge as an activity that does not create what is known but grasps what is already there."[47] "That which we grasp with the mind [thoughts] also exists independent of this activity, independent of the ideas and their alterations that are a part of this grasping or accompany it."[48] The thesis implicit in these remarks is that only Fregean realism is effective against the solipsistic circle.

Frege's aversion to subjectivity and idealism is most pronounced in the philosophy of mathematics. "Number is no whit more an object of psychology or a product of mental processes than let us say the North Sea is."[49] The entire realm of logical entities has the same independence of human construction as the oceans or the planets. But "in arithmetic we are not concerned with objects which we come to know as something alien from without through the medium of the senses but objects given directly to our reason and, as its nearest kin, utterly transparent to it."[50] The metaphor of givenness suggests that Frege justified mathematical knowledge claims by appealing to the immediate intuitions of reason. This suggestion is partly misleading. In actual practice, he relied almost entirely on logical deduction from allegedly evident axioms. But, at the level of his logical primitives, he does appeal to immediate evidence. What is epistemically given, in his foundational practice, are the set-theoretic premises and concepts and the logical laws on which the reconstruction of arithmetic rests.

According to Frege mathematicians cannot create at will. Their intellectual activity achieves the discovery not the creation of truth. Mathematics is like geography in that it discloses objective relations between objects that antecede its operation. The task of the mathematician is to mark out in sharp relief the objective relations that obtain between numbers and to provide referring expressions for both the numbers and their relations. "It is part of Frege's realism to believe that the mathematician discovers, he does not invent; or rather that his inventions and creations are not only invented for the sake of expressing his discoveries but in their very possiblity rest on discoveries. Fundamentally the mathematician is a Magellan or a Cook, not a Leonardo or an Einstein."[51] It is also part of Frege's realism to believe that there is no alternative to this generalized conception of science.

H. The Failure to Discern Alternatives

What Frege hoped to discover was the uniquely best system of philosophy that would ground the uniquely best system of logic on which in turn the uniquely best system of mathematics could be constructed. This he did not accomplish.[52]

Frege was a mathematician, a logician, and a philosopher. I have argued that he was primarily a logician whose entry into philosophy was motivated by theoretical interest in the foundations of mathematics. To understand Frege's intellectual development it is necessary to distinguish the different types of foundational inquiry he practiced. In the first instance, he had the familiar logician's concern for the axiomatization of arithmetic. Logic, as we have seen, is a general technique for bringing clarity, coherence, and rigor to science. The axiomatization of arithmetic was a special case of a common logical practice.

Frege's espousal of logicism combined logic as a science with logic as technique. It identified logical truths and concepts as the theoretical base for the axiomatization of arithmetic. This was hardly standard practice, for it committed Frege to a particular theory of mathematics not generally shared by logicians. The logicist thesis held that the *axiomatic foundations* of arithmetic are located in the science of logic; Frege first became a philosopher with this assertion of theoretical reducibility.

His contemporaries, as we saw, largely ignored Frege's foundational conclusions. He believed they could not understand logicism because they did not understand the science of logic. To repair this prior intellectual failure, Frege turned to metalogical reflections on the subject matter, method, and epistemic character of logic. This led him deeper into philosophical waters, for logic turned out to be both a science and a science of science. As a science it found its subject matter in the truths of all the other disciplines. Its laws were laws of truth; its methods deductive; its conclusions a prior and analytic. Frege's metalogical judgments were directly opposed to the psychologistic theories that had penetrated his discipline. His opposition to psychologism was twofold: Psychological premises and methods contribute nothing to the clarity or justification of logical truths; the psychologistic identification of truth-vehicles with ideas undermines the objectivity of all science.

In his critique of psychologism, Frege entered a new, nonaxiomatic level of foundational analysis. He was now seeking the necessary conditions of scientific objectivity as such. These metatheoretic principles were not axioms from which truths could be deduced but specifications of the essential properties of truth. Frege insisted that there must be an atemporal, invariant, and intersubjective realm of thoughts to provide the *transcendental foundation* of scientific practice. At its deepest level, science was the discovery, systemization, and permanent articulation of this timeless order.

Since science depends on language for its communal character, Frege felt compelled to coordinate epistemic with semantic objectivity. This led to a generalized semantics of sense and reference explicitly designed to preserve the objectivity of truth. From semantics, Frege proceeded to metaphysics and ontology. He developed a general account of objectivity modeled on the causal independence of natural objects and a complex ontology of functions and objects in harmonic relation to his philosophy of language. The various parts of his philosophical system were linked together to provide mutual support. Although Frege claimed his ontological discoveries were fundamental, they clearly rested, in part, on semantic principles that themselves were designed for epistemic purposes. The system was constructed so that you must accept it all if you want to keep any part.

Frege admitted that this complex structure of foundational levels, with arithmetic resting (axiomatically) on logic and logic resting (transcendentally) on the philosophical system, would be slow to gain acceptance. "I have moved farther away from the accepted conventions and have thereby stamped my views with the impress of paradox. I myself can estimate to some extent the resistance with which my innovations will be met, because I first had to overcome something similar in myself in order to make them. For I have not arrived at them haphazardly or out of a craving for novelty, but was driven by the nature of the case."[53] There was no credible alternative.

To support his philosophical theories, Frege repeatedly attacked empiricist principles that limit objective knowledge to what is directly or indirectly sensible. He repudiated the claim that objective entities must fall either within the outer world or the inner world. Although he did not have a detailed cognitional theory, he sketched a position to the effect that logical entities, being akin to reason, are directly given to it without sensible mediation. In its austerity, this sketch is suggestive but difficult to rebut or defend. What should be remarked is that starting from very modest concerns within a restricted theoretical context (the axiomatization of arithmetic) Frege advanced to an integrated philosophical system comprehending knowledge, language, mind, and existence. I share Rulon Wells's judgment that, despite his initially modest concerns, Frege advocated his philosophical system "immodestly." He did not propose it or the logical system it supports as the best available theory. For Frege it is the only system consonant with epistemic objectivity, just as logicism is the only adequate analysis of arithmetic. How does Frege justify these interrelated foundational assertions?

His justification of logicism would seem to have two strands: (1) he devises an apparently coherent axiomatic theory with sufficient scope to include arithmetic; (2) he criticizes destructively every recognized alternative to his position. Since the performance of the first strand would only provide Frege with *a* philosophy of mathematics, the achievement of exclusive adequacy hinges on the performance of the second. The destructive criticism of strand two is qualified by these considerations. First, the repudiation of a set number of alternatives does not preclude the existence of a non-Fregean axiomatic base. Under restriction one, Frege's criticism is limited by his lack of an effective way to review the entire class of alternative theories.[54] Second, Frege bases his criticism of rival theories on distinctions rooted in metaphysical realism. Yet there are grounds for rejecting psychologism, empiricism, and Heine's and Thomae's brand of formalism that do not embrace Frege's metaphysics. Even if Frege's objections to existing philosophies of arithmetic were compelling, there might be successful lines of attack incompatible with his philosophy and with logicism. One way to summarize Wells's criticism is that Frege confuses the achievement of an adequate philosophy of logic and arithmetic with the achievement of an exclusively adequate one.

Wells sharpens this challenge in a second article, "Is Frege's Concept of Function Valid?" He writes:

> Casting Frege himself in his chosen type of role, we would best regard him as a Columbus. Discover he did but he didn't discover what he thought he did.
>
> What Frege hoped to discover was the uniquely best system of philosophy that would found the uniquely best system of logic on which in turn the uniquely best system of mathematics could be constructed. This he did not accomplish.[55]

Frege's failure to discern the limits of his achievement is traced back to a certain blindness. "Frege was just blind to the leading idea of the English development, namely the idea of giving alternative interpretations to the same syntactical calculus. . . . I connect this blindness with his general insensitivity to alternatives and with his belief (a belief that I ascribe to him partly on the basis of his practice) that a best alternative could always be found.[56]

In the remainder of this chapter, I shall argue that "Frege's blindness" can profitably be understood in terms of the particular concept of science and scientific method he seems to have espoused. I credit these loyalties to him in the light of his informal commentary throughout the *Grundgesetze*. In the preface to the first volume of that work, he refers to "the ideal of a strictly scientific method in mathematics which I have tried to realize here,"[57] and cites the achievement of Euclid as a model for his own. He then proceeds to outline what he means by a "strict scientific method." The acceptable statement of a body of scientific knowledge requires (1) that everything definable within the science be defined, (2) that everything provable be proved, and (3) that every rule of inference used in its demonstration be specified.[58] The informal discussion of these requirements discloses that, for Frege, there are logically simple elements that cannot be defined and self-evident statements that cannot be proved. These logical primitives taken in conjunction with the rules of inference constitute the intratheoretic foundations of the science.

Frege believed that his contribution to mathematics was novel in two respects: the rigor with which he executed his proofs and the clarity with which he analyzed the conceptual foundations. Both contributions are seen as refined developments of the ancient Euclidean ideal. To that ideal, Frege was uncommonly loyal. I believe that his loyalty to the Euclidean model is also a cause of his "blindness," leading him to embrace the axiomatization of arithmetic but to reject the insights of modern formalism. The particular insight I refer to is the distinction between the axiomatization and formalization of a mathematical theory.

Euclidean geometry is the prototype of the classical theory of science. In his masterful work on the foundations of mathematics, E. W. Beth has thematized what that concept of science requires.[59] To be a strict science a system of sentences, S, must satisfy the following postulates:

1. *Reality postulate*—Any sentence belonging to S must refer to a specific domain of real entities.
2. *Truth postulate*—Any sentence belonging to S must be true.
3. *Deductivity postulate*—If certain sentences belong to S, any logical consequence of these sentences must belong to S.
4. *Evidence postulate*—In S are a finite number of terms such that
   a. the meaning of the terms is so obvious as to require no further explanation;
   b. any other term occurring in S is definable by means of these terms.
5. *Evidence postulate*—In S are a finite number of sentences such that
   a. the truth of these sentences is so obvious as to require no further proof;

    b. the truth of any other sentence belonging to *S* may be established by logical inference starting from these sentences.

Frege's statements in the *Grundgesetze* establish his intention to satisfy these five postulates. He insists:

1. That in a logically perfect language all the referring expressions have reference, and that this reference be made explicit.
2. That the sentences of this language be true descriptions of the items to which the expressions of the language make reference.
3. That the rules of the language permit inference from true propositions only to other true propositions.
4. a. That logically simple items cannot be defined;
   b. that whatever is not logically simple be defined in terms of what is logically simple.
5. a. That self-evident propositions (the axioms) require no proof;
   that whatever is not self-evident be proved on the basis of these axioms.

These convictions demonstrate Frege's loyalty to the Euclidean ideal. But the modern methodology of deduction has modified traditional Euclidean procedure. Frege failed to appreciate or make use of one consequence of this modification. What did he fail to see? (1) The axiomatic system can be developed in a purely formal way as a syntactical system of signs. The interpretation of the nonlogical signs is not part of the formal system as such. (2) "With formalization all the conditions imposed on the axioms by the old axiomatic system—such as self-evidence, certainty, ontological priority— become untenable. An axiom differs from the other sentences of the system in virtue only of the fact that it is not derived in the system."[60] Frege's foundational strategy is to offer conjointly a formal calculus and a particular philosophic interpretation of its meaning. He "offers us as a unit, an atom, what should be regarded as a package, or bundle."[61]

    Perhaps it is unfair to call this oversight *blindness*, because Frege anticipated to some degree the development of modern formalism and explicitly rejected it. This rejection occurs in his criticism of the formalistic theories of arithmetic proposed by Heine and Thomae. He wrote, "It is quite true that we could have introduced our rules of inference and the other laws of the *Begriffschrift* as arbitrary stipulations, without speaking of the reference and the sense of the signs. We would then have been treating the signs as figures."[62] This approach is rejected because it distorts "that train of thought which accompanied the affair for us and actually made it interesting."[63] The distortion is particularly grave with respect to the rules of the calculus. The formalist treatment makes the syntactical rules appear arbitrary. But Frege intends that the referents of the numerical signs (that is, numbers) provide the ontological ground for the rules governing the use of the numerals. The rules are founded in the nature of the numbers themselves and in their lawful relations to one another. Relying on his metaphysical realism and his metaphor of rational kinship. Frege maintains that our knowledge of the rules is grounded in our immediate knowledge of numbers and their relations. We rely upon this immediate knowledge in the formulation of the axiom system, and it guides procedure at every stage. Formalistic procedure is unnecessary because we have direct knowledge of numbers and misleading because it implies that we lack such knowledge.

I believe that Frege's real blindness is his uncritical commitment to metaphysical realism and the accompanying metaphor of immediate givenness. These commitments explain his refusal to separate the technical and philosophical dimensions of his foundational practice. His rejection of formalism *tout court* is based on philosophic principles that he never justified. What he failed to see was that formalism understood as a methodological device, not as a philosophy of mathematics, could admit divergent philosophic interpretations of which his own realism would be one. Fregean semantics and ontology are incompatible with a formalist philosophy that identifies numbers with symbols; but they are fully consonant with the adoption of a formalist method that separates the specification of the axiom system from the question of its ontological interpretation. With Frege,it is too often all or nothing.

The modern methodology of deduction explicitly distinguishes three stages in foundational practice. The construction of a syntactical calculus is prior to and independent of its semantical interpretations, which are themselves prior to philosophic arguments about the ontological import of standard and nonstandard models. When axiomatic method is practiced formally, the same calculus admits of divergent interpretations that are jointly acceptable to opposing philosophies of logic. Philosophical differences surface when admissible interpretations of a calculus are classified as nonstandard because they conflict with preassigned material interpretations of certain expressions in the calculus. A classic case of this three-tiered approach is the formal axiomatization of set-theory. The Löwenheim Skolem theorem implies that formalized set-theory admits of denumerable models. Platonist defenders of Cantor's results, in particular his existence proofs of nondenumerable sets, classify all the denumerable models of set-theory as nonstandard. The important epistemological and ontological conflicts thus emerge at this third level, where the different philosophies of mathematics confront each other.[64]

Extension of philosophic neutrality to the third level of foundational research does not occur within Frege's material axiomatics. For Frege, the axiomatic calculus and its philosophical interpretation are conjoined. The science of logic, broadened to include set-theory, is treated as an ordered body of truths bearing on an antecedently given subject matter. Different semantical interpretions of the sentences of logic are viewed as competing ontological accounts of the third realm. The divergent philosophies of arithmetic and logic are contrasted most sharply by comparing their semantical interpretations of logical and mathematical signs. "Everyone who uses words or mathematical symbols makes the claim that they mean something, and no one will expect any sense to emerge from empty symbols."[65]

Psychologism fails as a philosophy of logic by interpreting logical entities as either mental acts or ideas. Formalism fails by identifying the objects of arithmetic with uninterpreted inscriptions. Empiricism fails by interpreting arithmetic sentences as empirical generalizations about sets of sensible objects. Frege's semantical theory, the working center of his philosophical system, is designed to ensure both the objectivity of logic and the general objectivity of science. To preserve the objectivity of logic, he insists that its sentences refer to a timeless domain of abstract entities accessible to reason but independent of cognitional activity for their existence and character. To ensure the objectivity of science, he requires that the meaning of scientific sentences be timeless thoughts belonging to the same domain. Since all logical entities are independent of psychological activity clarification of their nature and properties is unaided by psychological research. Considerations of cognitional process conceal the ground of epistemic objectivity and promote the psychologistic confusion Frege critiqued.

Frege's final word on psychologism can be summarized in these terms. Psychologism is a substantive thesis in the philosophy of logic and a methodological thesis in metaphilosophy. The substantive thesis asserts that the subject matter of logic is subjective, its methods inductive, and its theories empirical generalizations. The methodological thesis asserts that philosophic inquiry into the meaning of language and the justification of knowledge must rely on psychological research. Both theses are mistaken. Yet the sympathetic reader who shares Frege's distaste for psychologism is left wondering. Must I endorse his entire theoretical system to secure epistemic objectivity? Are there no philosophical alternatives?

3

The Genesis of Husserl's Phenomenology—
From Descriptive Psychology
to Transcendental Idealism

A. Philosophy in Search of Itself

In the opening chapter, I briefly described the intellectual climate in Europe during the second half of the nineteenth century. Attention was directed to the decline of Hegel's speculative idealism under the pressure of developments in the natural and historical sciences. These sciences claimed all factual existence as their province of investigation; no region of reality, in principle, was exempt from their empirical methods of inquiry. Philosophy's future as a cognitive discipline was threatened by this comprehensive claim, for it appeared to deprive philosophy of a legitimate field of investigation. In response to this challenge, philosophy was reconceived as the analysis of knowledge, with the sciences themselves becoming the objects of philosophical study. Philosophy was restricted to the theory of knowledge at the same time that empirical science became the paradigm of human cognition.

Within Germany, three different approaches to epistemology struggled for ascendancy. The philosophical naturalists tried too make epistemology an empirical science; Frege treated it essentially as a program of logical reconstruction; the Marburg neo-Kantians took the transcendental route. The naturalists argued that scientific theories were the achievement of human minds. The task of philosophy was the descriptive and causal analysis of the psychological processes responsible for this achievement. They thought that theoretical investigation of the sciences of nature should be conducted by an empirical science using similar methods of research. The emerging discipline of experimental psychology was selected to explain the nature and existence of knowledge by genetically investigating the factual conditions under which scientific theories were developed, adopted, and revised. The neo-Kantians agreed that the primary task of philosophy was the analysis of knowledge, understood as the reflective examination of scientific theory. But they attributed to philosophy a special dignity with respect to the sciences of nature. They conceived of epistemology as a transcendental discipline disclosing the necessary conditions of science, conditions that are never to be confused with particular matters of fact, whether physical or mental. The necessary conditions of empirical knowledge are not items of experience, nor causes of experience to be inferred from their observable effects; philosophy moves at a radically different level from every factual science.[1]

Late nineteenth-century controversy about the nature of philosophy climaxed in the person of Edmund Husserl. Husserl stands at the point of intersection of important developments in psychology and logic; more than any person of his time, he was absorbed in the crisis of orientation that their joint emergence occasioned for philosophy. In fact, the burden of Husserl's career can be best understood as an extended reflection on the nature of philosophy: an attempt to define its field, to determine its methods, and to clarify the epistemic character of its results. Husserl's reflection ultimately led him in a transcendental direction, toward a repudiation of naturalism and of any attempt to conceive of philosophy as a species of empirical science.

To emphasize the philosophic limitations of naturalism, Husserl concentrated on the differences in goal and attitude between philosophy and the sciences of nature. He used a familiar metaphor to indicate their basic differences in goal: The natural sciences are concerned with achieving theoretical knowledge of the factual universe; philosophy is concerned with the foundations on which those scientific theories are erected.[2] From the beginning, Husserl conceived of philosophy as a foundational inquiry, searching after the ultimate grounds of human cognition. To clarify his concept of foundational analysis, he carefully distinguished among the objects of scientific knowledge, theoretical truths about those objects, and the noetic acts by which those truths are discovered and verified. For Husserl, natural science was absorbed in investigating the objects of knowledge but failed to reflect on the theories it asserted or the methods it used. Borrowing a distinction from Frege, we could say that science concentrates on the reference of theoretical discourse to the neglect of its sense. The first goal of foundational inquiry is to probe the implicit claim to rationality of natural science by clarifying the sense of scientific theories and appraising the reasonableness of its methods of inquiry. Philosophical analysis, at this level, is intrasystemic because it accepts scientific theory and methodology as they are given in scientific practice.

This difference in theoretical goals was correlated with a difference in epistemic attitude. Husserl contrasted the critical attitude of philosophy with the positive or "naive" attitude of natural science.[3] By *naive* Husserl meant that scientific inquiry is conducted within the natural attitude, an attitude framed by an unexamined epistemic assumption. Practicing scientists uncritically assume that through their theories they know reality as it in itself. The objects to which scientific discourse refers are presumed to exist independent of the noetic operations through which they are known. Scientists shift from the naive to the philosophic attitude when they confront the *critical problem*, when they realize that the relation of knowledge to an object that transcends the process of cognition is essentially problematic.[4] Husserl confronted the "naive realism" of natural science with the epistemological problem of transcendence. As classical philosophy found its origin in humankind's native intellectual wonder, so modern philosophy found its source in the spirit of critical reflection.[5] Like Descartes, Husserl believed that the exigencies of criticism could be satisfied only by epistemic certitude. He provisionally accepted the sceptical challenge to the epistemic status of science, in order to shape a concept of knowledge more rigorous than that of philosophical naturalism. The epistemic level of philosophy was extrasystemic because it challenged the scientists' implicit ontological assumptions about the object of natural cognition. Husserl's foundational philosophy had a twofold function: At the intrasystemic level, it clarified the sense of scientific theories; at the extrasystemic level, it determined the type of object of which those theories can be known with certainty to be true.

Husserl conceived of philosophy as a rigorous science (*ein strenge Wissenschaft*) whose findings were more certain than those of mathematics. For him, the burning issue was to devise a method that would satisfy philosophy's foundational concerns while yielding apodictic conclusions. In his search for this method, Husserl proved himself a child of his time. He was attracted from the outset to the use of psychology as a foundational method. "I began work on the prevailing assumption that psychology was the science from which logic in general, and the logic of the deductive sciences, had to hope for philosophical clarification."[6] But he came to realize that a "radicalization" of psychology was necessary to reach the philosophic dimension of thought.[7] At the climax of his development, he espoused a theory of cognition and a philosophical project explicitly opposed to the psychology and metaphilosophy of the naturalists. He maintained the thesis that philosophy is a rigorous science but he transformed the psychological methods needed to attain theoretical certainty. Like Descartes, he proposed a revolution in method for the sake of making philosophy a strict science. The reflexive turn to the cognitive subject gave that method a psychological cast, but when the reflexion reached the foundational level, Husserl passed from descriptive psychology to transcendental phenomenology.

This chapter will trace the evolution of Husserl's thought from its origins in intentional psychology to its term in transcendental idealism. I will use, as

Husserl did, issues in the foundations of logic and mathematics as both the point of departure and the thread of connection.

B. Dual Influences on the Early Husserl

The major intellectual influences on Husserl were provided by mathematicians and psychologists. Mathematical training focused his original interests; exposure to psychology stimulated a concern for questions of methodology. Both influences contributed to the formation of his ultimate philosophical position.[8]

As a student in the German university system, Husserl was fortunate to have two great mathematicians, Kronecker and Weierstrass, for his teachers. He originally intended to become a mathematician, doing his doctoral dissertation under Weierstrass on the calculus of variations. He was especially impressed by the certitude of mathematical knowledge, attributing this property to the clarity and rigor of mathematical methodology. Because of its rigor Husserl initially embraced mathematics as an exemplary instance of theoretical science. In his passionate enthusiasm for mathematics, Husserl was reenacting an adventure many earlier philosophers had experienced; the parallel cases of Plato, Descartes, Spinoza, and Russell are easily recalled. The direction of Husserl's interest did not tend towards the creative expansion of mathematics but towards foundational studies. This bent of his mind illustrated the influence of his teachers, whose specialized research emphasized foundational questions. When Husserl was eventually attracted to philosophy, his earliest projects were extensions of foundational research in arithmetic. During the first twenty years of his philosophic career, Husserl devoted himself to the philosophy of logic and mathematics, and he returned to these interests again in his maturity.

The shift to philosophy from mathematics can be traced to the study of psychology. Husserl had direct exposure to the major figures in the formative period of modern psychology, working with Wundt at Leipzig and Brentano at Vienna. Wundt adopted a causal, genetic approach to psychology, with methodological and theoretic ties to physics and physiology.[9] Brentano insisted on the importance of a preliminary descriptive investigation of genetic psychology's basic concepts. He did not exclude the legitimacy of causal analysis, but he argued that it employed certain basic terms that lacked a clear theoretical meaning.[10] Descriptive psychology was to conduct the conceptual clarification that genetic psychology presupposed but could not achieve for itself. Brentano's discipline sharply distinguished physical and psychological phenomena, classified the basic types of intentional act, and worked out their laws of serial combination. Unlike its causal counterpart, descriptive psychology used a method and evidential base not modeled on natural science. Brentano contrasted his method of "inner perception" with the sciences' reliance on empirical observation. He claimed that in inner perception the psychological subject achieved an immediate, selfevident awareness of his intentional acts and their contents. By restricting itself to this immediate evidence, descriptive psychology hoped to discover a set of conceptual truths epistemically more secure than the inductive findings of causal psychology.

After leaving Vienna, Husserl studied with Carl Stumpf at Halle. Stumpf employed both genetic and descriptive methods in psychology, contending that each method of investigation could make a fruitful contribution to the new science.[11] Unlike Brentano, he directed his psychological research to philosophical problems in mathematics, focusing on the psychological origin of the geometrical concept of space. He inspired Husserl with his heuristic belief that the philosophy of mathematics ought to be based on psychological investigations. Stumpf's influence can be discerned in Husserl's *Habilitation Schrift* on the concept of number, where he searches for the psychological roots of elementary mathematical concepts as a means to their philosophical clarification.

From Brentano, Husserl inherited the idea of philosophy as a rigorous science engaged in conceptual clarification through the use of a unique reflexive method. Stumpf encouraged him to apply both descriptive and genetic methods to conceptual questions in mathematics. Husserl has described his passion for philosophy as a foundational passion, the result of a desire to reach the ultimate and original sources of knowledge. Utilizing the motif of two influences, we can say that originally mathematics served as the object of foundational interest while descriptive psychology served as its method. Foundational inquiry was identified with conceptual clarification and foundational method with descriptive psychology.

A further debt to Brentano should be acknowledged. Brentano was ardently committed to restoring philosophy to the level of a fully rational science. As his student, Husserl became deeply affected by this project and pursued it with conviction throughout his career.[12] He saw in Brentano's program a return to the Cartesian ideal of philosophy as a rigorous science. Without a secure science of philosophy, he feared that the normative theoretical demand for clarity of meaning and certainty of judgment would remain unsatisfied. Natural science must be complemented by philosophy, for its own commitment to theoretical rationality is provisional.[13] According to Husserl, the positive sciences rely on their methods without justifying them, employ their concepts without clarifying them, and assume epistemic success without determining whether and how it is possible. Philosophy undertakes the justification, clarification, and epistemological reflection neglected by the first-order sciences. The charge of provisional rationality is applied to mathematics as well as the natural sciences. In his initial foundational project,

Husserl proposed to do for arithmetic what Brentano had done earlier for experimental psychology.

The *Philosophy of Arithmetic* was the outcome of Husserls's first venture in foundational thought.[14] The book bears a prophetic subtitle, *Psychological and Logical Studies*, which signals the dual perspective Husserl would bring to all philosophical analysis. The primary concepts of arithmetic provided the theme of the book; these are concepts that cannot be clarified by logical methods for they are the conceptual base on which all arithmetic definition rests. To secure clarity about them, Husserl shifted from logical to psychological analysis. Although logically primitive, these concepts have an intentional history; they are the intelligible term of a unique kind of genetic process. Conceptual genesis is not a causal process involving spatiotemporal objects but a process of concept formation. Conceptual analysis uncovers the set of noetic operations responsible for the formation of basic arithmetic categories. In his initial research Husserl simply assumed that concepts have a genetic dependence on intentional acts, that they are not atemporal abstract entities totally independent of the mind, as Frege had contended. The logical derivation of concepts practiced by Frege must be complemented by intentional psychology if complete conceptual clarity were to be achieved.

A special set of arithmetic concepts, the form-concepts or categories, are given extended treatment. They are contrasted with material concepts in both their matter and manner of origin. All concept formation rests on abstractive operations applied to concretely intuited phenomena. Material concepts result from abstractive reflection on the contents of sensory perception; form concepts result from abstractive reflection on noetic operations. The concepts of unity, plurality, and number are instances of form concepts that play a central role in the science of arithmetic. Numerical concepts are clarified philosophically by retracing their genesis through the network of serial formation procedures, including: the abstractive operations that divest the elements to be numbered of their concrete particularity; the act of synthesis that collects disparate elements together to form a unified set; and, the higher order act of reflection on the abstractive and synthetic operations. In the *Philosophy of Arithmetic*, the essence of foundational inquiry is the clarification of form-concepts, and the basic method is the genetic reconstruction of the process of concept formation.

Husserl's confidence in the adequacy of this approach diminished under critical attack. Frege, his most acute critic, wrote a damaging review in *Zeitschrift für Philosophie und Philosophische Kritik*, in which Husserl's concept of foundational analysis as well as his detailed arguments were challenged.[15] Frege claimed: Psychology had nothing to contribute to the foundations of arithmetic. Foundational questions are not questions of psychological origin, but logical questions bearing on the definition of concepts, the justification of rules of inference, and the selection of axiom sets.

Although basic concepts cannot be defined, this does not imply that they can be clarified by genetic analyses. Concepts are atemporal abstract entities without genetic origins and a fortiori without psychological origins. Because concepts are objective, independent of minds, submitting them to psychological analysis creates confusion rather than clarity about the nature of arithmetic. "If a geographer happened to read a hydrographic treatise which psychologically explained the coming to be of the sea, he would have the impression that someone had missed the point. I have the same impression of the present work."[16]

On matters of detail, Frege criticized Husserl's reliance on abstraction to account for concept formation and cited his ambiguous use of the term *vorstellung*. The ambiguity blurs the distinction between objective logical concepts and the psychologically immanent contents of individual mental acts, a confusion Frege had censured as psychologism. Although Husserl did not accept most of Frege's criticism, he was impressed by the argument against psychologism.

> I became more and more disquieted by doubts of principle, as to how to reconcile the objectivity of mathematics, and of all science in general, with a psychological foundation for logic. In this manner my whole method which I had taken over from the convictions of the reigning logic, that sought to illuminate the given science through psychological analyses, became shaken, and I felt more and more pushed towards general critical reflections on the essence of logic, and on the relationship in particular, between the subjectivity of knowing and the objectivity of the content known.[17]

Frege was wrong to neglect the subjective dimension of cognition but he was right to insist on the objectivity of the theoretic content that philosophy attempted to clarify.

In the ensuing years, Husserl steeped himself in the German and English literature on the theory of logic. The fruit of this reexamination was the *Logical Investigations* of 1900-1901.[18] The two volumes of the *Investigations* pursue different but related aims. Volume 1 which clearly reflects Husserl's response to Frege's criticism, attempts a refutation of psychologism by proposing a revised account of the science of logic. Volume 2 outlines a new foundational method for the clarification of concepts, a reformed version of the psychological pattern of analysis practiced in the *Philosophy of Arithmetic*. The new method testifies to Husserl's enduring judgment that logical analysis is insufficient for philosophical purposes and that foundational knowledge must terminate in a level of subjectivity consistent with the theoretical objectivity of science.

C. The Refutation of Psychologism

During his career Husserl used the term *psychologism* in two ways.[19] Both uses are critical, but one cuts deeper than the other. The less stringent use refers to a confusion about the subject matter of the science of logic. The deeper use refers to a confusion about philosophy, about the type of discipline it is and about the methods appropriate to its foundational objectives. The title of this section refers to the earlier and less fundamental use; it points to Husserl's attempted refutation of psychologism in the *Prolegomena to Pure Logic*, vol. 1 of the *Logical Investigations*.

Husserl began the *Prolegomena* by remarking that the philosophy of logic is in a state of controversy. There is no agreement about the field and method of logic or about the epistemic character of its theories. To remedy this disorder, Husserl proposed to delimit precisely the domain of logic, to distinguish its objectives from those of other scientific disciplines. Like Frege, he was hostile to the transgression of boundaries, to a misunderstanding of the field or method of a science. In the case of logic, the prevailing confusion revolved around four disputed questions.

1. Is logic theoretical or practical, a science or an art?
2. Is logic autonomous or essentially dependent on other sciences?
3. Is logic a formal or a factual discipline?
4. If logic is a science, does it contain a priori demonstrative or empirical inductive knowledge?[20]

In the late nineteenth century, the competing philosophies of logic were roughly divisible into two groups. The group with ascendancy in both numbers and influence adopted the psychological approach of Mill and Lipps, who conceived of logic as the art of thinking. Because all technically advanced arts presuppose supporting theories that intellectually order their materials, they believed logic must either be a branch of psychology or an applied form of it. Their position assumed that the art of logic had as its purpose the critical supervision of psychological activity. The empirical theory of the mind, covering both mental acts and their psychologically immanent contents, would provide logic with its theoretic foundations. The philosophy of logic derived from these assumptions can be simply stated: Logic is an art, dependent on the factual science of psychology, which is itself a species of inductive empirical knowledge.[21]

Husserl classified the opponents of Mill as the antipsychologists, citing Herbart and Jäsche as leading representatives of this movement. In contrast to Lipps, who viewed logic as the *physics* of thinking, the antipsychologists emphasized its normative function and treated it as the *ethics* of thinking. By treating logic as a normative discipline regulating rational conduct, they implied that it is not theoretical, that logic offers prescriptions for intellectual practice but not informative theories with a specific substantive content.[22]

Husserl's philosophy of logic is carefully distinguished from both of these opposing approaches. He contended that logic is not a factual science telling us how we *do* think nor a normative science prescribing how we *ought* to think but a theoretical science dealing with the propositional contents of specific intentional acts; it is independent of every factual science with respect to its foundations; it is a formal not a factual discipline; and its theories are instances of a priori knowledge. In arguing for these substantive theses, Husserl submitted his theoretic rivals to extensive criticism, aiming the sharpest criticism at the psychological theory of logic because of its controlling influence at that time.

Husserl defined psychologism in the philosophy of logic as the belief that the laws of logic refer either to actual mental events and processes or to their epistemically private and immanent contents. These events are taken to be real temporal occurrences with causes and effects that are part of a common time series. He charged psychologism with confusing essentially different types of investigation; different levels of evidence; the epistemic character of inductive and eidetic sciences; and, the subject matter of distinct disciplines. There are four reasons why logical laws are not reducible to those of psychology:

1. The laws of logic are exact and the concepts on which they are based precisely defined. The laws of psychology are vague, asserting approximate regularities of co-existence and succession between loosely defined mental phenomena.
2. Logical laws are known through eidetic insight making them a priori in nature. The psychological laws discovered through empirical induction are never more than probable.
3. Because of the apodictic evidence on which they are based, the laws of logic are necessary, whereas the empirical generalizations of psychology are irremediably contingent.
4. Psychological laws refer to the factual behavior of individual human beings—but logical laws neither assert nor imply propositions about matters of fact; they make no factual existence claims.[23]

Relying on these distinctions, Husserl concluded that logical laws differ in kind from psychological laws and that this difference of type disqualifies psychology from supplying the theoretical foundation of logic. No factual empirical science can be the theoretical foundation of a formal a priori science. If foundations are understood axiomatically, then the attempt to deduce logical laws from psychology would beg the question, for the principles of inference used in the deduction are themselves principles of logic. If foundations are understood to be principles of concept clarification, then psychologism attempts to clarify the precise by appeal to the vague. If foundations are understood epistemologically, then we are involved in a *petitio*, for the factual sciences require the very epistemic grounding they hope to provide for logic as an eidetic science.

The second part of Husserl's criticism is that psychologism consistently adhered to entails epistemic scepticism and relativism. Husserl exhibits this entailment while introducing his alternative concept of logic as the theory of science, which is to determine the necessary conditions that any scientific theory must satisfy. Like the neo-Kantians, Husserl insisted that the conditions of science are ideal not factual in character. To see this, we must distinguish between a scientific theory and the objects to which it refers. The objects of the factual sciences are temporally and causally related states of affairs with manifestly different properties from those of the theories through which they are known. According to Husserl, scientific theories are ideal propositional contents irreducible to factual occurrences, which emerge and then perish in time in accordance with causal laws. The objectivity of theory is undermined if theories are reduced to unique unrepeatable occurrences in the temporal order. Scientific theories must remain identical in content for all temporal inquirers to investigate, understand, and eventually appraise, but this condition cannot be satisfied if the psychological analysis of theories is accepted. Psychologism is branded as a species of scepticism, because "its theses announce expressly or imply analytically that the logical conditions of the possibility of theory in general are false."[24] Husserl treated psychologism as an outgrowth of philosophical naturalism; driven by its ontological constraints, naturalism reduces ideal theoretical content to real existents in the causal order. For Husserl, an essential precondition of natural science is the existence of propositional contents that themselves are not items within the order of nature. The logical order cannot be reduced to the naturalistic version of the real order without sceptical consequences that are epistemically absurd.

By its attempt to ground theoretically the laws of logic in those of psychology, Husserl finds psychologism also guilty of relativism. It makes the universal principles regulative of the order of truth dependent on the conduct of a biological individual or species.[25] If this dependence actually obtained, a variation in human psychological conduct would entail a change in logical laws. But these laws, as Husserl conceived them, apply absolutely and unconditionally to the complete range of theoretic truths; as such they are presupposed by the very psychological laws invoked to restrict their validity. As laws regulating the invariant realm of propositional truth, the principles of logic cannot be grounded in or derived from any factual discipline. In all of its versions, psychologism effaces the most basic epistemological distinction, that between ideal and real *noema* and ideal and real laws. This effacement is evident in the recurrent attempt to ground the absolute on the relative, the eidetic on the empirical, the necessary on the contingent. The relativization of the principles of truth to the unstable patterns of specifically human behavior would radically distort the meaning of all epistemic concepts. It would sabotage the very task of clarification assigned to the science of logic.

The refutation of psychologism in the *Prolegomena* is a central part of Husserl's comprehensive critique of empiricism. Like Frege, he viewed psychologism as the predictable outcome of theses embedded in the classical empiricist tradition.[26] But the biases of empiricism are not adequately overcome by the standard antipsychologistic position, which treats the laws of logic as normative prescriptions and conceals their primary theoretical character. Every propositional truth, regardless of discipline, is able to serve a normative function. The antipsychologists failed to distinguish a proposition's theoretical content from the various functions it can perform—"Due to envisaging their roles in the normalization of thought, we tend to speak of logical laws as laws of thought."[27] However, this idiom obscures more than it clarifies. "The proper contrary to the conception of natural laws as empirical generalizations based on existential or real results is not a norm conceived of as a prescription but an ideal or eidetic law based purely on concepts."[28] For Husserl, the propositions of logic are just such eidetic laws that assert the necessary conditions of objective scientific theory.

Husserl found the major failure of empiricism to be its inability to distinguish between ideal and real objects. This failure is critical in the philosophy of logic for it guarantees a misunderstanding of the sense and reference of logical laws. In the analysis of any discipline, three factors must be distinguished: the factual noetic operations of the practicing scientists; the propositional theories that are proposed, examined, and semantically appraised; and, the objects of the science to which the theories refer and that serve as the source of their truth-value.[29] Pure logic is not concerned with the noetic operations or subject matter of a first-order science. Its field of investigation is the concepts, propositions, and logically systematized network of propositions that constitute the theoretical content of science. The sense rather than the reference of scientific discourse constitutes the subject matter of logic. These propositional senses belong to the ideal not to the real order. They are independent both of the particular noetic acts in which they are"presented"[30] and the particular objects that determine their truth-value. The defining mark of an ideal entity is that it can serve as the common epistemic content for an indefinite number of noetic acts by an unrestricted community of noetic agents. Ideal senses, construed as the intersubjective vehicles of scientific truth, are not Fregean ideas. Essentially public and atemporal in character, they are not to be *identified* with real temporal contents or *individuated* by the acts or agents that apprehend them. Their functional role in Hussserl's theory of science is comparable to that of Fregean thoughts (*Gedanke*).

British empiricism inherited from Descartes the new way of ideas as a strategy for pursuing philosophy. It also inherited or promoted numerous confusions surrounding the concept of an idea. By the nineteenth century these confusions had eroded absolutely basic philosophic distinctions. Husserl's original critique of psychologism was a sustained attempt to restore the distinctions concealed by the multiple uses of the term *idea*. The term had been used ambiguously to refer to importantly different kinds of entity. Noematic objects of perception, noetic intentional acts, noematic propositional contents, and nonintentional states of awareness like physical sensations, were loosely classified under the rubric of *ideas*. When Husserl characterized theoretical contents as *ideal*, he restricted the term to the conceptional and propositional order. Only the entities of logic, what I have referred to as *formal terms of meaning*, are ideal; the other entities, carelessly referred to as *ideas*, are temporal items in the real order subject to genesis and perishing in conformity with causal laws. If scientific theories were reducible to temporal entities of this kind, the intersubjective and invariant truth-vehicles required for cognition would be lost. The root failure in empiricism is its collapsing of the difference between these propositional vehicles of truth and the other alleged ideas to which the category of truth does not properly apply. Frege's influence is apparent in the *Prolegomena* whenever Husserl attacks the proposed reduction of ideal theoretical contents to entities in the spatiotemporal order. Further parallels can be detected: Both coordinate their understanding of propositional contents with their theories of meaning and knowledge. They identify the objects of logical investigation with the intersubjective senses of indicative sentences and with the intentional contents of a species of nonperceptual noetic act. Thus, the propositional bearers of truth are related to linguistic inscriptions and intentional acts without being identified with either. By its neglect of these extralinguistic, extramental, logical entities, psychologism undermined an essential condition of theoretical science. The implications of classical empiricism, when carefully thought through, are inescapably skeptical.

The concept of evidence provides psychologism with an additional route of entry into the philosophy of logic. Because logical laws cannot be known through a process of inference, knowledge of their truth must in some sense be direct; their truth value must be immediately evident to anyone who understands their sense. But self-evidence, it is alleged, refers to a feeling of certainty experienced by an inquirer and feeling is the disciplinary concern of empirical psychology. Since the philosophy of logic must address the question of epistemic justification, a methodological dependence on the psychology of feeling seems inescapable.

Husserl countered this argument by insisting that evidence is an epistemological rather than a psychological concept, and one of legitimate concern to logic because the notion of scientific knowledge needs to be explicated in terms of evidence. If a person m is to know that p, not only must p

be true, but *m* must have sufficient evidence of *p*'s truth. As an example, suppose that *m* is a knower, *p* is a propositional content, and *e* is the evidence for the truth of *p* that *m* must have in order to know that *p*; and suppose further that *p* says something about object *r*. If *p* is true, then what *p* says about *r* is in fact the case; to know that *p* is true, *m* must experience *r* as satisfying the truth-conditions of *p*. Husserl defined "experience of evidence" as the immediate awareness of the truth of *p*. But *m* cannot know that *p* is true merely by experiencing *p*. Knowledge that *p* is true requires that *m*, who understands *p*'s truth-conditions, experience the referent *r* of *p* as satisfying those truth-conditions. In Husserl's idiom, evidence is the lived experience of perfect concordance between an intended meaning and the intuitive fulfillment of that meaning.[31] Whatever *m* feels in thinking about *p* is irrelevant to the experience of evidence. The project of clarifying the concept of evidence receives no support from the psychological analysis of feeling.

Husserl's critique of the psychological treatment of evidence concludes the critical portion of the *Prolegomena*. Beginning with Chapter 11, he developed a positive alternative to psychologism by structurally outlining an autonomous theory of pure logic.

D. The Autonomy of Pure Logic

The first nine chapters of the Prolegomena are designed to prove that no form of the psychologistic theory of logic is defensible. Husserl departed from the critical mode in Chapter 10 by connecting his theory of pure logic with that of major figures in the tradition: Leibniz, Bolzano, Lotze, and Kant. Chapter 11 of volume 1 schematizes the theory, which is then substantively developed in the six sections of volume 2. The following account of Husserl's theory of logic is drawn from these segments of the *Logical Investigations*.

At the outset, it is useful to recall Husserl's stand on the four disputed questions in logical theory. He held that logic was a theoretical discipline, independent of the factual sciences, formal in character, and achieving a priori results. The distinctive properties of logic as a theoretical science follow from the nature of its subject matter. Logic is eidetic not factual; it is a science whose objects are concepts and categorial combinations of concepts rather than concrete temporal individuals. Husserl's contrast between factual and logical disciplines recalls the distinction in scholastic semiotics between real and rational sciences. Real sciences use signs of first intention to refer to nonlinguistic matters of fact; the rational sciences, including logic, use signs of second intention to refer to signs of first intention. Like his scholastic predecessors, Husserl agrees that the primary referents of the signs of second intention are the nonlinguistic concepts and propositions that the scholastics had called *natural intentional signs*.

Husserl contends that the logician has access through intentional acts to a domain of intersubjective theoretical meaning about whose constituents he can make a priori judgments; he further contends that every factual science presupposes the contributions of logic as an eidetic discipline. The first principle grounds the claims that logic is theoretical and a priori; the second grounds the claim that logic is autonomous with respect to the factual sciences and formal in nature. When pure logic is defined as the theory of science,[32] it is given the task of identifying the elements, laws, and structures that a body of knowledge must satisfy to be scientific. The nucleus of the theory can be expressed in three statements:

1. Scientific theories are propositional in nature.
2. The form of their logical interconnection is deductive.
3. To constitute knowledge these theories must be true.[33]

Corresponding to these three conditions are three types of logical investigation. The first, pure logical grammar, investigates the necessary conditions for a proposition to be meaningful. The second, the formal theory of validity, investigates the necessary conditions for a deductively ordered set of propositions to be consistent. The third, the logic of truth, investigates the necessary conditions for a meaningful proposition to be true.[34] The a priori conclusions reached through these investigations are completely general. They constitute second-order or metalevel truths that are binding for propositions at all levels of discourse.

The factual sciences consist of first-order truths discovered and verified through accepted forms of empirical method. The second-order truths of logic abstract from all specific propositional content to assert the formal conditions every scientific truth must satisfy. Pure logical grammar classifies the elementary forms of predicative meaning (Husserl's semantic categories) and determines which forms of meaning can combine to form a proposition with sense. The principles of permissible combination, in effect, are a priori laws of propositional formation. The formal theory of validity classifies the basic types of propositional interconnection and determines the principles of consistency and consequence that obtain among propositions; these principles are the equivalent of syntactical transformation laws. Pure logic also constructs alternative sets of formal deductive system that can be appropriated by the positive sciences for the systematic expression of their results. In its first two capacities, logic articulates the essential conditions of scientific theory; in the third, it assists science by providing skeletal theory structures, for which the first-order sciences can supply the substantive content.

The network of distinctions carved out within the science of logic are derivatively but not fundamentally linguistic. Logical truths are not based on language, but on ideal elements of meaning.[35] Grammatical distinctions may serve as a point of departure for logical inquiry but the distinctions of meaning are epistemically prior; they ground and justify the grammatical laws. Both Frege and Husserl resorted to semantic ascent to clarify conceptual issues, but they contended that linguistic differences only indicate preexistent differences of sense. They believed that semantic ascent as a methodological strategy in logic should not be confused with the reductionist program that eliminates extralinguistic logical entities or explicates them in terms of freely adopted metalinguistic rules. The dependence of language on meaning in Husserl's semantics is evident in the fourth investigation, where the grammatical distinction between categorematic and syncategorematic signs is grounded in the prior distinction between independent and dependent meanings. The core of Husserl's argument is that the grammatical laws governing the combination of syntactical expressions are based on a priori laws that regulate the formation and combination of extralinguistic propositions.[36]

Husserl's comprehensive theory of meaning identifies five interdependent factors: the linguistic expression; the meaning-bestowing acts; the meaning (sinn) intended; the objects to which the expression refers by way of the intended meaning; and, the immediate intuitions through which meaning intentions are fulfilled.[37] Considered in isolation from intentional consciousness, the linguistic sign is merely a physical entity, a pattern of sounds, or a written inscription. It is endowed with the power to express meaning through the exercise of a meaning-bestowing act. Sense-giving acts intentionally constitute physical items as meaningful signs capable of expressing a sense and denoting a reference. Particular meaning-bestowing acts are temporal events in the intentional histories of human agents, but an indefinite number of agents can exercise the same species of act.[38] For example, the meaning-bestowing act of a German using the term *Begriff* is of the same type as that performed by an Englishman using the term *concept*. This *specific* though *non-numerical* identity of intentional acts transcends the differences of linguistic communities, permitting the translatability of languages and the communication of propositional meaning. Conventional differences among language communities at the level of signs, in principle, are overcome if their members share a common intentional life. The ground of a community of meaning is not a shared set of linguistic inscriptions but a common fund of dispositions in the field of intentional operations. These intentional acts are *private* in both the ontological sense and the empirical sense; they are uniquely attributable to particular individuals and they are not open to direct sensory inspection. But they are *public* in the decisive sense that the same species of act can be predicated of a community of persons who successfully exchange their meaning intentions with one another.

Contemporary theories of linguistic meaning can be divided loosely into two programatic models. In the *language* (*langue*) model the emphasis is upon the meaning of expression *S* in language *L*; semantical questions, on this model, are resolved by specifying the metalinguistic rules and conventions that regulate the use of *S* in *L*. Language is conceived as an abstract structure consisting of linguistic types governed by the full range of semiotic rules. This structure is available for an indefinite variety of social uses, in which those who have mastered the language can employ it in intersubjective communication. The *speech* (*parole*) model shifts the emphasis from *linguistic competence* to *communicative performance*. In the speech model, the controlling question is, What did speaker *M* mean by saying *S* to *N* in circumstances *C?* Knowledge of the meaning of *S* in *L* generally is a necessary but not a sufficient condition for determining the meaning intention of *M*. It can reasonably be argued that the two models are complementary rather than in opposition and that no single approach to questions of meaning is sufficient.[39] Husserl appears to have proposed his theory of meaning with a global intent. If I understand him correctly, he subordinated the language to the speech model because his deepest philosophical concern was with the generative sources of meaning. For him, metalinguistic rules are derivative from a priori laws regulating the combinations of intentionally generated senses. Intersubjective propositional senses are not causally dependent on particular sense-giving acts in the way that an individual temporal effect is uniquely dependent on the single causal series to which it belongs.[40] Unlike natural causation, intentional constitution generates the identical unity of sense through each meaning-bestowing act of the same species. The sense-giving acts stand to the species they exemplify as tokens in a language stand to the type that they token. Philosophical priority is given explicitly to intentional operations over linguistic inscriptions and rules.

An intentional subject who endows a linguistic sign with meaning expresses a distinct theoretical sense. As invariant atemporal entities commonly accessible through intentional temporal acts, logical senses are distinguished from the real objects and relations to which linguistic expressions may refer. Four of the five elements in Husserl's theory of meaning are real; only the intended meaning (*sinn*) is ideal.[41] Husserl was eager to distinguish his concept of the ideality of meaning from traditional theories. He differed from a conceptual realist, like Frege, by making the intended meaning essentially *dependent* on a species of intentional act. He differed from a a classical empiricist, like Locke, by making the intended meaning independent of any token of that species. For Husserl, ideal meanings are not private ideas peculiar to the individuals who bear them but the shareable contents of intentional acts attributable to numerically distinct intentional subjects. Husserl also clashed with the nominalists, ancient and modern, who attempted the reduction of semantics to the theory of reference, to a two-level study of words and objects—"Each expression not merely says something, but it says it of something: it not only has a *meaning* but *refers* to certain objects. This relation sometimes holds in the plural for one and the same expression. But the object never coincides with the meaning."[42] In propositional discourse, we not only refer to objects, but we communicate something about them through that reference. There exists an essential and irreducible distinction between the *referent* of discourse (what is spoken about) and the *theoretical content* of discourse (the thought expressed about that referent). Husserl concurred with Frege on the need for three-level semantics of sign, sense, and reference. But he sought to detach himself from Frege's intentional realism without surrendering the essential objectivity of the logical order.

Husserl's goal was to design an original theory of meaning delicately balanced between realism, psychologism, and nominalism. By situating the theory within his comprehensive investigation of logic he achieved two purposes. He clarified the thesis that logic is a science of objective *meaning*, and he undermined psychologism as a philosophy of logic by showing that it could not account for semantic objectivity. The integrity of the science of logic is preserved by clearly demarcating its investigative domain and by assigning specific tasks to its subordinate parts. In Volume 2 of the *Investigations*, Husserl insisted that philosophy do more than map the logician's field of inquiry: It must show how knowledge of that field is possible, how logic can be a *science* of meaning. The philosophy of logic must develop an epistemological dimension if extrasystemic foundational inquiry is to complete the intrasystemic defense of logic's autonomy. Two critical Husserlian themes dominate this new level of foundational research: the intentionality of consciousness and the phenomenological method. The themes are deeply interrelated and interdependent, for the substantive concept of the mind's intentionality provides partial justification for the methodological program.

E. The Clarification of Pure Logic

Husserl develops a philosophy whose first concern is to cut completely the ties between logic and psychology, but he seems to return endlessly to psychology, the analysis of consciousness, in order to found his logic and his phenomenology.[43]

Husserl assigned to philosophy the general task of understanding and appraising the achievements of positive science. To him, engagement in scientific inquiry does not require *reflection* on one's cognitive practice. The independence of practice from reflection explains why it is possible to have considerable knowledge about the objects of a science while remaining confused about its methods, theories, and epistemic attainments. Rational knowledge of the stars, for example, does not entail an equivalent theoretical grasp of the science of astronomy. Philosophical inquiry is needed to elevate the sciences to the level of objects of knowledge.

Not every *object* of theoretical investigation is itself a *science*. Because the stars and planets, for example, are not scientific theories, astronomy is a first-order inquiry; by contrast, logic is a second-order science whose primary objects are scientific theories of the first and higher orders. Logic is the scientific study of the universal properties of theory. By grounding every aspect of logic at a foundational level of reflection, the philosophy of logic completes the full requirements of rigorous theoretical reason. Observing the distinction between a theory and its object becomes difficult when the object is a theory with its own object, but the distinction is as fundamental and important as that between the sense and reference of a linguistic expression.

The theoretical project of clarifying logic remains ambiguous until we distinguish four levels of clarification. At the first level, Husserl articulated the *telos* or purpose of logic, by establishing that it is a science not an art, pursued by eidetic rather than inductive methods, bent on discovering the a priori conditions of scientific theory. A second level of clarity concerns the *objects* of logical investigation; that is, the complete ensemble of ideal theoretical contents. The distinction between ideal and factual entities is used to refute the different varieties of logical psychologism, which are treated as mistaken ontological accounts of the logical order. The errors of psychologism are further magnified when the *propositional content* of logical theories is made thematic. The semantical analysis of logical theories establishes indirectly the types of entity of which these theories could be true. The final level of clarity concerns the attainment of knowledge by the science of logic. How does logic achieve *scientific* knowledge of its *objects* through its *theories*? The epistemic level completes and integrates the preceding stages of philosophical analysis.

Using this four-part analysis, we can roughly divide the *Logical Investigations* into the following sections: Volume 1 is constructed to achieve clarifications of the first two types; the first four investigations of volume 2 thematize the sense and the reference of logical theories; the fifth and sixth investigations of volume 2 examine logic's epistemic status. A comprehensive philosophy of logic must secure clarity at every level. Husserl practiced eidetic phenomenology as his method for achieving the required clarity and thematized that practice as his way of announcing a new theory of philosophy.

The differences between Frege and Husserl are most pronounced at the metaphilosophical level. At the root of these differences are opposing concepts of the propositional vehicles of truth. Frege held that theoretical senses were abstract entities independent of the mind and its operations. These senses were hierarchically ordered in a pattern of receding logical priority. To clarify philosophically a posterior sense we must define or deduce it from a set of prior concepts and propositions. The primitive theoretical senses cannot be clarified logically by definition or deduction. Their elucidation is a complex affair, involving linguistic clues, which terminates in an appeal to immediate apprehension of their meaning. Epistemic justification of theoretical knowledge also is a matter of deductive inferences from axioms taken to be immediately evident. With the foundational base of concepts and axioms secured through direct insight, the philosopher can rely exclusively on logical operations for the third and fourth levels of clarity. But the vulnerable link in Frege's project is his ultimate appeal to the immediate insight of meaning and truth. With this appeal, philosophical practice ceases to be a purely logical affair. The cognitive relation between the mind and its semantic objects is not reducible to a logical relation between prior and posterior theoretical contents. For Frege, the givenness to reason of logically basic senses does not preclude their metaphysical objectivity. Through the act of understanding, reason alters propositional content no more than the eyes affect the moon in the act of perception. Frege expressly compared the mind's understanding of a thought (*Gedanke*) with the eye's perception of an object. As objective entities, both theoretical senses and perceptual objects are ontologically independent of the noetic acts that apprehend them. Frege never claimed that we intuit abstract entities, but his remarks on immediate evidence suggest that we understand logically primitive senses and know them to be true by a kind of direct acquaintance.

Husserl's theory of intentionality provides the substantive ground for his critique of Frege's philosophical strategy. The central importance of intentionality can be highlighted by contrasting two accounts of the mind's intentional awareness.[44] On both accounts, intentionality is the essential attribute distinguishing mental from physical realities. It is a constitutive feature of intentional entities that they bear a directed reference to an objective content distinct from themselves. The primary examples of such entities are noetic acts. On the neutral conception of intentionality, there is a psychological accusative or content for every intentional act, which that act is of or about.[45] The psychological subject becomes aware of intentional contents through the intentional operations of which it is the center and source. It is important to distinguish between the *object* of human knowledge and the *contents* of the intentional acts constitutive of the process of knowing. Although the successful completion of the cognitive process as a whole terminates in knowledge of an object, the intentional contents of the partial and successive acts in that process are not immediately known. Intentional awareness of a content is not in itself sufficient for knowledge of that content. Even in the terminal phase of cognitional process, when we affirm a proposition as true, we require the distinction between the affirmed proposition and the object known by means of the propositional judgment. Propositions can become objects of knowledge in their own right but only when they are known through other propositions of a higher order.

The neutral interpretation of intentionality is acceptable to both a conceptual realist like Frege and an eidetic phenomenologist like Husserl. This provisional neutrality is surrendered if we maintain that every intentional content is independent of mental acts with respect to both existence and character. Frege's logical realism appears to be based on his acceptance of this principle of objective independence. If I understand him correctly, he modeled his general account of intentional awareness on sense-perception. The object of propositional awareness, the thought, differs from the object of sight or hearing in its lack of temporality and concreteness, but both thoughts and things are equally independent of the subjective operations that apprehend them. Thoughts are no more dependent on the operations of mind than the North Sea.

Husserl rejected the realist's analysis of intentionality, insisting, instead, on a reciprocal interdependence between *types* of intentional act and *regions* of intentional content.[46] From the standpoint of the cognitive subject, all intentional contents become objects of awareness through a certain species of intentional act. Perceptual objects, for example, are the contents of acts of sensory intuition, whereas specific essences are apprehended through eidetic insights. *To be an intentional content is to be accusative to a type of intentional act but independent of particular tokens of that type*. Again, Husserl sought a delicate balance between Platonism and psychologism. By contrasting the type-dependent intentional content with the token-dependent immanent content, he hoped to resolve the ambiguity in the *Philosophy of Arithmetic* that Frege had censured.

The program of eidetic phenomenology rests squarely on this new concept of correlative intentionality, as Husserl's method of sense clarification reveals. Propositional senses are intentional contents correlated explicitly with types of intentional act. Through tokens of these types of act, an individual achieves theoretical understanding of a proposition. Both Frege and Husserl insisted on the proposition's objectivity. For Frege, this required an ontology of timeless abstract entities that the mind can grasp but cannot create. For Husserl, an ordered series of intentional acts cumulatively "constituted" the propositional content of the final act in the series. Frege clarified theoretical content by defining or deducing it from logical primitives. Husserl clarified the sense of a theory by explicitly reconstructing the intentional process beginning in sensory intuition through which the theory is progressively generated. This genetic reconstruction was executed at the *eidetic* rather than the *factual* level. An eidetic history recounts the serial order among types of intentional acts whose individual tokens are moments in a particular subject's life. The phenomenologist has access to this intentional process through reflection on actual or imagined noetic operations. For eidetic phenomenology, a theoretical proposition is adequately clarified when we can recount its eidetic history, when we can exhibit it as an ideal noematic content constituted through a specific series of intentional operations. In the Investigations, Husserl retained the emphasis on concept formation characteristic of the *Philosophy of Arithmetic*, but he refined his original method by carefully distinguishing between factual and eidetic inquiry and intentional and immanent contents. Frege opposed the phenomenological approach to semantical analysis because his concept of intentionality was strongly realistic. He held that the logical entities apprehended in propositional awareness were as ontologically independent of noetic activity as any object in the order of nature.

Husserl's theory of intentionality also sustained his phenomenological strategy on epistemic issues. Regardless of its modal character, every type of propositional knowledge requires a concordance between meaning intention and meaning fulfillment. The essential conditions of knowledge are satisfied when a knower directly experiences the referent of a proposition as satisfying the proposition's truth-conditions. When this principle is applied to logical knowledge, whose putative objects are propositional theories, it implies that a logician can *intuit* the objects of logic as perfectly concordant with the theoretical claims made about them. Husserl insisted that all epistemic justification ultimately rests on intuition. "Immediate 'seeing' (*sehen*), not merely the sensory seeing of experience, but seeing in general as primordial dator consciousness of any kind whatsoever, is the ultimate source of justification for all rational statements."[47] Once the term *intuition* was applied to the achievement of justifying evidence in logic, it is clear that Husserl was working on an analogical plane. To understand what Husserl meant by *intuition*, we must first understand how the analogical extensions of the term are related to the primary analogue of immediate perceptual awareness.

Permit me a critical remark before I attempt to establish these successive extensions. I think that Husserl's reliance on analogy to describe phenomenological method was a serious expository mistake. After numerous readings of his texts, I remain unclear about his pivotal concept of intuition. It is possible that Husserl knew exactly what he was doing, that he had a controlled sense of the scope and limits of his central analogy, and that the following distinctions rehearse a set of discriminations he had already achieved. If these suppositions are correct, then I am trying to be explicit where he was unduly obscure; if they are not correct, then I am trying to be accurate where he was, I suspect, confused.

The primary reference of the verb *to see* is ocular vision. At the ground level, seeing is something human beings do with their eyes when they are awake and looking at visible objects and their properties. In the standard case, the intentional content of acts of seeing are physical objects in a public world that is spatially, temporally, and causally ordered. Seeing of this kind often plays a significant role in human cognition, but it is not by itself epistemic.[48] For example, when John sees the *Mona Lisa* by da Vinci in the Louvre, he may not *see that* it is the Mona Lisa which he *sees*. The intentional content of epistemic seeing, seeing that, is abstract and propositional in nature, the intentional content of nonepistemic seeing is concrete and sensible. To see that it is the Mona Lisa at which you are looking entails that you see the Mona Lisa, but the converse does not hold. Let us call the primary sense of *seeing* nonpropositional perceptual awareness, or seeing[1].

Does seeing[1] provide a secure model for a general theory of intentional awareness? If we use seeing[1] as the analogical base, how far can we extend the analogy without compromising basic philosophical distinctions? Starting with sound extensions, we shall expand them progressively until they become indefensible.

All intentional acts resemble seeing[1] in their direct accusative relation to their contents; intentional contents are not separated from their acts by intermediary objects of awareness. Noetic acts may be described as intuitive if this means that *through* them all of the subject's direct intentional awareness is achieved. A second legitimate extension involves the requirements of consciousness. Intentional acts can be predicated only of a subject who is conscious at the time the acts occur. The radical differences in character and content of intentional operations are reflected in the four distinct levels of human consciousness: empirical, intellectual, rational, and existential. The idea of direct awareness is ambiguous because perceptual awareness, seeing[1] occurs at a different level of consciousness from epistemic awareness, seeing that. Seeing[1] is a recurrent component in cognitional process, but it is only a limited part of the larger epistemic whole. Not all forms of intentional consciousness in themselves are forms of knowledge. Although the different levels of consciousness are defined in terms of different intentional operations and stages of cognitional process, the requirement of consciousness is common to the entire field of intentional operations.[49]

Might further analogical extensions of seeing[1] be attempted? If the specific character of other intentional acts is modeled on vision, if the range of intentional contents are modeled on visible objects and their properties, or if all modes of consciousness are reduced to perceptual awareness, then the analogy has been overextended. The myth of the mental eye is the direct result of these incautious analogical extensions. According to the myth, eidetic structures and logical entities are "intuited" by an inner faculty that perceives them in the same way that vision perceives sensible objects. When Husserl claimed that we can "see" the essence of cognition or "intuitively experience" ideal meanings, was he embracing the fiction of intellectual intuition, or was he relying on imprecise language to make a different point?[50] Does the alleged intuition of essences and propositions reduce these objects of "intuition" to abstract particulars modeled on visible objects though without their spatiotemporal setting, or is Husserl using dramatic language to emphasize the great diversity of intentional contents? The noetic acts of perception, understanding, concept formation, and reflective judgment are equally intentional and conscious, but they are strikingly diverse in their character and content. For this reason, analogically based theories of intentionality are of highly restricted validity. When Husserl recognized specific differences in noetic operations, when he distinguished between sensory, general, and categorial *intuitions* and their correlative modes of noematic content,[51] was he bypassing the myth of intellectual intuition and recognizing the profound heterogeneity of intentional awareness, or was he succumbing to intellectual empiricism under the spell of the model of perceptual confrontation.?[52]

Similar questions arise when we shift attention from Husserl's concept of intentionality to his analysis of *consciousness*. By *consciousness*, I mean the subject's prereflective awareness of himself and his intentional acts, an awareness that is concomitant and correlative to his intentional awareness of objects. Does Husserl understand prereflective consciousness on the experiential or the perceptual model?[53] Experientially conceived, consciousness is not a distinct act of a psychological subject but an accompanying awareness immanent within each intentional act. Every intentional operation is marked by a distinction between subjective and objective modes of presence. The accusative content of an operation is objectively present to the subject through the act. But the intentional act, itself, is subjectively present to its agent, not through another intentional act but through a correlative and prereflective awareness constitutive of the intentional operation itself. Although each intentional act can become the objective content of a later reflexive analysis, even in this case, the acts of reflection themselves remain subjectively present to the person conducting the analysis. But when consciousness is conceived on the model of perception, it is treated as a further objectifying act. If true, this conception would make all awareness by subjects of their intentional operations dependent on reflecting acts of which the subjects would be unaware at the time of their occurrence. All awareness, all consciousness, would become objective intentional awareness; subjective presence, experiential consciousness, would cease to exist. When Husserl referred to an "intuitive awareness" of intentional operations, when he claimed for reflection the power to "see" mental acts, to what aspects of the seeing[1] model was he appealing? Does the reference to intuition entail the regress of the inner eye with which Locke's perceptual account of reflection was burdened, or does Husserl repudiate the perceptual model of consciousness and the act-content structure it treats as universal and exceptionless? Does the insistence on intuition merely acknowledge the subject's experiential access to his intentional operations as the precondition for phenomenological reflection, or is it an inherent part of an erroneous treatment of experiential consciousness, intentional analysis, and phenomenological self-knowledge?

Husserl clarifies the concept of intuitive awareness by contrasting it with mediated symbolic consciousness. Symbolic consciousness presupposes an immediate intentional content that signifies the object of which we are mediately aware. The reader of a text, for example, is directly conscious of the sign-designs on the page and symbolically conscious of the meaning they signify. But Husserl's distinction between the intuitive and the symbolic does not differentiate between the objective and experiential modes of direct awareness. These are concomitant and correlative modes of consciousness equally essential to an understanding of intentional operations and equally vital to a comprehensive theory of inquiry. Unfortunately, the idiom of *intuition* and the contrast between the intuitive and the symbolic obscure or neglect this distinction, leaving the project of phenomenological reflection in a state of serious ambiguity.

The threat of incoherence also overshadows Husserl's project of sense clarification and epistemic justification. The shadowy concept of intuition is again at the root of the problem. Consider the example of logical theories, the alleged intentional contents of categorial intuitions. What are categorial intuitions and through what intentional process do they and their contents emerge? We shall examine Husserl's answers momentarily, but the question itself points to a serious limitation in the use of analogical language. We know through Husserl's insistence that categorial and sensory intuitions are distinguished through different types of intentional content; categorial contents are ideal logical entities whereas sensory contents are concrete spatiotemporal particulars. But what do we know about categorial *intuitions* themselves? *Categorial* is a term applied to these acts in recognition of their distinctive content; *intuition*, once again, is unhappily ambiguous. Husserl's phenomenological method depends on a clear and nuanced theory of distinct kinds of intentional operations, but the language of analogy used in introducing the method compromises the project, forcing Husserl to rely on distinctions of intentional content in order to classify intentional operations.

How do these limitations affect the program of epistemic justification? Husserl required that all defensible knowledge claims ultimately be grounded in intuition. Symbolic operations play a major role in theoretical cognition but the terminal evidence in science is supplied by intuitive awareness. Husserl and Frege, in their epistemic projects, both depended on propositions whose truth values could be known directly. But the admission of direct propositional knowledge highlights a further ambiguity in Husserl's concept of intuition. According to Descartes, whose influence on Husserl's notion of intuition is appreciable, a proposition p can be known intuitively when the understanding of its meaning is sufficient to determine its truth-value.[54] Cartesian intuition converts the understanding of a proposition's meaning into knowledge of its truth without reliance on independent sources of evidence. It permits the determination of a proposition's truth-value through a grasp of its truth-conditions alone. I share Arthur Danto's judgment that the Cartesian theory of intuitive knowledge amounts to a "prayer for a logical miracle."[55] But intuition can be related to noninferential knowledge in a non-Cartesian way. Suppose that p is a proposition about r, an object of sense-perception. Once we understand the truth-conditions of p, how do we determine whether they are satisfied by r? By directly examining r to determine whether its properties satisfy the truth-conditions of p.[56] The direct perception of r is a case of sensory intuitive awareness that partially grounds the knowledge that p is true. Note, however, that we do not *intuit* that p is true. The legitimate object of intuition in this case is the sensible object to which p refers and not the proposition through which the object is known.

This non-Cartesian analysis of intuition clearly resembles Husserl's general theory of evidence. Can the theory plausibly be extended from knowledge of sensible objects to knowledge of abstract logical entities? Suppose that x is a logical theory about s, a first order scientific proposition. To know directly that x is true of s, s must be intuitively experienced as satisfying the truth-conditions of x. But how do I intuitively experience a scientific proposition, as I must, on this account, if I am to know that a logical theory about it is true? Categorial intuition is introduced to play the role in logical knowledge that sensory perception plays in empirical cognition. How clear is Husserl able to make this concept; how intelligible an account did he provide of the epistemic procedures of logic? The following answers are based on the position outlined in the second volume of his *Logical Investigations*.

Let us first distinguish among r, s, and q, where r is a brown chair in my living room, s is the proposition that a chair in my living room is brown, and q is the logical proposition that s is a first-order categorical proposition of the subject-predicate type. Our intention is to clarify Husserl's account of how I know that q is true.

Sensory intuitions have concrete particulars as their intentional contents. They are the original modes of direct awareness that provide the base for more complex forms of intentional operations and contents. Both eidetic intuitions and categorical operations presuppose sensory intuition as the intentional foundation on which they depend. Acts of sense-perception are classified as unfounded because they occur independent of predication, the most elementary level of categorial operation. Other types of intentional act are classified as founded to indicate their type-dependence on perceptual acts; a correlative distinction of levels applies to intentional contents. The objects of logical investigation are founded because they are not reducible to the contents of sensory intuition. In our example, r is an unfounded content, while s and q are founded. How does a knower proceed from the sensory intuition of r to the epistemic judgment that s, and from that judgment to the more complex logical judgment that q? A satisfactory answer to this question would provide us with a basic noetic theory of first- and second-order knowledge. I think that Husserl tries to construct such a theory but with partial success. The following paragraphs outline his basic approach, while criticism is reserved for a later chapter.[57]

Suppose we are asked on what grounds we assent to s. Before we can reply responsibly, we must understand the meaning of s. Because s is a proposition, we cannot clarify its sense by direct appeal to sensory intuition; rather we reconstruct s as a categorial content constituted by intentional acts performed upon the contents of sensory intuition. According to Husserl, propositional contents like s are formed by categorial operations t upon sensory content like r. A propositional sense is clarified when it is reconstructed as a founded content constituted by founded acts performed upon an originally unfounded base. Once we understand the meaning of s, we can assent rationally to its truth, if we experience r as satisfying the sense of s. By phenomenological analyses of this kind, first-order propositions are grounded semantically and epistemically.

How do we clarify and justify logical knowledge? Suppose we are asked on what grounds we assent to q. We clarify q by reconstructing it as a more complex categorial content formed by categorial operations t' on s. Second-order propositions like q are semantically analyzed by tracing their genesis to successive categorial operations upon unfounded and founded contents. Once we understand q, we can assent to its truth, if we experience s as satisfying the sense of q. Because we cannot sensibly perceive s, we must appeal within this framework to a new kind of intuition as the evidential ground for logical knowledge. Husserl claimed that by reflecting on the intentional acts constitutive of s, we could see immediately that s's subject-predicate structure is the outcome of predicative operations performed upon r. Through phenomenological reflection, we can achieve intuitive awareness of the series of intentional operations that account for the categorial structure of propositions at both the first and higher levels. Reflexive awareness of the operations constitutive of s provides the experience of s as satisfying the sense of q. Because categorial acts are intentional, the reflexive awareness of t also reveals the subject-predicate structure of s.

How do categorial intuitions function in this reconstructive program? Are they the logical operations of predication and conjunction, say, through which atomic and molecular propositions are constituted, or are they the acts of reflective awareness that take such logical operations as their content? Is the intentional object of a categorial intuition a propositional content, a categorial operation, or a categorial process constituting a propositional content? For categorial intuition to play the role in logical knowledge analogous to that of sense-perception in empirical cognition, the final alternative must be accepted. To experience s as satisfying q is to experience s as intentionally constituted by t. If categorial intuition is interpreted in this manner, then Husserl's general commitment to intuitive evidence can be preserved. Nevertheless, a final question remains. What does Husserl mean by intuitive awareness of categorial acts? Is such awareness intuitive because we can inspect categorial acts with an intellectual eye, as we inspect sensible objects with a sensitive eye, or is it because experientially conscious intentional operations can be objectified later through phenomenological reflection? In the first instance the "seeing" aspect of intuition is emphasized, though in ways that make phenomenology properly suspect to its critics. In the second case we are forced to recognize the correlative aspects of human awareness, both experiential and intentional, since the accusative consciousness of noetic acts presupposes their prior experiential immediacy.

These distinctions should remind us of earlier questions about Husserl's concept of intuition, which we recently explored though did not resolve. In concluding this section, I want to restate my original challenge. The perceptual model of phenomenological intuition, I think, is incoherent, and Husserl's resort to analogy in the explication of phenomenological method at best is an expository error of considerable gravity.

F. The Identification and Suspension of the Natural Attitude

From now on not only modern physicalistic naturalism, but every objectivist philosophy, whether of earlier or future times must be characterized as transcendental naivete.[58]

The *Logical Investigations* make two major contributions to philosophy. They safeguard the theoretical autonomy of logic by clarifying the eidetic distinction between the laws of logic and those of psychology. They provide an epistemic account of the science of logic by thematizing the types of intentional acts through which its objects are constituted and eventually known.

From the standpoint of method, the *Investigations* represent a clear advance beyond Husserl's practice in the *Philosophy of Arithmetic*. But judged by the standards that Husserl finally adopted, the *Investigations* fail to achieve philosophical stature. The semantic and epistemic analyses of volume 2 require a more radical treatment if they are to attain the foundational level of clarity. To appreciate the importance of Husserl's demand for radicalism, it is necessary to understand the tasks he set for philosophy. Husserl rejected the prevailing belief that the positive sciences had achieved theoretical autonomy. Although celebrated as the model for all authentic inquiry, they failed to satisfy the deepest norms of reason: they operated at a level of provisional rationality that failed to meet the requirements of rigorous science. Unless they are provided with the foundational support that only philosophy can offer, the modern aspiration to scientific knowledge would prove abortive. This caution applied even to an eidetic science like logic. By establishing logic's autonomy with respect to factual disciplines, Husserl did not exempt logic from further foundational scrutiny. For this scrutiny to be philosophical, it had to occur at a level of reflection distinct, in principle, from that of any positive inquiry. Husserl labored throughout his career to define this difference in principle, to *show* why the positive sciences were incomplete, and to show *how* philosophy could complete them.

The metaphor of foundations supplied Husserl with his image of the philosophical project. Foundations exist at a different level from the structures they support; the discovery and cognition of foundations vitally supplement any discipline that neglects to explore the deep ground on which it rests. Despite its posture of self-congratulation, positive science is charged with this neglect. Foundational analysis is mandated to remedy a twofold lack in logic and the natural sciences. At the intrasystemic level, theoretical categories are applied but not rationally clarified, and theoretical judgements are accepted without full disclosure of the necessary evidence. Philosophy's first contribution to these disciplines is to provide the conceptual clarity and rigorous justification that science demands. In volume 2 of the *Investigations*, Husserl adopted the method of genetic reconstruction to bring the categories and objects of logic to foundational clarity. The genesis in question was not causal, as in the natural sciences, nor deductive, as in logic and mathematics. According to Husserl, neither causal nor logical reconstruction is properly a foundational method;

neither the naturalists nor Frege had properly envisaged the philosophical project. Intentional genesis "constitutes" its objects as objects of awareness; it conditions their occurrence as intentional contents. Both the categories and objects of logic are grounded by disclosing the intentional process through which they are presented to consciousness. The intrasystemic deficiencies of logic are met through the program of intentional reconstruction.

Husserl's philosophical emphasis shifted after the completion of the *Investigations*. The extrasystemic limitations of science increasingly claimed the center of his concern; he accused the sciences of epistemic presumption and metaphysical naivete. What was the substance of these related accusations? To be a rigorous science, a discipline must conduct its inquiry without concealed presuppositions; it must be fully self-critical. Modern sciences pride themselves on their rigor and exactness, but Husserl contended that they suffer from a profound naivete. This naivete extends to both the objects and horizons of positive inquiry. All of these disciplines take for granted the prior givenness of their fields of research.[59] They presume that their subject matter exists independent of intentional activity, that it is already there in its full intelligibility before the operations of consciousness begin. The exclusive task of consciousness, then, is the causal or logical analysis of these preexistent fields of objects. The sensible world, the realm of nature, the logical order, the field of mathematical analysis—these are simply given to the mind for its theoretical scrutiny. In the *Investigations*, Husserl had already rejected this presumption for the science of logic. Unlike Frege, who postulated the ontological independence of abstract entities as a necessary condition of logic's objectivity, Husserl attempted to reconcile the intersubjective character of ideal objects with their dependence of intentional genesis. He sought to preserve epistemic objectivity without conceptual realism.

Beginning with *The Idea of Phenomenology*, in 1905, Husserl's thought repeatedly gravitated around the critical problem, around the question of the metaphysical status of the objects of knowledge. For him, the problem was set by two parameters: He was committed to preserving the objectivity of science with its logical system of timeless and unconditional truths; yet, he was equally committed to grounding this objectivity in a foundation of intentional operations. He wanted to detach scientific objectivity from metaphysical objectivism, the form of *naive* realism that uncritically assumed a receptive rather than constructive role for consciousness.[60] For the objectivist, human consciousness received what reality gave it in the way of objects, both concrete and abstract, both sensible and imperceptible. Frege had elevated this normally implicit presumption to the status of a metaphysical principle. All *objective* entities were *given* to reason or perception; none were constructed by rational or perceptual operations. Relying on his theory of intentional constitution, originally conceived for the field of logical entities, Husserl proceeded to a global assault on objectivism. Philosophy could not be critical unless it conducted a comprehensive reappraisal of the metaphysical status implicitly accorded the objects of positive science. What the objectivist took for granted became the central enigma for transcendental phenomenology.[61]

Husserl introduced this basic enigma by contrasting two opposing attitudes to the objects of inquiry, the natural and the transcendental. Because the natural attitude is a pervasive, implicit, precritical, metaphysical posture, its discovery and identification is a philosophical achievement. Raised to the level of an explicit principle, it states that the objects given to consciousness through intentional activity have their being independent of intentional operations. By virtue of their independent givenness, these objects are accessible universally and theoretical truths about them admit of intersubjective verification. Ontological independence of the mind becomes the defining mark of objective reality; no object can satisfy the conditions of rigorous science, which lacks the prescribed independence. To put the natural attitude into question is to suspend belief in these assumptions and in all forms of inquiry that proceed on the basis of their acceptance. According to Husserl, all nonphilosophic precritical inquiry is conducted within the framework of the natural attitude. It is the ruling presupposition that vitiates their claim to unqualified rigor. This indictment applies to mathematics and logic, the physical and historical sciences, practical reflection, and to nearly all of the "philosophical tradition." All are guilty of implicit objectivism.

For these reasons, Husserl found the project of philosophical naturalism to be absurd. The naturalist conceives of foundational epistemology as an empirical science conducted at the same level as the positive sciences it investigates. But a naturalized epistemology is as precritical as any discipline shaped by the natural attitude. For the purposes of philosophy, every epistemic assertion of natural science is moot. "If the meaning and value of natural cognition as such together with all of its methodological presuppositions and all of its exact foundations have become problematic, then this strikes at every proposition which natural cognition presupposes in its starting point and at every allegedly exact method of giving a foundation."[62] If a presuppositionless philosophy is to be possible, it must begin by thematizing and suspending the natural attitude. It must conduct its investigation of science from a standpoint that is not objectivist. The attitude and standpoint of rigorous epistemology must be transcendental.

In contradistinction to all natural cognition, philosophy lies within a new dimension; and what corresponds to this new dimension, even if, as the phrase suggests, it is essentially connected with the old dimensions, is a *new* and radically new method which is set over against the ('natural') method. He who denies this has failed to understand—what philosophy really wants to do and should do.[63]

Husserl denied that his earlier eidetic phenomenology had achieved the transcendental dimension. Although not explicitly objectivist, its intentional analysis of noetic operations was still precritical. Without a deliberate suspension of the principles of realism, they are presumed to be tacitly operative. No philosophy is genuinely rigorous unless it executes the transcendental turn, unless it identifies and brackets the implicit metaphysics of objectivism.

Moden philosophy, according to Husserl, has been essentially a struggle between objectivist and transcendental forces; his own conflict with naturalism and psychologism is seen as the climactic battle in a proctracted war. "The greatest of all philosophical revolutions must be characterized as the transformation of scientific objectivism into transcendental subjectivism."[64] Galilean physics began the modern era in philosophy by directly challenging the ontological status of the sensible world. Naive realism had taken the objects of sensory perception on trust. It had assumed unreflectively that these objects were real entities independent of the sensory process, that perception disclosed a given world already there. Following Galileo's lead, Descartes converted the objects of sense perception into ideas, into representations perceived by the mind.

The sensible world lost its ontological independence through this conversion; it became a domain of appearances inseparable from the perceiving subject. With this conversion, Descartes stood on the edge of transcendental thought. But on Husserl's reading he corrupted his insight by *treating these appearances as representations of an imperceptible objectivist world.* Real nature, true being, continued to be thought of as independent of the mind, although physical reality was now given to consciousness only through the mediation of sensible ideas. Physical naturalism replaced perceptual realism, one version of objectivism supplanted another, but the transcendental initiative had been lost.

Berkeley's subjective idealism and Hume's radical empiricism both developed a critique of philosophical naturalism. Berkeley denied the existence of Galilean nature, of a mind independent physical reality; he transformed the sensible world into a web of ideas, whose *esse est percipi*; he gave the central ontological place to the perceiving subject, to spirit. But the human spirit, though active in comparison with the inert ideas it perceives, itself is receptive with respect to the divine spirit, the imperceptible causal origin of the ideas of sensation. The divine ideas, the objects of divine intuition, provide the standard of truth and reality; for the human spirit, these ideas are the pregiven reality to which its true ideas must correspond. Although Berkeley overcame physicalist objectivism and perceptual realism, he failed to conceive of human subjectivity in transcendental terms. The objects of sensory perception were still understood, finally, to be representations of imperceptible being; human subjectivity was not the foundation of true existence; the mind remained a conditioned member of the causal order, now taken to be an order of spirits rather than bodies.

Hume struck boldly at Berkeley's objectivist concept of causation. His empiricist principles undermined any appeal to imperceptible causes of perception. Both mind-dependent physical causes and spirits were excluded from the sphere of philosophic reflection. True being is intuitable being, either impressions or ideas, whose *esse est experii*. Sensible objects were reduced to bundles of perceptions; causation was analyzed as the constant conjunction of ideas of a common type; the human subject was made the center of the philosophic universe. But Hume's reductionist fervor went too far. Instead of conceiving the subject transcendentally as the foundational origin of the intuited world. Hume reduced the subject to a second bundle of perceptions, on the model of his earlier reduction of sensible objects. By neglecting the intentional structure of consciousness and the asymmetry between the perceiving subject and the perceived object, Hume's radical empiricism became a universal leveling instrument. Both the subject and the object dissolved into the one-dimensional universe of ideas. The fundamental structure of consciousness explicitly conceived by Descartes, of a rational subject intending an intended content through an intentional act (*Ego-cogito-cogitatum*), therefore had been decimated. Hume collapsed Descartes's complex intentional structure to a one-dimensional series of intended contents, but because the constitutive elements in the Cartesian structure are defined reciprocally, the elimination of two of them leaves the third unintelligible.

Taking his point of departure from the dialectical struggle I have outlined, Kant tried partly to restore what Hume had undone. The three goals of transcendental philosophy were at the forefront of Kant's enterprise: to preserve the objectivity of knowledge and its objects; to eliminate the objectivist interpretation of the field of perception and cognition; and, to revise the traditional conception of mind as receptive rather than constructive. Despite the revolutionary solutions at which he arrives Kant's spirit was conciliatory rather than radical. His strategy was to integrate objectivism with transcendental principles rather than starkly to oppose it. This accounts for the numerous dualisms in Kantian thought. Kant resolved the problem of objectivity by his distinction between empirical realism and transcendental idealism. From the perspective of the empirical subject, *the subject in the world*, the world is already given to be perceived and investigated; but from the perspective of transcendental criticism, the empirical world itself is a web of appearance, whose *esse est experii* by the transcendental subject whose synthetic operations constitute it. The objectivism of the empirical subject is superseded by transcendental idealism. The world known through scientific cognition is a world fashioned to comply with transcendental categories and principles; it is a phenomenal not a noumenal world. Yet, this world is dependent materially on an imperceptible noumenal order that provides its primal sensory content. The true order of being still is independent of the human inquirer, though it is no longer perceptible or even accessible to cognition. The existence of transcendent being is conceded to the objectivist, but the concession is mitigated by the claim of its permanent unknowabilty. The world that we do know and perceive is dependent for its categorial structure on transcendental subjectivity. Although transcendental operations are made the foundation of the empirical world, they are inaccessible to direct intuition. A fine distinction is required between the empirical subject, a particular member of the phenomenal order, and the transcendental subject who is the constitutive ground of that order. Ground and grounded coexist at different levels, support different attributes, and are apprehended through different methods. Because the constructive operations of transcendental subjectivity are never items of experience, their contribution must be discovered through a process of regressive transcendental inference. This requirement, however, conflicts with a basic epistemic principle to which Kant was deeply committed; namely, that concepts without intuitions are epistemically empty—in Kant's critical idealism both the noumenal and transcendental grounds of empirical knowledge are postulated without intuitive corroboration. Kant's transcendental subjectivity and his objectivist in-itself (*an sich*) are both vulnerable to the internal criticism that their existence and nature cannot be known. The alleged foundations of scientific knowledge fail to meet the requirements of epistemic rigor. Because he was unable to secure apodictically his foundational principles, Kant's critical epistemology is not yet ready to "present itself as a science."[65]

The loss of epistemic rigor was more acute in the ensuing tradition of German idealism. There, speculative energies were given free rein and the insistence on intuitive verification was suspended. Philosophical naturalism with its insistence on a scientific epistemology was the predictable response to these unbridled rational conjectures. The naturalists' aspiration to make philosophy scientific was commendable; but the decision to achieve this by modeling philosophy on the positive sciences represented a relapse into the crudest form of objectivism. The lesson to be drawn from modern philosophy, according to Husserl, is that no earlier epistemology has satisfied the demands of a foundational discipline. Either they were uncritically objectivist, insufficiently rigorous, or excessively reductionist. Husserl did not spare himself in this indictment; both the *Philosophy of Arithmetic* and the *Logical Investigations* fail to accomplish a clear breakthrough into transcendental phenomenology. Even in these texts the transcendental turn is incomplete.[66]

Throughout his career, Husserl sought conceptual clarification through the study of intentional genesis. The *Investigations* purified this study by submitting it to the eidetic reduction, by conducting intentional analysis eidetically rather than inductively. Entities in the logical order systematically were correlated with the *typical* intentional processes responsible for their formation. After the *Investigations*, Husserl extended this pattern of foundational analysis beyond the sphere of logic. Having rejected conceptual realism, he began a systematic criticism of all recognized spheres of objectivity. Was it possible that every objective formation apprehended by consciousness was grounded in intentional operations, that the entire field of positive inquiry was founded in the processes of subjectivity? To raise this question seriously was to suspend the pattern of precritical metaphysical acceptance known as the natural attitude. It was to put on trial all objectivist assumptions, however deeply concealed. The systematic suspension of objectivism, given its universal hold on inquiry, required a concerted methodological strategy, the phenomenological reduction, or *epoche*.[67]

The purpose of the *epoche* was to purify intentional analysis of the central presupposition of all prephilosophic inquiry. Husserl struggled to make that presupposition fully explicit. He contended that every investigation is conducted from a distinctive intentional standpoint, from an intentional perspective taken for granted by the investigator. The examination of objects always occurs within a *horizon* of beliefs, assumptions, and acceptances that the examiner exempts from scrutiny. Natural consciousness is invariably directed away from the subject toward the field of objects; only through reflective analysis could the subject bring his own standpoint into relief. Deep critical reflection revealed that the "natural standpoint" presumes a comprehensive pregiven world of which the investigative subject forms a part. The world as a whole is *there* with its intrinsic intelligible structures; the investigator is an element in that world bent on discovering those structures. Even reflection on the intentional life of the subject has taken place within this ruling presumption. Intentional analysis, then, unless it is purified by the *epoche*, implicitly integrates subjectivity into the pregiven world. But when the world as the comprehensive horizon of inquiry is objectified, it thereby is converted or reduced into a totalized *noema* for a nonworldly consciousness.[68] The subjective standpoint that puts the foundation of the world as a whole into question, according to Husserl, must be a standpoint outside the world. Through the transcendental reduction all modes of objectivity are converted into aspects of a totalized mundane objectivity, which itself is converted into a global intentional content. Through this reduction the world and its objects lose neither their reality nor their intersubjectivity; what they do lose is their presumed independence of intentional operations. They become essential correlates of a nonmundane transcendental consciousness. Once the transcendental turn is executed, the field of foundational epistemology is revealed; it consists of the transcendentally reduced intentional structures in which all regions of mundane objectivity are correlated with their appropriate intentional acts. With the *epoche*, Husserl advances from an assumed dependence of consciousness on the world to an alleged dependence of the world on transcendental subjectivity.

To construe this dependence on the model of objective causation is to extend mundane categories beyond their legitimate sphere of application. Like Kant, Husserl confined causation to the realm of the objective world. The intentional relations between the transcendental subject and its noematic contents exist at a different level from all intrawordly relations. But unlike Kant, Husserl insisted that these foundational relations be brought to full intuitive clarity.[69] He saw no place within a rigorous philosophy for postulated subjects, elements, and relations. Husserl took the process of intentional reconstruction first developed in the *Investigations* and expanded it to cover all types of objective being. Intentional analysis re-enacts the step-by-step "constitution" of the sensible world, scientifically conceived nature,and the ideal order of logic. A radical shift in theoretical interest had occurred. Whereas the positive sciences investigate the causal or logical relations among their respective objects, philosophy examines the concrete intentional processes through which all objects of consciousness are given. This process begins at the level of pre-predicative perceptual experience and develops through successive intentional operations until it embraces the entire world. To be a constituted intentional content is to be the object of a founded intentional act or series of acts. The regulative principle of transcendental analysis within the epoche is this: All the intentional acts presupposed by a founded intentional act also are presupposed by its founded or constituted content. The foundational obligations of philosophy are met when every theoretical content and every object of positive science are exhibited intuitively in the process of their intentional constitution.

For reasons of clarity, three types of noetic investigation should be clearly distinguished:

1. Empirical psychology is an inductive study of mental acts that are taken to be singular, temporal elements in the causal order of nature. It is a discipline pursued within the natural attitude by empirical methods, using mundane categories, and without the benefit of either methodological reduction. It treats the ego as a

conditioned member of an all-embracing causal series, as a worldly element on a par with other natural objects.

2. Eidetic phenomenological psychology is a reflexive intentional analysis of the typical correlations between intentional acts and contents. It is pursued implicitly within the natural attitude, but it employs eidetic rather than inductive methods and classifies its objects in intentional rather than causal categories.

3. Transcendental phenomenology is foundational epistemology. It is an eidetic reflection on transcendentally reduced intentional structures, which seeks to reconstruct the pattern of their serial formation. It locates the ground of all objectivity in the transcendental subject and refuses philosophical stature to any examination of subjectivity still bound to the natural attitude. Logical psychologism resulted when the causal and logical orders were not distinguished eidetically. Transcendental psychologism is Husserl's critical term for any species of subjective investigation presenting itself as philosophical without the transcendental reduction.[70]

"If we disregard the *Philosophie der Arithmetik* of 1891, Husserl's work in logic can be seen to span some forty years, and, despite the undeniable evolution of thought, these works reveal a fundamental unity. The unity derives from Husserl's anti-psychologism."[71] How are we finally to understand his antipsychologism? Originally, it was Husserl's struggle to preserve the autonomy of the science of logic, to secure the independence of logical truths from naturalistic prejudices. Eventually, it became his struggle to preserve the unity of philosophy, to secure a field of foundational analysis totally liberated from presupposition and bias. Between the beginning and the end of this intellectual journey, a set of normative principles were held constant: Theoretic objectivity is to be protected; foundational clarity is imperative; such clarity is available through the genetic reconstruction of objective noematic content; the ultimate origin of true being is the intentional subject. By taking the transcendental turn into idealism, Husserl believed that he satisfied these principles while adumbrating a philosophy "able to present itself as science."

Wittgenstein began philosophy with the identical problem area, the foundations of mathematics, and a similar sympathy for transcendental methods, but he reached strikingly different conclusions. His successive linguistic turns oriented philosophy in a new direction, a direction that pointed analytic philosophers away from Husserl in both substantive content and method. In the next chapter, we will examine Wittgenstein's adventure in transcendental philosophy and the new frame he provided for metaphilosophical inquiry. In Chapter V, we will examine the full flowering of the new way of words and reassess Husserl's achievement from the perspective of linguistic philosophy.

4

Wittgenstein's Linguistic Turns

My work has extended from the foundations of
logic to the nature of the world.[1]

A. The Linguistic Turn

Wittgenstein shares with the philosophers we have examined a deep interest in
the theory of logic and metaphilosophy. In his *Tractatus* he makes an original
contribution to these fields by reconceiving their problems from the perspective
of language.[2] This transformation of perspective constitutes a minor revolution
in the history of philosophy, a revolution that has been celebrated and
condemned under the designation the *linguistic turn*.[3] The linguistic turn,
away from the older way of ideas to the new way of words, represented a
rejection of ideas as the focus of philosophic inquiry and an acceptance of
language as their replacement. One effect of this shift was to restore to
philosophy a public rather than private field of investigation. The reflexive
turn to the solitary subject and his private ideas first initiated by Descartes
suffered a deliberate reversal. In turning toward language, philosophers
turned away from themselves and their inner states and back toward the
world. But this return to the world and its objects remained mediated.
Philosophers continued to begin their analysis with entities in the logical
order, although that order was now conceived as an order of discourse rather
than an order of consciousness. The pioneers of linguistic philosophy exhibit
their Cartesian heritage by accepting the modern assumption that epistemic
access to the real order depends on a prior appropriation of the logical order
that symbolizes it.

The linguistic turn encouraged an increase in self-consciousness among philosophers. It prompted them to philosophize about language as well as by means of it. Wittgenstein's philosophical program displays this double aspect of practice and self-reflection. In his earliest work, he tried to solve the problems of philosophy by developing a comprehensive theory of language. He thought that questions in the philosophy of logic, metaphysics, and metaphilosophy could be settled if we correctly understood the nature of the proposition, the essential unit of language. A satisfactory philosophy of language would illuminate the differences between the propositions of logic and those of natural science and show why there are no specifically philosophical propositions. Wittgenstein's original philosophical convictions derived from his belief in a reciprocal mirroring relation between the deep structure of language and the skeletal order of the world. The underlying principles of his substantive argument can be outlined as follows:[4]

1. The propositions of natural language provide a complete and exact description of the world,
2. These propositions describe the world by picturing possible states of affairs,
3. The semantical content of a descriptive proposition is the possible state of affairs that it pictures,
4. Logical propositions differ from the propositions of natural science in that they have no semantical content,
5. Logical propositions say nothing because there are no logical facts that it is their special task to describe,
6. The propositions traditionally formulated by philosophers are pseudo-propositions,
7. Although they appear to describe the world, they exceed the limits of language, the limits of what can be said meaningfully,
8. They do this because they attempt to say what only can be shown, but whatever can be shown cannot be said,
9. Pseudo-propositions occur because natural languages are logically correct but lack perspicuity,
10. A perspicuous language will show what philosophers have attempted to say in a non-perspicuous language and release them from the temptation to say it.

My intention in this chapter is to explore the interconnections in the different stages of Wittgenstein's career between his theory of language, his philosophy of logic and his metaphilosophy. I hope to show that the account of propositional meaning advanced in the *Tractatus* as the core of a theory of language provides the backing for his original judgments on the nature of logic and the purpose of philosophy. Wittgenstein later revised both his concept of linguistic meaning and his method of semantical analysis. This revision led directly to a modified theory of logic and a reconstructed criticism of philosophy, which he vigorously applied to the *Tractatus* itself.

In both phases of his career, Wittgenstein contributed to the demise of psychologism. He did this in the *Tractatus* by making the legitimate concerns of all factual disciplines irrelevant to issues in philosophy. Logical psychologism is rebutted by the sharp distinction between logical and factual propositions. Philosophical psychologism is rebutted by the assertion that philosophy is not a factual science, that the connection between philosophy and empirical psychology is no closer than that between philosophy and botany. In the *Philosophical Investigations*, Wittgenstein made psychological research irrelevant to the project of conceptual analysis and epistemic justification. He recommended that we clarify concepts and justify knowledge claims by examining the use of language rather than by reflecting on mental acts and their imperceptible intentional contents. This methodological canon sets linguistic philosophy and phenomenology in direct opposition. It represents the culminating phase of a protracted process that began with the shift of philosophical inquiry from ideas to words. Reflection on their reasons for taking the linguistic turn eventually led analytic philosophers to question the nature of language itself. The philosophy of language then became the substantive base on which logical, metaphysical, and metaphilosophical theories were developed.

B. Logic as the Essence of Philosophy

It [philosophy] consists of logic and metaphysics, the former its basis.[5]

Frege and Husserl were attracted to philosophy through their original interest in the foundations of mathematics. Wittgenstein traveled a similar route. He began his philosophic career as a student of Bertrand Russell at Cambridge doing foundational research in both logic and mathematics. At that time, he and Russell shared a common belief in the importance of logic for the practice of philosophy and a common hope that the methods developed in foundational research could be put to philosophic use. Russell raised this belief to the level of a program in "Logic as the Essence of Philosophy."[6]

In that article Russell declared that philosophy needed a new method if it were to attain the status of a science. He urged that the appropriate method be borrowed from techniques of analysis developed in foundational research in mathematics. Claiming that rival philosophic schools are ultimately rooted in their logical theories, he anticipated a reconstruction of philosophy based on the modern revision and extension of classical logic. Russell's concept of logic consists of two parts: philosophic logic and mathematical logic. The aims of philosophical logic are to investigate the nature of propositions; to classify the different types of propositions; and, to develop the axioms and definitions needed for the logicist reconstruction of classical mathematics. The program of mathematical logic is to demonstrate the theorems of mathematics on the foundations supplied by the philosopher of logic. When Russell declared that logic is the essence of philosophy he referred to philosophical rather than mathematical logic.[7]

The primary focus of philosophical logic is on the nature of the proposition. In his theory of propositions, Russell made a sharp distinction between their forms and constitutive elements. The form of a proposition is determined by substituting free or bound variables of the appropriate type for the nonlogical constants that occur within it. Two propositions may have the same logical form but different semantic content; for example, "Cassius distrusts Caesar" and "Plato loves Socrates" are instances of the same propositional schema, which can be expressed as xRy. When the forms of two propositions are identical, their difference of content is based on a difference of constituent, a difference either in the individual and predicate constants the two propositions contain or in the order in which these constants are combined. Russell thought knowledge of logical forms was as essential to the understanding of a language as knowledge of its nonlogical vocabulary.[8]

Logic is concerned with propositions that can be used to make assertions about matters of fact. Russell made the crucial but unsupported assumption that there exists an identity of form common to propositions and the factual situations they describe.[9] Philosophical logic, by determining the full array of propositional forms, simultaneously discloses the possible forms of fact. This assumption of formal identity between propositions and facts permits Russell to separate effectively the aim of philosophy from that of the factual sciences. Whereas philosophy uncovers which forms of fact are possible, the sciences alone determine whether there are facts of that form. Both the sciences and philosophy preserve their autonomy through this assignment of related but independent objectives.

The specific objective of philosophy is to enumerate the range of propositional forms and thereby to uncover the possible forms of fact. According to Russell, this enterprise can be conducted without appeal to actual experience, and it produces conclusions that are wholly general and a priori. Since they are not grounded in experiential evidence, philosophical conclusions are not subject to revision by it. The possible forms of proposition are grouped under three basic headings, each with its own subdivisions: atomic, molecular, and general propositions.

In an atomic proposition an *n-adic* predicate constant is suitably combined with the appropriate number of individual constants. Within the class of atomic propositions there are an unlimited number of possible propositional forms as n ranges through the series of natural numbers. Note that Russell is not claiming that there *are* atomic facts corresponding to each *n-adic* atomic form but that facts of that form are logically possible. Only empirical investigation can decide whether there are such facts. Molecular propositions result from connecting atomic propositions by means of logical connectives such as conjunction, disjunction, and material implication. The use of the logical connectives indicates a difference in form between molecular and atomic propositions and, according to Russell, a parallel difference "in the nature of their correspondence with fact."[10] General propositions are propositions containing the quantifying expressions *all* or *some*. Russell takes pains to show that general propositions cannot be expressed as the logical product or sum of atomic propositions, that universally quantified propositions are not reducible to a finite conjunction of atomic propositions or existentially quantified propositions to a finite disjunction of atomic propositions.

This irreducibility becomes significant when Russell applies his techniques of analysis to the propositions of natural language. One striking conclusion of his analysis is that a proposition's grammatical structure may conceal its logical form. Classical instances of this concealment are propositions containing definite descriptions as constituent expressions and propositions containing *exists* as a grammatical predicate.[11] Russell's reconstruction of these propositions is intended to show that their logical form is that of general propositions although their grammatical structure bears a resemblance to propositions that are atomic or molecular in form. Since inferences to forms of fact are drawn on the basis of forms of statement, the method of propositional analysis has both logical and ontological significance. Russell's use of this technique in ontology is mainly deflationary. He used it to reduce to a minimum the number of categories required by an adequate ontology. The deflationary thrust of analysis is best illustrated in the search for logical constructions, in which Russell tried to analyze propositions about inferred entities into logically equivalent propositions about objects of direct or noninferential acquaintance.[12]

Without examining specific examples of logical construction, I can indicate the governing strategy behind this program. As a proponent of logicism Russell wanted to analyze the concepts of classical mathematics into logical concepts and to derive the theorems of mathematics from logical axioms using explicitly formulated principles of inference. The apparent achievement of this project in *Principia Mathematica* led him to believe that an equivalent reconstruction could be achieved for other fields of scientific knowledge. To render empirical scientific theories epistemologically secure, Russell sought to erect them upon what he considered an epistemic base of certainty. The base would consist of the propositions of logic and those atomic propositions in which primitive sensible predicates are attributed to bare particulars of immediate sensory acquaintance. He believed that by repeated applications of propositional analysis we could reach a foundation for science that was logically exact, empirically primitive, and epistemically secure.[13]

Although Russell's philosophical commitments were those of a logical empiricist, he shared many of Descartes's theoretical objectives. Like Descartes, he based his ontological claims on the conclusions of a prior epistemology. The division of Russell's ontology into two parts reflects both what is novel and what is traditional in his approach. Formal ontology is a theory of ontological possibility. It is based on an inference from the forms of propositions to the possible forms of fact, from the structure of the logical order to that of the real order. The warrant for that inference is the assumption of a structural isomorphism between propositions and what they describe. Material ontology, by contrast, is a theory of what in fact exists. It is based on the logically reconstructed propositions that we can endorse with certainty as true. The connective link between ontological possibility and actuality is scientific truth; the connecting discipline between formal and material ontology is epistemology. Russell's philosophical program, then, has two branches: The first begins in formal logic and ends in formal ontology; the second complementary branch extends from formal logic into empiricist epistemology and concludes in material ontology.

Given the purposes of this chapter, I do not intend to evaluate Russell's success in any of these ambitious endeavors. I cite them to show the range of problems that absorbed him and the use he made of logical methods and theories in dealing with them. I think a careful reading of Wittgenstein's *Notebooks* reveals the extent to which he shared Russell's interest in the intimate connection between logic and philosophy. One significant exception should be noted, however. Wittgenstein, in the Tractarian phase of his career, was far less concerned than Russell with the question of cognitive security. As Griffin[14] and others have argued, he shared Russell's' concern for analysis and the drive for irreducible simples, but the simples that concerned him were logical and ontological, rather than epistemological in nature. When Wittgenstein identified philosophy with logic and metaphysics, he accepted the first but not the second branch of Russell's program. Wittgenstein's ontology is a purely formal ontology. We learn from it what any possible world must be like but nothing of the actual world in its concreteness. The common interest that I wish to emphasize, then, is carefully circumscribed: their joint concern for the interconnecting links between logical theory, formal ontology, and metaphilosophy.

In his *Notes on Logic* in 1913, Wittgenstein wrote "Philosophy is the doctrine of the logical form of scientific propositions (not primitive propositions only). A correct explanation of the logical propositions must give them a unique position as against all other propositions"(NB93). To determine the logical form of scientific propositions, Wittgenstein believed that propositional analysis is necessary because ordinary factual discourse conceals its logical structure (TR 4.002). The grammatical form of a proposition need not be its logical form (TR 4.0031). "It is clear that the components of our propositions can be analyzed by means of a definition, and must be, if we want to approximate to *the real structure* of the proposition. When the proposition is just as complex as its reference then it is completely analyzed" (NB 46). Wittgenstein was confident that every proposition could be analyzed completely. This confidence rests on his understanding of the nature of the proposition. "My whole task consists in explaining the nature of the proposition. . . . in giving the nature of all facts whose picture the proposition is" (NB 39). Following Russell, Wittgenstein believed that the essence of language would be revealed in the essence of the proposition, which is the seminal unit of linguistic description. Moreover, because propositions describe the world, insight into their essence would simultaneously reveal the formal structure of reality. Wittgenstein devised a general theory of signification in the belief that it would decisively resolve the problems of philosophy. He conceived that theory as the answer to the question: What must a proposition that describes the world have in common with the world in order to be a description of it? The phrasing of the question indicates his close ties to Russell. Wittgenstein's answer sustained that close connection, but the implications he drew from the answer separate him from Russell and stamp his position as original. For our purposes two of these implications are particularly important:

1. A correct theory of symbolic representation explains the unique status of logical propositions. It grounds a philosophy of logic.
2. When we realize "that nothing that is necessary for the understanding of all propositions can be said" (NB 25), we also understand why there are no philosophic propositions, why philosophy cannot be a science.

C. Wittgenstein's Theory of Signification

Don't get involved in partial problems but always
take flight to where there is a free view of the whole
single great problem given even if this view is still
not a clear one. (NB 23).

In his preface to the *Tractatus*, Wittgenstein summarized the sense of the book in these words: "What can be said at all can be said clearly, and what we cannot talk about we must pass over in silence"(TR 3). This compressed summary highlights the contrast between significant discourse and discourse that aims to be significant but fails. Because what can be said must be said by means of a proposition, a study of the conditions of significant discourse concentrates on the nature of propositions. We can set a limit to what can be said by erecting a sharp distinction between sign combinations that are propositional and those that are not.

It is assumed without argument in the *Tractatus* that the single legitimate function of propositions is to provide descriptions of the world. Nonpropositional linguistic signs are used significantly only when they function in the context of propositional descriptions. We shall call this assumption *the descriptivist thesis*. The single great problem for a theory of language is to understand the essence of linguistic description. The semantic dimension of signs, their power to represent something other than themselves, is tied inextricably to their role in a propositional matrix. Only propositions have sense; only in the nexus of a proposition does a name have meaning[15] (TR3.3). The semantic connection between language and reality is secured by propositional description. Language acquires the power to represent the world through these descriptions, which bring language signs into coordination with the situations they are about (NB 53). Wittgenstein characterized the relationship between propositions and the situations they describe as that of picturing. Propositions describe possible states of affairs by picturing them.[16]

To say that a proposition pictures a possible state of affairs does not mean that the elements of the propositional sign iconically resemble the elements of the state of affairs. As in Russell's theory, an identity of logical form between picture and pictured, rather than a resemblance of constituents, is the core of the picturing relation. The relevant likeness is a likeness of structure. "The possibility of the proposition is. . . founded on the principle of signs as going proxy for objects. Thus, in the proposition something has something else as its proxy. But there is also the common cement" (NB 37). The identity of logical form between picture and pictured is the common cement. Although elements in the propositional sign represent correlative elements in the pictured situation, there is no linguistic *element* to represent the common logical form; nothing stands as proxy for the common cement. Propositions describe reality by picturing it, but what they must have in common with the reality they picture itself cannot be pictured. We cannot significantly discourse about logical form, even though significant discourse eventually rests upon it. In the strict sense, a general *theory* of representation is impossible, because we cannot describe the necessary conditions of significant description. For this reason the "propositions" of the *Tractatus* ultimately must be rejected as exceeding the bounds of sense they attempt to outline.

Wittgenstein agreed with Russell that propositions share a common form with the ontological situations they describe; he differed in maintaining that we cannot talk about this common form. "In order that you should have a language which can express or say everything that can be said, this language must have certain properties; and when this is the case, that it has them can no longer be said in that language or any language" (NB 107).

A logically correct language, one in which we can say everything that can be said and only what can be said, provides the resources for a complete description of the world. But it provides no resources for describing its own semantical relation to the world. Insofar as language is a complex of propositional signs that exist *within* the world it is a candidate for description like other factual complexes. But insofar as language is *about* the world, insofar as it signifies the world, it cannot be described by a language that is restricted to describing the world alone. Metalinguistic semantical discourse *about* descriptive language and object-linguistic descriptive discourse *about* the world are finally irreducible to one another. If a logically correct language is an object language completely without resources for its own metalinguistic characterization, then what Wittgenstein attempted to say in the *Tractatus* cannot be said.[17]

We provide a complete description of the world by means of the totality of true elementary propositions (TR 4.26). Elementary propositions are the residue that results from Wittgenstein's logical analysis of the propositions of natural language. An elementary proposition consists of names; it is a nexus, a concatenation of names (TR 4.22). Names are primitive linguistic signs, which cannot be dissected by means of a definition nor rendered more explicit by means of further signs (TR3.26). Within the linguistic order, they constitute the root level from which all linguistic combinations develop. They are the elements within a complex propositional sign that stand directly for objects. Names are the signs to which Wittgenstein referred when he said that the possibility of a proposition rests on signs going proxy for objects. An interesting reciprocity is at work here. The possibility of a proposition rests on names, but names have meaning only in the context of a proposition. Names stand proxy for objects only when they belong to an arrangement of names that collectively says something about an arrangement of objects. Both names and the objects to which they refer have form. The form of a name is identical with the form of its referent. Concretely, this means that the same normative laws regulate the combination of names to form propositions that regulate the combination of objects to form possible states of affairs. This principle explains the identity of logical form between language and the world. It guarantees that syntactically legitimate arrangements of names will have meaning through picturing possible states of affairs isomorphic in structure with them. The identity of structure between propositions and states of affairs ultimately rests on the identity of form between name and object. A completely analyzed atomic proposition consists only of names. "When the proposition is just as complex as its reference then it is completely analyzed" (NB 46).

The *Tractatus* proceeds on the explicit assumption that there are counterpart categories in the ontological order that correspond to the basic categories of language. This assumed isomorphism supports the thesis that logic is the foundation of metaphysics, an assumption shared by Wittgenstein and Russell and defended by neither. Names as primitive language expressions refer to objects; elementary propositions formed by combinations of names picture atomic states of affairs formed by combinations of objects. When the elementary propositions are true they picture atomic facts; when they are false they picture possible but nonexistent atomic states of affairs. Although names are the constitutive elements of atomic propositions, their semantical roles are importantly different. Wittgenstein emphasized this difference in contrasting his semantical theory with that of Frege. According to Frege, all proper names have a sense, and, in a logically perfect language, all of them would have a reference. All meaningful propositions have both a sense and a reference. The sense of a proposition is the thought (*Gedanke*) it expresses; the referent of a proposition is one of the two bivalent truth-values, the true or the false. Wittgenstein's position, by contrast, is that names have reference without sense and propositions, sense without reference. To say that propositions refer is really an elliptical way of saying that the names that constitute propositions refer. One outcome of this semantical difference for Wittgenstein is that naming and saying are clearly differentiated as linguistic functions. Propositions are not names and do not function semantically like names, although they depend on names for their functioning. States of affairs, the ontological counterparts of propositions, can only be described, whereas objects can only be named. Significant discourse occurs only at the level of saying, but the possibility of saying is founded on naming, on signs going proxy for objects.

The propositions of natural language do not contain names in the strict Tractarian sense. Names only occur in the nexus of elementary propositions (TR 4.23), which are not reached until propositional analysis is completed. If the essence of description is to be understood, the relation of unanalyzed to elementary propositions must be clarified. Wittgenstein's thesis is that all meaningful propositions are truth-functions of elementary propositions (TR 5). I shall call this the *thesis of extensionality*.[18] The complex object -language propositions of natural language are the logical outcome of truth operations upon elementary propositions (TR 5.234). The logical analysis of a natural language proposition exhibits it as the product of truth operation(s) carried out on a base of atomic propositions, on the analogy of an arithmetic product that is the outcome of a multiplication operation with prime numbers. The symbolic expression of this analysis displays the natural language proposition in a relation of mutual equivalence with a set of elementary propositions connected by specific logical constants. (For example, if S is a natural language proposition and p, q, and r are its constituent elementary propositions, then S is a truth function of of p, q, r, if $S \equiv (p \cdot q \cdot r)$.) If this pattern of reductive analysis were applied to all propositions, then the essence of description would be revealed by examining the semantical functions of the signs within the terminal analysand. In the chosen example, the signs in question are the elementary propositions, p, q, r and the logical constant '·'. We have seen that the elementary propositions consist exclusively of names that function semantically as direct representatives of objects and in combination as descriptions of possible states of affairs. The unresolved issue, then, is: How do the logical constants function? Wittgenstein's answer is unequivocal: "the possibility of propositions is based on the principle that objects have signs as their representatives. *My fundamental idea* is that the 'logical constants' are not representatives" (TR 4.0312). There are no "logical objects" (TR 4.441, 5.4).[19] The logical signs in a perspicuous language function neither as names nor as propositions. They do not represent objects or describe states of affairs. Their semantical contribution is to symbolize truth-operations. Wittgenstein cited as examples of truth-operations, negation symbolized by '∼', logical addition symbolized by 'v', and logical multiplication symbolized by '·'. He insisted that the number of truth-operations required for the complete description of the world depends solely on the notation employed (TR 5.474). It is possible to express every meaningful proposition "as the result of successive applications to elementary propositions of *the* operation '(————T) (————)'. This operation negates all the propositions in the right-hand pair of brackets, and I call it the negation of those propositions" (TR 5.5).

The Tractarian philosophy of language is a theory about the properties any language must have to provide a complete description of the world. If my interpretation is accurate, Wittgenstein's theory of linguistic signification can be stated as follows:

1. The essential function of language is to describe. The meaningful units of language are atomic propositions that describe the world (descriptivism).

2. Propositions must share an identical logical form with the states of affairs they describe. This identity is based on invariant laws regulating linguistic and ontological configurations (isomorphism).

3. Three distinct types of signs must be recognized, each with its unique semantical function. Every logically correct and perspicuous language must have signs of each type.

Sign	Semantical Function
Names	Refer to Objects
Elementary propositions	Picture atomic states of affairs
Logical constant(s)	Symbolize truth-operation(s) (semantical minimum)

4. All meaningful propositions are truth functions of elementary propositions (extensionality).

5. The relevant unit of semantical analysis is the proposition. Only propositions have sense; only in the nexus of a proposition does a name have meaning (moderate holism).

6. A theory of language, in the sense of a sct of propositions expressing theses one through five, is not possible (ineffability). "In order that you should have a language which can express or say everything that can be said, this language must have certain properties; and when this is the case that it has them can no longer be said in that language or any other language" (NB 107).

7. Wittgenstein's philosophy of language is not an empirical theory, nor are its theses supported by appeal to empirical evidence. His investigation is best understood as a transcendental argument in the Kantian sense. He is concerned with the conditions that must be satisfied if a complete, consistent, and semantically determinate description of the world is to be possible. Proceeding on the assumption that such a description is possible, he asks what language and reality must be like to ensure this possibility. Kant's *Critique of Pure Reason* aimed to establish the scope and limits of human knowledge. Wittgenstein's *Tractatus* proposed to determine the scope and limits of significant discourse, to set a limit to what can and cannot be said.[20]

Both Kant and Wittgenstein believed that the results of transcendental inquiry are necessary in a way that the disclosures of empirical science are not. As the conditions of the possibility of experience are not themselves items of experience, so the conditions of significant discourse are not susceptible of statement. The essential features of language that Wittgenstein is concerned to uncover cannot be described; the accidental features of language can be described in an empirical theory of discourse but this theory is without philosophical importance. The written and spoken forms of natural language are not essential to the possibility of propositional description. What is essential is that there be items in the elementary propositions standing for objects in a possible state of affairs. It would be a matter for empirical linguistics to determine the specific character of such items for any given language, but that there *must* be such a correspondence is not a matter of fact but a necessary requirement.

It does not go against our feeling, that we cannot analyze propositions so far as to mention the elements by name; no we feel that the world *must* consist of elements. And it appears as if that were identical with the proposition that the world must what it is, it must be definite. Or in other words what vacillates is our determinations, not the world. It looks as if to deny things were as much as to say that the world can, as it were, be indefinite in some such sense as that in which our knowledge is uncertain and indefinite.

The world has a fixed structure (NB 62).

The Tractarian theory of signification is a theory of the essence of language that discloses the necessary features any system of discourse must satisfy. It is the result of a transcendental inquiry into the conditions required for a complete and precise description of reality. With the completion of that inquiry, we finally realize that what a philosophical theory of language intends to say can only be shown.

D. Tautologies and Contradictions, Their Unique Status

Logic is not a body of doctrine but a mirror-image of the world (TR 6.13).

Wittgenstein's linguistic strategy in the philosophy of logic emphasizes the unique status of logical propositions among the totality of meaningful propositions that constitutes language (TR 4.001). Each proposition within this totality is a truth-vehicle with both truth conditions and a truth value. To understand its truth conditions is to understand under what circumstances it *would* be true. To know its truth value is to know *whether* these conditions are satisfied. Understanding the sense of a proposition, therefore, is a necessary but not sufficient condition for knowing its truth value. By the principle of extensionality every legitimate proposition is a truth function of elementary propositions (TR5). There are 2^n sets of truth conditions for a proposition that is the truth-function of n elementary propositions (TR 4.45). Among the possible sets of truth-conditions are two extreme cases. The truth-conditions of a proposition are tautological when the proposition is true for all the truth possibilities of the elementary propositions of which it is the truth function. The truth conditions of a proposition are contradictory when the proposition is false for all the truth possibilities of the elementary propositions of which it is the truth function (TR 4.46). A tautology is a proposition whose truth conditions are tautological; a contradiction is a proposition whose truth conditions are contradictory. In an exhaustive division of propositions on the basis of their truth conditions, tautologies and contradictions would be uniquely distinguished. Tautologies are the truth-vehicles whose truth value is true in all possible worlds, whereas contradictions are the truth-vehicles whose truth value is false in all possible worlds. All nonlogical truth-vehicles will be true in some possible worlds and false in others. Thus, Wittgenstein's controlling insights converge:

1. The correct explanation of the propositions of logic must assign to them a unique status among all propositions (TR 6.112).
2. The propositions of logic are tautologies and contradictions (TR6.1).

A clearer understanding of logical propositions can be gained by contrasting their properties with the propositions of natural science. All theories that make the propositions of logic appear to have content are false (TR 6.111). The semantic content of a proposition is the possible state of affairs that it pictures. All factual propositions have semantic content, but logical propositions have none. Logical propositions are not pictures of reality (TR 4.462); they do not represent any possible situations (NB 24); they have no subject matter (NB 48); they say nothing (TR 6.11). "Our fundamental principle is that whenever a question can be decided by logic at all it must be possible to decide it without more ado. (And if we get into a position where we have to look at the world for an answer to such a problem, that shows that we are on a completely wrong track) (TR 5.551).

Although tautologies and contradictions lack sense (*sinnlos*), they are not nonsensical (*unsinnig*). In clarifying their linguistic function, Wittgenstein returned to the metaphor of limits or extremities. The expressions of language can be divided into two classes, those that function as propositions and those that do not. Only the propositional expressions have sense and bear a truth value. As the limiting case of sign combinations that function as truth vehicles, the propositions of logic demarcate the bounds of sense. They also demarcate necessary from contingent truths, for their truth value alone is invariant across all possible worlds.

The most striking characteristic of nonlogical propositions is that their truth values cannot be determined by knowledge of their truth conditions (NB 127). It is impossible to tell from the proposition alone whether it is true or false (TR 2.224), for no propositions with sense are true a priori(TR 2.225). Logical propositions are peculiar in having the "property of expressing their truth or falsehood in the very sign itself" (NB 127, TR 6.113). Every tautology shows that it is a tautology (TR6.127). Since the word *tautology* is a metalinguistic predicate, we cannot *say* that a proposition is a tautology; what can be *shown* cannot be said. That a logical proposition invariably is true or false can be determined by merely examining the propositional sign. Wittgenstein insisted that this determination is not a matter of subjective certainty. Logical propositions are not to be distinguished from factual propositions by their degree of self-evidence (TR 6.1271). One can *calculate* algorithmically whether a proposition belongs to logic by calculating the logical properties of the propositional sign. The truth of a logical proposition is determined by the meanings assigned to the logical connectives within it. The meaning of the logical connectives is implicitly defined by the stipulation of their truth-tables. The calculation to which Wittgenstein referred is the use of the truth-table method as a decision procedure for determining logical truth and falsity. As Black remarked, "the need for known decision procedures for checking on putative logical truths is an integral and indispensable feature of Wittgenstein's philosophy of logic."[21]

Although the propositions of logic do not say anything about the world, something about the world is indicated by the fact that certain combinations of symbols are tautologies" (TR 6.124). This remark brings us to the ontological dimensions of Wittgenstein's philosophy of logic. In the *Tractatus*, logical propositions do not picture but mirror the logical structure of all possible worlds. By virtue of this mirroring, they retain an aspect of reference or intentionality. I have noted that, on Wittgenstein's account, language has both essential and accidental properties. The accidental properties can be described in factual propositions, but the essential properties can be shown only through logical analysis. Ontologically, there is a parallel distinction between essential and accidental features of logical space. The actual world is variable and contingent, but the *form* of the world is invariant and necessary; it is identical for all possible worlds. The language that we speak is contingent but the *logic* of language is identical for all possible languages. Outside logic everything is accidental; the only necessity that exists is logical necessity (TR 6.3). The essential features of language are logical features with ontological counterparts in the structure of reality. The propositions of logic mirror the world, not by picturing facts but by showing the essential properties of the universe. How is this done? The underlying assumption is Russell's thesis that propositions and the situations they describe share a common logical form. "If propositions are to yield a tautology when they are connected in a certain way they must have certain structural properties. So their yielding a tautology when combined in this way *shows* that they possess these properties" (TR 6.12). Given the assumption of isomorphism, this *shows* that the situations these propositions describe possess certain structural properties as well. Whatever is necessarily true of language corresponds to something necessarily true of logical space. Logic becomes the foundation of metaphysics when metaphysics is identified with the formal ontology of all possible worlds. However, the priority of logic to metaphysics in the order of knowing is reversed in the order of being. Existentially, the ontologically irreducible objects and their invariant laws of combination ground linguistic meaning and determine its syntactical and semantical articulation. Wittgenstein's metaphor for this unstatable but crucial correspondence is the great mirror. The propositions of logic are said to be connected with one another in an infinitely fine network, the great mirror (TR 5.511), which mirrors the a priori scaffolding of reality (TR6.124).

Before concluding this review of Wittgenstein's philosophy of logic, I want to comment briefly on his rejection of psychologism. Although the logical-psychological distinction does not receive the extended treatment in the *Tractatus* that it does in Frege's philosophy, Wittgenstein's position is staked out clearly by his theory of logical propositions. Psychological propositions are factual propositions of equal value (TR 6.4) with all the other propositions of natural science. They are no more closely related to the propositions of logic than are the propositions of geology or botany. Paraphrasing Wittgenstein's remark, we can say that "psychology is no more closely related *to logic* than any other natural science" (TR 4.1121). When Wittgenstein spoke of logical propositions, he was not referring, as Husserl did, to metalinguistic truths about ideal meanings. Husserl's concept of logic as the theory of science led him to treat the propositions of logic as second-order propositions about first-order theories. Wittgenstein rejects the possibility of a metalinguistic science of meaning. By logical propositions, he meant those complex object-linguistic truth-vehicles whose truth-values are invariant and effectively decidable. Knowledge of their truth values does not require a justifying phenomenological analysis, because an algorithmic test is always available

E. The Nature of Philosophy

Does not my study of sign-language correspond to the study of thought processes, which philosophers used to consider so essential to the philosophy of logic? Only in most cases they got entangled in unessential psychological investigations, and with my method too, there is an analogous risk (TR4.1121).

Wittgenstein's purpose in the *Tractatus* is "to set a limit to the expression of thoughts" (TR 3). This limitative project is singularly important because, once achieved, if offers a final solution to the problems of philosophy (TR 5). When the limits of significant discourse are understood, the special task of philosophy has been completed. One sees the world aright (TR 6.54).

   Wittgenstein thought that to determine the limits of discourse it was first necessary to understand the essence of language. The essential features of language are the properties language must have to provide a complete description of the world. To do this, language must consist of propositions that share an identity of form with the states of affairs they describe. What is essential to language is this identity of logical form, the common cement that binds language to the world.

Why is Wittgenstein confident that this requirement extends to every possible language? As I have noted, his theories were not based on empirical research. He did not distill the essence of language by abstracting a set of common features from a judicious selection of natural languages. Rather, he cautioned that the empirical study of language is unsuited to his purpose. The essential features of language are necessary; empirical research is restricted to the contingent. Even if empirical inquiry disclosed characteristics common to all languages, these findings would lack the required necessity. "Even if they were true, their truth could only be the result of a fortunate accident" (TR 6.1232). If philosophy is to discover the essence of language, its methods must be different from those of natural science.

In the *Tractatus*, Wittgenstein did not thematize his method, but his inferential procedure can be construed as a form of transcendental argument. Given certain assumptions about the objectives of language, what conditions must obtain for those objectives to be realized? If these necessary conditions can be discovered, supposedly the essence of language will be known. But how do we determine whether the transcendental argument is successful? According to Wittgenstein, we cannot appeal directly to the grammatical structure of natural languages for confirmation. In these languages grammatical structure conceals logical form. "Distrust of grammar is the first requisite for philosophizing"(NB93). "Everyday language is a part of the human organism and is no less complicated than it. It is not humanly possible to gather immediately from it what the logic of language is" (TR 4.002). Since the grammatical form of a proposition need not be its logical form, philosophy is set an additional task—the critique of language (TR 4.0031). The two functions of philosophy are complementary. In its transcendental role, philosophy discovers the foundational requirement of the identity of logical form between the sign and signified; in its clarificatory analytic role, philosophy exhibits the true logical form of the propositions of natural language.

Wittgenstein described this second function of philosophy as the "logical clarification of thoughts" (TR 4.112). We clarify a thought logically when we display the logical form of the proposition in which it is expressed. Wittgenstein's rhetoric suggests that everyday propositions are to some extent unclear until this activity is accomplished. "Without philosophy thoughts are, as it were, cloudy and indistinct: its task is to make them clear and to give them sharp boundaries." Philosophic or logical analysis does not issue in metalinguistic philosophical propositions but rather in the clarification of object-linguistic descriptive propositions (TR 4.112). By presenting clearly what can be said, we signify indirectly what cannot be said and begin to establish, in piecemeal fashion, the limits of significant discourse (TR 4.115; TR 6.53).

A cardinal tenet of Wittgenstein's *Tractatus* is that philosophy is not a science but an activity of clarification. Every science consists of a logically organized corpus of propositions, but there are no philosophic propositions. The world divides into facts, but there are no philosophic facts. What is of philosophic interest is the a priori structure of language and reality. "The great problem around which everything I write turns is: Is there an order in the world *apriori*, and if so what does it consist in?" (NB 53). The *Tractatus* answers this question affirmatively, but with a peculiar twist. "Propositions can represent the whole of reality but they can't represent what they must have in common with reality in order to be able to represent it—logical form" (TR 4.12). The a priori structure of reality finds its reflection in language, but language cannot be used to describe this structure. Propositions show the logical form of reality. (TR 4.121). But what can be *shown*, cannot be said (TR 4.1212). The a priori order of the world cannot have anything as its proxy (NB 37). Everything properly philosophical, as everything properly logical, belongs to what can only be shown. In principle, there can be no philosophical propositions.

What traditional philosophers have attempted to say is already mirrored in the propositions of natural language. They failed to see this because the grammatical surface of language disguises thought (TR4.002). In its clarificatory function philosophy can remove the mask of grammar by rendering the logical form of a proposition perspicuous. The perspicuous expression of a thought presents it in fully analyzed form, in which the essential features of language and reality are made manifest. In a perspicuous language we could dispense with all logical propositions. "If we know the logical syntax of any sign language then we have already been given all the propositions of logic" (TR 6.124). The only propositions in a perspicuous language would be atomic propositions and molecular combinations of atomic propositions. The a priori mirroring of the essence of reality, performed by logical propositions in a nonperspicuous language, would be taken over by the atomic propositions in a perspicuous language. This would be the correct method of doing philosophy: "to say nothing except what can be said, i.e. propositions of natural science— i.e. something that has nothing to do with philosophy—and then whenever someone else wanted to say something metaphysical to demonstrate to him that he had failed to give a meaning to certain signs in his proposition" (TR 6.53).

Wittgenstein recognized that he has not observed these strictures in his own performance. The *Tractatus* is of a piece with traditional philosophy in its attempt to say what cannot be said. It distinguishes itself from the tradition with its candid acknowledgment of failure. "My propositions serve as elucidations in the following way: anyone who understands me eventually recognizes them as nonsensical, when he has used them—as steps—to climb up beyond them" (TR 6.54).[24]

F. The *Tractatus* as an Ethical Deed

The book's point is an ethical one. I once meant to include in the preface a sentence which is not in fact there now but which I will write out for you here, because it will perhaps be a key to the work for you. What I meant to write then, was this: My work consists of two parts: the one presented here plus all that I have not written. And it is precisely this second part that is the important one.[25]

In his preface to the *Tractatus*, Wittgenstein cautioned the reader of the book's difficulty. He observed that its sense might be intelligible only to those who have already thought the thoughts it expresses. Subsequent interpretations of his text indicate that he had legitimate cause for concern. The *Tractatus* later became a seminal document for both Viennese positivism and the program of philosophical analysis centered at Cambridge. In situating Wittgenstein's achievement within the philosophical tradition, both of these schools took their cue from the debt to Frege and Russell acknowledged in the Preface. Guided by this landmark, they identified Wittgenstein's purpose with that of his predecessors in foundational research. Substantial textual evidence supports their assumption, since the *Tractatus* focuses largely on topics in philosophical semantics and ontology. If the central purpose of the *Tractatus* were determined by the textual emphasis accorded to its major themes, it would properly be classified as a work in the philosophy of language, a treatise on the proposition.

Recent studies on Wittgenstein's cultural background and his published correspondence with Engelman and Von Ficker, however, raise justified doubts about the adequacy of the received interpretation.[26] This material forces us to situate the *Tractatus* against a Viennese rather than an English background. It compels us to see Wittgenstein as a figure of prewar Hapsburg Vienna, as a participant in the Viennese modernist movement, as a student versed in the post-Kantian ethical tradition stretching from Schopenhauer to Kierkegaard and Tolstoy. Taken collectively, these sources revise the accepted judgment of Wittgenstein's intention. The logical analysis of language is now seen as a means to an ethical end. "The book's point is an ethical one."[27] Not only is Wittgenstein's declared intention respected by this shift of perspective, but the integrity of the *Tractatus* as a whole is restored. The Tractarian propositions one through 6.4 now are united with the oracular remarks on ethics and value that complete the work. The primacy of the ethical intention intimated in the Preface is affirmed explicitly in its mysterious conclusion. "And if I am not mistaken in this belief, then the second thing in which the value of this work consists is that it shows how little is achieved when these problems are solved" (TR Preface).

Just as in the *Critique of Pure Reason* Kant limited knowledge to make room for faith, so in the *Tractatus* Wittgenstein limited meaningful expression to protect the integrity of the inexpressible. The comparative silence of the *Tractatus* on ethical questions, seen in the light of Wittgenstein's strategy, is no indication of marginal or subordinate status."Propositions can express nothing that is higher" (TR 6.42). Wittgenstein's preoccupation with the limits of linguistic expression had its ground in his attempt to isolate ethics from rational discourse and argument. This is not to be an arbitrarily postulated separation but one grounded rigorously in an insight into the essence of propositional representation. Frege and Russell, with their research into the foundations of language, inspired him to find a technical solution to the problem of fixing the limits of the sayable. The problems and difficulties that haunt the *Tractatus* are Viennese in origin but their strategic solution lies not in the methods of Vienna but in those of Jena and Cambridge.

"For now, I would recommend you to read the *preface* and the *conclusion*, because they contain the most direct expression of the point of the book."[28] Wittgenstein's advice to Von Ficker is helpful in trying to comprehend the *Tractatus* as a whole. The leading principles of the work, adumbrated in the Preface, reach their climax in the Conclusion. The whole *sense* of the book might be summed up in the following words: What can be said at all can be said clearly, and what we cannot talk about we must pass over in silence (TR Preface). "What we cannot speak about, we must pass over in silence"(TR7). The reader's bridge between the beginning and the end of the text is erected out of the Tractarian propositions themselves. Once these propositions are understood, the logic of our language becomes transparent and the distinction between what can and cannot be said is grasped firmly. To honor this distinction is to say only what is sayable, to be silent about the inexpressible, and to realize tacitly why silence is more expressive than speech. Even though the propositions of the *Tractatus* are nonsensical (*unsinning*), they can have an effective use. They can serve as a connecting medium gradually transporting the reader from speech to silence, not the silence of confusion and unrest but that which results from seeing language and the world aright, the silence of peace.

In the *Tractatus* language can be seen from two complementary perspectives: as a series of pictures that are facts *in* the world and as a series of truth-vehicles that are pictures *of* the world. The logical analysis of language abstracts from its factual dimension. It concentrates exclusively on the internal properties and relations of propositional pictures; these properties are transcendental in character, determinable a priori, and common to all possible languages. Since these attributes are metalinguistic in nature they cannot be expressed *in* propositions although they are shown *by* the propositions whose properties they are. The factual analysis of language, by contrast, abstracts from its logical or semantical dimension. It concentrates exclusively on the external properties and relations of propositional signs, which are factual in character, determinable empirically, and restricted to a particular natural language. These object-linguistic properties are expressible in the propositions of empirical linguistics.

Logic and empirical linguistics stand, respectively, to the analysis of language as formal ontology and science stand to the investigation of the world. Formal ontology is concerned with the internal, transcendental properties common to all possible worlds; science, with the totality of contingent facts into which the existing world divides. Whereas empirical linguistics and science consist of meaningful propositions that describe both linguistic and extralinguistic facts, the putative propositions of logic and metaphysics are technically without sense and value. They fail to picture any possible or actual state of affairs.

These principles suggest a possible reading of *Tractatus* 6.4-7, a reading that integrates the central argument of the work with its conclusion. Suppose we extend the logical and metaphysical distinctions generated by propositional analysis to the world as a limited whole. As propositions with both internal and external properties have sense and truth value, so the world, with both internal (logical) and external (factual) properties, might possess a meaning and value of its own expressible in language. This extended analogy between propositions and the world may not succeed, but an insight into the source of its failure could lead us to see the world aright and to enjoy the expressive silence such seeing brings.

Given the required conditions of the analogy, the meaning of the world must lie outside the world as the sense of a picture lies external to the picture. Now, all propositional pictures are of equal value (6.4). There is no hierarchical structure of propositions, because all of them are equally meaningful and the states of affairs they picture equally contingent. As the sense of a proposition is a function of its internal properties rather than its external properties, so the meaning of the world, as well, would be a function of its internal features. Because all possible worlds have the same internal features, the sense of the world would be entirely independent of the facts. In the world everything occurs contingently, but the sense of the world is not contingent. (6.41).

As every proposition with sense has two possible truth values, so the value of the world is equally bivalent; it is said to wax and wane with the action of the will. (6.43). This action, though independent of the world's internal and external properties, may not be independent of the way the will sees and feels the world. The value of the world alters with the action of the will toward the world as a whole. In referring to the will, Wittgenstein introduced psychological categories into the *Tractatus*, categories he had intended explicitly to exclude.

The will of which he speaks is not the will of empirical agents who exist within the world. The reference rather is to the will of the transcendental ego that serves here as a unifying limit of the world, as it had served earlier in Kantian theory. Only the transcendental ego that stands outside the world can see and judge it as a limited whole. The willing attributed to the transcendental or metaphysical subject is not an event within the world; it leaves the world as it is while altering its value. As the facts in the world determine the truth value of a meaningful proposition, so the action of the transcendental will determines whether the world is happy or unhappy, independent of its factual content (6.43).

Because propositions with sense are restricted to describing states of affairs within the world, the sense of the world as a whole cannot be put into words. There are no ethical propositions (6.42). Propositions cannot express either the internal properties of language and the world (the *deeper* conditions of logic and ontology) or the sense and value of the world as a whole (the *higher*, that is, ethics and aesthetics).

As logic is independent of empirical linguistics, so ethics is independent of science. The factual composition of the world is a matter of indifference to the transcendental will and to the value of the world that this will determines (6.432). Ethical reward and punishment, so to speak, lie within ethical action itself(6.422). The world as the totality of facts remains the same, whether the exercise of the will is good or bad. The world is a happy world for the good will and an unhappy world for its contrary. But for both exercises of the will the substance of the world is unchanged, and no reasons, no arguments, no propositions can be used to justify one ethical action rather than the other. Ethical action, willing, since it alters the world only at its limits, alters what language cannot express or defend. In what does that action consist? It is very difficult to say with confidence, but it appears that the choice of the will is between the affirmation and negation of life as a whole regardless of the factual forms it may take. The good will says yes to life, the bad will says no. At the heart of ethics is an elemental yes or no that lies entirely beyond the reach of reason and discourse.

Thus, Wittgenstein can say that the solution to the problem of the meaning of life lies strictly beyond the limits of science (6.4321). Science says *how* things are in the world, but this is a matter of complete indifference for what is higher (6.432). The facts of the world contribute only to setting the problem of the meaning of life; they contribute nothing to its solution. It is not *how* things are in the world that is mystical—inexpressible—but *that* it, the world, exists. (6.44). Seeing and feeling the world as a limited whole, it is this that is mystical (6.45). Only when the world is seen in this way can we raise the question of its global meaning and value. But the question itself indicates the limits of our analogy between the world and the proposition, and this leads to the disappearance of the question. When we see the world aright, we see it as a limited whole, *sub specie aeterni*. We thereby see what can and cannot be said about the world. Nothing can be said about the world as a whole other than a sequence of statements about the facts it contains. But when an answer cannot be put into words, neither can the question it answers. The question about the meaning of the world cannot be answered sensibly.

It is important to remark that Wittgenstein's conclusions do not support ethical skepticism, for skepticism is nonsense when it tries to raise doubts where no meaningful question can be asked (6.51). When all possible scientific questions have been answered, the question of the meaning of life remains untouched. But then there are no questions left to ask. The vanishing of the problem of the meaning of life, taken as a problem with a discursive answer, is the solution to the problem. The solution to the problem of the value of the world is the vanishing of the problem as a problem with a solution (6.52).

What cannot be put into words makes itself manifest (6.522). The propositions of science *show* the conditions under which discourse is possible. Their complete silence with respect to what is higher *shows* the radical difference between science and ethics, between matters of fact and the value of being. The final solution to all the problems of philosophy, logic and metaphysics (the deeper), ethics and aesthetics (the higher), is their disappearance as problems. To see the world aright is to be released from the desire to say what cannot be said. The ethical deed achieved by the *Tractatus* is its concluding silence, a silence Wittgenstein struggled to observe in his withdrawal from philosophy from 1918 to 1929. During that period he ceased talking about philosophy and began to practice it.

G. From Meaning to Use

*It is interesting to compare the multiplicity of the
tools in language, and of the ways they are used,
the multiplicity of kinds of word and sentence, with
what logicians have said about the structure of
language. (Including the author of the Tractatus
Logico-Philosophicus).*[29]

A particular picture of the essence of human language dominates the *Tractatus*. "In this picture of language we find the roots of the following idea: every word has a meaning. This meaning is correlated with the word. It is the object for which the word stands" (PI 1). The *Philosophical Investigations* does not entirely repudiate that account of language, but it sets severe limits to its application. In the second phase of his linguistic turn, Wittgenstein charged that his earlier theory of meaning "has its place in a primitive idea of the way language functions; but one can also say that it is the idea of a language more primitive than ours" (PI 2). The danger in such a picture is that it "surrounds the working of language with a haze which makes clear vision impossible" (PI 5). To dissolve the haze, to provide us with "a clear view of the aim and functioning of words" Wittgenstein introduces surveyable linguistic models, called language games, as objects for inspection. A language game is an actual or imagined form of life in which words are used, a context "consisting of language and the actions into which it is woven" (PI 7) He urged us to examine a broad selection of these language games. The purpose of this survey is to break the hold on our imagination of primitive ideas of language use, to show us that the uses of linguistic signs are as diverse as the uses of tools (PI 11) and that the occasions of linguistic practice are as heterogeneous as those of human practice generally. The one-sided descriptivism of the *Tractatus* prevented us from seeing this elementary truth.

The manifest diversity of linguistic use is overlooked in an abstract or noncontextual examination of language. When we isolate language-expressions from the occasions of their employment, from the forms of life in which they function, we tend to be struck by their uniform appearance and to disregard their distinct operations (PI 11). The *Tractatus* was guilty of this oversight in its account of propositional use. The only admissible propositions were the factual propositions describing possible states of affairs and the logical propositions that mirrored the a priori structure of reality. Language was restricted to providing descriptions of the world, "whereas in fact we do the most various things with our sentences" (PI 27). Against the telelogical monism of the *Tractatus*, the *Philosophical Investigations* opposes a picture of linguistic pluralism. There is no essential purpose of language.

We are led to adopt an overly simplified theory of language whenever we fail to keep the multiplicity of language games in view (PI 23). This one-sided picture captivates the imagination. If actual practice fails to confirm it, we argue that everyday language disguises thought (4.002), that the purpose of philosophic analysis is to uncover the simple pattern of functioning necessarily operative in natural languages though concealed by their grammatical surface. We search for something that is not there, and failing to find it, we argue that it *must* be there. The *Tractatus* contrasted the deep and surface structures of language. In the *Philosophical Investigations*, nothing of importance is hidden, though we may have to look from different and contrasting perspectives to see what is open to view.

Wittgenstein suggested that the philosophic investigation of language is unusually prone to the conceit of concealment. By studying language when it goes on holiday, when it is not actually being used, we tend to "sublime the logic of our language" (PI 38). This tendency is illustrated in the Tractarian claim that there are no names in natural language as it actually operates. According to the Tractatus, names occur only in completely analyzed propositions, where they stand proxy for the elemental objects that give them meaning. The reference (*Bedeutung*) of a name is the object it represents. The sense (*Sinn*) of a proposition is the possible state of affairs, formed by the concatenation of objects, that the proposition describes. This is the core of Wittgenstein's semantical theory in the *Tractatus*. The *Philosophical Investigations* challenges this account by encouraging us to think about the concept of meaning in a new way. "For a large class of cases-though not for all—in which we employ the term 'meaning' it can be defined thus: the meaning of a word is its use in the language" (PI 43). "Doesn't the fact that sentences have the same sense consist in their having the same use" (PI 24). "Look at the sentence as an instrument, and at its sense as its employment" (PI 421). These quotations testify to a critical shift of emphasis within Wittgenstein's thought. The primacy accorded to propositional description has been rejected, to be replaced by a working analogy between linguistic signs and instruments. Language is located squarely within the world of practice, in the multiple contexts of making and doing in which it plays a role. With the shift from the theoretical to the practical offices of language, a new model of semantical analysis emerges. The *Tractatus* explicated sentential meaning (*Sinn*) in terms of truth conditions. Propositions were essentially vehicles of truth whose sense depended on metaphysical atoms subject to universal and invariant normative laws. The foundations of linguistic meaning were set in an irreducible level of being radically independent of human deliberation and choice. The conditions of meaning were *given* to men rather than *formed* by them in their collective activity. By contrast, the *Philosophical Investigations* conceives of linguistic meaning in terms of practical function or use. Meaning belongs to linguistic expressions by virtue of the intersubjective conventions, tacit or explicit, that regulate their use in the language games to which they belong. These rules of use are variable and not rigidly binding, and they derive their authority from the community of practice that promulgates them. The foundations of meaning have become sociological rather than metaphysical, paralleling the shift from invariant logical laws to historically conditioned grammatical rules. To see all this clearly we must focus on the details of language use, to look at our language games "from close to" (PI 51).

The tension between this new approach to language and that of the *Tractatus* is addressed directly:

> "You talk about all sorts of language games, but have nowhere said what the essence of a language game, and hence of language is: what is common to all these activities and what makes them into language or parts of language. So you let yourself off the very part of the investigation that once gave you yourself most headache, the part about the general form of propositions and of language." "And this is true.

Instead of producing something common to all that we call language, I am saying that these phenomena have no one thing in common that makes us use the same word for all. (PI 65)."

"What we call 'sentence' and 'language' have not the formal unity that I imagined" (PI 108). The assumption that there *must* be something common to all languages makes us unable to see how different sentences really work (PI 93). To offset our repeated urge to misunderstand, an urge rooted in essentialist and transcendental expectations, we must look directly into the workings of our language and examine the function of words in the language games that are their original homes (PI 109, 116).

The *Philosophical Investigations* restores an ostensibly empirical dimension to the logical analysis of language that is absent from the *Tractatus*, but it is not an empirical work in the standard sense. The *Philosophical Investigations* appears to be empirical because of its explicit rejection of the transcendental modes of argument favored in the *Tractatus*. Perhaps, it is best understood as a work of grammatical analysis in Wittgenstein's specialized use of that term. In Wittgenstein's later philosophy *grammar* is used as a term of art and contrast. The variable grammar of different language games is deliberately contrasted with the uniform logic of language espoused in the *Tractatus*. Where the logic of language was allegedly hidden beneath the surface of language, Wittgenstein now urges us to look to the surface and not into an illusory depth. The purpose of Wittgenstein's references to actual or imagined uses of language is deflationary not informative. They are meant to deflate a particular concept of the foundations and functioning of language not to assemble evidence for a new philosophic theory. "What we are supplying are really remarks on the natural history of man: not curiosities however, but rather observations on facts which no one has doubted and which have only gone unremarked because they are always before our eyes."[30]

In shifting from his earlier semantical realism to use analysis, Wittgenstein has substituted one metaphor for another. The metaphor dominating the *Tractatus* was that of language as an isomorphic picture of reality. The metaphor dominating the *Philosophical Investigations* is that of language as a set of humanly shaped instruments characterized by their use in the conduct of life. The metaphor of the *Tractatus* is semantical, that of the *Investigations* pragmatic. The use of an expression is not a distinct entity for which the expression is supposed to stand on the model of a name going proxy for an object. By emphasizing the pragmatic significance of language, Wittgenstein suggested a new way of picturing the relation of language to reality. "How do sentences manage to represent?"[31] The answer might be, "Don't you know? You certainly see it, when you *use* them." For nothing is concealed—nothing is hidden (PI 435). The single great problem at the axial center of the *Tractatus*, the problem of propositional representation, has lost its urgency and mystery.

As the model of propositional pictures loses its force, the transcendental objects essential to the model disappear.

H. The Crystalline Sphere

How can logic-all embracing logic, which mirrors the world—use such peculiar crotchets and contrivances? Only because they are all connected with one another in an infinitely fine network, the great mirror. (TR 5.511)

The *Philosophical Investigations* persuades us to think about language in a new way. A direct consequence of this shift of perspective is the introduction of an alternative concept of linguistic meaning. The decision to construe the meaning of an expression as its rule governed use within a language game leads to a modification in the Tractarian philosophy of logic. The *Tractatus* endowed logic with a universal significance by making the essential properties of language and reality logical properties. "Logical investigation explores the nature of all things. It seeks to see to the bottom of things and is not meant to concern itself whether what actually happens is this or that. It takes its rise...from an urge to understand the basis or *essence* of everything empirical" (PI 89).[32] Logic is not concerned with contingent facts but with a priori structure, "the order of possibilities which must be common to both world and thought" (PI 97). Although we cannot meaningfully describe what is a priori, it shows itself obliquely in the propositions of everyday language and in the fact that certain combinations of those propositions prove to be tautologies and contradictions. "This order, it seems, must be utterly simple. It is prior to all experience, must run through all experience; no empirical cloudiness or uncertainty can be allowed to affect it. It must rather be of the purest crystal" (PI 97).

If natural languages were perspicuous, we could immediately discern that their constituent propositions mirror this a priori structure. But natural language propositions are logically opaque; the identity of logical form between picture and pictured lies hidden beneath their grammatical surface. Since this identity of form constitutes the essence of language, propositional analysis is required if the essence of language is to be disclosed (PI 42). It is "as if our usual forms of expression were, essentially, unanalyzed; as if there were something hidden in them that had to be brought to light. When this is done the expression is completely clarified and our problem solved" (PI 91). When a proposition is completely analyzed, the isomorphic correspondence between picture and pictured is displayed fully. If all propositions were analyzed to the limit we would achieve a state of complete exactness: the infinitely fine network, the great mirror, the real goal of our investigation (PI 91).

Between the completion of the *Tractatus* and the composition of the *Philosophical Investigations*, Wittgenstein ceased to believe in this ideal logical order. "The more narrowly we examine actual language, the sharper becomes the conflict between it and our requirement. (For the crystalline purity of logic was, of course, not a result of investigation: it was a requirement) (PI 107). The shift from normative requirement to detailed examination of linguistic practice parallels the shift from the transcendental to the quasi-empirical or grammatical mode of inquiry. The emphasis in the *Philosophical Investigations* on examining language in its concrete employment makes the earlier demand seem increasingly implausible. The transparency exclusively assigned to perspicuous languages in the *Tractatus* is liberally assigned to all languages in the *Philosophical Investigations*. "Since everything lies open to view there is nothing to explain. For what is hidden, for example, is of no interest to us" (PI 126). Nothing is concealed about the relation of sentences to reality. Whatever is involved can be seen directly in the use of sentences within a public context (PI 435). However, poorly chosen forms of expression, primitive images of signification, obsessive metaphysical assumptions, or deceptive analogies seduce us into thinking that something queer must be achieved by propositions, that something out of the ordinary is taking place when they are used. To correct this misapprehension, we can substitute one form of expression for another, or suggest a contrasting analogy, but this method of rhetorical substitution is quite different from the propositional analysis outlined in the *Tractatus*.[33] "You say the point isn't the word but its meaning, and you think of the meaning as a thing of the same kind as the word, though also different from the word. Here the word, there the meaning, the money, and the cow that you can buy with it (but contrast money and its use)" (PI 20).

The picture theory of language supports the preconceived idea of crystalline purity. To shake the hold of that fixed idea on our thinking about logic and language, Wittgenstein urged us to "turn our whole examination around" (PI 108). "There must not be anything hypothetical in our considerations. We must do away with all explanation and description alone must take its place" (PI 109). In our descriptions of linguistic practice, we should focus on "subjects of everyday thinking," for there is nothing extraordinary, nothing sublime about our language games or the grammar of the expressions they contain.

If we want to understand the fundamental concepts of the *Tractatus*— proposition, language, thought, world (PI 96)—we have to describe the way these terms are used in the language games where they appear regularly. "We are not analyzing a phenomenon (e.g. thought) but a concept (e.g. that of thinking) and therefore the use of a word" (PI 383). Wittgenstein stressed the garden-variety status of these concepts when he wrote, "If the words 'language', 'experience', 'world' have a use, it must be as humble a one as that of the words 'table', 'lamp', 'door'" (PI 97). In these passages, Wittgenstein introduced a new model of conceptual analysis. Concepts now are conceived as rule-governed roles played by the expressions in a public language. They are to be clarified or analyzed by observing their use in a language game and by articulating the rules that define correctness of use. As these rules change, so do the concepts they loosely define. Richard Rorty has labeled this new canon of analysis *methodological nominalism*. The notion that language (or thought) is something mysterious is a misunderstanding caused by the forms of expression that we use in talking about them. By investigating these concepts outside their context of application, we tend to sublime their actual function, to make them appear part of a imperceptible process accessible only to a recondite form of inquiry.

A primary purpose of the *Philosophical Investigation* is to release us from this misunderstanding. Wittgenstein proposed his new technique of clarification with a therapeutic intent. Ask yourself, Is the disputed expression "ever actually used this way in the language game which is its original home?" (PI 116). After applying this technique to the central concepts in the philosophy of logic, Wittgenstein concluded: "The philosophy of logic speaks of sentences and words in exactly the sense in which we speak of them in ordinary life." "We are talking about the spatial and temporal phenomenon of language, not about some non-spatial, non-temporal phantasm" (PI 108). The force of the intended contrast becomes clear when we realize that the spatial and temporal phenomena of language are meant to be replacements for Frege's *thoughts*, Husserl's *ideal propositional meanings*, and the possible states of affairs of the *Tractatus*.[35] With these remarks Wittgenstein was trying to lay to rest the ghost of the *Tractatus*. But in his obsession with an earlier failure, he overreacted to past errors. The excesses of Tractarian descriptivism are highlighted by the linguistic pluralism documented in the *Philosophical Investigations*. If that pluralism is to be genuine and thorough it must include both descriptive and nondescriptive forms of first-order discourse, as well as distinctively metalinguistic discourse in which semantic and epistemic predicates occur. Predicates like *knows*, *means*, and *true* do have garden-variety status in the sense that we use them often and easily, but they occur at a different level of language from object-linguistic predicates like *table* and *door* and they perform a radically different semantic function. Logic is a science of propositions not a science of things. A philosophy of logic that assimilates propositions to tools and blurs the distinctions between signs of second and first intention and between signs and things that are not signs is itself a victim of deceptive analogy.

According to the *Tractatus*, the propositions of logic say nothing, but they mirror the a priori structure of reality. The shift from the semantic to the pragmatic metaphor robs logical propositions of their ontological import by denying the existence of the crystalline sphere. In his Tractarian phase, Wittgenstein based transcendental ontology upon logic. In the *Philosophical Investigations*, the logical analysis of language is stripped of ontological privilege. Conventionalism and pragmatism supplant the earlier semantical realism, and the doctrine of showing loses its referential aspect.

I. Mathematics Forms a Network of Norms

There is not any question at all here of some correspondence between what is said and reality; rather is logic antecedent to any such correspondence; in the same sense, that is, as that in which the establishment of a method of measurement is antecedent to the correctness or incorrectness of a statement of length. (RFM,I,155).

The *Philosophical Investigations* requires philosophers to examine linguistic expressions within the forms of life that give them purpose. By exhibiting the specific function of these expressions and the rules regulating that function, we adequately clarify their sense of meaning. Wittgenstein's *Remarks on the Foundations of Mathematics* applies this methodological canon to the philosophy of mathematics. His purpose in the *Remarks* is not to increase our mathematical knowledge but to change our way of viewing it (RFM II, 18; II 81-82). The philosophy of mathematics is mathematically idle (RFM IV, 52). It does not add new theorems or proofs to the language of mathematics but clarifies the use of existing signs and exhibits their interrelation to one another and to their fields of application. It is not "that a new building has to be erected or a new bridge has to be built but that the geography as it now is has to be judged" (RFM IV, 52).

To understand the sense of mathematical sentences requires close attention to context, because the correct understanding of a mathematical proposition is not guaranteed by its isolated verbal form (RFM IV, 25).[36] It is easy to make a mistake in the description of a mathematical language game. "The descriptions which immediately suggest themselves are all misleading— that is how our language in this field is arranged" (RFM II, 85). Traditional approaches to the philosophy of mathematics have erred either by abstractly examining mathematical propositions (RFM II, 26; IV, 16), or by operating with a restricted concept of meaningful sentence employment.[37] Both the *Philosophical Investigations* and the *Remarks* remind us that sentences can be meaningful without being used to describe reality. "To resolve philosophic problems one has to compare things which it never seriously occurred to anyone to compare" (RFM V, 12). The central recommendation of the *Remarks* is that we compare mathematical sentences with rules rather than with factual descriptions. Emphasis on the regulative character of these sentences is intended to release us from basic misconceptions that dominate our thinking in this area (RFM III, 11).

The first misconception is the myth of Platonic realism. According to Wittgenstein, the Platonist thinks of the science of mathematics as the natural history of mathematical objects (RFM II, 11-13), "Except that it is not really a natural history since the relevant objects are not natural objects and the methods of investigation are not experimental."[38] Mathematical sentences are construed as theoretical descriptions of atemporal abstract entities. "What is before our minds in a vague way is that this reality is something very abstract, very general, and very rigid. Logic is a kind of ultra-physics, the description of the 'logical structure' of the world, which we perceive through a kind of ultra-experience" (RFM I, 8). This passage recalls Wittgenstein's references to the great mirror in the *Tractatus*. It indicates the ontological component of his earlier philosophy of logic, although his Platonic sympathies, even then, were much weaker than those of Russell or Frege. The *Philosophical Investigations* and the *Remarks* make the break with Platonism complete. They repudiate the Platonic "myth" that mathematical propositions are descriptions of mathematical objects and that mathematical inquiry is an investigation of their lawful relationships (RFM IV,16).

Wittgenstein attacks Platonism frontally by denying that mathematical sentences express assertoric propositions.[39] Mathematical theorems do not state facts, not even the sui generis facts to which the Platonist appeals.In the region of mathematics there is no knowledge of objects, because there is nothing at all to which knowing could refer. The apparatus of logic and mathematics is deprived of ontological import by denying any referential function to logical and mathematical propositions. "Even if the proved mathematical proposition seems to point to a reality outside itself, still it is only the expression of acceptance of a new measure of reality" (RFM II, 27). The proposition proved by means of the proof serves as a rule or norm, not as a description. Mathematics is a collection of rules, a motley of techniques, a network of norms with practical application, not a science of imperceptible objects accessible only to the vision of reason. The anti-Fregean character of these remarks became evident when Wittgenstein asserted that the "mathematician is an inventor not a discover" (RFM I,167).

The Platonist is accused of misinterpreting the hardness or invulnerability of a rule as the hardness or uniqueness of a special subject matter. Mathematics is normative, but *norm* does not mean the same as *ideal* (RFM V, 40). Wittgenstein's position here is the direct antithesis of Husserl's in the *Prolegomena*. Husserl had argued that mathematics was essentially a theoretical science of ideal objects and only derivatively a network of norms.

Wittgenstein's attack on the assertoric character of mathematical propositions is a rejection of both Frege's ontological realism and Husserl's intentional conceptualism. For want of a modal distinction, the Platonist invokes a material distinction,[41] recognizing that mathematical propositions are not empirical, but mistakenly assuming they are supraempirical, that they refer to a domain of eternal objects inaccessible to empirical inquiry.

The *Remarks* attempt to subvert Platonism by comparing mathematical propositions with rules. But a rule qua rule is as detached from significance as a measuring instrument with nothing to measure. What gives the rule importance is the facts of daily experience (RFM V, 3). Although the facts of experience are essential to the application of mathematical propositions, they do not constitute their semantic content. "Wittgenstein strongly opposes the opinion that the propositions of mathematics have the function of empirical propositions, but the applicability of mathematics, in particular of arithmetic, rests on empirical conditions."[42] Wittgenstein wanted to deontologize logic without reducing it to social psychology. The second misconception that the *Remarks* oppose might be called *anthropologism*. A philosophy of mathematics is guilty of anthropologism when it treats mathematical propositions as descriptions of mathematical behavior. "Are the propositions of mathematics anthropological propositions saying how men infer and calculate? Is a statue book a work of anthropology telling how people of this nation deal with a thief?" (RFM II,6J). The techniques of calculation depend upon certain general facts of experience, but the expressions used in the calculations do not refer to these facts. If certain facts were altogether different, the rules of mathematics would have lost their application and, with that loss, their meaning and importance. Without embracing an empiricist philosophy of mathematics in the classical sense, in the *Remarks* Wittgenstein required close attention to matters of fact. "An empirical regularity lies behind a mathematical law. The mathematical law does not assert that the empirical regularity obtains, because we do not treat it as we treat an assertion of empirical fact, but as a necessary statement; all the same what leads us to treat it in this way is the empirical regularity since it is only because the regularity obtains that the law has a useful application."[43]

Wittgenstein's insistence that we distinguish between a mathematical proposition and its useful application is balanced by the demand that mathematics have an application. "It is essential to mathematics that its signs are also employed in mufti. It is the *use* outside mathematics and so the *meaning* of the signs that makes the sign game into mathematics" (RFM IV, 2). These remarks offer an explicit alternative to both Frege's relational theory of numerical meaning and the inscriptional formalism to which he opposed it. Not every adoption of a rule qualifies as a move in mathematics. Mathematical statements have the dignity of rules, but rules must be applicable[44] to be important and to be of interest. The principle use of the rules of mathematics is as normative measures of calculation. They furnish standards of correctness for calculation operations in nonmathematical contexts. As norms they do not asset matters of fact, but were certain facts to change, calculation would cease to be a useful activity. The analogy with measuring instruments is helpful here. If rulers behaved like flies rather than like stable rods, they would be useless in measuring the lengths of objects. To adopt a measuring instrument is to rely tacitly on certain features of the world remaining relatively constant. The conventional freedom in selecting alternative norms of measurement is offset by the factual constraints on useful selection. In the *Remarks*, Wittgenstein attempted to integrate conventionalist instrumentalism with pragmatism. The requirement of effective use moderates the arbitrariness of choice by making choice responsive to considerations of practical success.

By treating mathematical propositions as rules rather than descriptions, Wittgenstein pictured mathematical activity as an affair of proposal and decision rather than discovery. When we accept a network of propositions as a proof, we treat the proof's conclusion as unassailable; we deposit it among the norms of our language. Such a move is based on a free decision. Nothing compels us to accept a proof as a paradigm; nothing can put the move to a paradigm out of the reach of criticism.[45] Philosophers are mistaken to demand a foundation for mathematics other than our ongoing mathematical practice, for mathematical practice is its own foundation. It does not require additional theoretical support. "The danger here is one of giving a justification of our procedure where there is no such thing as a justification and we ought simply to have said: *That's how we do it*" (RFM II, 74).

When ontological significance is attributed to the propositions of logic and mathematics, they are treated as special cases of theoretical discourse. Like other theories they submit to semantical analysis of their truth conditions and truth values. To speak of their foundations is to refer to the field of reality that is the source of their truth value. When the assertoric character of mathematical discourse is denied, foundational inquiry ceases to be semantical and ontological. Frege's truth-conditional analysis of mathematical meaning then yields to Wittgenstein's rehearsal of the practical uses to which the sentences of mathematics are put. Foundational inquiry becomes a reflection on recurrent patterns of human social practice. If mathematics is not a special instance of theoretical knowledge, then epistemic justification of its propositions is irrelevant; the only pertinent mode of appraisal becomes pragmatic. Because mathematics has an extrasystemic use, we justify the adoption of its rules in terms of efficiency, simplicity, or expediency. The ultimate court of justification becomes our common forms of life, our recurrent social practice, what we do.

Though the propositions of mathematics are grammatical not empirical, Wittgenstein's foundational remarks are clearly empirical in tone and content. They assert what "might be called intuitively known empirical facts" (RFM

III, 44). "What we are supplying are really remarks on the natural history of man" (RFM I, 141). Measured by Frege's criterion, Wittgenstein's new outlook is psychologistic because it locates the foundations of mathematics in variable rules of procedure human beings are free to accept or reject on pragmatic grounds. Even if we concede to Wittgenstein his attack on classical foundational programs (RFM V, 13), his own solution remains unsatisfactory. Despite his repeated return to the question, he never succeeds in explaining what the relation is between the empirical regularity and the proof that induces us to put the proof in the archives.[46] He fails to provide an intelligible rationale for the decisions of the mathematical community. Although he suggested that these decisions are not arbitrary, his remarks on this point are not really persuasive.

J. Philosophy as Captive and Escape from Captivity

*A picture held us captive. And we could not get
outside it, for it lay in our language and language
seemed to repeat it to us inexorably.(PI 115)*

Both the *Tractatus* and the *Philosophical Investigations* testify to the centrality of language within Wittgenstein's thought. Both connect the objectives and methods of philosophic activity with the logical or grammatical scrutiny of language. But there are major differences between these two works, based on opposing conceptions of logic, and opposing conceptions of how logic contributes to philosophy. The *Tractatus* is concerned with the invariant essence of language. It contains a set of substantive theses about the permanent nature and purpose of human discourse. It identifies the great problem of philosophy, the problem around which all other philosophical issues revolve, with the nature of the proposition (NB 23, 39, 53). The *Tractatus* attempts decisively to resolve the axial problem by a transcendental determination of the properties propositions must have to describe the world completely. The transcendental argument yields a set of a priori knowledge claims about the foundational requirements of language and the world. Reality must consist of elements subject to invariant laws of combination; language must consist of counterpart elements subject to the same laws. Given these foundations the limits of the sayable are fixed eternally.

The *Philosophical Investigations* fiercely opposes the a priori theories advanced in the *Tractatus*. "I have been trying in all this to remove the temptation to think that there must be."[47] "Don't say: 'there *must* be something common—but look and see whether there is anything common to all" (PI 66).

"Don't think, but look." The assumption that there must be something common to all propositions makes us unable to see how particular propositions really work. To correct this assumption, Wittgenstein urged us to examine a collection of diverse language games. The language games are "set up as objects of comparison which are meant to release us from the preconceived idea that there is a single, unchangeable model to which language and reality must conform (PI 131). The *Tractatus* suffers from a radical Procrustean urge.

In the *Philosophical Investigations*, Wittgenstein portrayed traditional philosophy, including the *Tractatus*, as a victim of prejudices and preconceived ideas. These prejudices have many sources. Some are rooted in language, some in history, some in powerful images and analogies that ensnare our imaginations, and some in the theoretical exigence for universal knowledge itself. The purpose of the *Philosophical Investigations* is to release us from these obsessions and the philosophic "problems" they breed. To distinguish the tradition under attack from the weapons used against it, we can classify philosophies into two types. Philosophy₁ represents the philosophic tradition insofar as it has been subject to the Procrustean urge. Nearly all of Wittgenstein's examples of philosophy₁ are drawn from the *Tractatus*, the foundational investigations of Frege, Russell, and Carnap, and the Cartesian tradition in epistemology and the philosophy of mind. Philosophy₂, represented by the *Philosophical Investigations*, draws its problems from the questions that torment philosophy₁. These questions perplex and obsess philosophy₁ and bring its activity into question by philosophy₂ (PI 133).

In the *Tractatus* Wittgenstein took seriously many of the great problems of philosophy. He devised a new approach to their solution with the striking result that its conclusions could not be asserted. The sentences of logic, metaphysics, and ethics were senseless because they attempted to say what only could be shown. But there *was* something to show and the effort to say it, although futile, was not without merit. In the *Philosophical Investigations*, he concluded that the great problems are pseudo-problems that demand dissolution rather than ineffable solution. Philosophic sentences are not senseless but pointless. And the task of philosophy₂ is to release us from their spell by showing how they arise through misunderstandings of the way language works (PI 109, 133). Philosophy₂" is a battle against the bewitchment of our intelligence by means of language" (PI 109).

The methods employed in the *Philosophical Investigations* are grammatical rather than logical, purely descriptive rather than transcendental.[48] Philosophy₂ leaves everything as it is. The purpose is not to justify language, to supply new information about it, or to unify it theoretically, but to assemble reminders so that actual patterns of our linguistic practice are made clear (PI 124,127). "An unsuitable type of expression is a sure means of remaining in a state of confusion" (PI 338). Philosophy₁ is held captive by the pictures those unsuitable expressions evoke. The release of a philosopher₁ from captivity is to be achieved by arranging what we already know in a new way. The activity of philosophy₂ consists in matching the rearrangement to the type of confusions that require it. It is a form of art, a type of therapy, an individually ordered enterprise, like Socratic maieutics, carefully suited to a particular audience rather than a science expressible in a universal treatise.

Both the *Tractatus* and the *Philosophical Investigations* declare that philosophy is not a science (TR 4.111; PI 109). They also presume that the central task of philosophy is linguistic clarification, although they conceive of such clarification differently. According to the *Tractatus*, natural language propositions need to be clarified because they conceal logical form. Propositional analysis is necessary because the logical structure of language is hidden beneath its grammatical surface. According to the *Philosophical Investigations*, what is philosophically significant about language already lies open to view. Both the forms of expression that bewitch us and the contrastive forms that shall liberate us lie on the surface of language. No single method will produce clarity, but a variety of methods is needed, each related to particular types of philosophic preconception.

1. For philosophers perplexed by questions about essence and the use of sortal predicates, Wittgenstein introduced the metaphor of family resemblance (PI 67).
2. Ontological preconceptions about meaning are dispelled by assimilating meaning to use (PI 43).
3. Difficulties in the philosophy of mind are allayed by emphasizing the asymmetry between first and third person psychological discourse.
4. The demand that we justify our linguistic practice is said to be superfluous, "the danger here, I believe, is one of giving a justification of our procedure where there is no such thing as a justification and we ought simply to have said: That's how we do it" (RFM II, 74). When practice takes primacy over theory, foundational questions are transformed into reflections on what human beings do within the community of language they share. "What has to be accepted, the given, is—so one could say—forms of life" (PI 226).

A final point of overlap between the *Tractatus* and the *Philosophical Investigations* should be noted. Both represent attempts to conclude philosophy, to bring the history of philosophy to a halt. The *Tractatus* claimed to have found, on all essential points, the final solution of philosophic problems (TR 5). We see the world aright by recognizing and honoring the limits of significant discourse (TR 6.54). The clarity the *Philosophical Investigations* is aiming at, "is indeed complete clarity. But this simply means that the philosophical problems should completely disappear" (PI 133). Wittgenstein's later philosophy expressly repudiates the positive goals set for philosophy in the *Tractatus*. The essentialist objectives, the transcendental logic and ontology, the permanent solutions, the expressive silence are all rejected. "Where does our investigation [philosophy2] get its importance from, since it seems only to destroy everything interesting, that is, all that is great and important [philosophy1]. What we are destroying is nothing but houses of cards and we are clearing up the ground of language on which they stand" (PI 118). The method of propositional analysis is preserved but with a new purpose and a new set of tactics. The purpose of clarification in the *Philosophical Investigations* is to release traditional philosophy from its prejudices, from the pictures and theoretical compulsions that hold it captive. The basic tactic is to describe actual or imagined occasions of use for the specific linguistic expressions we are prone to misunderstand. These descriptions are therapeutic rather than theoretical in purpose. By its highly negative critique of the tradition, of philosophy1, the *Philosophical Investigations* encourages the emergence of a postphilosophical culture.[49]

> The sickness of a time is cured by an alteration in the mode of life of human beings, and it was possible for the sickness of philosophical problems to get cured only through a changed mode of thought and of life, not through a medicine invented by an individual.
>
> Suppose the use of the motor car produces or encourages illnesses, and mankind is plagued by such illness until, from some cause or other, as the result of some development or other, it abandons the habit of driving. (RFM II, 4).

5

The New Way of Words

Since the late nineteenth century, philosophers from opposing traditions have mounted an intensive campaign against psychologism. Despite internal divisions about what psychologism is and why it is mistaken, it is possible to identify a common core in their criticism. Psychologism is the metalevel thesis that logic and philosophy are psychological disciplines or disciplines that receive their ultimate clarification or confirmation through psychological research. As a metalogical thesis, psychologism is mistaken because it confuses the subject matter, investigatory methods, and results of logic with those of psychology. Philosophers who oppose psychologism as a theory of logic endorse this critical objection without sharing a common conception of the disciplines they thereby distinguish. As a metaphilosophical thesis, psychologism is mistaken because it confuses the disciplines of epistemology and semantics with the practice of psychology. The opponents of psychologism in metaphilosophy, though united in their critical perspective, remain deeply divided in their understanding of what philosophy is and ought to be.

The new way of words is a deliberate attempt to avoid psychologism in both its metalogical and metaphilosophical form. In speaking of the new way of words, I mean the development of a formal linguistic approach to philosophical problems. The emphasis on language constituted a deliberate departure from the Cartesian tradition that had made ideas the subject matter of philosophy. It represented a shift in philosophic focus from the intro-spectable contents of mental acts to public intersubjective linguistic structures. In the course of this chapter, I offer a schematic history of the movement as it evolves from the *Tractatus*, through Carnap, to reach mature form in the writing of Wilfrid Sellars. Sellars's critique of psychologism is particularly interesting in light of the history of this problem. The earliest charges of psychologism were leveled against naturalistic interpretations of logic and philosophy. Sellars' linguistic strategy allowed him to fashion a more sophisticated naturalism explicitly designed to avoid psychologistic errors.

The chapter concludes by reexamining the linguistic turn from the standpoint of contemporary philosophical controversy. At its inception, the analytic movement sought to define the task of philosophy and clarify its essential difference from natural science in terms of a special methodological dependence on language. But contemporary analytic philosophers, divided by incompatible theories of language, have adopted conflicting metaphilosophical strategies, so that even opposition to psychologism no longer unites them.

A. Pure Semiotic and the Formal Mode of Speech

Philosophy is not one of the natural sciences. The word "philosophy" must mean something whose place is above or below the natural sciences, not beside them.[1]

It is difficult to overestimate the impact of the *Tractatus* on subsequent analytic philosophy. The *Tractatus* raised to thematic status the issues in semantics, ontology, and metaphilosophy that have since dominated analytic thought. In this chapter and in Chapter VI, I want to focus on Wittgenstein's thesis of a sharp distinction between philosophy and natural science. Analytic metaphilosophy in the period bounded by the *Tractatus* and Quine's *Two Dogmas of Empiricism* was effectively united by that principle.[2] Perhaps the best way to understand the metaphilosophical divisions within contemporary linguistic philosophy is to appreciate why analytic philosophers have adopted or rejected Wittgenstein's distinction. At the root of their conflict is a basic disagreement about the theory of linguistic meaning. Wittgenstein's successors are still struggling with the "single great problem" he hoped definitively to resolve.

The decisive and immediate influence of the *Tractatus* on the program of the Vienna Circle is evident in Carnap's *Logical Syntax of Language*, where he credits Wittgenstein with five contributions of permanent philosophical importance.[3]

1. Wittgenstein was the first to exhibit the close connection between philosophy and logical syntax.
2. He made clear the formal linguistic character of logic. "Logic can only be studied with any degree of accuracy when it is based on linguistic expression (sentences) for which it is possible to lay down sharply defined rules"[4] (LSL 1-2).

3. He emphasized that the rules and proofs of syntax should make no reference to the meaning of symbols. "A theory is called 'formal' when no reference is made in it to the sense of the expressions, but simply and solely to the kinds and order of the symbols from which the expressions are constructed"[5] (LSL 1).
4. He showed that the sentences of metaphysics and ethics are pseudosentences.
5. He insisted that philosophy is critique of language.

Carnap's substantive position in the *Logical Syntax of Language*, despite its obvious debt to the *Tractatus*, differs from Wittgenstein's in these important respects. Two theses limiting the scope of discourse dominate the central portions of the *Tractatus*.

1. Propositions cannot represent logical structure. What is presupposed by propositional description cannot itself be meaningfully described.
2. Philosophy is not a science. As an activity of logical clarification, philosophy's task is to make other propositions clear not to formulate theories of its own. Philosophers are properly concerned with the semantical relations between language and the world. Yet, when they correctly understand these relations, they realize that they cannot be expressed in language. These relations can be shown but not said, and they would be shown in the perspicuous language resulting from the performance of logical analysis.

Let us call these two negative theses *Wittgenstein's ineffability results*. Carnap deliberately rejected the ineffable component of the *Tractatus*. He abandoned both Wittgenstein's refusal to talk about logical structure and his belief in an all-pervasive logic. For Carnap, the problems of logic are resolved by choosing among alternative sets of linguistic rules. We have in every respect complete liberty in making this choice. The logical structure of a language, fully determined by its metalinguistic rules, is the appropriate subject of philosophical discourse. Philosophy, therefore, is not ineffable; it can be a science with an exact method and positive theses of its own. But it is a science of conventional human structures that admit alternatives, not a theory of the invariant structure of logical space.

Carnap accepted Wittgenstein's claim that neither logic nor philosophy is a factual science. Philosophy, on Carnap's interpretation of its history, is a patchwork of three subjects, conceptually distinct but historically inseparable: metaphysics, psychology, and logic.[6] What can be salvaged from the tradition in a reconstructed philosophical science? Metaphysics is denied scientific status because its propositions are unverifiable.[7] The propositions of traditional metaphysics are existential sentences asserting the existence of entities for which there is no conceivable empirical evidence. Judged by the standards of the verification principle of meaning, they are condemned as cognitively meaningless, as empty assertions that only appear to make intelligible claims. If they were verifiable existential propositions, they would belong to empirical science. The elimination of metaphysics from the province of knowledge reduces the content of traditional philosophy to psychology and logic. Carnap adopted the Tractarian thesis (TR 4.1121) that psychology is a factual science, no more closely related to philosophy than any other factual discipline. His reconstruction of traditional philosophy turns out to be a demolition job. Once philosophy is purified of non-scientific and factual elements, only logic remains. "Philosophy is reduced to logic alone in a wide sense of the term 'logic'" (PLS 31). The logical analysis of the language of science takes the place of the tangle of problems historically identified with philosophy (LSL 279).

To understand Carnap's thesis identifying logic with philosophy, it is essential to grasp his extended use of the term *logic*. In the narrow sense, the science of logic comprises the propositional calculus, quantification theory, and some portions of classical mathematics. We need to distinguish, for this restricted concept of logic, between formalized object-languages taken as uninterpreted calculi and the syntactical metalanguages in which their formation and transformation rules are formulated.[8] The uninterpreted calculi provide the subject matter of logic in the narrow sense, and their metalinguistic syntactical rules are the sentences constituting logic as a distinct science. Logic in the broad sense comprises the syntactical analysis of both these uninterpreted calculi and the explicitly interpreted object-linguistic sentences in which the results of the natural sciences are expressed. By reflexive application, metalinguistic syntactical sentences themselves are subject to syntactical analysis with the results formulable in a metasyntactical language. The philosopher's task is to examine the syntactical character of the terms and sentences used in all of these levels of languages and to formulate their respective formation and transformation rules. The scientific sentences of philosophy are the complete set of metalinguistic sentences in which the results of syntactical analysis are formulated. The predicates of philosophy are metalinguistic syntactical predicates used to characterize the formal properties of linguistic expressions.

Carnap proposed a simple schema to organize the array of cognitively meaningful sentences(PLS 60).

1. Real object sentences are the object linguistic sentences of the factual sciences that refer to extralinguistic objects.
2. Syntactical sentences are the metalinguistic sentences of logic that state the syntactical properties of linguistic expressions. If we adopt the terminology of medieval logical theory, then Carnaps' real

object sentences are complex truth vehicles containing signs of first intention; and his syntactical sentences are complex truth-vehicles containing signs of second intention that refer to the signs of first intention occurring in the real object sentences. At this point, the ambiguity cited in note 4 becomes significant. If we confuse the methodological principle that permits us to abstract from the sense of linguistic expressions in syntactical analysis with the substantive thesis that the signs clarified by syntactical analysis are actually uninterpreted signs, then the distinction between signs of first and second intention collapses and the metalinguistic sentences of syntax are metalinguistic in name only.

3. Psuedo object sentences resemble real object sentences in form but syntactical sentences in content. Although they appear to describe extralinguistic objects, they actually are unperspicuous classifications of linguistic expressions. Carnap contends that pseudo object sentences can be translated into equivalent syntactical sentences in the formal mode of speech.

Carnap "assign[s] to the material mode of speech any sentence which is to be interpreted as attributing to an object a particular property, this property being quasi-syntactical, so that the sentence can be translated into another sentence which attributes a correlated syntactical property to a designation of the object in question. In contrast with the material mode of speech of the quasi-syntactical sentences we have the formal mode of speech of the syntactical sentences" (LSL 237-238). Any sentence that is not a real object sentence or that cannot be translated into the formal mode of speech is without cognitive meaning.

How do the theories of traditional philosophy fit within Carnap's schema? He divided the sentences of metaphysics into two classes: meaningless real object sentences that are empirically unverifiable (for example, statements about God and the soul), and pseudo object sentences in which there occur quasi-syntactical predicates like *object*, *property*, and *relation*. The sentences of empirical psychology are recognized as significant, but they are transferred from philosophy to a factual scientific discipline. The remaining theories are pseudo object sentences deceptively formulated in the material mode of speech. Carnap recommends that we translate all legitimate philosophical discourse into the formal mode to emphasize its explicitly metalinguistic nature and to indicate that these syntactical sentences are relativized to the particular language system that contains them. Philosophical theories are metalinguistic classifications of the syntactical properties of the expressions of a humanly constituted language.

The restriction of philosophy to syntactical analysis alone severely limits its scope and importance. Carnap's successors, while accepting the logical analysis of language as philosophy's appropriate project, proceeded to enlarge their conception of the enterprise. This less restrictive tendency is exemplified by Charles Morris in *Foundations of the Theory of Signs*. Morris identified philosophy with either the theory of science or the theory of signs.[9] The two conceptions are taken to be equivalent because theoretical examination of science is a comprehensive investigation of scientific language. *Pure Semiotic*, Morris' name for the unified theory of science, is divided into three disciplines:[10] syntax, the study of the intralinguistic relations between signs; semantics, the study of the relations between linguistic signs and the objects they signify; and, pragmatics, the study of the relations of signs to sign users or interpreters. Although there are distinctive syntactical, semantical, and pragmatic concepts, a complete semiotic inquiry regards each branch as a partial aspect of the unitary process of sign use. In *Foundations of the Theory of Signs*, Morris offered the following account of semiosis. S is a sign of D for I to the extent that I takes account of D in the presence of S. In the semiotic matrix S is the sign; D, the designatum of the sign; and I, the sign's interpreter.

The concept of a language rule is the central concept of pure semiotic. We construct artificial languages by stipulating the metalinguistic rules that define their properties, and we semiotically clarify existing natural languages by discovering and formulating their operative metalinguistic rules. The concepts of philosophy make their initial appearance in these semiotic rules. Pure semiotic analyzes these concepts and the intersecting patterns of connection between the metalinguistic rules that contain them. If philosophy is identified with the logical analysis of the language of science, then it should include all three semiotic disciplines and not simply the syntactical branch affirmed by Carnap.[11]

Morris, like Carnap and Wittgenstein, drew a sharp distinction between philosophy and natural science. He hoped to differentiate philosophical analysis from any natural scientific investigation of language. Rather than emphasizing the difference of level between object-linguistic and metalinguistic discourse, he located the essential difference in the contrast between pure and empirical methods of linguistic analysis. Morris's distinction between pure and descriptive semiotic is a linguistic analogue of the contrast between pure and applied mathematics. Pure semiotic or philosophy is a conceptual analysis of the entire battery of metalinguistic concepts needed to clarify the nature of language as such; descriptive semiotic is the application of these analyzed concepts to the expressions of natural language. If Morris had grasped Wittgenstein's basic distinction between sign designs and symbols, between signs *in* the world and symbols *of* the world, he would have identified pure and descriptive semiotic with pure and applied philosophy. But he blurred the difference between a factual analysis and a logical analysis of language and converted his distinction into that between a philosophical theory and a natural scientific theory of signs.

B. Philosophy as Logical Syntax

The *Logical Syntax of Language* was the earliest and, for a time, the most influential attempt to develop philosophy as a species of pure semiotic. Carnap, who deeply wanted to make philosophy scientific, thought he had found an exact method for philosophy in syntactical analysis. But syntax, as Morris argued, is only a branch of pure semiotic; it operates with a purely formal conception of language, abstracting from the relations of signs to objects or to interpreters. Carnap originally believed that "all philosophic problems that have any meaning belong to syntax" (LSL 279); the other branches of semiotic are not required for the solution of genuine philosophic problems.

The first task of logical syntax is to define the essential metalinguistic concepts that apply to a formalized object language. The syntax of an object language L is formulated in the metalanguage L' by stipulating the formation and transformation rules of L. The terms, sentences, proofs, and theories expressed in L are logically clarified with the aid of these metalinguistic concepts. The concept of a sentence in L is defined by listing the vocabulary of L and stating the formation rules of L in L'. The concept of logical consequence in L is defined by listing the axioms of L and stating the transformation rules of L in L'. The other syntactical concepts are defined in terms of these conceptual primitives. Among the syntactical concepts defined in terms of sentence and logical consequence are the following: analytic, synthetic, contradictory, L-determinate, content, equipollent, and synonymy. In the *Logical Syntax of Language*, concepts like synonymy and analyticity, generally held to be semantical in nature are treated as part of syntax. All the sentences of logical syntax in which these concepts occur are formulated in the formal mode of speech. Carnap segregated philosophy from natural science by framing philosophic sentences in a way that excluded extralinguistic reference.

Carnap divided the reconstructed domain of philosophy into three regions: pure logic, epistemology, and the theory of meaning. The central concept of pure logic is the concept of deductive consequence. We formalize the conditions of valid inference for language L by defining the concept of deductive consequence for L. An essential feature of Carnap's concept of logic is that formation and transformation rules are always relative to a given language system. There is no single correct logic, no invariant science of logical syntax. The formation and transformation rules of a given language express conventions freely adopted not deep structures of language or reality that have been theoretically uncovered. In the *Tractatus*, Wittgenstein held that the syntactical forms of perspicuous sentences are isomorphic with the ontological forms of the states of affairs they picture; there is a unique logic common to all possible languages that mirrors the invariant ontological structure of logical space. By adopting a conventionalist account of syntactical rules,[12] Carnap abandoned the ontological thrust of Wittgenstein's philosophy of logic while preserving its emphasis on language rather than ideas or abstract meanings. The conventionalist twist permits Carnap to conceive of philosophical differences as contrasting *proposals* regarding the choice of syntactical rules, rather than as conflicting *theories* about a common subject matter. Philosophical problems raise questions of convenience and suitability not questions of correctness. Later in his career, when Carnap extended the scope of philosophy from syntax to semantics, he extended his pragmatism as well, holding that philosophical questions call for decisions rather than discoveries.[13] Carnap's abandonment of an ontological foundation for logic signals a steady shift toward pragmatism in linguistic philosophy, the marked pragmatism of the later Wittgenstein and the pervasive pragmatism espoused by Quine and Rorty.

The semiotic thesis, that philosophic questions are exclusively about the properties of language, is difficult to reconcile with traditional approaches to epistemology. But Carnap contended that classical epistemology is a polyglot enterprise: partly empirical psychology, partly syntactical analysis, partly meaningless speculation. What is philosophically relevant in epistemology is the logical analysis of the formation and verification of scientific statements (PLS 83). Epistemology is concerned with the deductive connections between the complex theoretical statements formulated in language L and the epistemically primitive statements of L. Like Russell and other logical empiricists, Carnap was committed to a form of epistemological reductionism whereby each cognitively meaningful statement is equivalent to some logical construct upon sentences that report matters of immediate experience.[14] These epistemically primitive statements of L constitute its verification base. Since each meaningful sentence in L is thought to be logically reducible to these primitive statements, L is assigned a decision procedure such that, in principle, all of its statements are verifiable or falsifiable by appeal to immediate experience. The epistemologist contributes to the *clarification* of scientific statements by logically reducing them to their verification base; and to their *verification* by disclosing which statements in L are logically reducible to the observation sentences immediately verified as true. Epistemology, a la Carnap, is an empiricist's version of applied logic.

All diachronic questions about how scientific knowledge is discovered and developed are dismissed as matters of empirical psychology.[15] The familiar Tractarian theme recurs; factual questions are not the concern of logic. Philosophy is confined to the linguistic formulation of scientific knowledge, and denied access to the cognitive operations that make scientific knowledge possible. Carnap insists on a rigid separation of logic and psychology. "The logical analysis of verification is the syntactical analysis of those transformation rules which determine the deduction of observation sentences. Hence epistemology—after elimination of its metaphysical and psychological elements—is a part of syntax"

Carnap's comprehensive ambition in the *Logical Syntax of Language* is dramatized by his syntactical approach to the theory of meaning. Morris had held that questions about meaning were the special province of semantics; that syntax, with its exclusive concern for intralinguistic relations, could not provide an adequate analysis of properly semantical concepts. Carnap displayed virtuosity, if not good judgment, by attempting to settle questions of meaning by the purely formal methods of syntax. He restricted himself to defining the concept of identity of sense for both the terms and sentences in *L*. The pivotal concept in his analysis of meaning is the concept of content. Two sentences have the same content if the class of nonvalid logical consequences for each sentence is the same; such sentences are said to be equipollent (PLS 57). If two terms have the same sense they are synonymous."Two expressions are called mutually synonymous, if the content of any sentence containing one of them is not changed if we replace that expression by the other" (PLS 58). Paralleling his earlier treatment of epistemology, Carnap dismissed as psychological, and thus as philosophically irrelevant, any further questions concerned with linguistic meaning.[16]

The *Logical Syntax of Language* announced a philosophical program with both positive and negative intentions. Positively, it was contructed to prove that the questions of pure logic, epistemology, and the theory of meaning were exclusively syntactical. Negatively, it reinforced the hermetic separation that Wittgenstein had urged between philosophical and factual inquiry, particularly psychology. Until Quine's *Two Dogmas of Empiricism*, its negative intention was largely accepted within the analytic tradition. After the dissemination of Carnap's criticism, analytic philosophers took it as a principle of faith that logic, in both the broad and narrow sense, was indifferent to psychological theory. Carnap's positive purpose, however, was not received uncritically even within analytic ranks. Most analytic philosophers accepted the restriction of philosophy to the formal mode of speech, but they rejected its confinement to the sphere of logical syntax.

C. The Pure Theory of Empirically
Meaningful Languages

The work of Wilfrid Sellars exemplifies the drive in recent analytic philosophy to extend the formal mode of speech beyond logical syntax. To appreciate both the continuity and the development of his philosophical program, I have chosen to develop it chronologically, beginning with a series of early papers in which his basic ideas were introduced and concluding with later texts in which the same ideas were refined and consolidated.[17]

Sellars used Carnap's work as his point of departure, just as Carnap had earlier used Wittgenstein's. Like Carnap, Sellars was intent on distinguishing philosophy from the factual sciences. While acknowledging the intimate relation between philosophy and the investigation of language, he insisted on a sharp distinction between the concepts of empirical linguistics and those of pure semiotic. The basic distinction is between an object-linguistic or factual investigation of language and a metalinguistic or philosophical approach. Since the term *language* may be systematically ambiguous, referring both to sign-designs as physical objects in the real order and to these same signs as players of intentional roles, discourse about language suffers from a related ambiguity.

> We have insisted that two irreducibly different usages of the term "language" must be distinguished, namely, the factual and the formal or more suggestively, the *descriptive* and the *constitutive*. In the factual-descriptive usage, a language is a set of socio-psychologico-historical facts. In this context the concepts in terms of which we describe a language are factual concepts such as *goal-behavior, substitute stimuli*, etc., together with a strong dose of statistics. The "metalanguage" in terms of which we describe a language thus understood is a "metalanguage" in a purely factual sense; from the formal standpoint it is no more a metalanguage than is language about non-linguistic socio-psychologico-historical states of affairs (PPE, 198)18.

Sellars brought an original and provocative slant to metaphilosophical inquiry. He chronicled the historical development of philosophy as the progressive achievement of increasingly appropriate questions (RNWW 4241). He believed that casting a philosophical problem in the proper form rather than providing an answer to that question is the heart of the philosophic enterprise. The major obstacle to the correct understanding of philosophical questions has been their confusion with factual questions, particularly in psychology. Sellars devoted a set of early papers to the job of reconstructing the heuristic program of philosophy. "The aim of these early papers is to provide a general framework in terms of which specific problems of formulation and argument in epistemology can be discriminated from questions relating to matters of fact and their status as capable of definitive solution clarified" (PPE 188). The result of Sellars's reconstruction is a revised concept of epistemology as the pure theory of empirically meaningful languages. The proposal and execution of this heuristic strategy constitute the major contribution of linguistic philosophy to the program of combating psychologism.

We develop a pure theory of empirically meaningful languages by identifying the invariant features proper to any sign-system to which the complete set of philosophic predicates applies (PPE 195). If a philosophic predicate is applicable to an expression, then the expression belongs to a formal linguistic system whose signs are regulated by metalinguistic rules (PPE 181). Philosophic predicates are the metalinguistic predicates introduced in these rules that define the conceptual roles a sign-design can play (ENWW 648). The enterprise of philosophy cannot be restricted to one branch of semiotic. Formal linguistic systems are not uninterpreted calculi to which only syntactical predicates apply. Unless the predicates of pure semantics and pragmatics were applicable to formal systems as well, they could not be called *languages* in the humanly relevant sense (PPE 183). Carnap had contrasted a formal system of signs with an interpreted calculus; Sellars contrasted a formal linguistic system with language as behavioral fact. Measured by Sellars' standards, Carnap's uninterpreted calculi really are not languages and the concepts applicable to them are not *metalinguistic* concepts strictly speaking.

A cluster of distinctions is needed to clarify the specifically philosophic aspect of linguistic analysis. The term *language* has three distinct senses:

1. Sense one refers to language as norm or type. Language as norm is language as posited or constituted by explicit metalinguistic rules. The pure theory of empirically meaningful languages is designed to clarify the metalinguistic predicates that have as their domain expressions in a language that is a model or norm. Languages in sense one are deliberately constructed languages (PPE 189). The metalinguistic predicates that apply to them are decidable by immediate appeal to the language's constitutive rules. Because of the requirement of formal decidability the sentences of pure semiotic are either analytic or self-contradictory.

2. Language as behavioral fact is the subject matter of numerous factual inquiries that treat the sign-designs of language as spatio-temporal objects in a network of causes, but systematically disregard the metalinguistic rules that constitute these objects as the players of conceptual roles. These investigations include causal studies of the origin and transmission of language as well as descriptive statistical studies of the matter of factual uniformities in which sign-designs are involved. In the investigation of language as behavioral fact, the relevant methods are empirical, the applicable concepts are object-linguistic, and the conclusions are formulated in synthetic object-linguistic sentences.

3. The third use of *language* refers to language as actual discursive behavior *qua* token of language as norm or type. Language in this sense is the subject matter of applied semiotic (PPE 198-199), which

deals with existing natural languages rather than with artificially constructed systems. To achieve a clear concept of these natural languages we need to distinguish:

a. the sign designs of the language,
b. the descriptive properties of those sign-designs considered as spatiotemporal objects,
c. the factual relations in which these sign-designs are involved,
d. the metalinguistic rules that constitute the sign-designs as players of conceptual roles,
e. the object-linguistic predicates that apply to the sign-designs under dimensions *b* and *c*.
f. the metalinguistic predicates that apply to the sign-designs under dimensions *c* and *d*.

In the case of the pure semiotic of constructed languages, we focus on the metalinguistic rules abstracting from actual linguistic behavior. In a behavioral science of language, we focus on patterns of linguistic behavior and neglect the constitutive metalinguistic rules. In the semiotic analysis of natural languages, we uncover the metalinguistic rules *d* by attention to the relevant factual relations *c* and we apply the philosophic predicates *f* to the appropriate sign-designs *a* in the light of these constitutive rules. The relevant methods of applied semiotic are both empirical and formal, the applicable concepts are metalinguistic, and the conclusions are formulated in irreducibly metalinguistic sentences. The critical point on which Sellars insisted is that we can employ empirical methods in determining the application of both philosophic and object-linguistic predicates to the sign-designs of a natural language.[19]

If we compare Sellars's concept of pure semiotic with Carnap's, we find these differences. Sellars accepted Carnap's allocation of logic in the narrow sense to pure syntax, but he rejected the exclusively syntactical treatment of epistemology and the theory of meaning. He also rejected Carnap's assignment of uninterpreted inscriptions as the terms of logical relations. For Sellars, the relations of logic hold between interlinguistic propositional senses expressed by sentential expressions in different natural languages. Though uninterpreted signs are not logical entities, in the calculational dimension of pure syntax we can deal with the sign-designs as inscriptions only and disregard the propositional roles they play. Carnap's pure syntax was concerned with the syntactical rules that define the formal structure of a calculus, but his calculi do not qualify strictly as languages. Languages are defined by three levels of applicable semiotic predicates with each level adding a new dimension of calculus structure. Without decidable semantical predicates, questions about designation and truth do not apply to calculi; without decidable pragmatic predicates questions about verification and confirmation do not apply. Sellars transformed Carnap's metaphilosophical program by assigning the theory of meaning to pure semantics and epistemology to pure pragmatics. Pure semantics explicates the philosophic concepts of *true*, *false*, and *designates* and clarifies their relation to the formal systems they partially define. Pure pragmatics performs a similar function for *confirmable*, *verifiable*, *verified*, *confirmed*, and *meaningful* (PPE 182-183).

Wittgenstein's *Tractatus* limited the positive function of philosophy to the analytic clarification of the descriptive sentences of natural language. The epistemological program of Sellars also restricts philosophy to conceptual analysis, but with an important difference. Epistemology does not analyze the descriptive sentences of science and common sense but the metalinguistic concepts with which we classify and appraise descriptive and explanatory discourse. Carnap had initiated this development by rejecting the ineffability principles of the *Tractatus* and assigning to philosophy the clarification of syntactical concepts. Sellars deepened and clarified the program Carnap had begun. The expansion of philosophic possibility corresponds to an expansion of the realm of meaningful discourse, a realm that Wittgenstein had limited to descriptive and logical propositions. Sellars endorsed the irreducibility of factual and metalinguistic discourse asserted by Carnap, but he insisted on the added irreducibility of semantical and pragmatic predicates to those of syntax.

Pure pragmatics is a formal theory about the relation of a meaningful language to the world. Its aim is "to give a formal reconstruction of the common sense notion that an empirically meaningful language is one that is about the world in which it is used" (PPE 187). In this phrasing Sellars captured the double sense of *language* I have remarked since the beginning of this chapter. Language as a system of signs is simultaneously *in* the world and *about* the world. If we study language as something *in* the world and abstract from its role of talking *about* the world, we abandon the metalinguistic approach to language and confine ourselves to a factual empirical investigation. If, for different reasons, we treat language as a set of uninterpreted formal inscriptions, we achieve exactly the same result. The crucial insight in the philosophy of language is to remark the legitimacy of these complementary perspectives without blurring their essential differences.

The first task of pure pragmatics is to set formal restrictions on the calculi to the expressions of which epistemological predicates are applicable. Such calculi must be P-lawful systems with specified confirmation rules (PPE 189). In addition to rules of formation and transformation, empirically meaningful languages are defined by their rules of confirmation, which "specify for each non-relational predicate in the calculus the relational predicates which can participate in sentences with one and the same individual constant which is conjoined in a sentence with the non-relational predicate in question" (PPE 189). These metalinguistic rules together with appropriate material rules of inference provide a decision procedure for the metalanguage's epistemic predicates. The objective of the epistemologist is to distinguish and relate four strands of language: the sentences of the object language to which epistemic predicates apply; the network of metalinguistic rules by reference to which they are decidable; the epistemic metalinguistic sentences in which those predicates are used; and, the sentences used by the epistemologist to clarify their specific semantical role. The irreducibility of epistemic predicates to object-linguistic predicates is founded on the irreducibility of object-linguistic discourse to rule-prescribing discourse. But metalinguistic rules, though they ground the difference between object-linguistic and metalinguistic statements, are sui generis. They connect these two levels of discourse without converging with either.

The expressions of a calculus have determinate meaning in the semiotic sense only by virtue of the metalinguistic rules regulating their use (PPE 190). The semantical statements in which the theory of meaning for a natural language is expressed are metalinguistic. They are related but logically irreducible to the factual statements asserting statistical correlations between linguistic expressions and the circumstances of their use. The central concept of pure semantics, *designates* or *means*, is a metalinguistic concept. There is a deep philosophical temptation to construe semantical statements as relational, as asserting a unique semantical relation between the expressions of a formal system and the domain of real objects that serve as its designata. Sellars, following the later Wittgenstein, insisted that this inclination be resisted. Pure semantical statements concerning the relation of language to "the world," in fact are metalinguistic statements whose essential purpose is to *classify* linguistic expressions with respect to the semantical roles that they play. "The pure theory of empirically meaningful languages as formally defined systems which are about worlds in which they are used has no place for *the* world but only for the world designated by the story which is the meaning base of a given language" (ENWW 657).

(I want to emphasize, at this juncture, two principles that connect the early and later stages of Sellars's thought. The first is his insistence on the irreducibility of factual and philosophic discourse. The second is his intention to explicate metalinguistic discourse as essentially classificatory and nonrelational in character. The surface grammar of metalinguistic semantical statements makes them appear like relational sentences, but this apppearance dissolves under rational reconstruction of their deep structure. Because these sentences are not relational they cannot express a semantical connection between the linguistic order and the real order. In his earliest papers, Sellars established this point through his reconstruction of sentences containing *means* and *true*. In his later work, he offers a parallel analysis of *names*, *refers*, and *denotes*. But he complements his reconstruction of semantical statements by coordinating them with a level of factual discourse that does assert factual relations between linguistic and extralinguistic objects. See the distinction between signifying and picturing in *Science, Perception and Reality*.)

A basic task of pure semantics is to explicate the rubric "'E' (in L) means..." that is used to clarify the sense of linguistic expressions. To preserve this rubric for philosophy, we must distinguish its uses in pure semantics from those in behavioral linguistics. The psychologistic intrusion into philosophy stems principally from a factualistic interpretation of the philosophical concept of meaning. By sharply distinguishing semantical from psychological approaches to meaning, Sellars hoped to blunt the leading edge of psychologism and secure for philosophy its proper autonomy as the pure theory of language. "The essentially new feature of the new way of words is that it does not commit the mistake of psychologism in either of its forms" (ENWW 431).

D. Two Species of Psychologism

From the perspective of semiotic analysis the history of psychologism can be recounted in this sequence (PPE 181). The issue was first joined regarding the concepts of logic and mathematics. Frege, Wittgenstein, and Carnap attacked psychologism by rejecting a factual analysis of these disciplines. They argued that logic and mathematics were not factual sciences nor branches of any factual science, but they disagreed in their substantive explanations of this claim. Frege defended logic's autonomy by appealing to its abstract and atemporal subject matter. Wittgenstein classified logical propositions as tautologies and contradictions and distinguished their semantic and epistemic properties from those of descriptive factual propositions. According to Sellars, Carnap finally resolved the issue by developing the theory of pure syntax. He clarified the concepts of logic by locating them within the formation and transformation rules definitive of a natural or constructed language. These rules constitute, for the language they define, a normative standard of implication and deducibility. Logic is a normative rather than a factual discipline, but the ground of its norms is to be found in humanly conceived rules rather than in invariant laws governing an extralinguistic region of being.

Because Carnap restricted pure semiotic to syntax, he failed to prevent the incursion of psychologism into the other regions of philosophy. A decisive victory over psychologism requires an attack at its roots. Sellars believed that the basic error of psychologism has been the treatment of philosophic concepts as factual rather than metalinguistic (PPE 183). Philosophical psychologism has confused formal metalinguistic predicates with the factual predicates involved in the psychological description of thought. The different versions of philosophical psychologism can be traced to competing theories of meaning, but they commonly assume that the analysis of meaning is essentially a psychological issue. The complete avoidance of psychologism cannot be achieved until a clear distinction is drawn between the philosophical and the factual senses of *meaning*. We need that distinction to clarify the three senses of *language* remarked earlier.

The defining feature of the new way of words is the sharp division it maintains between the framework of semiotic analysis and the framework of empirical psychology. Although the philosophic use of *meaning* is a reconstruction of the psychological use, the two must be kept conceptually distinct. Confusion of the formal and factual frames of reference with respect to the theory of meaning and epistemology has been the underlying cause of *philosophical* as opposed to *logical* psychologism.

Sellars isolated two species of philosophical psychologism for close scrutiny; logical nominalism and ontological realism. "To be guilty of psychologism is to suppose that 'means' in such sentences as A means B stands for a psychological fact involving symbol A and item B, whether the psychological fact be analyzed in terms of [*wesen*] schau, acquaintance or plain experience. Psychologism underlies Platonism, Humean and nineteenth century nominalism and the conceptualistic attempts at compromise" (RNWW, 430).

All the species of psychologism in semantics identify the meaning of a linguistic expression with an object of immediate awareness. Logical nominalism, the narrow type of psychologism attacked by Frege and Husserl, restricts the objects of immediate awareness to immanent ideas, to private, nonrepeatable mental contents. Having identified the sense of a linguistic expression with a private idea in the mind of its bearer that varies for each individual on each occasion of the expression's use, logical nominalism effectively precludes the intersubjectivity of language. But is this a price nominalism as such has to pay? Sellars did not think so. He distinguished three species of nominalism, of which only the logical variety excludes linguistic intersubjectivity. The *ontological* nominalist denies the existence of extralinguistic abstract entities and rejects their postulation as linguistic meanings. The *psychological* nominalist denies that we learn the meaning of linguistic signs through direct intellectual awareness of the abstract entities that they are claimed by the realist to signify. (Sellars's alternative proposal is that we learn the meaning of language by gradually mastering the rules that regulate the use of linguistic expressions.) The *logical* nominalist accepts a relational theory of meaning but he rejects the alleged mental experience of abstract entities. He then identifies the extralinguistic terms of semantical relations with subjective private ideas and thus loses publicity of linguistic meaning.

The ontological realist recognizes the need for intersubjective discourse.

But, like the logical nominalist whom he opposes, he is trapped by his acceptance of a relational theory of meaning and by his taking objects of direct acquaintance as the extralinguistic terms of the semantical relation. If the senses of linguistic expressions are to be properly intersubjective, they must be publicly accessible entities that remain constant over time and space, providing common access to the speakers of different languages and cultures. The ontological realist secures these conditions for them by making them objects of intellectual intuition rather than sensory perception. He rejects Sellars's psychological nominalism in order to defend logical realism, and tries to account for the intersubjective meaning of language by positing as its field of designata a domain of abstract entities of which any person can have immediate intuitive knowledge. These abstract entities play the double role of the intersubjective *senses* of linguistic expressions and the intentional *contents* of classically conceived mental acts. Sellars branded as epistemologism (RNWW 430) any psychological theory that asserts the possibility of direct intuitive apprehension of abstract entities. He explicitly accused Husserl of epistemologism (RNWW 430-431) while acknowledging that Husserl's conceptualism differs from ontological realism by making objective noematic contents distributively but not collectively independent of mental acts. He wavered about Frege's status as an ontological realist. "Although Frege insists that the entities he calls senses have a being which is independent of being conceived by particular minds on particular occasions—thus correctly insisting on their public character—he does not seem to take the tough early Russell line that they are independent of thought altogether."[20] In order to preserve intersubjective linguistic meaning, (that is, logical realism), both ontological realists and conceptualists enlarge the domain of direct awareness to include concepts and propositions as well as perceivable objects and private ideas.

Sellars charged that the common error uniting these different approaches is the confusion of the semantical and psychological frames of reference. We need to distinguish

> between "meaning" as a term belonging to the framework of epistemo-
> logical or logical analysis and "meaning" as a descriptive term in
> empirical psychology relating to habits of response to and manipulation
> of linguistic symbols. The classical conception of mind as apprehending
> universals and propositions is based on a confusion of these two frames
> of reference. To deny that universals exist when speaking in the logical
> frame is as mistaken as to assert that universals exist when speaking in
> the framework of the psychological description of thought. (RNWW
> 444).

The insistence that it is nonsense to speak of meanings or senses as data, as intuited objects of any kind, constitutes the essential difference between psychologistic and semantical analyses of meaning, between the linguistic reformulation of Platonism and Platonism itself. (ENWW 699). "Epistemologism has the virtue of preserving philosophical content (intersubjective senses) though at the expense of constructing a fictitious psychology. Psychologism in the narrow sense lacks merit as philosophy, although the philosopher and psychologist can join hands in approving its avoidance of pseudo psychology" (RNWW 431). Sellars applauded Husserl's effort to distinguish philosophy from empirical psychology, but he contended that this objective should be secured not through the reductions of transcendental phenomenology but by the pure theory of language.

The formal linguistic alternative to psychologism is the endorsement of logical realism together with ontological and psychological nominalism. The general strategy is to connect realistic talk about universals with nominalistic discourse about linguistic expressions, while preserving a sharp distinction between semiotic and psychological analysis. The acceptance of logical realism does not entail Platonism nor the eidetic intuition of ideal contents. The new way of words provides an alternative understanding of the familiar metaphorical claim that the mind apprehends universals. The twist is to turn the contents of classically conceived mental acts into the intensions of linguistic expressions, and then to treat intensions as interlinguistic rather than extralinguistic in character. The interlinguistic framework of intensions does not involve a commitment to Platonism in either its psychological or ontological form.

Sellars's intensions are linguistic entities in the special sense of language as type.[21] They need to be distinguished from the specific sign-designs that embody them in existing natural languages. The sign-designs of natural language token these types when they are governed by the same metalinguistic rules that define the interlinguistic intensions.[22] Because model linguistic types are capable of realization in different languages, we have a formal method for dealing with interlinguistic questions of identity of meaning. *Rojo*, *rot*, and *rouge* all express the same conceptual intension, ·red·, if they play the same linguistic role in their languages that *red* plays in English. Expressions between the asterisks (*rot*) refer to sign-designs in a given natural language. Dot quoted expressions, (·red·) are "sortal predicates used to classify the items which play the role played in our language by the sign-design between the dot quotes." Descriptively different sign-designs in the same or different languages are able to play the same semantic role. Metalinguistic rules define types of linguistic roles but they leave undetermined the factual character of the sign-designs that can be used to play that role. The implications of this indeterminacy for a naturalistic interpretation of conceptual acts are explored at the conclusion of this chapter.

Dot quoting is a special device used in specifically semantical contexts.

To appreciate its illuminatory power, recall the semantical rubric with which we began, "'E' (in L) *means*..." In a battery of arguments and papers spanning nearly thirty years, Sellars labored to distinguish the *meanings* of meaning in properly semantical contexts.[23] His first principle was the irreducibility of the semantical predicate *means* to an object-linguistic psychological predicate. His second principle was that *means* as a semantical predicate plays significantly different conceptual roles in different linguistic contexts.[24] These roles include:

1. *Means* as a translation rubric,
2. *Means* as "stands for",
3. *Means* as "names",
4. *Means* as "connotes",
5. *Means* as "denotes".

He focussed attention on the means as "stands for" rubric, that rubric in which "'E' (in L) *means*" was equivalent to "'E (in L) stands for its sense." In the standard analysis of these contexts, the expression to the left of *stands for* was a scare-quoted expression in a particular natural language and the expression to the right of *stands for* was an abstract singular term in the same or another natural language; for example, "'Dreieckig' (in German) stands for triangularity." Sellars argued that the standard analysis was syntactically nonperspicuous, philosophically misleading, and in need of rational reconstruction. Without rehearsing all of the steps in the proposed reconstruction, we can review its basic premises.

1. The abstract singular term *triangularity* can be reconstructed as the distributive singular term *the ·triangular·*.
2. The dot quoting device indicates that it is a special sort of distributive singular term, namely a metalinguistic distributive singular term.
3. The expression *stands for* is a nonperspicuous classificatory copula used to classify the expression on the left-hand side in terms of the linguistic role it plays. The role is named on the right-hand side by the metalinguistic distributive singular term.
4. When correctly analyzed, distributive singular terms in the predicate position are seen to be special types of classificatory predicates; and metalinguistic distributive singular terms are seen to be sortal predicates that classify a linguistic expression in terms of the conceptual role it plays. The conceptual role itself is defined by the appropriate set of metalinguistic rules.

If these critical premises are accepted, then the perspicuous reconstruction of "'dreieckig' (in German) stands for triangularity" is "'dreieckig' (in German) is a ·triangular·." The metalinguistic sortal predicate *a ·triangular·* can be used to classify the sign-designs in any language which play the same conceptual role played in the base language by **triangular**. Semantical statements of this classificatory type require for their full understanding an insight into three irreducibly different types of linguistic statement.

1. The first are statements asserting matter-of-factual uniformities involving sign-designs and the circumstances of their use. These empirical generalizations do not involve *means* as a semantical predicate and are not semantical statements in the strict sense, but the truth-value of the related semantical statements is dependent on their being true. These statements are object-linguistic relational statements that assert a significant statistical connection between linguistic items in the spatiotemporal order and the extralinguistic occasions of their use.

2. The second are semantical statements in the strict sense containing *means* or *stands for* as irreducible metalinguistic predicates. Correctly reconstructed, these statements are not relational but classificatory in character. They are used to classify sign-designs in terms of their rule-governed conceptual roles. Although logically irreducible to factual statements asserting semantical uniformities, they entail statements of that sort.

3. The third type of statements are metalinguistic rules constituting the conceptual roles played by the sign-designs. In the case of language as type, they are stipulated rules explicitly formulated in the metalanguage. In the case of language as *token* of language as *type*, they are the operative but implicit metalinguistic rules that we can discover empirically and then formulate explicitly to clarify the sense of contested linguistic expressions.

The outcome of this highly ambitious reconstruction is a many-leveled linguistic theory that preserves logical realism within a framework of ontological and psychological nominalism. Sellars's strategy is to adopt the three-dimensional semantics of Frege, but to incorporate within it the analysis of meaning developed in the *Philosophical Investigations*. This unusual conjunction of realism and nominalism sets him apart from logicians like Quine, who abandon the theory of meaning for the theory of reference, and from semanticists like Carnap, who preserve the rubrics of the theory of meaning but give them a relational interpretation. Sellars's arresting and highly original strategy is to modify Carnap by constructing a nonrelational semantics and to correct Quine by showing that the theory of reference presupposes Sellars's reconstructed theory of meaning.[25]

E. Naturalism without Psychologism

To complete the scientific image [of man] we need
to enrich it not with more ways of saying what is
the case, but with the language of community and
individual intentions.[26]

The revisionary energies of the new way of words are not exhausted in reconstructing the problem of abstract entities. Analysis of the status of linguistic intensions leads directly to issues in the philosophy of mind. The central problem in the philosophy of mind is to provide an adequate account of the intentionality of mental acts. Sellars structured the problem of intentionality in openly linguistic terms. It is "the problem of interpreting the status of the reference to objects and states of affairs (actual or possible)... which is involved in the very meaning of the 'mentalistic' vocabulary of everyday life."[27] His approach accepts the irreducible intentionality of mentalistic discourse while directly opposing classical philosophies of mind. As an alternative to classical theories, he proposes a semantic analysis of intentional discourse that provides support for a naturalistic interpretation of mental acts. Acceptance of intentionality as the mark of the mental is consistent with a naturalistic account of humanity in the full employment of its powers. In forging a naturalistic theory of mind, Sellars hoped to avoid both substantive and logical behaviorism as well as the traditional versions of mind-body dualism. It is important to remark that Sellars's concept of intentionality is naturalistic not behavioristic. His analysis of mentalistic discourse is designed "to show exactly in what sense it includes something (reference or aboutness) which is not to be found in the language of behavioristics."[28] My purpose in this section is to outline his semantic approach to the philosophy of mind, to show how it effectively integrates scientific realism with a many-leveled linguistic pluralism and thus achieves the larger goal of a nonpsychologistic naturalism.

Sellars regularly pursued philosophical clarification by way of contrast. He constructed models of opposing substantive positions, and then gradually modified them until they were transformed into his own theory. The preliminary model of the classical theory of the mind he devised is built around three principles, formulated partly in the material mode and partly in the formal mode of speech:

1. There exist overt linguistic episodes that can be characterized in semantical terms.
2. Over and above these, there exist certain inner episodes, mental acts, properly characterized by the traditional vocabulary of intentionality.

3. Semantical discourse about overt linguistic performance is to be *analyzed* in terms of discourse about the intentionality of the mental episodes "expressed" by these overtly linguistic acts.[29]

The critical difference between Sellars's theory and the classical model is thesis three. To dramatize the similarities and contrasts between his theory and the classical model, Sellars proposed an alternative set of principles, which we shall call *the semantic theory of intentionality*.

The semantic theory of intentionality is based on three decisive reconstructions. It reconstructs classically conceived mental acts as inner speech episodes; it reconstructs the intentional contents of those acts as the interlinguistic intensions of both outer and inner speech; it reconstructs Carnap's relational interpretation of semantical discourse along the lines developed in Section D. The reconstructed categories of philosophical semantics then are used to analyze the intentionality of mental acts reconceived as episodes in inner speech. Before we introduce the theory as an organized series of propositions,[30] certain complex conceptual discriminations are required. The term *express* as used in philosophical contexts is systematically ambiguous.[31] Express₁ is the *causal* use of express; overt speech is said causally to express₁ the mental acts that are its efficient cause. Express₂ is the *semantical* use of express; linguistic episodes semantically express₂ their sense or meaning. Express₃ is the *action* use of express; people express themselves in linguistic actions when they *decide* to use certain words to express₃ their intentions or beliefs. A second related ambiguity involves the term *thought*. Thought₁ refers to mental acts or episodes; this is the event use of *thought*. Thought₂ refers to the propositional intensions expressed₂ by sentential linguistic episodes; thoughts₂ are linguistic roles rather than mental events. There is a final distinction to be drawn between the because₁ of analysis and the because₂ of explanation. "If a concept x is to be analyzed in terms of y, it would be incorrect to say of anyone that he had the concept x but lacked the concept y". This stricture of conceptual priority does not apply to the *because₂* of explanation.[32] If x is the explanatory cause of y, it is surely possible to be aware of y and ignorant of x. The conceptual priority of y to x from the standpoint of analysis is consistent with the ontological priority of x to y from the standpoint of explanation.

With these important distinctions in mind, let us turn to the semantic theory of intentionality.

1. Meaningful overt linguistic acts are the expression₁ of inner episodes, thoughts₁.
2. The thought₁ that p is an inner speech episode which might be referred to as the mental saying that p.

3. $Thought_1$ episodes are essentially characterized by the categories of intentionality.

4. $Thought_1$ episodes are not overt speech episodes but are $expressed_1$ by overt speech episodes.

5. All speech episodes, inner and outer, are meaningful utterances because they $express_2$ $thoughts_2$.

6. Although speech episodes mean states of affairs $because_1$, they $express_2$ $thoughts_2$ about states of affairs, it is important not to confuse this thesis with the claim that they mean states of affairs $because_1$ they $express_1$ $thoughts_1$ about states of affairs. This distinction is crucial because Sellars claimed that it is possible to understand and to analyze semantical discourse about overt speech even if we have no idea that imperceptible inner speech episodes are the efficient cause of overt speech.

7. Although they are conceived on the model of postulated theoretical entities, $thoughts_1$ are not merely theoretical entities, since we can have direct noninferential knowledge of what we are thinking.

8. The framework of $thoughts_1$ is introduced as a theory "to explain the fact (among others) that a person's verbal propensities and dispositions change during periods of silence as they would have changed if he had been engaged in specific sequences of candid linguistic behavior."[33] When it is first learned, the language of $thoughts_1$ is solely theoretical; but language users who have mastered it can be trained in an avowal or reporting use of the framework of mental acts.

9. The analogical model for the theory of $thoughts_1$ is semantical discourse about overt speech. $Thoughts_1$ are conceived analogously as "inner speech" episodes that although not descriptively similar to overt speech acts are functionally similar. The same semantical categories that apply to their analogues in overt speech can be applied correctly to them. The original categories of the theory of $thoughts_1$ are analogical functional categories that characterize $thoughts_1$ not in terms of their intrinsic descriptive properties but in terms of the semantical roles they play.

10. The semantical vocabulary in which we talk about overt linguistic episodes can be *analyzed* without appealing to the explanatory framework of mental acts. This thesis directly contradicts thesis three of the classical model.

11. The basic rubric of semantical discourse "'E' (in L) $expresses_2$ the $thought_2$ that p" is an irreducible feature of all semiotic discourse, applicable to both overt and inner speech episodes. This semantical rubric cannot be reduced to object linguistic factual discourse without psychologism.

12. It is essential to distinguish between semantical statements, metalinguistic rules, and semantical uniformities. Although semantical statements of the form "'E' (in L) expresses₂ the thought₂ that p" do not *assert* behavioral facts they do *imply* certain facts about the place of *E* in the behavioral economy of the users of *L*. The semantical uniformities are the descriptive factual core of meaningful speech.

13. The *fundamentum* of an anlogical theory of thoughts₁ is meaningful overt speech understood in terms of the semantical statements, rules, and uniformities outlined in 12.

14. The culminating thesis of Sellars's theory is that the categories of intentionality are nothing more nor less than the semantical categories in terms of which we talk epistemically about overt speech as they appear in the framework of mental acts conceived on the model of overt linguistic episodes.

The explicit contrast between ontological and conceptual priority provides the strategic foundation for Sellars's philosophy of mind. He exploited this contrast to situate himself between a classical theorist like Descartes and a logical behaviorist like Ryle. From Sellars's perspective, Descartes confused the causal or ontological priority of mental acts with their conceptual priority. Although mental acts, in fact, are the cause of linguistic behavior, our concept of the mind and its acts is derived from concepts pertaining to the observable use of language. The Cartesian concept of imperceptible mental acts is an analogical concept based on a behavioral model of overt speech.

Logical behaviorists, like Ryle, recognized the conceptual priority of psychological concepts pertaining to linguistic behavior or dispositions toward such behavior. But they mistakenly concluded that this conceptual ordering undermines the ontological commitment to imperceptible intentional acts. The conceptual priority of the Rylean level of discourse is compatible with the causal priority of inner speech episodes. In the order of being, the imperceptible cause precedes the observable effect, but in the order of understanding the pattern of priority is reversed. Sellars modified this ancient Aristotelian principle to construct a semantical alternative to the classical model of mind.

In its bare bones, his revisionary account can be summarized as follows: To each person there belongs a stream of inner intentional episodes. The subject of these episodes has privileged but not invariable nor infallible epistemic access to them. Inner intentional episodes can occur without being expressed₁ by verbal behavior, but verbal behavior in an important sense is their natural fruition. Candid linguistic behavior is the typical manifestation at the overt level of these imperceptible intentional acts. The semantic concepts applied to overt speech episodes appear in the framework of thoughts$_1$ as the categories of intentionality. The fact that the model for thoughts$_1$ is semantical rather then behavioral discourse about overt linguistic episodes explains why intentionality is an irreducible feature of thoughts$_1$. The behavioral facts about linguistic expressions that are implied though not asserted by semantic statements are the model for the behavior of thoughts$_1$ as episodes in the order of causes. Although semantical language conveys undergirding behavioral information, it cannot be translated into exclusively behavioral terms. A naturalistic theory of mind can avoid psychologism by acknowledging the irreducibility of discourse containing metalinguistic semiotic predicates to the language of behavioral or neurophysiological description.

F. Linguistic Pluralism and Scientific Realism

The manifest pluralism of the *Philosophical Investigations* has left its mark on Sellars's approach to linguistic philosophy. He insisted that we recognize a number of irreducible modes of discourse (for example, descriptive and explanatory, normative, and metalinguistic) that are functionally complementary but not logically continuous. Sentences about intentional episodes cannot be translated or regimented into a physicalist (Quine) or behaviorist (Ryle) language. Discourse about the intentionality of mind requires that we supplement factual discourse with semiotic categories. A sophisticated naturalism can accommodate this linguistic plurality without succumbing to ontological dualism. Intentional discourse about thoughts$_1$ resembles discourse about chess when we are stating the rules of the game and envisaging permissible moves within the rules but neglecting to describe the physical properties of the chess pieces with which the game will be played. Descriptive, rule-prescribing, and metalinguistic discourse supplement each other, without being logically reducible to a common vocabulary. When we construe the intentionality of thoughts$_1$ on the model of semantic categories applied to overt speech, we treat thoughts as players of conceptual roles, we deal with them at the semiotic level. The descriptive properties of the sign-designs that play these roles are left indeterminate, to be investigated by factual rather than semiotic inquiry. The *aboutness* of thinking is essentially a semantical matter; what thinking is *descriptively* is a question of fact.

As a scientific realist and ontological naturalist Sellars identified thoughts$_1$ with neurophysiological episodes in the central nervous system. In *propria persona* the inner conceptual episodes of the framework of thoughts$_1$ are complex events occurring in the cerebral cortex. The scientific image of a human being is able to coordinate a nondualistic psychology of the higher mental processes with a clear differentiation of logical, factual, and ethical strands of discourse. Sellars's comprehensive strategy is to combine scientific realism with linguistic pluralism, thus avoiding the dialectical impasses of both ancient and modern theories of the mind.

How does a scientific realist like Sellars differ from a phenomenologist like Husserl? Both agree on the intentionality of mental acts; both agree that intentionality is the defining feature of the mental; and both believe that an adequate understanding of the mind's intentionality cannot be achieved within empirical psychology. Sellars understood the intentionality of the mind in terms of the applicability to mental acts of semiotic categories. Husserl understood intentionality in terms of the absolute irreducibility of human consciousness to the categories of nature. For Husserl, mental acts are radically distinct from natural occurrences within the matrix of space, time, and causality. For Sellars, mental acts can be adequately *described* in physical terms, but this description does not indicate their intentional role. Events in the central nervous system are characterized as intentional only when classified and appraised in semiotic categories. Husserl was correct to insist on the irreducibility of intentional categories to those of nature. But, according to Sellars, he was mistaken in taking them to be higher-order ontological categories. If he had realized that intentional categories are in essence metalinguistic, he could have preserved his basic philosophical insight in a form compatible with ontological naturalism.

For the purposes of description and explanation, the scientific realistic views the human person as a complex of physical particles and understands all human activities, including thoughts, as a matter of these particles changing in state and relationship. But something about persons clearly seems to be omitted on this naturalistic view. According to Sellars, the need to capture the specifically human within the framework of scientific realism is the basic task confronting modern philosophy. He rejected as unacceptable three strategies that enjoy broad currency today[34]:

1. Ontological dualism, in which humans as scientific objects are contrasted with the disembodied minds that are the source and principle of their existence as persons,

2. A rejection of the reality of persons in favor of the exclusive reality of scientific objects (whether this rejection was intended or not, Sellars believed that it is logically entailed by those forms of naturalism that exclude intentional idioms and intensional discourse,)

3. An affirmation of the primacy of persons that relegates the scientific theories of humankind to a limited calculational function. This ontologically purified view is favored by the various instrumentalist interpretations of theoretical science.

The alternative strategy endorsed by Sellars is to enrich the language of scientific description and explanation with the language of intentions, the language of semiotics and ethics. The irreducible core of the framework of persons is not expressible in descriptive discourse. "The conceptual framework of persons is the framework in which we think of one another as sharing the community intentions which provide the ambience of standards and principles (above all those which make rational and meaningful discourse possible) within which we live our own individual lives."[35]

If scientific realism is enriched by the insights of ethics and philosophical semantics and if it preserves the crucial distinctions among the different levels of human discourse, then it can embrace the discoveries of neurophysiology, resist the collapse of philosophy into science, and recognize the special status of human persons to which the classical tradition was deeply committed. This ambitious vision is the program and the promise Sellars offered to those who would join him along the new way of words.

G. The Linguistic Turn and the Philosophy of Language

Philosophical problems are problems which may be solved (or dissolved) by reforming language or by understanding more about the language we presently use.[36]

The way of words was a new way because it deliberately abandoned the way of ideas. The shift to language from ideas occurred chiefly because the older tradition had brought pervasive confusion rather than order to philosophy. From this centuries-old impasse there seemed no exit. This conclusion is the common theme uniting philosophers as diverse as Frege, Husserl, Wittgenstein, and Sellars. Frege rejected the confusion of abstract senses with private ideas and located this intellectual disorder at the center of philosophical empiricism. Husserl rejected the confusion of ideas with ideal meanings and insisted that a philosophic theory of meaning be based on a foundation of intentional acts. Wittgenstein rejected ideas for linguistic expressions and thereby restored to philosophy a public subject matter open to empirical investigation. Sellars accepted human discourse as the appropriate subject matter of philosophy but preserved a sharp distinction between philosophic and factual theories of language. He cautioned that the way of words could lead to linguisticism, just as the way of ideas had led to psychologism, unless this sharp distinction were observed. An attentive student of modern philosophy, he knew the different senses that the term *idea* had expressed in

British and Continental thought. He detected comparable ambiguities in the term *language* and related expressions in the theory of signification. He saw in the linguistic turn the opportunity to unite the naturalistic movement in psychology with the important developments in contemporary logical theory. Naturalistic psychology, released from its self-imposed bondage to phenomenalism, could become the core of a scientific theory of humankind. Complemented by the insights of a comprehensive theory of language, the scientific image could achieve "that articulated and integrated vision of man in the universe" which had been the goal of philosophy from the beginning. But these potential fruits of the new way of words depended on the development of an adequate theory of signification. The rush into language like the rush into ideas would prove philosophically barren unless the necessary distinctions within the web of discourse were observed; as always in philosophy, the alternative to distinctions is confusion.

Contemporary linguistic philosophers lack a common theory of signification. Although they practice philosophy through the medium of language, they disagree about what language is and why it is philosophically significant. Differences in their metaphilosophical programs spring from these opposing philosophies of language. We can isolate the divisive metaphilosophical issues but we cannot resolve them until we understand the conflicting theories of meaning in which they are rooted. Sellars provided the matrix of distinctions needed for a clear statement of the problem.

"An empirically meaningful language is one that is *about* the world *in* which it is used." Discourse, the subject matter of philosophy, jointly satisfies two relations to the world. It is simultaneously *in* the world and *about* the world; these relations are complementary but irreducible. Insofar as discourse is *in* the world it is the subject matter of factual analysis and insofar as discourse is *about* the world it is the subject matter of semiotic inquiry. The two modes of investigation are also complementary but distinct.

According to linguistic philosophers, philosophy finds its distinctive subject matter not by abandoning the world for a domain of abstract objects, ideal meanings, or mental acts but by locating within the world those entities (namely, intentional signs) that also are *about* the world. The field of philosophical inquiry is the set of natural entities to which the categories of intentionality apply. Although Husserl's basic insight was correct, he misunderstood the categories of intentionality that served to demarcate the subject matter of philosophy. According to Sellars, he failed to realize that they are the semantical categories first applicable to overt speech given analogical extension to mental acts. They bear no special ontological or epistemic burden. The fact that inner and outer speech are irreducibly intentional does not preclude their being *in* the world and thus appropriate objects for empirical scientific analysis. Because the intentional and factual properties of discourse are linked but easily confused, there is a permanent ambiguity in the concept of language and in the concept of discourse about language.

An entity in the natural order is a linguistic sign only if it satisfies the following set of conditions:

1. As a sign-design, the entity has certain descriptive properties,
2. It is lawfully correlated in its social use with other sign-designs and sets of extralinguistic states of affairs,
3. It plays a specific conceptual role in a language game that is defined by the metalinguistic rules, explicit or implicit, that specify its correct use,
4. Participants in the language game use the sign-design in the way they do because they have learned the rules that constitute the sign as intentional,[37]
5. The relevant metalinguistic rules must include formation rules, transformation rules, confirmation rules, material rules of inference, and semantical rules of both the ought-to-be and ought-to-do types,[38]
6. These rules define a standard of correctness for a particular language game, but they admit of historical development and coexistent alternatives; language games have a history.

The concept of discourse about language is comparably complex. Strictly speaking, discourse is not metalinguistic unless it applies to expressions that satisfy all of the stipulated conditions. If we think of each condition as specifying a particular dimension of discourse, then we can classify the forms of talk about language by citing the specific dimensions to which they refer. Factual discourse about language refers to sign-designs conceived under dimensions one and two. Metalinguistic discourse refers to sign-designs whose use is regulated by metalinguistic rules. The more complex modes of metalinguistic discourse presume more complex patterns of applicable rules. The decidability of epistemic predicates, for example, may require close attention to the entire set of metalinguistic rules. The many species of discourse about discourse are complementary but discontinuous ways of talking about the range of conditions that define the complex human structure we call *language*.

Adequate theories of complex structures must distinguish, order, relate, and unite the elements ingredient in those structures. Inadequate theories can be classified by indicating their omission or confusion of essential elements and relations. Philosophical theories of language refer to structures of extraordinary complexity. A careful scrutiny of contemporary positions supports Leibniz's remark that philosophers tend to be right in what they affirm and wrong in what they deny or omit. Inadequate theories of language omit or confuse one or more of the dimensions constitutive of language. Inadequate metaphilosophies omit, confuse, or fail to integrate one or more of the modes of discourse about language. In so doing they deny or neglect a distinctively philosophical mode of speech. Chapter VI, "The End of Epistemology," locates the ground of this denial in an imperfect understanding of language and a limited acceptance of linguistic pluralism. The philosophic aspiration for self-knowledge requires a sustained reflection on our own performance. Practitioners of the linguistic turn will remain incomprehensible to themselves until they better understand the medium in which they work and the variety of forms their chosen medium can assume.

6

The End of Epistemology

What would be the effect if knowing and doing were brought into intrinsic connection with each other? What revisions of the traditional theory of mind, thought and knowing would be required and what change in the idea of the office of philosophy would be demanded?[1]

A. The Crack in Tradition

Tradition is the basis of continuity in human time. It is the willed inheritance of the past that illumines the present and future. When it loses its authority, its power to convince and illuminate, the human mind wanders in obscurity.[2] A break in tradition is often the source of cultural crisis, of a division in historical time that separates human beings from what has been and what is to come. The passionate concerns of our ancestors fail to engage us as they formerly engaged our fathers. We have the uneasy sense that projects once fully alive have come to an end; we no longer know our way about.

The heightened philosophical self-consciousness of this century is a sign that our tradition has lost its authority, that we no longer rely on it for firm intellectual guidance. There is a risk, of course, of crying crisis as the hireling in the ancient legend repeatedly called wolf. A balanced knowledge of history is needed to protect against this abuse. But recent assessments of the practice of philosophy seem to converge in the judgment that a historical turning point has been reached, that the philosophical project begun by Descartes has finally run its course and that the time is ripe for something fundamentally new.[3] This judgment rests on the shared conviction that the Cartesian strategy of subduing skepticism through the attainment of certainty has not served the interests of either science or culture. Rather, it has isolated philosophy from fruitful interaction with both. Given Descartes's intention to ground modern culture on a foundation of philosophical truth, this isolation threatens the continuance of the Cartesian project. But the implications of disengagement would be more threatening if that project were identified with the enterprise of modern philosophy itself. Does surrender of the quest for certainty mean more than the death of Cartesianism? How deep is the crack in tradition caused by the widespread rejection of Descartes?

A philosopher's answer to these questions will vary with his vision of the nature and value of the philosophical past. To some, what is now required is a critical appropriation of modernity, a thoughtful assessment of its limitations and achievements. To others, the necessary liberation must be more radical. The tradition should be overcome by deconstructive criticism and then deliberately abandoned. The shared conviction that we stand at a historical benchmark does not preclude conflicting accounts of how we arrived there nor opposing appraisals of where to go next.

The renewed historical awareness provoked by this crisis has had a divisive effect on analytic thought. The central issue concerns the meaning and value of the linguistic turn. Has it put philosophy on the sure path of science by recasting and then solving traditional problems, as Frege and Russell once hoped? Or has its major value been therapeutic, leading to the dissolution of inherited problems and the liberation of culture from the tradition that originally fostered them? Richard Rorty, drawing his inspiration from the later Wittgenstein, has argued persuasively for a therapeutic assessment of the analytic movement. In his anthology, *The Linguistic Turn*, he criticized the scientific aspirations of analytic philosophy while locating them in an historical continuum traceable to Descartes.[4] Rorty was not dismayed by the failure of analytic thinkers to raise philosophy to the level of science, since he viewed that familiar goal as a dialectical dead end, a false start.[5] In Rorty's eyes, the merit of the linguistic turn was that it "succeeded in putting the entire philosophical tradition. . . on the defensive. . . . This achievement is sufficient to place this period among the great ages of the history of philosophy."[6]

In a succeeding work, *Philosophy and the Mirror of Nature*, Rorty was not content to challenge the vitality of the tradition.[7] He now insisted that we permanently destroy it by bringing epistemology, the paradigm instance of modern systematic philosophy, to an end. Following the example of Dewey and Heidegger, whose criticisms of philosophy he greatly valued, Rorty offered his own revisionary account of epistemological history. The purpose of this account was to put the classical problems of knowledge into question on both cultural and technical grounds. If scientific epochs are defined by the theoretical answers they take as paradigmatic, then philosophical epochs should be defined by their outstanding questions and problems.[8] Rorty believes that the most interesting philosophical change occurs not when a new way is found to deal with an old problem but when a new set of problems emerges and old ones begin to fade away.[9] The scandal of modern philosophy is that it took the Cartesian problematic so seriously for so long. By combining the critical insights of recent linguistic philosophy with a subversive pragmatic historicism, Rorty hopes to terminate that scandal and transfigure the philosophical landscape. Polemical resources borrowed from Dewey and the later Wittgenstein give added force to Rorty's sombre vision of the past.

> I should wish to argue that the most important thing that has happened in philosophy in the last thirty years is not the linguistic turn itself but rather the beginning of a thoroughgoing rethinking of certain epistemological difficulties which have troubled philosophers since Plato and Aristotle.... If the traditional spectatorial account of knowledge is overthrown, the account of knowledge which replaces it will lead to reformulations everywhere else in philosophy, particularly in metaphilosophy. Specifically, the contrast between "science" and "philosophy" may come to seem artificial and pointless.[10]

Rorty's power as a critic of epistemology stems from three sources. He has mastered the analytical arguments against empiricism first developed by Sellars and Quine; he has combined the technical facility of linguistic philosophy with a historical range notably lacking in most analytic thought; and he has acquired Wittgenstein's flair for framing unexpected analogies with striking rhetorical force. "To resolve philosophical problems one has to compare things which it never seriously occurred to anyone to compare."[11] *Philosophy and the Mirror of Nature* brings these assembled powers to bear on the theory of knowledge with unnerving effect. Dewey had criticized the epistemological tradition in order to promote a redescription of knowledge in naturalistic terms. Quine's rejection of logical empiricism had opened the way for a naturalized epistemology based on the discoveries of empirical science. But Rorty's purpose is more radical than either of his philosophical allies. He seeks to eliminate epistemology, not to transform it into an empirical discipline. His governing purpose is to liberate philosophical energies from an extended cultural impasse and to release them for more modest and less rigid intellectual tasks. As Dewey predicted, a major change in the idea of knowledge invites a radical reconception of the office of philosophy. Rorty's texts are full of interesting reasons for rejecting our inherited concepts of mind and knowledge as well as the underlying metaphors on which they are based.

Rorty's perspective on the tradition, like Dewey's, is that of the self-conscious outsider. He casts the history of epistemology in a new light and evaluates it by unfamiliar standards. Classical principles and distinctions are subverted by patently genetic arguments. "The best way to revolt against inherited distinctions is to point out that they are imposed by the tradition for specific cultural reasons but have outlived their usefulness."[12] Rorty is piqued by the Kantian assumption that philosophy should serve as the tribunal of culture, passing critical judgment on art, morality, and science. He reverses this conceit by making cultural criteria the measure by which philosophy is judged. The history of epistemology then appears as an episode in European culture to be preserved or abandoned in the light of its cultural vitality and value. Divorced from its assumption of cultural authority, philosophy becomes a single voice in the conversation of humankind, and no longer the decisive arbiter of historical change.

Rorty owes a major debt to Dewey for his iconoclastic reading of history and for his vision of a culture whose primary values are aesthetic. But his strength as a critic is equally dependent on the technical arguments of his analytic peers. Quine's holistic critique of empiricist dogmas, Sellar's attack on the myth of the given, and Wittgenstein's linguistic behaviorism give a depth and detail to Rorty's polemics that make them more formidable than Dewey's. Using the resources of analytic thought, he has refined Dewey's ontological naturalism while retaining his historicist perspective. In outlining a legitimate office for philosophy in a post-epistemological culture, he, together with Wilfred Sellars, has mounted the most forceful American response to the present crisis of tradition.

Although I share Rorty's belief that our tradition has lost its authority, I do not share his desire to destroy it. His strategy is more radical than is necessary and he blurs or rejects distinctions I think should be revised or retained. But I am not unmoved by the power of his historical vision. In this chapter, I shall tell the story of the rise and fall of epistemology as it looks from the intellectual perspective shared by Rorty and his closest allies, Dewey and Wittgenstein. Their perspective, the perspective from which this story is told, is not finally my own, but I have adopted it for the purpose of this reconstructive account and tried to honor its inner coherence and integrity. In Chapter VII, I shall propose a more tempered response to the crisis of philosophy we commonly share.

B. Platonic Imagery and Aristotelian Principles

Forget this transcendent certainty which is connected with your concept of spirit.[13]

The following dialectical narrative is a deliberate attempt to synthesize Dewey's genetic reconstruction of Greek philosophy with Rorty's critical remarks about modern epistemology. Attention is focused on the assumptions and images that traditionally have been linked to the concept of knowledge, and the deliberate interweaving of cultural and technical arguments is intentional. Although the story is designed to "save the ancient appearances," it deliberately casts them in a shadowy light. My own version of epistemological history would be very different from this one, but for present purposes, I have restricted my occasional dissents to the chapter's footnotes.

Socratic-Platonic philosophy originated with the decline of Greek religion. Economic and political changes in Mediterranean culture had combined with the new naturalistic cosmology to weaken the credibility of the inherited religious myths. The sophists appreciated the instability of the mythical tradition and sought to replace theological and cosmic explanations with humanistic ones. They intended to make human beings rather than gods the effective measures of all things. Socrates and Plato vigorously opposed the humanistic relativism of the sophists, but they realized that a secular replacement was needed to assume the cultural functions of Greek religion and poetry. They therefore accepted the sophistic emphasis on rationality and discourse, but they attempted to use reason for conservative ends. They invented philosophy as a discursive rational discipline to legitimize the inherited religious morality.[14] In accepting the primacy of *logos* over *mythos*, they sided with the new and emerging cultural impulse. But in employing reason to justify inherited custom, they revealed the deeper conservative purpose to which they were loyal. Even as they claimed for philosophy epistemic privilege over other human practices, they made its cultural function apologetic rather than critical.[15]

Platonic philosophy sought an ontological guarantee of morality to replace the discredited gods. It found its ontological substitute in the forms or ideas (*eide*) of the middle and late dialogues. These forms were transcendent, atemporal standards of value intended to serve as inflexible measures of human conduct. They were meant to take the place of the divine laws and sanctions that had lost their inherited authority. Because the forms were invisible they could not be readily discovered by ordinary citizens. A special class of men was needed to turn away from the visible world and to apprehend the forms in their undiluted purity and brilliance. These men were the true philosophers who enjoyed exclusive access to the highest objects of knowledge and value. The Platonic philosopher thus became the secular substitute for the Greek priest. His immediate rational intuition of the forms took the place of priestly divination and prophecy.

Platonic philosophy, even more than the mythical tradition it displaced, is based on a series of diremptions that separate the temporal and eternal orders.[16] At the metaphysical level is the fundamental bifurcation between transcendent forms and spatiotemporal things. At the epistemic level is the radical separation of knowledge from opinion. The superiority of knowledge (*episteme*) as a state of the soul derives from the ontological superiority of its object. Because forms, unlike things, are invariant and immutable entities, knowledge has a security and certainty that opinion (*doxa*) lacks. Metaphysical, epistemic, and ethical privilege are correlated eternally for the philosopher in a timeless order protected from change. Because the philosophers enjoy privileged knowledge of these transcendent harmonies, they are properly the rulers of the nonphilosophers with whom they share the city. There is a remarkable symmetry to this many-levelled holistic scheme that finds clearest expression in books six and seven of the *Republic*.[17] In these books, the full range of Platonic dualisms is artistically displayed. In order to survey only the most prominent of these dualisms, consider the following elaborate proportions: Being is to becoming as form is to thing; knowledge is to opinion as certainty is to fallibility; eidetic intuition is to sense perception as intelligible idea is to sensible particular; intellect is to sensibility as the ruling power of the soul is to the faculty ruled; contemplation is to action as eternity is to time; human virtue (*arete*) is to craft (*techne*) as excellence of the soul is to that of the body. The philosopher is to the nonphilosopher as the leisure class of rule is to the laboring class that materially sustains it. In the Platonic scheme of things, social and political hierarchies are invariably justified on ontological and epistemic grounds.[18]

Dewey's startling revision was to invert the Platonic rationale. He claimed that Plato read existing social inequalities based on economic divisions into his supposedly timeless metaphysical scheme. Plato took a transient political and social arrangement and gave it the highest philosophical sanction. He invented an unforgettable myth with exceptional poetic power to legitimize an institutional order favorable to an aristocracy of intellect. To break the grip of this Platonic myth on our historical imagination, we need to create a counter story that reveals the Platonic dualisms in a deliberately unattractive light. The core of the Platonic account is its concept of transcendent immaterial being. The Platonic idea (*eidos*) is said to endure eternally, to be known with certainty, and to provide for the philosopher who intuitively experiences it a permanent standard of value and judgment. Dewey labeled this part of Plato's myth the *spectator theory of knowledge* and traced its origin to the aesthetic encounter with the beautiful and serene.[19]

Two damaging assumptions essential to the myth become part of the classical tradition: That knowledge discloses an invariant reality prior to and independent of the process of inquiry; that the desire to control the quality of temporal objects has no part in the purposes for which we inquire.[20] The explicit aim of Platonic cognition is the conquest of passion by reason in the agonal struggle for the philosopher's soul. The true object of cognition, being essentially immutable, is unaltered by the activity of knowing it. Plato justified the separation of knowing from doing, of contemplation from craft, by appealing to the form's transcendence. But Dewey saw the intellectualism of the spectator theory as a compensation for practical impotence.[21] Aesthetic vision, because it is unable to transform the material environment through action, takes refuge in a domain of poetic fantasy. Here, the ideal exists securely and permanently, without reliance on creative human energies. Lacking the technical capacity to realize ideals in the realm of fact, Plato proposed, instead, that we exemplify them in our souls. The Socratic principle that knowledge is virtue rests on the power of aesthetic vision to transform the psyche of beauty's beholder. The contemplative mind comes gradually to share in the timeless excellence of its object.

Now, beyond question, Plato was a superb poet and a remarkably gifted thinker. He dominated the ensuing tradition of European philosophy by inventing certain images and assumptions to which there seemed no alternative. This intellectual domination has been particularly acute in the field of epistemology. Both Dewey and Rorty traced back to Plato the following important assumptions:

1. That the difference between knowledge and opinion is based on a metaphysical difference in their respective objects.[22]
2. "That the acquisition of knowledge presupposes the presentation of something 'immediately given' to the mind, where the mind is conceived of as a sort of 'immaterial eye' and where 'immediately' means at a minimum without the mediation of language" (the spectator theory of knowing).[23]
3. That the object, organ, and operation of authentic knowledge exist outside of nature and are inaccessible to sensory observation.
4. That theory and practice are mutually exclusive activities requiring different faculties and engaged with ontologically disparate objects.[24]
5. That there is a permanent hierarchy of ontological value and dignity in which being is superior to becoming, knowing to doing, the invariant to the changing, and the contemplative mind to every other human capacity.
6. That the foundations of human cognition are the ideal transcendent forms with which the true philosopher has immediate acquaintance and that propositional knowledge of necessary truths is caused by prior eidetic intuition of these forms.
7. That philosophy, the highest level of theoretical activity, climaxes in intuitive experience of the most perfect being. In contemplating (*theorein*) the supreme reality, the philosopher participates in the blessedness of eternity and achieves the knowledge necessary for the critical judgment of time.

Plato's philosophical successor, Aristotle, was both a disciple and a critic of his master. He articulated the first systematic theory of knowledge under the spell of Platonic imagery and poetry. In Aristotle's epistemology, Platonic images are transformed into explicit principles; aporetic Socratic conversation gives way to a succession of truth claims. The following discussion reveals how Aristotle simultaneously preserved and modified each of the central Platonic assumptions about knowledge.

1. There is a basic distinction between knowledge and opinion but it is not founded on two levels of existence. Opinion differs from knowledge as the man of experience differs from the man of science. Experience knows *that* something is the case; science knows *why* it is so. Although opinion and knowledge concern the same sensible substances, the man of science can explain their existence and properties as the man of opinion cannot. He who genuinely knows can teach. For each object of scientific knowledge, he can produce an essential definition and a demonstration of its necessary attributes. Ultimately, knowledge is related to opinion not as separable form to sensible thing but as the intelligible cause is related to its sensible effect.[25]

2. The mind knows intelligible forms not by confrontation but by identity. Aristotle rejected the Platonic image of an immaterial mind directly intuiting a transcendent form. Although he used the analogy of sight to clarify the act of understanding, he insisted that knowledge occurs through abstraction and not intuition. The Platonic image of the mind as an "immaterial eye" is replaced by the Aristotelian image of the mind as "the place of intelligible forms." Knowledge depends on the existence of a likeness between the knower and the known. The intelligible form is present in the sensible thing under conditions of materiality and individuation. When understanding takes place a numerically distinct but specifically identical form becomes present in the mind under conditions that are immaterial and universal. Through the process of abstracting intelligible forms from sensible images, the mind, which was empty at birth, achieves a modified identity with its object. The human mind by its very nature is open to the substantial forms of all things.

Rorty traced the classical picture of mind as the mirror of nature back to this Aristotelian model.[26] The mind receives the intelligible forms of natural things without altering their properties and without being changed in its own specific nature. To function as the mirror of existence, the mind must be made of the most pure and subtle substance; it must have a glassy essence. Whether we adopt the Platonic image of the mind as directly observing universals or the Aristotelian image of its as receiving intelligible likenesses, we must concede to the organ of knowledge a unique ontological status, unlike that of anything else within the natural order. The ancient metaphysical contrast between mind and body, therefore, has its origin in the epistemic distinction between the faculty for apprehending or abstracting universals and those more limited powers through which we deal with sensible particulars.[27]

A further important corollary should be noted. The epistemological conflict between realism and representationalism is directly suggested by the clash of the two images. In the Platonic picture, the mind knows its object by immediate intellectual vision; on the Aristotelian account, the mind knows its object by receiving an intentional likeness of it. It should be noted, however, that the Aristotelian object of knowledge is not the likeness in the mind but the intelligible form of the sensible substance in nature. Although we know by means of forms in the soul, what we know, in truth, are the natures of corporal things.[28]

3. One of Dewey's strongest criticisms of Plato was that he made the object, organ, and operation of cognition ontologically transcendent and thus unnatural. Dewey's revisionary epistemology had as its central goal the naturalization of knowledge, the incorporation of the entire process of cognition within the physical order.[29] In his effort to naturalize the Platonic theory of knowledge, Dewey had a partial ally in Aristotle. Aristotle agreed with Plato that the proper object of cognition is the intelligible form, but he believed that forms are immanent within the natural order and not transcendent of it. Aristotle accepted the immateriality and immutability of intelligible forms, but he denied their separate existence.

According to Aristotle, the mind is the principle of cognition in the human person. It is the highest power of the intellectual soul that, itself, is the substantial form of the human body. In general, the powers of the soul are seated in bodily organs and rely on organic functioning for their exercise. The operation of the mind in understanding and judgment is a noteworthy exception. Although the object of understanding is the intelligible form of a corporeal object, the act of understanding is independent of any corporeal organ. No part of the body serves intellection as the eye serves sight or the ear hearing. The act of understanding presupposes the existence of corporeal objects and antecedent corporeal operations, but it itself is an immaterial act. The process of human cognition essentially depends on the human body, but the major cognitive power remains, for Aristotle, immaterial.[30]

4. Aristotle carefully distinguished between the activities of the theoretical and the practical intellect.[31] The ground of the distinction is twofold. Theoretical operations are concerned with objects whose

causal structure is invariant; because these objects do what they do always or for the most part, they provide the subject matter of science. The purpose of theoretical science is disinterested knowledge of reality's causal structure. Scientific knowledge, then, leaves its proper object entirely unchanged. What is changed through science is the mind of the inquirer, which becomes like its object in the course of knowing it. The speculative intellect is perfected by intentionally becoming its object, thereby actualizing its essential nature.

The chief practical activities of human beings are making and doing. Both of these activities transform the objects with which they are engaged. Making adds a new durable artifact to the world; *praxis* or action adds a new deed or speech to the political realm. The knowledge required for excellence in practical activities is not disinterested. Truth in the practical order is not sought for its own sake, for the intrinsic perfection of the mind; rather, it is sought as a necessary means to the practical operations that it directs. As theoretical knowledge changes and perfects the mind of the knower, so practice changes the world.

5. Aristotle shared Plato's conviction that the order of being is an order of excellence. His metaphysical scheme extends in a hierarchical pattern from God through the celestial substances to the mortal beings of this earth. On earth, the hierarchical order continues from human beings through the animals and plants until it terminates in inanimate terrestrial things: The most perfect reality, God, is immaterial, and completely actualized. God, the standard of ontological perfection, admits into its nature neither becoming nor change and into its activities neither making nor doing. The Aristotelian God is an eternally actualized contemplative substance, a selfthinking thought.

Every natural substance strives to imitate God in accordance with its nature. Human nature is more complex than that of God, since people have bodies as well as souls and within their souls, vegetative, sensitive, and intellectual powers that require cultivation and development. There is a hierarchy of value within this complexity, so that the soul is more perfect than the body and the intellect more perfect than other human psychic capacities. But Aristotle balanced this hierarchical pluralism of psychic powers with a principle of functional complementarity. The soul depends on the body for its being as the exercise of mind depends on the antecedent performance of lesser psychic operations. In the human case, becoming is for the sake of being, doing for the sake of knowing, and change for the sake of development and virtue. Only in a fully actualized reality like God is change intrinsically an ontological defect. In the human sphere, change is necessary for human actualization and thus serves as an indirect good. But since the ultimate standard of excellence is God and not humankind, the Platonic priorities are essentially sound. The ontological condition of humanity is not the model by which the values of being are measured.[32]

6. Aristotle offered a dual perspective on the foundations of cognition, but he failed to integrate his views into a coherent whole. The primary perspective is *metaphysical*. What are the ontological conditions required for human knowledge? Aristotle's guiding principle is a maxim inherited from the pre-Socratic tradition: Like is known by like.[33] A likeness or identity of form between knower and known is necessary, so that in the process of knowing the known retains its identity while the knower acquires the identity of the known without surrendering its own nature and being. The mind of the knower must be *like* a mirror in that it actualizes its own nature in the very act of reflecting the nature of its objects. If the foundations of cognition are understood as the metaphysical conditions required for knowledge, then Aristotle's foundational thesis holds that there must be knowable things constituted by intelligible forms and there must be intelligent minds that can abstract and receive the forms of the known. Aristotle's theory of cognition, in large measure, is a direct extension of his metaphysical categories to the special case of human understanding.[34]

From the *logical* perspective, Aristotle conceived of science (*episteme*) as a systematic order of truths about a determinate subject matter. The fundamental distinction among scientific truths is between the demonstratively prior and posterior. In the order of inquiry, the last truths to be discovered are the axioms and definitions of a discipline. But in the order of demonstration, these truths have an explanatory priority. They serve as the base or foundation for deductive demonstration of the discipline's theorems. Logically speaking, the axioms and definitions of a science are its foundational principles. We shall call these *the logical foundations of knowledge* to distinguish them from the metaphysical constituents of intelligent mind and intelligible nature. The science of logic has its own basic principles in the axioms of identity and noncontradiction; they serve as universal principles regulating the intelligibility of predication and judgment.

Aristotle's epistemology would be strengthened considerably if the connecting ties between the metaphysical and the logical analyses of knowledge were drawn more carefully.[35]

7. Aristotle and Plato shared the belief that the best human life is philosophical. It is the life closest to the divine; it achieves the purest realization of human nature. As a complex activity, philosophy involves human beings in public argument and discussion and in private reflective study, but it attains its climax in the contemplative understanding of God. Theoretical activity is humanity's highest attainment, and the supreme theoretical act is the contemplation of the divine nature and all things in their relation to God. This is the wisdom that, by their nature, all persons seek. If the nature of a being is revealed in its *telos* or perfected state, then human nature is best described as that of a mortal god. Human beings share mortality with all other terrestrial substances, but they share contemplative activity with the divine alone.[36]

Despite Aristotle's evident effort to modify the Platonic principles, deep lines of continuity can be discerned between them. Both of them think of the human mind as a unique psychological power whose uniqueness is required to explain the possibility of cognition. Both of them view theoretical knowledge as a disinterested achievement that connects human beings with the gods rather than the beasts. Both of them identify philosophy as the highest cultural activity, to which all other human practices are subordinate. The enduring influence of these beliefs burdens Western thought with an excessive intellectualism that effectively separates the finest human knowledge from world transforming power. Greek philosophers sought to conquer their own natures through the achievement of theoretical knowledge but their intellectual virtues left the material world essentially unchanged. In this respect, the experience of the aesthetic observer is given precedence over that of the productive artisan. In both Plato and Aristotle there is a profound reluctance to honor the labor of the body and the work of the hands, through which life is sustained and the world transformed.[37]

C. The New Way of Ideas

The decline in credibility of Greek religion was the occasion for the Platonic initiative, an initiative consolidated by Aristotle and systematized in his classical theory of science. By the late sixteenth century, a new tradition had formed out of Hebraic and Christian as well as Hellenic sources. It attempted to synthesize the theological beliefs of the Christian religion with the cosmological and metaphysical theories of Aristotle. The stability of this synthesis was shaken by the Protestant Reformation and the occurrence of the Scientific Revolution. Neither the Christian Church nor Aristotle ever again held such cultural authority.

The modern philosophical project can be usefully understood on the model of the ancient experience. Once again, philosophy offered itself as a secular replacement for theology and religion. But the originating spirit of modern thought was critical rather than conservative. Representatives of the new science actively sought liberation from ecclesiastical and scholastic authority. They began to shape an independent cultural realm governed by reason rather than by faith and tradition. The methodically purified reason celebrated by Descartes in the *Discourse on Method* was an explicit secular substitute for a weakened traditional faith.

A crisis in traditional belief often stimulates original minds but such minds are clearly the exception. The great majority of people experience varying degrees of deception, doubt, and disbelief. At least for a time, they are pulled toward skepticism. The religious and philosophical disarray that prevailed in Western Europe throughout the seventeenth century generated skeptical doubts of unprecedented depth. The new Galilean science challenged more than the ancient cosmology and the Aristotlian physics. It explicitly undermined the common human faith in the truth-revealing capacity of the senses.[38] If the new science correctly described the real structure of nature, then the sensible world of waking life must be a dream, a web of illusory appearance. Descartes seized upon the motif of dreams and illusions in order to accelerate the process of cultural change. If the world disclosed to our senses and confirmed by traditional belief is a dream world, then it has no authority over those who are awake. The function of the new physics was to release human beings from the ancient dream about nature and reveal to their reason its true being. The constructive intention of Cartesian thought has two related objectives: to secure a realm of autonomous reason where ecclesiastical authority and traditional philosophy no longer rule; and to legitimate Galilean science by demonstrating the certainty and truth of its geometrical vision of nature. Descartes framed the project of modernity so that the enlightenment ideal of secular autonomy was yoked to an epistemological thesis about the nature and purpose of scientific theory.[39]

The puzzles and perplexities of modern philosophy received memorable expression in the Cartesian texts, especially the *Meditations*. All of Descartes's successors have wrestled with the philosophical and cultural problems he created and then struggled to resolve. Dewey believed that Cartesian philosophy failed because Descartes had not been sufficiently modern. He attempted to comprehend seventeeth-century science, self-consciously novel in both its method and content, with the aid of epistemological principles inherited from the classical Greeks. Despite his avowed radicalism, Descartes did not break cleanly from ancient prejudices. In describing the object and aim of science, Descartes was a bona fide representative of modernity; but his theory of the organ and operation of cognition was hopelessly archaic. By making the subject matter of science temporal becoming rather than eternal being, he naturalized the cognitive object. And he qualified his inherited intellectualism with openly pragmatic themes: knowledge and power were identified; successful theories were to be confirmed by their fruits and works.

Where, then, according to Dewey, did Descartes go wrong? In his theory of the mind and its operations.[40] He shifted the ideality and value Plato had assigned to the object of science to the cognitive subject and the process of cognition. He removed mind entirely from the natural world and located its operations and ideas in a realm of such epistemic privacy that no one but their individual subjects could observe them. Cut off from nature and the powers of the body, the operations of mind were reduced to viewing (intuition) and willing. Descartes rehabilitated the classical spectator theory but modified its epistemic import. The immediate objects of the mind's intuition were no longer Platonic ideas but Cartesian ones.[41] Plato's ideas had been mind-independent transcendent forms, the exemplary objects of theoretical cognition. Cartesian ideas were dependent mental particulars antecedently caused by objects external to the mind in which the ideas reside. Their epistemic function was to represent these objects, which were veiled from the mind's direct acquaintance by the very ideas they caused to come into being. The first task of rational inquiry was to distinguish which of the mind's mediating ideas correctly represented the external world. When the spectator theory of knowing is coupled with a representational model of awareness, how can such a distinction possibly be made? By the defining conditions of the problem, the mind can never compare the internal representation with what it represents externally in order to determine its accuracy. But if the mind cannot tell which of its many ideas are true, then the unavoidable conclusion appears to be skepticism. The potential irony of the Cartesian project is thereby revealed. Will Descartes's concentrated effort to conquer skepticism only increase its sway over modern minds? Will his hyperbolic doubt undertaken for the sake of certainty only create a permanent atmosphere of distrust?

Both Dewey and Rorty agreed that the ruling purpose of modern philosophy was to silence permanently the epistemic skeptic. By making skepticism global and unlimited, Descartes hoped to destroy it once and for all. Once radical doubt was applied to all received beliefs, the attainment of certainty became a matter of singular urgency. Only the discovery of indubitable truth could remove the philosophical initiative from the malignant demon, the nightmare figure of modern epistemology. Descartes's discovery of the mind as the locus of epistemic indubitability served both of his constructive intentions. It certified the mind's independence as an autonomous agent of scientific cognition and it provided a conclusive answer to the skeptical challenge.

As Rorty has noted, it is important to distinguish between the ancient and the Cartesian conceptions of mind. Both Plato and Aristotle effectively contrasted mind (*nous*) with sensibility, the other major human cognitive power. Mind is the soul's faculty for the intuition or reception of intelligible forms. Sense is the psychic faculty for the perception of changing temporal particulars. Intellect and sense are complementary forms of human awareness, differentiated by their intentional operations and objects. The Cartesian mind, by contrast, is the seat of consciousness generally. It is the ego or subject of human awareness as such and not the specific faculty of the person whose proper activity is understanding and judgment. For Descartes, the mind is no longer contrasted with sensibility but with the human body as a whole.[42] Ontologically speaking, a mind is a thinking thing (res cogitans) and a body is an extended thing (res extensa). Each is defined so that it lacks the characteristic proper to the other. For both Plato and Aristotle, the immateriality of mind was a derivative property flowing from its essential function of understanding intelligible forms. For Descartes, the mind's immateriality and consciousness were equally essential and mutually entailed. The contrast between intellect and sense is reduced to the difference within consciousness between clear and distinct representations and those that are vague and unclear.

Epistemically speaking, Descartes's position was even more radical. The ancient philosophers had argued that God and the soul were the most difficult realities for a human being to know. Although first in the order of ontological excellence, they were the last in the order of human inquiry. But Descartes contended that the individual mind provides for its subject a realm of ideas in which error is impossible. When the mind refrains from judgments about external realities and confines its attention to its own operations and ideas, it cannot be deceived.[43] The mind has an infallible awareness of whatever it immediately examines, such that, were it to restrict its knowledge claims to objects of intuitive inspection, its judgments would be invariably true.

If this claim for the mind's self-certainty were sustained, Descartes would have defeated global skepticism, but the problem of the external world would still remain. The alleged infallibility of judgments about the ego's ideas does not extend to claims about their representative accuracy. How are the true Galilean ideas about nature to be distinguished from their Aristotelian rivals? Without a satisfactory answer to this question, the legitimation of the new physics has not yet been achieved. Descartes's solution to the problem created by his representational theory of mind won few adherents. He believed that the mind, after critical inspection of its ideas, could select those among them which were indubitable and, therefore, certainly true. He postulated the occurrence of self-authenticating[44] intuitions that could determine the truth-value of an idea merely by examining its representative content. Supposedly, the mind could determine the truth of an idea by inspection of its phenomenal properties; all ideas possessing clarity and distinctiveness assuredly are true. When the spectatorial account of knowledge was joined to Descartes's representative theory of consciousness the logical result should have been solipism. It is a sign of Descartes's deep confusion that he found in this hybrid conjunction an alleged solution to skepticism about the external world.

For Descartes, scientific knowledge is the logically ordered system of true ideas that accurately represents the causal order in nature. Each idea in the system must either be evidently true or be sequentially related to true ideas through a succession of operations that evidently preserve truth. Science achieves a perfect correspondence between the humanly ordered pattern of ideas in the mind and the divine order of things in the world. To construct a systematic order of truths, the mind must identify those elemental ideas and axioms whose truth value can be determined by a single self-authenticating act. These privileged internal representations are the foundations of Cartesian science.[45] Being indubitable, they provide a permanent repository of truth that is immune from epistemic revision. They also provide the self-evident principles required for a system of knowledge modeled on deductive geometry. The task of foundational epistemology is to discover these ultimate truths, to establish their certainty, and then to erect the edifice of knowledge upon them. In this way, philosophy legitimates the objective validity of natural science and secures its claim to knowledge of reality. In these privileged representations, philosophy possesses a litmus test for all possible interpretations of the world. The epistemic validity of every system of ideas is determined by its coherence or conflict with the foundational truths of Cartesian science.

Although Descartes overturned the basic principles of Aristotelian cosmology, he considered the foundational ideas of the new physics to be permanently secure. Cartesian mechanics was intended to be the final epistemic revolution at the axiomatic level. The tree of science could grow progressively upward because it rested on secure philosophical roots.

Descartes's theory of science was a mixture of ancient and modern principles. In its logical structure, its correspondence theory of truth, and its insistence on immaterial cognitive operations, it retained classical themes, though in a significantly altered form. But in its rejection of tradition, its reliance on hyperbolic doubt, its radical distrust of the senses, its concept of representative awareness, its ontological and epistemic assumptions about mind, and in its espousal of theoretical pragmatism, it was distinctively modern. It combined the ocular imagery of Plato with the receptive intellect of Aristotle, the classical language of substance and essence with the modern idiom of the veil of ideas and the external world. Seen in retrospect, it was an eclectic amalgam of things old and new, jumbled together in the name of clarity and certainty. This was a philosophical mixture far too powerful to ignore but so thoroughly confused that it took centuries to unravel. Descartes formulated the set of problems that dominated the horizon of modern thought; though he could not solve the problems he created, his model of a solution cast a spell over everyone who tried.

From the time of Aristotle to the appearance of Descartes, metaphysics was the preeminent philosophical discipline. Questions of knowledge were regularly cast in metaphysical terms and resolved by appeal to its universal principles. It is a measure of Descartes's historical significance that he overturned this state of affairs. He made ideas rather than things the starting point of philosophical reflection and thus subordinated metaphysics to the theory of knowledge. Classical theories of the mind had been based on a prior understanding of forms as the object of human cognition. In modernity this order was reversed. Judgments about the mind and the epistemic value of its contents effectively determined the solution to metaphysical problems. The self-reflective, methodically purified mind of the solitary individual, in effect, had become the measure of all things.

D. Kant's Transcendental Turn

The things that pass for epistemology all assume
that knowledge is not a natural function or event
but a mystery.[46]

It is important at this juncture in our story to repeat that I am narrating the history of epistemology from an external perspective. I am trying to capture the critical perception of this discipline common to Dewey and Rorty, thinkers who wanted to reform the theory of knowledge or to eliminate it altogether. Thus, the presentation of Kant that follows is not cast in exclusively Kantian terms. Kant's central position in the history of epistemology is recognized; yet, given a critical assessment of that history, such recognition clearly is ambivalent. The story is complicated further by an ultimate difference in purpose between our two critics. Dewey wanted to naturalize epistemology by transforming it into the empirical theory of inquiry. Experimental logic, his name for that theory, would jettison many of the assumptions of the traditional discipline, but it would preserve the philosophical centrality of knowledge. Dewey proposed to reconstruct philosophy on the foundation of his new logic. He thus retained a community of purpose with the traditional theorists he opposed. Rorty's objective clearly is more radical. He intended to deconstruct epistemology and eventually to bury it. He proposes the elimination of the problems that haunted Descartes rather than their resolution. As a result, Kant figures less favorably in his version of the story than in Dewey's, though there is considerable overlap in many of their judgments. I shall begin this stage of the narrative by rehearsing the perceptions of Kant that they share and then indicate the chief respect in which their critical perspectives diverge.

For Kant, the proper function of philosophy was the critique of reason. Enlightenment culture had accepted reason as a secular replacement for a unified religious faith. Its leading representatives, the *philosophes*, hoped to overcome the institutional order of Europe through rational criticism of its legitimating beliefs and to replace it with a new order whose foundational principles were those of modernity. The claim of reason to cultural sovereignty was based on its striking success in natural science. Descartes had hoped that pure theoretical reason, liberated from the weight of tradition and authority, could achieve demonstrative knowledge of nature and man. He adopted the strategy of hyperbolic doubt to validate scientific theory, but the unintended effect of that strategy was to strengthen the spirit of skepticism. Skepticism about the power of reason found eloquent expression in the writing of David Hume, who shared the secular ideals of the enlightenment but lacked its faith in reason's constructive capacity. Hume learned from Descartes and Pascal the critical force of reason and applied that lesson with equal skill to both ancient and modern theories. Appearing at the climax of the Enlightenment, Kant believed that both Descartes and Hume represented unacceptable extremes: Descartes, because he promised more than human reason could ever deliver; Hume, because he slandered reason's powers and promised nothing. An enlightened age demanded a critique of reason that would establish, on a basis of strict principles and arguments, the scope and limits of rational power. Although Kant rejected Descartes's rational psychology, he shared the Cartesian confidence in a reason's capacity for self-knowledge. The faculties, a priori content, and distinctive operations of reason could be known with apodictic certainty.[47]

Kant accepted the classical ideal of theoretical science as true, certain knowledge of causal necessity. To refute Hume's academic skepticism, he intended to demonstrate *that* and *how* pure mathematics and natural science satisfied these classical norms. Euclidean geometry and Newtonian physics were to be permanently secured as theoretical achievements. The critical investigation of reason would put them beyond the reach of skepticism forever. But the same critique that legitimated mathematical physics supported Hume's skeptical doubts about *transcendent* metaphysics. Knowledge of the *transcendental* conditions of science revealed the impossibility of knowledge beyond the range of confirming intuition.[48] Although human reason had an ineradicable need to *think* beyond the limits of knowledge, these thoughts could never satisfy the requirements of theoretical science. In demonstrating the failure of metaphysics, the most honored philosophical discipline, Kant created a successor discipline to replace it. Transcendental epistemology assumed the position in Kant's philosophical architectonic that metaphysics had occupied in Aristotelian thought. It was conceived as a rigorous science of pure reason that would articulate the necessary conditions and evaluate the validity of every epistemic claim. It would establish rigorously when the criteria of science had been met and when, in principle, they could not be satisfied.

By setting strict limits to theoretical knowledge, Kant left room for rational faith in the territory of ethics and theology. While validating the autonomy of theoretical reason, he also curtailed its scope of operation. Kant did not want to eliminate belief from its appropriate place in human life. His purpose, rather, was to put an end to modern uncertainty by strictly defining the boundaries of knowledge and belief and guarding them against trespass by one another. Kant thus restored the ontological difference between knowledge and opinion, but he reversed the traditional Platonic hierarchy. For Kant, human knowledge is restricted to the realm of sensible appearance; the ontologically prior noumenal realities forever elude our theoretical grasp. The most important matters in human life, those on which the practice of morality rests, are matters of faith. As a theoretical discipline, philosophy can clear the ground for faith, but it can never take possession of it. Human dignity does have its source in reason, but the reason that establishes our unconditional worth is practical not theoretical. The most liberating insight critical philosophy offers to an age of enlightenment is that science poses no threat to the freedom required by the moral life.

Kant's philosophical vision has a grandeur often obscured by the complex detail of his thought. The human purpose of the Kantian texts, like those of Wittgenstein, frequently is lost in the passionate effort to follow the line of argument.[49] Neither Dewey nor Rorty in their references to Kant attempted a careful exegesis of his work. Their concern was solely with his historical contribution to the history of epistemology. They focused on Kant because he changed the inherited concepts of mind and knowledge and redesigned the architecture of philosophy. In each instance they wanted to preserve his critical arguments without endorsing the successor concepts he proposed.

The Kantian theory of mind was designed to reconcile the insights of empiricists and rationalists. It recognized three cognitive faculties—sensibility, understanding, and reason—and three types of representations—intuitions, concepts, and ideas. It distinguished the different types of representations by appeal to their genetic origin and cognitive function. In the theory, pure intuitions, concepts, and ideas are innate possessions of the mind; empirical representations are acquired through the functioning of human receptive sensibility. Kant corrected the modern tendency to blur the difference in kind between concepts and intuitions, and he insisted on their interdependence for the achievement of cognition. "Concepts without intuitions are empty; intuitions without concepts are blind."[50]

The novel features of Kant's theory are these:

   1. It restricts the activity of intuition to sensibility and explicitly denies

the possibility of intuitive intellectual acts. Ocular imagery is preserved in Kant but it is withdrawn from the depiction of intellect. The assimilation of understanding to a quasi-visual power is rejected with the attendant denial of any intellectual encounter with transcendent reality. In this respect, Kant's theory of mind is overtly anti-Platonic.

2. Kant preserved the receptive aspect of human cognition but he limited receptivity to the faculty of sense. He thus denied Aristotle's thesis that human understanding can receive intelligible forms; this breaks the back of the mirror imagery based on the Aristotelian concept of the receptive intellect.[51]

3. He rejected the Cartesian assertion that the mind can know itself through immediate inspection. The pure a priori representations and operations of the mind are not available for external or internal viewing; they must be discovered through a process of transcendental inference. The character of the mind may be known only through its distinctive operations. Because these operations are not open to intuitive inspection, we must infer their nature and order from the epistemic objects and products they make possible.

4. Although Kant failed to break cleanly with the spectator theory of knowledge, he denied that immediate sensory intuitions are ever sufficient for cognition. Human intuitions without concepts and judgments are always blind.

5. A new image of the intellect is proposed within the general framework of representationalism, that of the mind as a constructive and synthetic power. The discrete empirical intuitions received by sensibility need to be synthesized into coherent and unified objective wholes. The pure concepts of the understanding are rules of synthesis that ensure the automatic and invariant performance of this task. There is an unfortunate tendency, owing to Kant's reliance on the idiom of representations, to blur the difference between the mind's constructive formation of propositional judgments and its fabrication of perceptual objects.[52] This confusion weakens Kant's general insight that knowledge is a relation between persons and judgments rather than a perceptual encounter between minds and things. Although Kant used the empiricists' idiom of experience, he made pure a priori concepts and intuitions a necessary condition of any perceptual occurrence that qualifies as cognitive.

6. Relying on the metaphor of constructive mind, Kant inverted but failed to abandon the correspondence theory of knowledge. His Copernican revolution in the eyes of his critics therefore is a half-hearted affair. In order to account for true synthetic judgments about nature known a priori, Kant reasoned that there must be a

necessary conformity between knower and known. But he denied the assumption of Aristotle and Descartes that the form or representation in the intellect must correspond to the independent nature of the thing known. What if, instead, the object of knowledge must conform to the a priori representations in the mind? That would permanently ensure for every object of cognition invariant features of a structural or relational character. At one stroke, it would permit a *transcendental* metaphysics of empirical objects and rigorously exclude a *transcendent* categorization of things in themselves. Because the pure Kantian categories are rules of constructive synthesis, his version of the correspondence theory, unlike those of Descartes and Locke, cannot involve a literal resemblance between idea and object. Kant, like Aristotle before him, supported a notion of epistemic correspondence incompatible with the original-copy model favored by his immediate predecessors. In fact, Kant's theory is profoundly Aristotelian in structure, though the source of intelligibility now resides in the transcendental subject rather than in mind-independent things. In Aristotle's epistemic realism, the natural world informs the mind of the knower; in Kant's critical idealism, the transcendental subject informs the phenomenal world with its relational structure and unity.[53]

7. Kant retained the traditional epistemological emphasis on the foundations of knowledge but he clarified what had been obscured in the representationalist tradition. The privileged representations on which science rests are not intuitions or concepts but judgments. They are neither caused by immediate acquaintance with intelligible forms nor validated in self-authenticating intuitions. Kant's foundational principles are pure propositional representations, innate rules of the mind that it imposes on nature in its constitutive function as nature's legislator. Like all the mind's a priori possessions, they are assumed by Kant to be invariant, unrevisable, and universally valid. They admit no development and compete with no rivals.

8. By rejecting the transcendent metaphysics of the Greeks, the speculative theology of the medievals, and the rational psychology of the moderns, Kant often appeared to his contemporaries as the great destroyer of traditional philosophy. This was not his self-perception. He thought that he had discovered a rigorous philosophical science carefully distinguished from both mathematics and physics. Kant introduced transcendental epistemology, the scientific critique of reason, as the permanent guardian and judge of the domain of knowledge. Critical philosophy should ensure that the rigor of science is observed strictly, but it should also defend the

realms of human life in which theoretical reason has no rightful claim.

Dewey welcomed many of Kant's departures from the epistemological tradition: the rejection of intellectual intuitions and ocular imagery, the adoption of constructive metaphors for the mind, the subordination of theoretical to practical purposes. But he claimed that Kant did not extricate himself sufficiently from the tradition he criticized. In particular, Kant shared its lack of historical consciousness. This was apparent in his passion for epistemic certainty, his insistence on invariant categories and principles, and his absolutist treatment of Enlightenment science. What Dewey found lacking in Kant he discovered later in Hegel, the first philosopher fully to honor temporal becoming and change.

Dewey also opposed Kant's withdrawal of reason from nature and its relocation within the transcendental ego.[54] As Dewey saw it, Kant had mystified the process of cognition by divorcing its operations from biological and social occurrences in space and time. The Kantian epistemic subject, the pure ego, is the transcendental source of nature; its acts of constructive synthesis bring into being the empirical world. Transcendental epistemology has for its subject matter an extranatural, extraempirical subjectivity, to which neither the forms of intuition nor the Kantian categories themselves apply. By naturalizing the mind and its operations, Dewey preserved the constructive emphasis of Kantian psychology but lessened its ontological import. The mind does not create the natural world, but is itself the evolutionary outcome of natural processes over time. Its constructive function is re-creative rather than creative. The mind guides the re-creative operations through which human beings transform the world with the aim of more fully enjoying it.

With the cognitive subject relocated in nature, Dewey believed that many of the basic Kantian dualisms would dissolve. The sharp dichotomies between pure and empirical sources of knowledge, a priori and a posteriori forms of cognition, and noumenal and phenomenal modes of existence do not make sense within a comprehensive naturalism. The idiom of ideas can be retained but it should be separated from the representational framework Kant had inherited from Descartes. The ideas that regulate cognitive operations are not innate possessions of an atemporal ego but practical suggestions for the solution of specific historical problems. They are conscious and artful proposals for reorganizing the human environment, not rules for the constitution of the natural world.[55]

The final benefit of converting from transcendental to experimental logic is that the life of the mind becomes a matter for public inspection. Cognitive activity becomes a species of observable behavior, as subject to empirical scrutiny as any other form of organic activity. When knowledge is examined behaviorally, it loses the aura of mystery that philosophers since

Plato had imposed on it and which Kant, more than anyone else, perhaps, had strongly reinforced.

Rorty shares Dewey's desire to demystify the facts of knowledge. He welcomes his robust historicism and his rejection of metaphysical dualism. But he is leery of one aspect of Dewey's strategy. Rorty thinks that we do not need an empirical science of inquiry to replace transcendental epistemology and to perform the cultural functions Kant had assigned to it. The cultural practices of modernity can take care of themselves perfectly well. Behavioral description of epistemic activity, certainly is legitimate, but its appropriate purpose is to release us from inherited pictures and metaphors that surround the facts of cognition with an impenetrable haze. We do not need a successor science to take the place of epistemology, nor a metaphysical redescription of mind and its object, nor the assimilation of human inquiry to the adaptive behavior of lower animals. Instead, we require a deliberate rejection of the very idea of a *philosophical theory of knowledge*. There is no foundational discipline that rationally governs the turbulent history of intellectual change. There is simply the extravagant myth of this enterprise first invented by Plato in the *Republic*, a myth that has unfortunately become part of philosophy's self-image.

E. A New Concept of Secular Reason

The superior enlightenment on which the moderns prided themselves was credited to the exercise of secular reason. The ideal of the new humanism was an institutional order founded on principles of reason and progressively satisfying rational norms. Kant's critique set limits to the achievement of theoretical reason, but it essentially preserved the classical theory of science. Kant recognized that practical reason could not satisfy theoretical require- ments but he insisted that the moral law share the exceptionless rigor of the laws of nature. Pure reason, whether theoretical or practical, was a source of universally binding laws to which all rational beings were subject. It was the ground of whatever is a priori in human life.

In the *Discourse on Method*, Descartes provisionally distinguished the norms of theoretical and practical reason, the first requiring metaphysical but the second merely moral certitude. Theoretical reason, if it adheres to Cartesian canons, should only assent to ideas that are indubitably true. The policies of practical reason, by contrast, are based on probability rather than certainty. Practical judgments endorse whatever course of action is most likely to secure desired goods. But Descartes anticipated an emergent historical future in which theoretical reason would effectively guide human practice. Indubitable knowledge of nature's laws would then regulate practical activity, raising the condition of human beings to that of lords and possessors of nature.

When the mechanical arts are founded on scientific principles, the ancient human longing to control natural forces at last would be satisfied, not by magic but by science.

There is a tension in Descartes's *Discourse* between two conceptions of the purpose of reason. Descartes inherited the Greek theoretical ideal that knowledge is an end in itself, and he apparently subscribed to that principle during the provisional separation of theory and practice. But in the concluding sections of the *Discourse*, he supported Bacon's union of knowledge with power and his pragmatic suggestion that fruits and works are the ultimate test of a theory's truth. It is characteristic of Descartes's eclecticism that he blithely juxtaposed classical canons of science with pragmatic criteria of technical control. The text as a whole does not make clear which is the true norm of Cartesian rationality, epistemic certainty or practical effectiveness.

Descartes's ambivalence about the normative standards of reason deeply affects the modern interpretation of science. If the theoretical discoveries of science must be certain and indubitable, then the skeptic's reservations about their epistemic validity are warranted. If the canons of rationality require that all beliefs pass the test of hyperbolic doubt, then few, if any, of the conclusions of modern science would survive. The skeptic who adopts the Cartesian ideal of certainty as the true standard of reason can put all of modern science and practice into question. But if the test of rationality is an increase in practical security, rather than the permanent attainment of certainty, then our appraisal of the scientific enterprise clearly will be more favorable. Skeptical doubts about the rationality of science are blunted when a pragmatic conception of reason becomes the norm. Rational judgments within a pragmatic context are comparative appraisals of conflicting beliefs; they no longer require the submission of truth-claims to the extravagant epistemic standards imposed by Descartes.

Dewey believed that the self-understanding of the Enlightenment had been distorted by the Kantian and Cartesian theories of reason. Modern culture appealed to reason as the source of its distinction and merit but its actual rational practice diverged from philosophical requirements. When skeptics judged the achievements of modernity by philosophical standards, they questioned their claim to embody complete rationality. But when practical persons examined the normative standards of philosophy, they challenged their right to intellectual authority. Dewey's reconstructive aim was to undermine the authority of the inherited theories of reason and to legitimate the pragmatic, experimental reason already at work in modern science and industry. Once the required bond between reason and certainty had been broken, the isolation of reason from economic and social activity would lose its justification. Only that isolation had given plausibility to the Cartesian picture of a solitary ego or to Kant's transcendental subject with its invisible world constituting operations. The lingering self-doubts of modernity could not be overcome until a new concept of secular reason had been formulated and openly defended. Its differences from traditional theories of reason were numerous and unmistakable. For Dewey, reason is social rather then solitary, historically rooted rather than timeless, experimental and pragmatic rather than theoretical, and empirically surveyable rather than hidden in its constructive operations. Dewey's experimental logic advocates a revolution in the understanding of the human mind.

On what grounds did Dewey justify his appeals for radical change? He held that knowledge of a thing's nature comes only through a study of its functions. We learn what modern reason *is* through investigating what it *does*. Logic is the descriptive science of the operations of reason, and contemporary logical theory is the ground on which major philosophical differences are gathered together and focused.[56] The historic isolation of human cognition from nature had been the result of defective logical theories. A revised experimental logic based on the model of empirical science would undercut that isolation and the inherited dualisms to which it gave support. Dewey believed that the received distinctions between mind and body, knowing and doing, being and becoming, science and craft no longer were tenable in the light of modern intellectual practice. The philosophical tradition had converted functional differences within the comprehensive context of human inquiry into rigid conceptual oppositions. Classical theories of knowledge had concealed the profound continuity between the organic adaptations of animals to the natural environment and the purposive conduct of rational agents. Cognitive operations had been separated from bodily events; the cognitive object had been isolated from temporal becoming. Dewey's logic was designed to prove that human inquiry should be conceived as a continuum. The operations of inquiry are ontologically continuous with biological processes.[57] The method of investigating reason is continuous with experimental method, whose features are writ large in scientific practice.[58]

Dewey identified philosophy with the study and criticism of rational practice. By his lights, modern philosophy was a failure because it used Greek images and concepts to interpret distinctively modern practices, particularly in the field of science. To dramatize his criticism, he constructed the model of an opposing logical theory to serve as a foil for his own account of reason. This counterlogic, which he labeled *the spectator theory of knowledge*, was a particular version of naive realism, blending the classical commitment to an invariant cognitive object with the Cartesian image of knowing as looking. According to the spectator theory, human reason is a passive contemplator of timeless and invariant objects, and human knowing is the result of gazing directly at those objects until a representative likeness of them is imprinted on the knower's mind. Although modern scientific practice bore no relation to this ocular model, the prevailing logical theories had failed to adjust to this evident disparity.

The distinctive feature of scientific inquiry is its active experimental character. Dewey chose experimental science as his example of rational activity, and he constructed a general theory of reason around this model. He was deeply impressed by the analogies between scientific method and the process of making or building. His logical theory, which conceives of knowing as a species of doing, has as its polemical target the spectator theory and as its guiding model the experimental procedures of science.

The core of Dewey's experimental logic is his notion of the pattern of inquiry.[59] He believed that this pattern was omnipresent in rational conduct but clearest in the practice of science. Human inquiry always begins with a problematic situation arising out of lived experience. Individual and collective life present an authentic problem when they fail to satisfy an actively felt desire, interest, or need. The purpose of inquiry is to resolve these troubling situations by actively transforming them under the direction of practical ideas. The occasion and enduring focus of inquiry is a concrete problem situation embedded in a context of familiar experience.[60]

The second phase of inquiry is the analytic resolution of the difficulty: The troubling features of the original situation are identified, and strategies are proposed for remedying them. Dewey called these strategies of action *hypotheses* or *ideas*. Rational ideas are proposed policies of conduct conceived in response to particular problems and aimed at their solution. Ideas normally arise together with alternatives, and the task of critical reason is to choose the best of the available options.

The third phase of inquiry is the active reconstruction of the original situation through overt operations guided by the preferred idea. Experimental actions causally transform the surrounding environment; the rational ideas guiding those actions are tested by putting them directly into practice. The investigating subject who has embraced the proposed course of action deliberately reshapes the surrounding world.

In inquiry's final phase, the adequacy of the directive idea is evaluated by determining whether the transformed situation now satisfies the original purpose. If the enacted change is successful, the idea is endorsed as true. The effective solution of the problem completes the cycle of inquiry but not without cumulative effect. Successful ideas are retained as guides to later action and as tested maxims of experience useful in the solution of future problems.

In Dewey's logic, the rational subject is the human organism consciously adjusting to changes in its complex environment. The operations of reason are that subject's concrete attempts to restructure the environment as a locus of personal satisfaction. The objects of knowledge are the resulting changes in the world brought about through these rational transactions. Despite his differences with Kant, Dewey could agree with the central Kantian maxim: "We only know what we have made after a plan of our own."[61]

Dewey's logic is intended to explain the confusions in traditional theories of knowledge. On his account, earlier logics were based on the selective extraction of particular factors in the pattern of inquiry from the comprehensive whole that provides them with meaning.[62] These factors are misunderstood when isolated from the temporal antecedents and consequences that qualify their contribution to the structure as a whole. Dewey's pragmatic logic is meant to liberate modernity from the idealism, intellectualism, and realism of earlier theories of science. Idealism is a mistaken theory of rational operations; intellectualism, a distorted account of the motive and purpose of inquiry; realism, a false description of the objects of knowledge and their epistemic relation to rational ideas. What are the pragmatic alternatives?

Against the idealist theory of immaterial mental acts known through introspection or transcendental reflection, Dewey opposed a naturalistic account of cognitive operations. The operations of mind are overt physical actions directed by the organism's practical ideas. These actions are intelligent because they are performed consciously and deliberately, but they are no longer mysterious and shadowy because their occurrence is open to direct public scrutiny. Against the intellectualism that distinguishes the desire to know from other human appetites and makes the discovery of an antecedent reality the final purpose of science, Dewey opposed a pragmatic account of rational purpose. The governing purposes of inquiry are not finally cognitive. Inquiry is an active mediating process between troubling immediate experiences and reconstructed alternatives that are richer in meaning and aesthetic quality. We appraise inquiry by judging its outcome in the light of noncognitive standards. The purpose of science, and of rational activity generally, is to increase human control over nature without relying on fate, fortune, or the blessings of divine providence. It is to assume active responsibility for our temporal destiny on the earth. Against the realism that looks to science for disclosure of a reality antecedent to inquiry and that tests ideas by their fidelity to this mind-independent given, Dewey opposed an instrumentalist account of scientific ideas.[63] The objects of knowledge do not antecede the process of inquiry; rather they are to be identified with the altered physical consequences in which the pattern of inquiry concludes. Knowing is a form of deliberate making in which the object to be known is brought into being through the process of environmental transformation. Ideas are not theoretical representations of the world to be judged by their correspondence to mind-independent things but directives of action, guiding reconstructive operations and appraised in the light of their consequences.

There are two distinct but related senses in which the pattern of experimental inquiry is a continuum. From the metaphysical perspective, the organ, operations, and objects of cognition are fully restored to the natural order. All versions of metaphysical dualism are renounced for a picture of mental acts as rationally guided physical events causally reshaping the material world. All human activities belong to the same ontological continuum as the objects of nature. Within that continuum there are important differences in the degree of control an agent exercises over its organic operations. The biological evolution of human intelligence means the increase in directive mastery gradually achieved by *homo faber* over his natural and social environment.

From the methodological perspective, all forms of reflection are special cases of the pragmatic method of inquiry. Rational practice in everyday life, in the economic and social sphere, in politics and ethics, in experimental science and philosophy always exhibits the same general features. The differences within the methodological continuum are in the scope and significance of the inquiry, not in its structure or purpose. Dewey consistently espoused a monism of rational method.

The behavioral basis of Dewey's theory of reason is explicitly contrasted with the transcendental method of Kant. Kant's reconstructive analysis reached behind scientific theories and objects to uncover the hidden operations and rules that were their invisible source. Kant's transcendental intuitions and categories are conditions of possible experience, but they cannot themselves become objects of empirical investigation. They are inaccessible to the method of empirical science. To discover these pure a priori representations and the pattern of their transcendental interaction requires a philosophical method that is declared to be sui generis. For Dewey, however, as later for Wittgenstein and Rorty, nothing of philosophical importance is hidden. The process of inquiry, like other natural processes, is open to public inspection from beginning to end. It consists of overt temporal activities redisposing observable situations to produce a richer and more satisfying human environment. The method of logic is simply the general method of rational inquiry applied to the investigation of rational practice. Because human knowing is metaphysically continuous with other types of natural occurrence, the investigation of cognition is continuous with the universal model of experimental inquiry.

What is the fate of the spectator theory and the traditional reliance on ocular imagery in the wake of Dewey's logic? The core of that theory can be stated in two principles: Knowing is a form of looking; the immediate objects of knowledge are objects to be looked at. Variations on the central theme can be stated with equal brevity: Granted that knowing is perceiving, are there *intellectual* and *rational* as well as *sensory* modes of intuition? Granted that the objects of knowledge are immediately perceived, is it *reality* that we directly intuit, a *representation* of reality, or merely a state of internal consciousness with no representative significance? These questions dominated the history of modern epistemology and absorbed the attention of philosophers from Descartes to Kant.

Kant abandoned the spectator theory because he did not believe in intellectual intuition and because he emphasized the mediating factors in human cognition that the traditional theory neglected. Although he failed to break cleanly with modern representationalism, he insisted that human knowing demands more than intuition of the given. He thought of knowing as a complex process of unification and synthesis climaxing in the formation of true propositional judgments. The major synthetic operations of the mind take place covertly and unconsciously. Only through regressive analysis of the products and objects of cognition can we raise to awareness the hidden operations on which perceptual experience and propositional knowledge depend. Kant's transcendental theory maintained that the mind is both active and passive in the process of cognition. The constructive operations of transcendental reason order and unify the given manifold of discrete sensations to produce the empirical world of spatiotemporal objects and the epistemic judgments through which these objects are known. There is partial agreement, therefore, between Kant and Dewey that the object of human knowledge is the final result of antecedent operations of reason on a prerational given.

In Kant's transcendental logic the constructive operations of cognition are uniformly rule-governed. The rules of synthesis, or categories, are initially as remote from consciousness as the ordering operations they regulate. Transcendental analysis makes these operations objective and explicit by formulating the rules that implicitly define them. These rules and the operations they govern are universal and invariant. They are innate endowments of pure theoretical reason, immune from time and historical change, automatically operative whether actual persons are conscious of their contribution or not.

Dewey borrowed from Kant and Hegel the concept of the mind as an active power, but he externalized, naturalized, and historicized the other features of critical Idealism. Kant's hidden synthetic operations became overt physical activities and his a priori rules became Dewey's experimental ideas. These ideas resemble the Kantian categories in their function of guiding cognitive operations. But unlike the timeless, a priori rules of understanding, Dewey's ideas have a history. They originate in individual subjects as projected solutions to particular historical problems. In Dewey's naturalized version of reason, ideas are stripped of their universality, innateness, and invariance, the very properties that make them rational for Kant.

Perhaps the greatest difference between Dewey and his predecessors was the historical sensitivity he acquired in studying Hegel. He contrasted the conservative impulse of classical philosophy with the essentially progressive character of modern thought. The cultural function of Greek philosophy was to justify traditional political institutions and moral beliefs. It provided rational sanction for a religious inheritance that previously had been sanctioned by custom. By contrast, the scientific influence on modern thought made its dominant spirit critical and progressive. At its best, modern philosophy shared that spirit with its opposition to inherited values and principles and its lack of reverence for traditional beliefs. Critical resistance to one's philosophical inheritance is a sign of cultural vitality. "I think it shows a deplorable deadness of imagination to suppose that philosophy will indefinitely revolve within the scope of the problems and systems that 2000 years of European history have bequeathed to us."[64]

In addition to the critical divestiture of the past, a further experimental office is open to philosophy—to shape a new and compelling cultural vision based on distinctively modern values, the vision of a democratic social order in which the secular, experimental, and pragmatic reason of modernity finally has come into its own.

F. Quine's Holistic Empiricism

Each man is given a scientific heritage plus a continuing barrage of sensory stimulation; the considerations which guide him in warping his scientific heritage to fit his continuing sensory promptings are, where rational, pragmatic.[65]

The naturalistic movement that came after Dewey shared his ambivalent perspective on Kant. Its active leaders, like Quine and Sellars, borrowed many Kantian ideas but divested them of their transcendental standing. This flexible strategy is clearest in those forms of naturalism that restated Kant's insights in the idiom of the linguistic turn. The different varieties of linguistic Kantianism are united by these common traits. They assume that human knowledge requires the integration of sensory experience into antecedently acquired conceptual structures. But they treat these structures as historical formations, subject to cultural modification and transmission, and open to causal explanation like other natural phenomena. Unlike Kant's transcendental representations, the new categorical frameworks are embedded in natural languages, learned by mastering those languages, and revised in the course of cultural change. They are the cumulative heritage of linguistic communities that preserve their identity through the education of successive generations. For many contemporary naturalists, these linguistic structures or the language games from which they are abstracted, have become the major focus of philosophical inquiry.

The transition from the way of ideas to the new way of words has not had the desired effect of eliminating philosophical controversy. Kant had insisted on sharp distinctions between pure and empirical representations, among intuitions, concepts and principles, and between analytic and synthetic judgments; there are equivalent distinctions proposed for the internal structure and properties of natural languages. Sellars, following Carnap, drew a basic contrast between the object-linguistic sentences of a particular language and the metalinguistic sentences used to talk about them. He further distinguished the descriptive and explanatory predicates of factual discourse from the semantical and epistemic predicates with which analytic philosophy is concerned. He even preserved subject-matter dependent, necessary truths, though he relativized them to restricted conceptual schemes. Sellars assigned to human languages a complex polydimensional structure arguing that irreducible linguistic pluralism is fully consistent with the metaphysical continuity espoused by the naturalists. His work is replete with warnings against linguistic versions of the naturalistic fallacy, in which intensional idioms are reduced to the language of fact.

Where Kant and Sellars actively sought to preserve philosophical distinctions, Dewey and Quine sought to blur or deny them. Dewey urged naturalists to support an ontological and methodological continuum of inquiry. Quine urged them to endorse a continuum of discourse in which the sentences of mathematics and logic, theoretical science and common sense, and epistemology and ontology differ only in degree and not in kind. Quine's holistic continuum of empirical discourse is created by denying a cluster of principles at the center of Carnap's philosophy. As we shall see, those principles are the correlates within logical empiricism of analytic divisions directly traceable to Hume. Quine's critique of traditional empiricism strikes at dualistic contrasts so central to modern thought that they cut across the familiar epistemological lines.

Carnap thought of a linguistic system as a set of sensible inscriptions governed by metalinguistic rules. In his early writing, he admitted only syntactical rules, but later he accepted semantical rules as well.[66] He sharply contrasted two intellectual perspectives on language. In one case, we speak from within the language, having accepted its vocabulary and metalinguistic rules; in the other, we speak from outside the language, debating the adoption of its rules against those of alternative systems. Questions raised from within a language are said to be internal; those raised from without are labeled *external questions*. According to Carnap, internal questions are effectively decidable by appeal to linguistic rules and empirical evidence. External questions, by contrast, are decidable only on pragmatic grounds of efficiency and utility. The answers to internal questions are truth-bearing propositions subject to epistemic appraisal; but external questions are met by practical decisions for which the question of truth does not arise. Pragmatic considerations do not apply to internal questions because they possess an effective decision procedure. But external questions must be answered pragmatically, since empirical evidence does not determine the categorical scheme it is best to employ. Carnap identified the sharp cut between internal and external questions with the contested interval between cognitively meaningful scientific matters and the undecidable speculations of metaphysics. For Carnap, ontology can never be a science because it lacks a decision procedure to resolve ontological conflicts.

Within the realm of internal scientific questions a second sharp distinction is to be observed. The answers to internal questions are either analytic or synthetic statements. They are analytic if they are decidable by appeal to the language's metalinguistic rules without recourse to empirical evidence. Synthetic statements are decidable by appeal to the rules and the empirical evidence taken together. The division is exhaustive and exclusive; all truth-bearing statements are either analytic or synthetic. The cognitively meaningful sentences of philosophy are without exception analytic; all sentences reporting matters of fact, by contrast, are synthetic.

To decide the truth value of a factual sentence, we must investigate the extralinguistic world. But the truth value of philosophical sentences is determined by the metalinguistic rules governing the use of a particular language. Analytic philosophical sentences are in the formal mode of speech because their range of reference is restricted to the linguistic order. Synthetic statements are in the material mode of speech because they refer to extralinguistic objects and events. There are synthetic statements that refer to linguistic inscriptions, but these are object-linguistic factual reports whose truth-value is decided on empirical grounds. The philosophical and factual sciences are *discontinuous* in their subject matter, method of confirmation and discursive results.

Carnap's theory of language combines pragmatic, empirical, and fallibilist perspectives, but it applies each perspective selectively. Questions about the vocabulary and rules of a language are external questions decidable on pragmatic grounds. Synthetic statements are object-linguistic factual reports, decidable and revisable in the light of sensory evidence. Analytic statements are indifferent to sensible evidence, devoid of extralinguistic reference, and decidable by appeal to linguistic rules. The theory rests on a series of sharp and irreducible distinctions.

1. There are distinctions between the rules of a language that are not subject to epistemic appraisal and its truth-bearing statements that are.
2. There are distinctions between analytic and synthetic statements, differentiated by considerations of referential import, method of confirmation, and epistemic revisability.
3. There are distinctions between the contingent truths of empirical science and the necessary truths of mathematics, logic, and philosophy.
4. Philosophical sentences, as special cases of analytic discourse, are

decidable metalinguistic sentences stating the syntactical and
semantical properties of written and spoken linguistic inscriptions.

The web of discourse displays a triple discontinuity between truth-
bearing object-linguistic and metalinguistic sentences and non-truth bearing
linguistic rules.

Striking parallels connect Carnap's logical empiricism to the psychological empiricism of Hume. Although Carnap sharply segregated psychology
from philosophy and insisted that all meaningful philosophical sentences are
metalinguistic, his cleavage between analytic and synthetic statements mirrors
Hume's division of the objects of inquiry into relations of ideas and matters of
fact. Both men appeal to the same criteria to justify their distinctions,
referential import, method of confirmation, and epistemic revisability. We
need only shift the idiom from ideas to sentences and the correlations match
perfectly. For Hume, knowledge of relations between ideas lacks existential
import, is discovered by thought alone, and achieves intuitive or demonstrative
certainty. It corresponds in each respect to the necessary analytic truths of
Carnap. By contrast, knowledge of matters of fact has existential bearing, is
based on the testimony of the senses or the records of memory, and lacks
rational certainty and justification. It corresponds to Carnap's class of
contingent synthetic truths, Whereas Hume based these distinctions on
allegedly factual claims about human nature, Carnap based them on the
constitutive principles of his philosophy of language. Despite this dramatic
metaphysical opposition, their shared commitment to empiricism accounts for
the substantial overlap. Both psychological and logical empiricism recognize
an unalterable division in the realm of truth.

Despite his evident sympathy with empiricism, Quine rejected as
dogmatic the epistemic dualisms of Hume and Carnap. He directed his explicit
criticism against Carnap but all of modern empiricism fell within the scope of
his arguments. Quine argued that the analytic-synthetic distinction rested on
two false assumptions[67]:

1. Because truth depends on both language and extralinguistic fact, we
   are tempted to suppose that the truth of each statement is analyzable
   into a linguistic and a factual component. Analytic statements
   would be those limiting cases whose factual or empirical content
   was null. In the limiting case, only the linguistic component
   determines its truth value.
2. Because synthetic statements have a factual component attributable
   to their empirical import, we are tempted to suppose that each
   synthetic statement has a precise portion of empirical evidence that
   is uniquely its own. If this were true, then each factual claim could be
   confirmed or disconfirmed by direct appeal to a specific series of

sensory events. This is the explicit assumption of logical reductionism that underlies empiricist attempts to reconstruct science on a foundation of protocol or observation sentences.[68]

The first assumption supposes that there are true statements without extralinguistic reference; the second assumes the precise empirical specification of each synthetic statement's referential import. Both principles presume that we can allocate empirical evidence sentence by sentence. Quine contended that this is the unquestioned dogma of logical empiricism. In abandoning the term for the statement as the unit of empirical significance, logical empiricism was overly conservative. The linguistic unit of empirical significance is the whole web of beliefs to which a particular culture subscribes. "Taken collectively science has its double dependence on language and experience, but this duality is not traceable into the statements of science taken one by one."[69] "Our statements about the external world face the tribunal of sense experience not individually but only as a corporate body."[70]

If we adopt Quine's holistic empiricism, then Carnap's sharp distinctions immediately blur. Empirical evidence is relevant to all the sentences in the web of belief when they are taken collectively rather than distributively. Since sensory evidence applies everywhere, so does extralinguistic reference. This undercuts the fixed distinction between analytic and synthetic statements; there are no statements whose truth-value is decided by exclusive reliance on linguistic rules. The internal structure of truth-bearing language is a continuum in which the statements of mathematics, logic, natural science, and philosophy belong together. All truth-bearing sentences have referential import, all are appraised by appeal to empirical evidence, and all are subject to pragmatic criteria with respect to their acceptance or rejection. The evidence of observation bears on the structure of belief as a whole, but it is insufficient to determine its content. Holistic empiricism leads to pervasive pragmatism and fallibilism when we realize that sensory evidence can conflict with our web of belief but cannot decide which belief(s) must then be revised. The pragmatic norms Carnap restricted to ontological questions are now extended to all levels of epistemic practice. "Carnap maintains that ontological questions and questions of logical or mathematical principle are questions not of fact but of choosing a convenient conceptual scheme; and with this I agree only if the same be conceded for every scientific hypothesis."[71] Carnap's external ontological questions become continuous with all the inquiries of science. Quine took Carnap's empiricism, pragmatism, and referential import and gave them pervasive rather than selective application to the web of human belief.

A major effect of Quine's epistemic holism is to blur the Tractarian boundary between natural science and philosophy. Analytic philosophers, from the early Wittgenstein until Quine, had concurred in maintaining a difference of level between philosophy and the factual sciences. Philosophy enjoyed a special relation to language, however difficult it might prove to define, that distinguished it in principle from every factual discipline. Carnap had identified that boundary with the cut between the material and the formal modes of speech. Logic, semantics, and epistemology fall on the formal side of this cut because their sentences lack extralinguistic content and are indifferent to sensory evidence. Quine challenged Carnap's defense of the Tractarian principle, insisting that the device of semantic ascent was used throughout the web of belief and not uniquely in philosophy.[72] We engage in semantic ascent when we talk directly about language rather than about the world. But semantic discourse about language, restricted to the rubrics of the theory of reference, is just an oblique way of talking about the extralingustic.[73] There is a legitimate distinction between the formal and material modes of speech, but it will not serve Carnap's classificatory purposes. The use of metalinguistic discourse is not peculiar to philosophy and should not tempt us into claiming for it a unique subject matter and evidential base. Logic, ontology, and epistemology are integral parts of empirical knowledge, differing only in degree from the other regions of the continuum of discourse. For various reasons, philosophers use semantic ascent more extensively than natural scientists, but we should not infer from this difference a discontinuity of motivation, method, or discursive result.

Logic and ontology, the theory of linguistic reference, rely heavily on semantic ascent, but they are not sciences of language. Their sentences carry a referential import comparable to that of physics or biology. Epistemology also is concerned with language but not to the exclusion of questions of fact. Carnap, Russell, and the other logical empiricists had uncritically adopted the Cartesian quest for certainty with its correlative requirement of foundational truths. Carnap located the foundations of knowledge in direct reports of sensory experience. He assumed that all meaningful synthetic statements were logically reducible to this privileged empirical verification base. But the denial of logical reductionism and the recognition that theoretical beliefs are underdetermined empirically has permanently undermined foundational epistemology. No logical reconstruction from an unrevisible empirical foundation will guarantee the certainty of scientific belief. It is hopeless to ground natural science upon immediate experience in a firmly logical way. Every empiricist version of the quest for certainty is bankrupt.[74]

What remains of epistemology once empiricists abandon the pursuit of cognitive certainty? The sharp division between psychology and logic, between the causal genesis of belief and its epistemic justification, must be relaxed. In its post-foundational phase epistemology merges with empirical psychology and linguistics. It becomes the empirical science of the factual process through which human beliefs are generated, adopted, and revised. Its goal is an explanatory theory of the logical, causal, and pragmatic factors that intervene between the thrust of the natural world on the sensory organs and the tentative acceptance by the linguistic community of the web of belief that is its heritage. The traditional empiricists were right in holding that scientific evidence must be sensory, and Hume was right to insist on a logical gap between the available evidence and our scientific theories. The task of epistemology, then, is to understand how the gap between sensation and accepted theory actually is closed. Philosophy cannot justify our collective beliefs but it can help to explain why we hold or discard them. Within a naturalized epistemology our existing procedures of verification become part of the causal theory. Justification comes to an end in what we do and agree to accept. "I see philosophy not as an *a priori* propaedeutic or groundwork for a science, but as continuous with science. I see philosophy and science in the same boat.... There is no external vantage point, no first philosophy. All scientific findings, all scientific conjectures that are at present plausible, are therefore in my view as welcome for use in philosophy as elsewhere."[75] The rationality of belief depends on sensory evidence, logical inference, and pragmatic choice. Philosophy derives its rationality from the same set of sources as its neighbors in the web of belief.

For Quine, every sentence subject to epistemic appraisal is a sentence of science. The internal structure of scientific discourse is a holistic continuum that submits to epistemic appraisal as a corporate body. All of its parts are responsive to empirical evidence. Each sentence is revisable in the face of evidential conflict and thus bears referential import. Because sensory evidence underdetermines the corporate whole, revisions of the web of belief are appraised by pragmatic norms. The criteria of rational choice include simplicity, economy, familiarity, and predictive power. Quine insists that a uniform policy of extensionality is a privileged application of these general pragmatic norms. Sentences within the continuum of discourse occur exclusively in truth-functional contexts. The Tractarian ideal of a fully extensional language is broadened to include philosophical as well as factual discourse. Uniform extensionality ensures simplicity of propositional construction, ease of algorithmic computation, and unlimited substitution of extensional equivalents *salva veritate*. But it excludes from epistemic appraisal both intentional and intensional forms of language. Quine justifies these exclusions on the pragmatic ground that scientific discourse can survive without intensional idioms and intentional episodes. But a major reason Quine is able to regiment language within his discursive continuum is that he excludes from its membership whatever violates his stipulated constraints.

Nevertheless, a considerable range of language is preserved: the truths of logic and mathematics, beliefs of common sense and natural science, and the acceptable portions of genuine philosophy, naturalized epistemology, and the theory of reference. These statements share a common evidential base in sense perception and a common mode of pragmatic verification and revision. Their differences "are merely variations in degree of centrality to the theoretical structure and in degrees of relevance to one or the other set of observations."[76] Quine's holism can countenance different degrees of entrenchment, familiarity, and responsiveness to sensory evidence in the web of belief without surrendering the extensionalist continuum that is the logician's ideal. But at what price in clarity and plausibility is this supervening ideal secured?

It would seem that both Dewey and Quine exaggerate the claims for continuity they make in the name of naturalism. "Philosophically, I am bound to Dewey by the naturalism that dominated his last three decades. With Dewey, I hold that knowledge, mind and meaning are part of the same world they have to do with and that they are to be studied in the same empirical spirit that animates natural science."[77] Recent naturalistic theories have revealed problems in both sets of continuity theses:

1. Rational operations may be discontinuous with biological events, if they are intentional episodes and the biological events are not. If intentional categories are ontologically neutral, as Sellars has argued, then this categorial difference is compatible with the metaphysical naturalism favored by Dewey and Quine.

2. Science and philosophy might be discontinuous, if science is a factual discipline concerned with causal relations and philosophy is a metalinguistic discipline concerned with logical or linguistic relations. This discontinuity would be compatible with the empirical requirement that both disciplines test their purported conclusions against an intersubjective evidential base.

3. Cognitional theories might restrict themselves to methodological behaviorism without endorsing the substantive behaviorism advocated by Dewey.[78] He held that all cognitive operations are publicly observable physical events. But naturalistic theories of the mind, like Sellars's semantic theory, can accept imperceptible mental acts to which intentional categories apply. These intentional episodes are as remote from sensory observation as the synthetic operations of Kant, though they have a markedly non-Kantian ontological status.

4. The acceptance of pragmatic features in science does not require subordination of theoretical to practical purposes. Naturalistic theories of knowledge are not committed to instrumentalism or to the pragmatic explication of truth claims. Peirce objected to Dewey's account of the purpose of inquiry in the earliest days of pragmatism; Sellars, whose naturalism derives partly from Peirce, reinforced his objection by defending a realistic interpretation of scientific theories.

5. Quine's elimination of linguistic intensions and intentional acts cannot be justified on purely naturalistic grounds. Sellars has shown how both are consistent with the metaphysical and methodological requirements of science. Unlike Quine, Sellars sought to reconstruct rather than abandon the carefully wrought insights of the tradition.

6. Quine tended to blur the difference between object-linguistic discourse about the causal order and metalinguistic discourse about the logical order. This allowed him to assimilate epistemic predicates, which are metalinguistic, to causal psychological predicates, which are not. The ambiguity is most striking in Quine's reference to the "evidential" gap between sensation and theory.[79] For Quine, psychology studies the causal processes that intervene between the physiological stimulation of the sense organs and the organism's subsequent utterance of a connected string of physical sounds. But epistemology is concerned with the evidential grounds that justify persons in their assertion of truth-vehicles. The ontological identity between physical utterances and sentential assertions is fully compatible with a categorial difference between psychological and epistemic predicates.[80] There is a conceptual division between metalinguistic predicates like *theory, evidence, ground,* and *justification* and object-linguistic predicates like *sensory input, causal processing* and *audible outcome.* Philosophical clarity is lost in Quine's naturalized epistemology when that distinction is ignored. The ambiguous notion of evidence in Quine's theory threatens to rehabilitate the confusions of psychologism that Sellars had struggled effectively to overcome.

7. Matters of causal explanation may be the legitimate and exclusive concern of science. If they are, then scientific discourse could comply with the thesis of extensionality, providing a genuine continuum of descriptive and explanatory language. But matters of rational justification clearly are the proper concern of epistemology. Justificatory discourse, whether ethical or epistemic, includes intentional categories and intensional contexts. It has a different logical character from the extensionally regimented language of science. The Kantian distinction between theoretical and practical *Vernunft*, between explanatory causes and justificatory reasons, needs to be restated in a linguistic idiom and protected against naturalistic reductions. Kant's ontological gap between phenomena and noumena can be closed without abridging the distinction between causal laws and normative rules. Sellar's great contribution to naturalism is to show how this might eventually be done.

G. Groundless Belief

*It is so difficult to find the beginning. Or better it is
difficult to begin at the beginning and not to try to
go further back.*[81]

Modern philosophy has presented itself to the world as the voice of critical reason. Since the ascendancy of Descartes, it has required our inherited cultural practices to submit to its epistemic appraisal. A distinctive picture of human life has supported philosophy's claim to this ultimate judicial function. It has been assumed that every valid human activity rests on a cognitive foundation, which itself rests on a privileged bedrock of certainty. This bedrock is the locus of all epistemic authority; it sanctions the human activities bound to it through a network of logical justification and invalidates those not connected so securely. The task of modern philosophy is to identify this privileged epistemic ground and to explain the source of its authority. To be authoritative, to serve as a ground, the foundational mode of knowledge must satisfy the strictest requirements of Cartesian reason. Unless immune to epistemic revision, it cannot support the edifice of knowledge nor the weightier edifice of culture that rests upon it. Closely allied to this institutional picture of stratified knowledge is an image of reason grasping the foundational truths through acts of direct intuition. The decisive human activities are pictured as solitary operations of the mind, and the highest rational episodes are moments of assured theoretical vision.

Dewey's pragmatic theory of inquiry tried to separate Enlightenment ideals from this Cartesian concept of the mind. Quine made pragmatic rationality an integral part of the process of epistemic confirmation. Both challenged the project of foundational epistemology and the quest for certainty that inspired it. But the most profound reversal of Cartesian assumptions and imagery occurs in the posthumous writing of Wittgenstein, particularly in his text *On Certainty*. Wittgenstein rejected three principles at the core of Cartesian epistemology:

1. He argued that inherited linguistic custom is a precondition for the exercise of reason and cannot be tested by it;
2. He made knowledge rest upon an evidential base of belief acquired through the precritical mastery of language;
3. He restricted philosophy to the description of linguistic practice and ridiculed its attempt to explain or justify our given forms of communal life. With these rejections, Wittgenstein altered the modern picture of the place of reason within the human condition. In so doing, he changed our understanding of humankind and our familiar appreciation of ourselves.

What is the alternative picture Wittgenstein offers? Our image of human life should not begin with knowledge or theoretical reason nor with a solitary individual's relation to the world through vision or sight. We should begin with the human person as a member of a language community already embedded in the natural world. That community shares a common history and a common form of life. For its newest members, this shared linguistic heritage is something to be accepted rather than justified. Theirs is an acritical rather than an uncritical acceptance, for the activity of criticism presupposes a prior mastery of language.[82] The language games into which one is born are for each person the ultimate locus of epistemic authority. They are not based on grounds (OC 354); They are neither reasonable nor unreasonable. They are simply there, like our life. The rational activity of giving grounds must come to an end some time. "But the end is not an ungrounded presupposition: it is an ungrounded way of acting" (OC 110). "Giving grounds...justifying the evidence, comes to an end; -but the end is not certain propositions striking us immediately as true, i.e. it is not a kind of *seeing* on our part; it is an *acting*, which lies at the bottom of the language game" (OC 204).

Our language games, our common forms of life, do not rest upon knowledge. "Language did not emerge from some kind of ratiocination" (OC 475, 477). Rather, our cognitive practice takes them as its point of departure. The conceit of traditional epistemology is that there exists a foundational level of knowledge prior to our shared linguistic practice that can justify or undermine what we say and do. But the bedrock from which critical reflection begins are the primordial forms of being in the world and being with others that we enter through our linguistic apprenticeship.[83] This finite, contingent, historically conditioned situation, rooted in agreements and practices we inherit but do not control, strikes critical reason as a scandal and drives it to seek a deeper foundation for human life. For critical reason with its origin in doubt, rather than acceptance or trust, the conduct of life on a foundation of unjustified belief is profoundly unsatisfying. To the discontent of reason Wittgenstein replied that "the difficulty is to realize the groundlessness of our believing" (OC 166)- to begin at the beginning and not to try to go further back (OC 471). At the foundation of justified belief lies belief that is not justified (OC 253). We need openly to acknowledge the facts of our epistemic situation. "I did not get my picture of the world by satisfying myself of its correctness; nor do I have it because I am satisfied of its correctness. No: it is the inherited background against which I distinguish between true and false" (OC 94). Mastering a language is the precondition for the exercise of cognitive operations; it cannot be explained or justified by reference to them. Linguistic competence is not primarily a matter of amassing propositional knowledge. It means acquiring a broad range of conceptual capacities and internalizing a complex network of mutually supporting beliefs. These beliefs form a holistic framework of personally untested truths.

The empirical propositions in our language do not form a homogeneous mass (OC 213). Although there is no fixed boundary between different sets of propositions, there is a fundamental contrast in the way propositions are learned, revised, and used. There is a meaningful division of empirical propositions based on their contrastive roles in our cognitive practice. "In philosophy what is interesting is how we use propositions." Wittgenstein gave qualified assent to the traditional imagery of foundations. He accepted, for each language, a foundational set of propositions consisting of both empirical and mathematical sentences. These propositions are learned in the original acquisition of language. The members of a language community accept them on trust from their teachers and masters. "We belong to a community which is bound together by science and education" (OC 298). From the internal perspective of the community, to understand the meaning of these propositions is to accept them as true.

Epistemic certainty is attached to these basic beliefs, not because they are *indubitable* or because we possess incontrovertible evidence of their truth but because the exercise of doubt does not apply to them. "The cases in which doubt plays no role are cases in which we do not let doubt play a role-not cases with respect to which we are in a different psychological state";[84] "doubt gradually loses its sense; the language game is just like that" (OC 56). "My life consists in my being content to accept many things" (OC 344).

The limited acceptance of foundationalism in *On Certainty* is qualified by Wittgenstein's relativism, historicism, and holism. The foundational beliefs of a particular community, its governing picture of the world, are not timeless a priori truths, the universal endowment of all rational creatures. Rather they are a variable fund of historically conditioned beliefs transmitted through time by the teaching and learning of a particular language. As language games change through time, their fund of basic beliefs and their central vocabulary alter (OC 65, 256, 336). Moreover, the constituent elements in the fund are reciprocally interdependent. "What I hold fast to is not one proposition but a nest of propositions" (OC 225). "When we first begin to believe anything, what we believe is not a single proposition, it is a whole system of propositions." "What stands fast does so not because it is intrinsically obvious or convincing; it is rather held fast by what lies around it" (OC 141). The linguistic foundations of human inquiry are carried by the whole network of ungrounded beliefs and not by some epistemically privileged part.

Although truth values are assigned to these groundless beliefs, most of the important epistemic concepts are not. The concepts of inquiry, hypothesis, doubt, evidence, justification, and knowledge presuppose the acceptance of a fiduciary framework and cannot be used to explain or justify its adoption. The individual exercise of reason presupposes a communal fund of belief that provides for an existing society its foundations of research and action. For its present members, these beliefs are not the result of research and testing, although at an earlier time some of them might have been. They now constitute the frame of reference for inquiry and investigation, the inherited background against which to appraise the validity of contested epistemic claims.

Wittgenstein's revisionary thesis is that the entire array of cognitive operations-asking questions, framing hypotheses, raising doubts about truth, assembling evidence, testing beliefs, justifying knowledge claims, achieving knowledge, and correcting mistakes-takes place within the framework of a language game whose basic vocabulary and evidential base have been accepted on trust. In the end the practice of rational inquiry rests on a foundation of groundless belief. Because of their foundational prerogatives, we do not treat the denial or questioning of basic beliefs like challenges to an empirical hypothesis. To doubt or deny the truth of these beliefs is either to misunderstand their meaning or to be mentally disturbed. To doubt these beliefs is senseless, because they provide the required background against which we identify and settle reasonable doubt. Wittgenstein seemed to adopt the implicit principle that the legitimate moves in a language game are those for which we have established criteria of success. Skeptical doubt is treated as senseless because it puts established criteria into question without sufficient reason and fails to provide an accepted strategy for the resolution of doubt. "The reasonable man does not have certain doubts" (OC 4, 24, 56). The basic epistemic concepts hang together as a unit. If our foundational beliefs are beyond doubt, they are also beyond evidence, justification, proof, and knowledge. Justification and explanation are rational practices that eventually come to an end (OC 204). According to Wittgenstein, they terminate within the fiduciary framework of an evolving language game that provisionally determines for its members what it is to be rational.

On Certainty recognizes the epistemic priority of foundational beliefs. But it rejects the attempt to provide a metaphysical or psychological explanation of their privileged role. Wittgenstein implicitly subscribed to what Rorty has called *the Principle of the Relativity of Incorrigibility*: "That a given sentence is used to express incorrigible knowledge is not a matter of a special relation which holds between knowers and some object referred to by the sentence, but a matter of the way the sentence fits into the language of a given culture, and the circumstances of its user at a given time."[85] The ultimate source of conceptual and epistemic authority is the continuing game taken as a whole. The epistemic authority of particular sentences derives from their role within the game. There are no prelinguistic forms of epistemic awareness, no rational intuition of objects or truths, that either explain or justify our incorrigible beliefs. No form of human cognition is antecedent to propositional knowledge. Persons are credited with such knowledge when they are able to give adequate grounds for their contested beliefs. No person achieves this capacity without mastering a language game. Thus the authority of moves within the game cannot be derived from prelinguistic episodes of cognition, be they sensory, intellectual, or rational. If we understand the rules of a language game we understand all that is to be understood about why moves in that game are made. No ground of cognitive meaning is prior to or deeper than the existing level of our linguistic practice. Significant saying does not rest upon seeing, but upon social agreement about what can and cannot be said.

Wittgenstein's new picture of the epistemic situation offers a direct challenge to Platonic and Cartesian imagery. It displaces the image of a disembodied mind contemplating ideas with a view of human beings sharing in public linguistic activities. Epistemic practice loses its traditional primacy in human affairs; it is assigned a more modest role as one species of cultural activity, on a par with others. The rational activity of justification remains significant, but it is no longer foundational. It presupposes an inherited framework of belief to which questions of justification do not apply. The designation of philosophy as the highest form of human conduct seems unjustified once Enlightenment prejudices about reason's cultural role are no longer maintained.

Philosophy's preeminence had rested on its claim to be the most rigorous mode of knowledge, deeper and stricter than either science or common sence.Foundational epistemology was expected to reveal the final level of epistemic authority and to reconstruct less rigorous strata of knowledge from this hidden ground. Wittgenstein treated these aspirations to rigor and purity as a type of illusion. "A picture held us captive. And we could not get outside it" (PI 115). That picture is one of philosophy providing a critical foundation for human life. "Philosophy may in no way interfere with the actual use of language; it can in the end only describe it. For it cannot give it any foundation either. It leaves everything as it is" (PI 124). The rational practices of explanation and justification come to an end in our prephilosophical modes of cognition. The hope that philosophy might extend reason to a deeper level of insight is vain. "Philosophy simply puts everything before us, and neither explains nor deduces anything.—Since everything lies open to view there is nothing to explain" (PI 126).

For the philosopher, especially, it is difficult to begin at the beginning and not to try to go further back. And where is the beginning, the foundation of human life? It lies in the full variety of linguistic practices in which we publicly engage, in our common forms of life that already lie open to view. If philosophy is concerned with the ground of cognition, then its subject matter is remarkably simple and familiar. "There must not be anything hypothetical in our (philosophical) considerations. We must do away with all *explanation* and *description* alone must take its place" (PI 109). But what is the point of these linguistic descriptions if what is being described is already familiar? "If one tried to advance theses in philosophy, it would never be possible to question them because everyone would agree to them" (PI 128). Part of the point is the very hiddenness of the familiar. "One is unable to notice something because it is always before one's eyes. The real foundations of his enquiry do not strike a man at all. . . we fail to be struck by what, once seen, is most striking and most powerful" (PI 129). Wittgenstein's behavioral descriptions get their value from the recurrent temptation in philosophy to seek what is most important, not in the obvious and the ordinary but in the allegedly subtle and hidden. Philosophical problems, in their demand for something that does not exist, are not empirical problems. They arise from a refusal to begin at the actual beginning, from a demand that we go further back than human beings are able to go. They can only be solved by a return to the beginning, to the concrete workings of our language, in such a way as to make us recognize those workings despite an urge to misunderstand them (PI 409). The dilemmas of traditional philosophy are solved, not by giving new information but by arranging what we already know in a manner that conveys its importance. Wittgenstein's work consists in "assembling reminders" for the purpose of recovering and assenting to our basic situation as human beings (PI 127). He invited his readers to acknowledge what they already know but appear to have forgotten. Like Socrates, he thought of philosophical discovery as recollection and of his own teaching as reminding. The final purpose of philosophical recollection is to give human beings peace, the peace that comes from full acceptance of our humanity. We can disengage ourselves from the practice of traditional philosophy once we acknowledge the truth of our condition and cease demanding that it become something other than it is. With the full recovery of self-knowledge, philosophy should come to an end (PI 133).

H. From Epistemology to Hermeneutics

Explaining rationality and epistemic authority by reference to what society lets us say, rather than the latter by the former, is the essence of what I shall call "epistemological behaviorism."[86]

Wittgenstein's alusions to a postphilosophical era have deeply influenced the thinking of Richard Rorty. Rorty's goal is to bring an end to the cognitive domination of Western culture and the picture of philosophy that reinforced the undue emphasis on knowledge. He actively seeks a new, less rigid phase of the Enlightenment, liberated from the vocabulary and imagery of traditional epistemology. Rorty compares his revisionary objectives with those of Freud. Freud's therapeutic criticism of religious imagery and belief provides a model for Rorty's attack on foundational epistemology. Like Freud, he believed that his intended target is profoundly embedded in the history of Western consciousness. The deconstruction of epistemology, therefore, requires sustained and simultaneous pressure on many fronts. Traditional philosophy has survived the emergence of modernity because it incorporates a comprehensive account of human nature and culture. According to that account, a human being is essentially a rational animal who uses reason to know the nature of things. Theoretical knowledge, the supreme human achievement, reaches its climax in philosophy, the purest expression of rationality where the human likeness to the divine is revealed most fully. Noncognitive cultural practices derive their dignity from rationality and are subject to judgment by it. Epistemology is the philosophical discipline that protects the purity of reason, preserves the rigor of science, and tests the degree to which the institutions of culture have satisfied reason's exigent norms.

To subvert a cultural vision of this magnitude is not a task for one person or even one century. Rorty places his work in a context of criticism that reaches back to Hegel. He openly acknowledges his critical debts: to Hegel, for his insistence on the philosophical importance of history; to Dewey, for his naturalization of Hegel and his pragmatic opposition to intellectualism; to Quine, for his epistemic holism that subverted the basic dualisms of modern thought; to Sellars, for his vision of human beings as linguistic animals, a vision that locates the rational life within the horizon of the life of discourse; finally, to Wittgenstein, for his linguistic pluralism and his behavioral model of therapeutic philosophy. Rorty's philosophical heroes are not those like Plato, Descartes, and Kant who shaped the traditions of philosophy, but these reactive, therapeutic thinkers intent on overcoming our inherited intellectual legacy. Rorty proposes an alternative vision of human life based on his concept of culture as the continuing conversation of mankind. Human beings are primarily conversational animals, creatures of discourse. Rational argument is simply one form of human speech, with no greater rights or privileges than any other. It takes place in the regions of language, where there is common agreement about the resolution of conflict. But the chief purposes of conversation are not cognitive and there are no canonical standards to measure new species of linguistic practice. People participate in conversation, as they participate in culture, for purposes of pleasure and delight. Philosophy is not the guardian of culture's rationality, but a single voice in the human conversation intent on keeping it lively and keeping it going. Rorty's vision preserves the secular humanism of the Enlightenment but divests it of the Cartesian mythology that was first used to justify its emergence. The best way to survey the scope of Rorty's project is to rehearse his revisionary views on reason, knowledge and philosophy. This will allow us to identify the positions he opposes as well as the substitute notions he would put in their place.

The Platonic concept of reason as the spiritual faculty through which human beings experience the absolute is repeatedly subject to Rorty's polemics. He objects to Platonic *Nous* on two ground. It pictures rational operations as essentially intuitive in nature, and it portrays the objects of reason as universally binding transcendent forms. The ocular imagery conceals the linguistic nature of rational episodes; the mystique of transcendence conceals the social origin of human norms and their continuous evolution and development. Plato's quest for transcultural, transhistorical standards of judgment is treated as a flight from human historicity. There is no common fund of exigent norms to which rational beings are essentially bound. For Rorty, human beings are subject to normative standards only when they enter a language community where a particular game is played. These standards are social conventions adopted for pragmatic reasons. They change as the needs and desires of society evolve. In the cultural struggle out of which philosophy emerged, Rorty's loyalties are clearly with the Sophists rather than Socrates. Plato, unfortunately, was the more compelling poet, but in Rorty's view, Protagoras had the sounder understanding of cultural life.[87]

The Cartesian account of reason combines the Platonic imagery of vision with the Aristotelian emphasis on likeness. For Descartes, reason is the immaterial substance that discovers unrevisable truths. It is the locus of scientific knowledge, a rigidly structured edifice of ideas resting on incorrigible foundations. Rorty has both metaphysical and epistemic objections to the Cartesian theory. Metaphysically, he denies the existence of immaterial things and events; embodied persons, rather than minds, are the legitimate bearers of knowledge. On the epistemological side, he accepts relatively incorrigible beliefs within a given language community, but traces their privileged standing to existing social practice. All human beliefs are revisable, though some are more deeply entrenched in the epistemic web than others. The holistic fallibilism of Quine and Wittgenstein is the proper alternative to Cartesian foundationalism. It preserves the notion of epistemic privilege but dissociates it completely from the myth of the given.

Kant divorced the faculty of reason from the ocular imagery of Plato and Descartes. He replaced the traditional emphasis on intellectual vision with legislative and constructive metaphors. Transcendental reason remained an a priori power, however, though it was made the originating source of universal laws rather than their infallible witness. In Kant, the historical bond between reason and strict universality was maintained explicitly. Along with Dewey, Rorty objects to the ahistorical, transcendental character of Kantian reason. When reason is ontologically naturalized and its operations reduced to linguistic episodes, the philosophical aura surrounding it finally should dissolve. For Rorty, reason is an acquired rather than an innate capacity. We become rational beings by mastering the practice of language. The norms of reason are internal to language, and they vary with linguistic change. Estimates of the rational validity of belief are relative to the customary practice of a particular language at a particular stage in its history. Reason is thereby purged of its traditional association with eternity and universal validity. In its origin, acquisition, and exercise, it is entirely temporal.

The new concept of secular reason is explicitly historical, pragmatic, and conventional. The exercise of reason occurs within a holistic matrix of conversation. The rational sectors of the matrix are those for which we have shared criteria of agreement. Although all forms of conversation are equally legitimate, original discourse, for which there are no antecedent criteria, stands or falls by its power to attract adherents. The distinction between normal and original discourse is not a disciplinary distinction between cognitive and noncognitive practices. Rather, it marks the contrast between the culturally familiar and the culturally strange, a contrast as applicable to science as it is to art or politics. Human practice strikes us as rational when we share customary ways of understanding and evaluating it. To elevate reason to humanity's highest faculty is to celebrate unduly the residue of custom and to diminish the value of what is original, unexpected, and strange.

The linguistic community is the measure but not the cause of all things. Authority within the community is distributed democratically. There is no privileged stratum of discourse on which the other layers depend for their legitimacy. All attempts at linguistic reduction through translation to a foundational vocabulary are rejected as versions of cultural imperialism. The linguistic pluralism favored by Wittgenstein and Sellars is endorsed warmly, even celebrated, by Rorty. "Let a thousand discourses bloom!"

Rorty owes a second debt to Wittgenstein for his linguistic behaviorism. Both of them deliberately explicate philosophical concepts in terms of observable linguistic practice. The regulative principle guiding this strategy is that nothing of philosophical importance is hidden. All versions of realism and idealism are denounced for mystifying what is essentially simple. Linguistic behaviorism is recommended, in part, as a means of avoiding the inconclusive struggles of modern philosophy.

Although Rorty occasionally is critical of idealism, his major polemical target is semantic and epistemic realism. The realistic model of semantical analysis is traceable to Frege's philosophy of language. For Frege, the major purpose of language is the articulation and communication of truth. The meaning of linguistic expressions is based on their contribution to the truth conditions of the sentences in which they appear. To understand the meaning of a sentence is to know under what actual conditions it would be true. The statement of sentential truth conditions provides the proper method for the explication of language. In the *Tractatus*, Wittgenstein largely accepted Frege's theory of sentential meaning. But he later rejected the emphasis on sentential descriptions and the relational conception of meaning. In the *Philosophical Investigations*, the meaning of a linguistic expression is not an extralinguistic entity to which language is tied, but the use or uses to which the expression is put within a given linguistic economy. We explicate meaning by describing the conduct of language games. We explicate contested linguistic predicates by specifying the intersubjective criteria within the game(s) regulating their use. These criteria are socially determined in the course of linguistic practice. All that we need to know about linguistic meaning resides on the surface of the language game. There is no deeper stratum of mind or being to which we need appeal. Nothing of importance is hidden.

When these methodological principles are used to explicate epistemic predicates, the results are revolutionary. For the epistemic realist, a factual proposition is true only if its truth conditions are satisfied by an extralinguistic object of reference. The source of truth lies outside of language in the reality to which language refers. Truth is a relation of satisfaction between an order of reality independent of discourse and an order of intentional signs used to refer to reality and make determinate claims about it. The realist's theory of knowledge complements his account of meaning and truth.[88] Propositional truth is the medium through which reality is known. Persons know the extralinguistic world by making true judgments about the properties and relations of its objects. When a person determines that the truth-conditions of a sentence are satisfied by its referent, then the person has knowledge of the referent by knowing that the sentence is true of it. We steadily increase our knowledge of objects by increasing our knowledge of propositional truths about them.

By contrast, Rorty and Wittgenstein explicate linguistic meaning without truth conditions, truth without extralinguistic sources of truth value, and knowledge without intentional relations between persons and objects. The truth of a contested belief is a matter of its agreement with the groundless beliefs that serve as the evidential base of the language game. "What does agreement with the facts consist in, if not in the fact that what is evidence in these language games speaks for our propositions" (OC 203). The idea of agreement with reality has no clearer behavioral application than the logical coherence of problematic beliefs with those that are relatively incorrigible (OC 215).[89] Questions of truth and objectivity are solely intralinguistic affairs, to be settled behaviorally by appeal to accepted linguistic practice. The behavioral treatment of knowledge fits the same pattern as the earlier account of meaning and truth. Knowledge is a relation between persons and beliefs divested of all reference to extralinguistic objects. A linguistic agent knows that a proposition is true if he can justify the proposition in the face of critical challenge and provide evidence for its truth from the accepted network of supporting beliefs. "In characterizing an episode or a state as that of knowing, we are not giving an empirical description of that episode or state; we are placing it in the logical space of reasons, of justifying and being able to justify what one says."[90] Human understanding and knowledge are dispositional properties of persons, a matter of their demonstrable linguistic capacities. Like the related concepts of person, evidence, ground, and objectivity, they should be interpreted wholly within a framework of accepted social practice. It is not that our public linguistic activity provides confirming evidence for an antecedent cognitive state; rather, there is no more to our cognitive condition than our dispositions to such activity.

In contrast to Quine, Rorty insists on preserving Sellars's sharp distinction between the causal genesis of belief and its epistemic justification. There is a categorial division within language between causes and reasons. No genetic account of the formation of belief can establish the existence of truth or knowledge, because epistemic and causal categories are irreducible to one another. Since the entire framework of justificatory reasons has been relativized to language, it is possible to explicate its structure only in linguistic terms. The concepts of truth and knowledge and the correlative concept of the world lie entirely within that categorial space. "The only intuition we have of the World as determining truth is just the intuition that we must make our new beliefs conform with a vast body of platitudes, unquestioned perceptual reports and the like."⁹¹ The epistemological idealist recognizes the gap between the *causes of* and the *reasons for* belief but mistakenly ɩreats it as an ontological division between natural and transcendental causes. According to Rorty, his rival, the realist, tries to close the gap by describing epistemic episodes as causal encounters between cognitive objects and minds. For the idealist, the operations of the transcendental subject bring the object of knowledge into being; for the realist, the natural world itself causally generates knowledge by producing a representative likeness of itself within the human knower. The idealist is in error because linguistic practice is the measure but not the cause of reality; the realist is mistaken because no causal episodes in and of themselves are either epistemic or rational. It is not that Rorty denies causal relations between persons and natural objects; he, rather, believes that these relations are irrelevant to the concepts of knowledge and truth. Realism treats causal relations as though they were inherently epistemic and claims to find epistemic relations where there are none to discover.

Rorty, Sellars, and Wittgenstein were united in their denial of spurious philosophical relations and terms. Semantic meaning is a matter of linguistic use, not a relation between language and an extralinguistic region of sense or reference; truth is a matter of agreement among beliefs, not a relation of satisfaction between sentences and their ontological sources of truth value; knowledge is a matter of justified belief, not an intentional relation between persons and the concrete universe of being. The radical rejection of philosophical relations undercuts the basic imagery of the tradition. The spectator theory of knowledge cannot survive the denial of an epistemic relation between persons and objects; the picture of the mind as the mirror of nature cannot survive the rejection of the correspondence theory of truth. The radical skepticism of Descartes loses its sting against a behavioral treatment of knowledge based on groundless belief. If knowledge is what we have the right by current standards to believe, then skeptical doubt rather than familiar belief requires justification. With skeptical doubt placed on the defensive, the quest for certainty and the search for incorrigible representations begin to seem pointless. The behavioral concept of foundations as relatively incorrigible beliefs within a linguistic community preserves the notion of evidential privilege without the need for a transcendental deduction. Kant's elaborate reconstructive arguments are unnecessary, wasted motion if epistemological behaviorism is true.

After Rorty's systematic deconstruction of the principles and metaphors of traditional epistemology, there remains the holistic pragmatic conception of knowledge patterned on the insights of Wittgenstein and Thomas Kuhn.[92] Knowledge is predicated of persons who are capable of justifying their problematic beliefs within an inherited framework of propositional evidence. The purpose of human inquiry is not the correct understanding of mind-dependent reality but the increase of prediction and control over the surrounding environment. Pragmatic considerations must decide the controversies of revolutionary science when competing paradigms are in conflict. But prediction and control are not the paramount purposes of human life. Alternative purposes inspire noncommensurable forms of discourse, with the same cultural legitimacy as the languages of science. There is no hierarchy of conversational purposes but an indefinite range of vocabularies, whose survival is determined in the free market of conversational exchange. There remains a constant temptation to select a privileged vocabulary and set of beliefs and to attempt the reduction of legitimate discourse to this arbitrary standard. In modernity, this vocabulary has been taken from the discipline of physics and elevated to the rank of a universal language of science. Then, an attempt has been made to integrate the results of inquiry by translating them into the foundational language. Whatever regions of discourse resist the translation become epistemically doubtful. For Rorty, this is the specifically linguistic version of the traditional epistemological project—the attempt to prove that our existing criteria of successful inquiry are not just our criteria, but an absolute standard by which all conversation must be measured. Epistemology, in all its variations, wants to constrain in advance the freedom of conversation by confining human discourse to what we already understand. The arbitrary nature of this constraint has not prevented the emergence of conversational pluralism, but it has gradually eroded the prestige of philosophy. Epistemology increasingly resembles a dethroned monarch who continues to issue commands that no one any longer obeys.

What is the likely fate of philosophy if Rorty's linguistic behaviorism prevails? The result will be a paradigm shift of revolutionary dimensions, described by Rorty as the end of epistemology and the beginning of hermeneutics. The competing philosophical paradigms in this shift are appropriately described in the favored behavioral idiom. Human conversation is most fruitfully divided into two regions of discourse, though the division is provisional and alters with time. The first class is the domain of normal discourse, the regions of language that embody shared criteria of agreement; in the second class of abnormal discourse, such agreement is provisionally lacking. This division is based entirely on an appeal to existing linguistic practice. Where discourse is familiar, where we know our way around in it, it qualifies as normal; wherever discourse is strange, when we are perplexed about how to evaluate it, it is abnormal. The distinction cuts across our cultural practices and provides minimal support for familiar demarcations of the cultural terrain. Traditional epistemology concentrated its attention on instances of normal discourse. Characteristically, it selected some privileged segment of familiar conversation to serve as the measure of cultural activity. The purpose was to systematize human speech by reducing its various forms to a common vocabulary where mutual agreement already existed. Why should one piece of normal discourse be assigned this singular foundational role? Various myths were devised to justify this exceptional privilege. They all attempted to make an existing social practice appear to be something grander and more permanent than it actually was. The common strategy was to ground legitimate discourse by translating it into the foundational idiom and then to ground the foundational stratum in a unique cognitive relation between objects and minds. "The picture which holds traditional philosophy captive is that of mind as a great mirror containing various representations, some accurate, some not, and capable of being studied by pure non-empirical philosophical methods."[93] The theories of traditional philosophy are the mythical attempts to ground a particular species of normal discourse in order to legitimate its foundational position.

The image of philosophy as a *Fach*, a pure, nonempirical discipline, prior to and regulative of scientific research, was the direct result of searching for an *arche* of discourse beyond discourse.[94] The central thesis of linguistic behaviorism is that intersubjective linguistic practice is its own ground, that there is no concealed foundation on which it rests. The central thesis of linguistic pluralism is that the regions of human conversation are relatively autonomous and are not reducible to any stratum of normal discourse. Taken together, these principles subvert the foundational strategy of traditional philosophy and deprive its theories of their accustomed honor. "What we are destroying is nothing but houses of cards, and we are clearing up the ground of language on which they stand"(PI 118).

Does the end of epistemology mean the permanent withdrawal of philosophy from the historical scene? Not if philosophy is willing to accept a more modest cultural role. It no longer can be the guardian of rationality, the monitor of science, and the overseer of culture; it no longer can underwrite our discourse by proving its correspondence to the structure of nature.[95] Philosophy must go forward without the traditional imagery and aspirations that Rorty, Dewey, and Wittgenstein have subverted. This will not be easy, for to a great extent the identity of philosophy has been inseparable from what it must now abandon. In setting aside epistemologically centered philosophy, we are changing our image of humanity, our concept of rationality, and our notions of epistemic objectivity.[96] Given the historical place of philosophy in the West, a crisis in its ranks cannot fail to be a cultural crisis as well.

Rorty looks to Dewey and Kuhn for guidance at this point in the story. Dewey had a vision of what the West might become if it ceased to be centered around the pursuit of knowledge. If science becomes one cultural practice among others, then the discourse of science becomes embedded in the greater cultural matrix of conversation. The effort to systematize and normalize scientific discourse has absorbed traditional philosophers for the past three centuries. Kuhn's historical research has shown how the revolutionary moments in science resist such logical systematization. He has urged us to focus on abnormal discourse in science and to appreciate its incommensurability with the inherited vocabularies from which it departed self-consciously. Rorty follows Dewey's lead in shifting philosophical attention from science to other cultural practices, and he follows Kuhn's example by emphasizing the importance of abnormal discourse. When philosophy advances from epistemology to hermeneutics, it stops trying to commensurate the different regions of conversation, it ceases to be essentially systematic. For Rorty, the cultural function of the new philosophy should be one of edification.[97] Philosophy can play this role in a variety of ways: by therapeutically liberating us from outworn vocabularies and dualisms, by trying to render abnormal discourse intelligible without reducing its strangeness to familiarity, by adding original contributions of its own to the conversation of humankind. In its hermeneutic posture, philosophy becomes a cultural intermediary rather than a sovereign judge. It joyfully accepts human historicity and the human capacity for linguistic novelty. It ceases its attempt to arrest time and becoming and decides to flow with it. It joins the contemporary conversation of the West as a cultural equal after finally surrendering its ancient Platonic pretensions to rule.

Platonic philosophy came on the scene as the savior and judge of classical culture. Ever since that decisive origin, philosophers have been tempted to reenact the Platonic experience—to evaluate history from an allegedly nonhistorical standpoint, *sub specie aeternitatis*. The crisis in contemporary philosophy has become acute, according to Rorty, because the Platonic paradigm is now laughable in the extreme. Within the mainstream of cultural life today, philosophy appears to be either irrelevant or unjustifiably vain. It has lost its critical prerogatives to artists and persons of letters, cultural observers who are content to be edifying rather than systematic. But philosophers cannot bear to be ignored by their contemporaries for long;

eventually and ironically, they may allow culture to save or rescue them by offering them an equal place in its continuing conversation. Will they be modest enough to accept it? Only time will tell.

I. After-thoughts

I want to conclude this already lengthy chapter with some brief critical reflections. Their immediate purpose is to disengage us from Rorty's vision of the philosophical past. Their strategic objective is to prepare the ground for Lonergan's markedly different account of philosophic method.[98]

1. Rorty's revisionary history of epistemology was written from the standpoint of the outsider, bent on overcoming the tradition. This is a valid perspective, but one that does little to reduce the strangeness of the unfamiliar. Given Rorty's stress on hermeneutic sympathy, it is surprising how little he displayed in his critical narrative. No serious effort was made to pass over to the intellectual perspective of those he criticized or to benefit from the insights that perspective might afford.[99] Rorty encourages his reader to be tolerant, even actively sympathetic, to the unfamiliar discourse of the present, but he seems reluctant to extend this interpretive principle to the philosophical past. This is a questionable stance to adopt toward a tradition in crisis. It makes sense if one's fixed goal is to overcome the tradition, to blur its distinctions, abandon its imagery, and dispense with its vocabulary wherever possible; but the question remains whether that is the wisest goal to pursue. A contrasting approach to cultural crisis is what Bernard Lonergan calls *the critical appropriation of the tradition*. This requires sympathetically passing over to the past in order to understand it, before passing back to the present to judge it with fairness. The goal of this intellectual passage is to discern both the achievements and the limitations of our predecessors, to revise or restate their distinctions rather than merely to abandon them. It is a way of intellectually becoming at home in the old as well as the new, a way of being historically conscious without lapsing into historicism. "It is easy to break a tradition, but not so easy to renew it."[100]

2. Rorty's treatment of reason fails adequately to distinguish between two epistemic values traditionally associated with it: universal validity and certainty. Among the Greeks, reason was the faculty for discovering universally binding truths; among the moderns, reason was the faculty for discovering incorrigible certainties. The contrast

is significant, since a stress on human fallibility leads readily to a critique of certainty but not necessarily to an espousal of relativism. Relativism denies the universal validity of the claims of reason; fallibilism cautions that such claims are always liable to error. Kant's theory of reason combined these different properties, which are historically and logically separable. But post-Kantian epistemologists, like Michael Polanyi, stress the revisability of our rational beliefs, even though we hold them with universal intent. It is possible to liberate ourselves from Cartesian and Kantian accounts of apodictic reason while retaining the Greek allegiance to universal principles.

3. Following Sellars, Rorty places great stress on denying the myth of the given. The decisive point of their denial is to establish the epistemic priority of propositional knowledge. It is to reject epistemological analyses that made knowledge *that* causally or conceptually posterior to knowledge *of*. If belief in the given is the belief in knowledge by immediate acquaintance, the belief in self-authenticating intuitions, or a variation on the image of the mental eye, then its rejection is of considerable philosophical value. But Rorty and Sellars appear to make a much stronger claim. They both deny the existence of prelinguistic intentional episodes, as though intentional and epistemic consciousness were one and the same. Moreover, they reduced all intentional acts to linguistic occurrences. This makes the notion of a nonlinguistic intentional operation equivalent to a category mistake. But without intentional sources of cognitive meaning, there is no way to make linguistic change or revision intelligible. Despite Sellar's stress on conceptual change and Rorty's emphasis on linguistic originality, they have almost nothing to say about the intentional origins of these recurrent and important developments.

4. There is a serious ambiguity in Rorty's critique of epistemic realism. In his version, there appear to be two types of realism, both equally unacceptable. Naive realism is an instance of the spectator theory; it reduces human knowledge to the mind's immediate intuition of an extramental object. Rorty concedes the existence of causal relations between persons and objects, but he denies any epistemic relations between them. For him, knowledge is a matter of social practice, an affair between persons and propositions within a specific language game.

The other defective form of realism is representational. In this account, linguistic or mental representations, propositional truth-vehicles, stand in a mirroring relation to the extralinguistic sources of their truth value. Rorty ties the correspondence theory of truth inseparably to the mirror imagery of the new way of ideas. When sentences are identified as the appropriate bearers of truth value, it becomes difficult to imagine how they might significantly resemble the real entities to which they refer. As long as the relation of correspondence is identified with visual resemblance or sensible likeness, it becomes an easy target for criticism. Rorty scraps the correspondence theory entirely, insisting that the truth of a sentence is a matter of its agreement with the broadly accepted beliefs of the language community. Truth is not an intentional relation between discourse and the world, but an intralinguistic relation between sentences. The practice of the language community determines what is true. The realist's conviction that the source of truth lies in the objects of knowledge is fatally compromised by Rorty, who conflates all realism with its naive or representational forms. If these were the only versions of epistemic realism, the surrender of that conviction might be necessary. But Rorty's objections are powerless against critical realism, with its concept of truth as reflectively grasped satisfaction. Critical realism restores genuine intentional relations between persons and objects and epistemic relations between truth-vehicles and their extralinguistic sources of truth value.[101] A critical realist can accept Rorty's opposition to the spectator theory and spurious notions of language-world correspondence without endorsing his behavioral alternatives.

5. The denial of epistemic realism strongly colors Rorty's concept of science. Following Dewey, he makes the major purpose of scientific inquiry pragmatic. Science becomes the most effective means for predicting and controlling the world, rather than the collective human effort to understand it. The human capacity and desire for disinterested knowledge, which receives vivid expression in the history of science, simply disappears from view. But pragmatic theories of inquiry are extremely implausible to anyone who takes scientific practice seriously. Pierre Duhem, who had deep reservations about the ontological import of scientific theory, struck the right note about pragmatism. "Yes, science and in particular the physical sciences have a utilitarian value, indeed one that is considerable. But that is a small matter alongside their value as disinterested knowledge. And to sacrifice this aspect to the former is to bypass the general nature of physical science."[102] We can respect and support Rorty's commitment to cultural pluralism without endorsing his pragmatic conception of knowledge.

6. Rorty's therapeutic treatment of traditional philosophy is based on Wittgenstein's dictum that nothing of importance is hidden. Philosophical theories of meaning and knowledge were vain attempts to

find an explanatory or legitimating ground beneath or beyond our linguistic behavior. If there is no such ground, then there is no special method by which to uncover it and no privileged theories in which to describe it. Without a field and method of investigation, philosophy ceases to be a distinct theoretical discipline. What survives is the behavioral description of human conversation undertaken for therapeutic or hermeneutical purposes. Since philosophy leaves everything as it is, all cultural practices are granted full autonomy; they are freed from any philosophical attempt to confine them within the limits of the familiar.

There is a profound tension though in the double stress on behaviorism and historicity. How is a marked change in linguistic behavior to be rendered intelligible, if criteria of intelligibility are internalized within normal discourse? Rorty cautions repeatedly against absolutizing existing criteria, but he has no way of accounting for the intelligent and rational operations at the source of linguistic development. By confining philosophical attention to the surface of linguistic behavior and by refusing in principle to trace linguistic change to an intentional ground, he leaves linguistic originality shrouded in mystery. Sir William Hamilton has said:

In the process of tunnelling through a sand bank. . . it is impossible to succeed unless. . . almost every inch of our progress be secured by an arch of masonry before we attempt the excavation of another. Now language is to the mind precisely what the arch is to the tunnel. . . . Though. . . every movement forward in language must be determined by an antecedent movement forward in thought, still unless thought be accompanied at each point in its evolutions by a corresponding evolution of language, its further development is arrested.[103]

Linguistic behaviorism has no access to the antecedent movement forward in thought through which the tunnel of knowledge is advanced. It can provide descriptions of different historical placements of the arch, but it cannot account for the intentional process that moves the arch of language forward. Rorty and Wittgenstein want to leave all causal explanations to science and confine intentional operations to the field of linguistic episodes. But this allocation of territory leaves the intentional core and sources of meaning without a home. Perhaps, something of philosophical importance is hidden after all; namely the interior life of intentional consciousness.

7. In assessing Rorty's critique of foundationalism, it is necessary to be clear about his concept of a foundational ground. Generally, he thinks of an epistemic foundation as a privileged set of beliefs or truths. These truths are considered immune from revision because of some internal feature they possess or some special causal relation tying them to equally privileged objects of knowledge. Their foundational function is to provide a permanent neutral framework of inquiry against which all truth claims are to be judged. Foundationalism is a threat to historical development because it isolates the normal discourse of a given period and raises it to the level of eternal truth. For Rorty, there are relatively incorrigible beliefs within a social context, but they are as subject to historical change as the context that actually sanctions them. The only viable notion of an epistemic foundation is the holistic and language-relative version sketched by Wittgenstein in *On Certainty*. But these foundational beliefs are neither neutral nor permanent; they simply are the provisional verification base of a particular historical community. They provide a temporary common ground for the practice of its members, but for no one else.

Rorty thinks of verification or justification as the basic operation of reason. He, therefore, tends to think of a rational foundation as an invariant stratum of propositional evidence that can be used to resolve epistemic conflict. It would be a case of permanent truths framed in an equally permanent vocabulary, a procrustean grid constraining conversational freedom.

But is this the only conceivable notion of a cognitive foundation? What if the foundations of human knowledge are not permanent propositional truths but the structure of intentional operations through which all truths are discovered, confirmed, and revised? What if these foundations are the source of intelligible historical development rather than an obstacle to its occurrence? What if the common ground shared by human beings at all times is not a fixed vocabulary or deposit of evidence but an *arche* of discourse beyond discourse, precisely what Sellars and Rorty refuse to allow? "Prior to analysis, to concepts, to judgments, there are the native endowments of intelligence and reasonableness and the inherent structures of cognitional process. These are the real *principles* on which the rest depend."[104]

Perhaps, the time has come, both historically and in the course of our expository development, to test these important suppositions. After all, when philosophers stop at linguistic behavior, have they really arrived at the beginning?

7

The Need for Cognitive Integration

*Every mind by its inner unity seeks the
integration of all it knows.*[1]

A. In Search of Common Ground

*Multiplicity which is not reduced to unity is
confusion. Unity which does not depend on
multiplicity is tyranny.*[2]

Since its origin in ancient Greece, Western philosophy has enjoyed a symbiotic
relation with the culture that has served as its home. At historic junctures,
major cultural changes have created an agenda for philosophy; philosophical
language and imagery continually have haunted and energized cultural
practice.[3] The interdependence is sufficiently deep that a profound cultural
shift will invariably create philosophical disquiet. We have been studying such
a period of change and uncertainty, grave enough to be commonly recognized
as a crisis of identity. The practice of philosophy, since the end of the
nineteenth century, has taken place within a greatly altered cultural context.
The magnitude of this change has required philosophy to redefine its
theoretical function and its relation to other cultural activities. But Western
culture also has suffered from the decline in philosophical vitality. Philosophy
exists to meet the native human demand for the integration of knowledge. The
cultural need for cognitive integration has remained unsatisfied while
philosophy adapted to its new historical situation. Serious doubts now exist
whether that need can be met, whether philosophy or any human activity can
order and unify the extraordinary pluralism of our time.

The Canadian philosopher Bernard Lonergan has made a memorable attempt to address these disturbing doubts.[4] He has devoted himself to understanding the cultural transition we are presently experiencing and working out its implications for the authentic practice of philosophy. I know of no more important or impressive effort in contemporary thought. This chapter explores Lonergan's conception of a philosophical project adequate to the exigencies of our culture and continuous with philosophy's historical purpose.

Hegel's *Phenomenology of Spirit* marked a turning point in the philosophical tradition. For the first time, temporal becoming and change became the central concern of theoretical reflection.[6] Attention shifted from the classical emphasis on the abstract and universal to the historical concern for concreteness and particularity. The concrete, factual development of the human spirit through time, the accepted subject matter of historiography, assumed equal importance in philosophy. As Western culture grew historically sensitive it also became increasingly empirical. The transition from classical to historical consciousness coincided with the appearance of the empirical human sciences: psychology, sociology, and anthropology.[6] Classical theories of humankind investigated the constant, ahistorical essence universally shared by human beings. But the new empirical theories stressed the unfinished, developmental aspect of the human condition. They concentrated on humans as social and cultural beings and emphasized the plurality of social contexts distributed throughout time and space. The heuristic ideals of classical culture had been those of unity, constancy, and identity. The goal of theoretical reflection was to seek unity within plurality and invariance in the context of change. But the heuristic aspirations of historical consciousness violate classical ideals. They seek the intelligibility of human life in the numerous expressions of human pluralism, in the stages of dynamic development, personal and historical, and in the arresting differences among cultures and peoples. From the cultural perspective of history, classical ideals appear immobile and excessively homogeneous. In emphasizing universal and eternal truths, they seem to confine attention to what is static and already finished.

The transition from classical to historical consciousness represented a radical shift in heuristic emphasis. Classical thinkers had sought explanatory intelligibility in timeless essences; the new human sciences seek illumination and insight in the empirical study of concretely situated historical beings. This heuristic reversal has had a profound effect on the understanding of science. The classical theory of science was framed from the atemporal perspective of logic.[7] As viewed by the logician, the essence of science is the systematization of immutable truth. Science is a permanent propositional achievement expressing certain knowledge of causal necessity. It is the terminal goal in which human inquiry concludes, a region of epistemic closure and rest. The essence of science is revealed in its finished or perfected axiomatic-deductive form. The new concept of science is based on an empirical investigation of its history. As viewed historically, science is an ongoing process of collective inquiry, marked not by the discovery of immutable truth but by the relentless quest for fuller understanding. The spirit of this dynamic enterprise is one of fallibility rather than certainty. Discoveries are formulated hypothetically, maintained in a provisional spirit, and subjected to revisions of scope and theoretical formulation. Modern empirical science provides the most vivid existing expression of the collective dynamism of human intelligence. It is an ongoing historical process unified by canons of method and by an evolving fund of critically controlled beliefs. Logical operations play a major role in disclosing the presuppositions and implications of existing discoveries, but they cannot adequately account for science's progressive, developmental character. The rationality of the scientific enterprise cannot be reduced to its admittedly significant logical profile.[8]

The empirical study of modernity reveals the growing independence of cultural practices from philosophical prescription. In science, politics, the arts, and religion, the moderns increasingly have demanded autonomy of initiative and self-definition. The concept of philosophy as a higher discipline prescribing methods, vocabulary, and purposes for docile intellectual subordinates has vanished from the scene. Any attempt to restore philosophy to its role as cultural sovereign would be dismissed as tyranny. But this dismissal leaves undetermined the proper function of philosophy within a pluralistic age where human practices look after themselves. Our distinctive emphasis has been on the new relation that obtains between philosophy and empirical science. The primary purpose of modern epistemology had been to monitor the compliance of scientific theories with the classical theory of science. The shift to historical consciousness made that project obsolete while leaving the theoretical function of philosophy in doubt.

To a limited extent, Lonergan's assessment of our historical situation coincides with Rorty's. Philosophy is now at a turning point because the paradigmatic projects of modernity were tied to a classical theory of reason and knowledge that no longer commands assent. All the basic epistemic notions—rationality, objectivity, truth, and knowledge—need to be reconceived independent of Cartesian assumptions. Philosophy must take account of cultural pluralism and autonomy and surrender its attempt to integrate discourse by the method of logical reduction. In fact, all logical strategies of discursive integration become questionable once linguistic pluralism is taken seriously. There is no privileged propositional stratum of evidence to which legitimate discourse must be reduced. The identity between philosophy and logic, actively celebrated by Carnap, ceases to be credible once philosophers take time and history into account.

As a replacement for epistemology in both its psychological and linguistic versions, Rorty offers a behavioral explication of epistemic concepts and a hermeneutic approach to linguistic pluralism. But his behavioral analyses are of restricted credibility; they derive their limited force from Rorty's elimination of the alleged epistemic alternatives: the spectator theory and representational realism. However, these positions do not exhaust the post-Cartesian alternatives to epistemological behaviorism. As this chapter attempts to establish, Lonergan's critical realism is a case in point. A critical realist can endorse Rorty's objections to both idealism and the spectator theory without accepting his favored behavioral substitutes.[9]

Philosophical hermeneutics, as conceived by Rorty, actively celebrates linguistic pluralism and novelty. It encourages the acceptance of linguistic originality and strangeness and refuses all efforts to absolutize normal discourse. But it leaves the intentional sources of original meaning entirely concealed, and it effectively abandons the project of discursive integration. Rorty opposes the goal of reducing multiplicity to unity because his concept of reduction is exclusively logical. Because he rightly fears the tyranny of logical reduction, he is prepared to embrace the confusion of unintegrated pluralism. Once again, his choice is attractive only in comparison to its putative rivals. By refusing to seek foundations of discourse beyond discourse, Rorty lacks access to the dynamic intentional structures that would ensure historical continuity without imposing the rigidity he properly distrusts. Rorty's historical relativism is completely in tune with the temper of the times. But it lacks sufficient appreciation of the classical attention to unity, identity, and invariance. Rorty would abandon these heuristic ideals rather than discover a fresh way to achieve them. This is the deepest point of opposition between his concept of philosophy and Lonergan's.

Lonergan continued to think of philosophy as a foundational inquiry committed to the integration of knowledge. The emergence of historical consciousness requires philosophy to shift its theoretical sights from the objects and terms of cognitive meaning to the intentional subject and that subject's normative pattern of intentional operations. Philosophy continues to seek a common ground out of which the specialized developments of cognition arise. But it does not locate the foundations of development in a privileged vocabulary or stratum of discourse. Rather, it locates its concrete foundational invariants in the dynamic structures of intentional consciousness. The universal foundations of cognition are not privileged terms of meaning, as both Descartes and his conceptualist critics assumed. Since Rorty denied the existence of timeless propositional truths, he abandoned the concept of foundations and the allied project of discursive integration. But, unfortunately, this leaves unmet the cultural need for cognitive synthesis and exaggerates the rupture with the philosophical tradition. By contrast, Lonergan's strategy of foundational analysis respects the specialized differentiations of consciousness without leaving them a disordered aggregate. His understanding of a cognitive foundation is that of a common intentional ground that conditions the possibility of continuous cognitive development across categorial and disciplinary lines. By appropriating the invariant structure of cognitional process, philosophy traces cognitive change to its deepest roots and secures for itself the critical base from which to integrate the multiple aspects of cognitive meaning.

B. The Priority of the Intentional Subject

From the beginning of philosophy, the quest for cognitive integration has involved a concern for principles (*archai*). Greek and medieval philosophers identified foundational knowledge with metaphysics. They sought in nature, the Good or God, the causal principle on which the cosmos depends or from which it originally proceeds. Metaphysics, though last in the order of discovery, was considered the foundational science because it concerned what is first in the order of being.[10] Starting with Descartes, modern philosophers shifted the focus of foundational inquiry from the principles of being to the principles of knowledge. They sought a base of indubitable truths on which the structure of science could be logically erected. These privileged truths, immune to criticism and exempt from revision, were identified with the foundations of knowledge. After philosophy had guaranteed the clarity and certainty of its axioms, it could logically unify the remainder of knowledge within a single deductive system. Descartes's geometric model of knowledge was challenged by Hume, who argued that the foundational science is actually the science of human nature. "Even mathematics, natural philosophy and natural religion are in some sense dependent on the science of man; since they lie under the cognizance of men and are judged of by their powers and faculties."[11] Hume's suggestion directed foundational analysis away from the objects and terms of cognitive meaning toward the inquiring subject.

The belief in psychology as the basic philosophical science can be traced to Hume's call for an empirical theory of human nature. But the nineteenth-century response to that call yielded little in the way of reliable knowledge. In the wake of Hume's reductive analysis, empiricist theories of the subject collapsed the distinctions within the matrix of cognitive meaning and dissolved the cognitive subject into a bundle of impressions and ideas.[12] The campaign against psychologism was the inevitable reaction to these empiricist confusions. To secure the objectivity of knowledge, critics of psychologism like Frege insisted that foundational analysis abandon its concern for the cognitive subject. Frege confined foundational inquiry to the analysis and reconstruction of the propositional structure of science.[13] He promoted the concept of philosophy as the logical analysis of thoughts (*Gedanke*), which later climaxed in the new way of words. The Tractarian principle that philosophy consists of logic and metaphysics, the former its basis, derived its inspiration from Frege's example. The merits of the analytic tradition, stemming from Frege and the early Wittgenstein, are undeniable, but it suffered from one major flaw. It concentrated philosophic attention on the expressions and terms of meaning but left the theory of cognitional performance in a state of neglect.

Brentano and Husserl attempted to remedy that neglect through descriptive psychology and phenomenology.[14] Husserl insisted that philosophers go beyond the logical products of cognition to their sources in cognitive acts. He identified the foundations of cognitive meaning with the noetic operations of the transcendental subject, but he failed to clarify the precise relation between the transcendental ego and the finite, factual intentional subject of inquiry. This failure, combined with the idealist tendencies in transcendental psychology, sparked a naturalistic reaction. This second phase of naturalism combined the analytic program of logical analysis with a behavioral approach to cognitive psychology.[15] It preserved Frege's interest in the logical structure of science but rejected his search for the invariant conceptual foundations of that structure. It sustained Dewey's interest in a behavioral theory of inquiry but identified the basic cognitive operations with forms of linguistic activity. The foundational principles of contemporary naturalism are distinctively methodological. They restrict legitimate theoretical inquiry about cognition to the intersubjective evidential base of language or behavior.[16] The point of this restriction is to model philosophical reflection on the canonical methods of empirical science. Naturalism restored the cognitive subject to the domain of surveyable fact, but its behavioral bias concealed the full reality of the subject's intentional consciousness.

The history of foundational analysis has paralleled the cultural transition described in the preceding section. The foundations of knowledge no longer are sought in invariant propositions or epistemic objects but in the structural invariants of the cognitive subject. Lonergan characterized the heuristic transition from the objects of knowledge to inquiring subjects and from terms of meaning to their originating sources as the passage from logic to method.[17] The new foundations, like their classical antecedents, are unchanging and universal. But unlike static concepts and abstract propositional principles, the dynamic patterns of intentional life are the originating source of cognitive development and change. These patterns are already operative in the cognitive activity of intentional subjects. Yet, they are rarely acknowledged, investigated, and brought to the level of full articulation. Lonergan believed that this failure of cognitive self-appropriation is momentous, because it deprives philosophers of the critical base from which they might unify and organize the diverse fields of cognitive meaning. The critical integration our culture demands can be achieved from a position of comprehensive self-knowledge. Even in our own time, the authority of the ancient imperative remains in force: Philosopher, know thyself.

C. Personal Appropriation

For certain readers, the phrase *intentional subject* may be unfamiliar but the reality it refers to is not. It refers to our own reality insofar as we are conscious subjects of experience. The classical tradition treated the human being as a metaphysical substance distinguished from other natural beings by his psychological attributes and powers. But the emphasis of intentional analysis is on human beings as psychological subjects: finite, factual, historically situated conscious persons. From the metaphysical perspective, the human being is a substance whether awake or asleep. But psychologically speaking, persons are only subjects when they exist as centers of consciousness. The intentional subject is the experiential center of the desires, operations, and dispositions constitutive of conscious life.

There are significant differences between the intentional subject and the Cartesian and Kantian egos. Unlike disembodied Cartesian minds, human persons are metaphysically unified, incarnate beings;[18] unlike Kantian transcendental subjects, they are historically situated beings embedded in particular cultural contexts.[19] By virtue of their temporality and facticity, they admit of historical analysis as Kant's transcendental ego does not. By virtue of their ontological unity and embodiment, they avoid the intractable dilemmas attendant on Descartes's substantive dualism. Nor is the intentional subject an exclusively cognitive and rational being. Human consciousness is inherently polymorphic in nature. Hunger and thirst; dreams and fears; desires and emotions; religious, aesthetic, and moral experiences claim equal place with inquiry in the stream of human consciousness. The subject's intentional life, when it is not haphazard and rhapsodic, follows distinctive patterns of experience: biological, aesthetic, artistic, dramatic, practical, and intellectual.[20] The sequence of intentional operations within such a pattern is purposively ordered toward the satisfaction of its governing desires and goals. When human beings are in the intellectual pattern of experience, their intentional operations follow a dynamic pattern governed by the disinterested desire to know. The central thesis of Lonergan's cognitional theory is that every successful enactment of inquiry follows a transcendental method, "a normative pattern of recurrent and related operations yielding progressive and cumulative results."[21] The strategy of personal appropriation requires intentional subjects to objectify their polymorphic consciousness: first, to discover and differentiate the various patterns of their conscious experience; then, to identify the distinctively intellectual pattern of consciousness; and, finally, to recognize and affirm the normative structure in which cognitive life within that pattern unfolds. Philosophy is the flowering of the individual's intentional conscious-ness in its coming to know and take possession of itself.[22]

The basic elements of cognitional structure are intentional operations.[23] Cognitive acts are intentional because they are *of* or *about* something; they take a psychological accusative; they have objects. These are different ways of saying that intentional acts embody the basic distinction between a subjective intending and an object intended. Cognitional operations by their intentionality make objects psychologically present to the human subject. Through the operation, the subject becomes conscious of the object, which is its intentional content. "Just as operations by their intentionality make objects present to the subject so by consciousness they make the operating subject present to himself."[24] Clarifying the facts of consciousness as they apply to cognition requires a firm hold on a number of subtle distinctions. Failure to draw these distinctions often has turned cognitional theory into a bog. Behaviorists choose to avoid the bog by ignoring consciousness and focusing on the publicly observable dimensions of human inquiry. I shall try to avoid it by drawing the essential distinctions.

The first distinction is between two modes of intentional presence.

> There is the presence of the object to the subject, of the spectacle to the spectator; there is also the presence of the subject to himself, and this is not the presence of another object dividing his attention, of another spectacle distracting the spectator; it is presence in, as it were, another dimension, presence concomitant and correlative and opposite to the presence of the object. Objects are present by being attended to but subjects are present as subjects, not by being attended to, but by attending. As the parade of objects marches by, spectators do not have to slip into the parade to be present to themselves; they have to be present to themselves for anything to be present to them.[25]

Experiential consciousness is the name for the subject's prereflexive nonintentional awareness of himself and his intentional acts. All objective intentional presence presupposes an act of intending of which its subject is prereflexively aware. There is no intended without an intending; nor an intending without an intender whose presence to himself is not initially intended. Consciousness, then, is not a psychological subject in its own right, as Descartes had argued, nor a particular psychological episode but a constitutive property of dispositional states and occurrent episodes in the lives of persons. Conscious occurrences like pains, emotions, and intentional acts differ intrinsically from such nonconscious episodes in a person's life as the growth of hair, the circulation of the blood, and the normal functioning of the nervous system.[26]

The subject's experiential presence to himself in the performance of intentional acts is not to be confused with introspection or intentional analysis. In introspection subjects intentionally attend to their conscious acts and states; they concentrate their thematic reflection upon them. Attention to one's conscious life heightens its presence to the subject but it does not constitute that presence. In fact, without the prior experiential presence of intentional life, introspection would be impossible. Through intentional analysis what was originally an act of intend*ing* becomes an object intend*ed*. In the conduct of reflexive inquiry subjects continue to be present to themselves as subjects, but by attending to their own conscious acts they also become present to themselves as objects. The reflexive operations of intending and the intentional acts intend*ed* remain ontologically distinct; they cannot be collapsed into a single ontological episode without losing the intending-intended structure constitutive of the entire intentional field. Although any conscious act can become the object of intentional analysis, in each reflexive investigation the reflecting acts themselves are not reflected upon.

As introspection presupposes experientially conscious antecedent operations, so personal appropriation presupposes the successful performance of intentional analysis. Neither experiential consciousness nor introspection by itself is sufficient for the achievement of self-knowledge. For subjects to know their own cognitional structures, they not only have to attend to the data of consciousness but to understand what they attend to and pass judgement on the correctness of their understanding.[27] Experientially conscious intentional performance, reflexive intentional analysis, and affirmation of what is understood through reflexive inquiry are necessary, distinct, and complementary stages in the passage to cognitive self-appropriation.

Since the intentional operations of subjects differ in kind and functional connection, we need a further distinction among levels of intentional consciousness. Sensitive, intelligent, and rational consciousness are different types of psychological presence defined by successive levels of cognitional operations. Each level is specified by a particular range and series of cognitive acts. Subjects raise the level of their consciousness by performing the operations definitive of that level. Sensitive consciousness is defined by the operations of perceiving, imagining, and remembering; intellectual consciousness, by questioning, thinking, discovering, and conceiving; rational consciousness, by critically reflecting, weighing the evidence, grasping its adequacy, and judging. The appropriation of our intelligent and rational consciousness presupposes a prior engagement in cognitive acts that are themselves intelligent and rational. It demands a double development in the intentional subject who applies the reflexive operations as intentional to the experience of the operations as conscious.[28] The priority of self-knowledge from the standpoint of critical cognitive integration is consistent with its being irrevocably posterior in the chronological order of inquiry. The theory of knowing that results from intentional analysis can be only as comprehensive as the range of prior cognitive experience reflected upon.

To these remarks on the presuppositions of self-appropriation, let me add a note on the process. Intentional analysis begins with human beings in their full concreteness and historicity. It occurs when they shift the focus of their inquiry from the objects and terms of cognitive meaning to the cognitive subject and his methods of knowing. A simple question announces that shift: "What am I doing when I am pursuing knowledge?"[29] The use of the personal pronoun accurately reflects what is distinctive about this investigative enterprise. The data from which it begins and the evidence that bears on its resolution are distinctively personal. In intentional analysis, subjects want to understand and affirm the structure of knowing they experience in themselves when they inquire. "In no other way would we have come to knowledge of these acts did we not first experience them in ourselves."[30]

"Personal appropriation is a development *of* the subject and *in* the subject and, like all development, it can be solid and fruitful only by being painstaking and slow."[31] Lonergan's masterful work, *Insight*, is a philosophical essay written to aid the process of self-knowledge in its readers. It gradually assembles the elements and relations of cognitional process until the subject can identify them with ease and from personal conviction and discriminate the structure of cognition from the other patterns of intentional experience.[32] The pedagogically ordered process of appropriation culminates in a decisive judgment of fact: "Yes, that is the pattern of operations in which I engage when I seek the correct understanding of experience." With this act of self-affirmation, the subject takes cognitive possession of himself as a knower. Philosophical self-appropriation is an explicitly limited and modest endeavor. It recognizes the existence and importance of the noncognitive features of the self without requiring their full thematization.[33]

In his *Philosophical Investigations*, Wittgenstein encouraged something akin to personal appropriation as a way to end the practice of philosophy. The intended effect of rehearsing our common linguistic experience was to liberate us from misleading imagery and fixed ideas, to quiet the theoretical urge. For Lonergan, self-appropriation is not merely therapeutic; it is the necessary beginning of a total strategic campaign with important implications for both epistemology and metaphysics. To grasp the basic facts of human cognition and to discern their operative presence in our own inquiry is to secure the strategic ground on which to develop a critical and comprehensive philosophic position. Before examining Lonergan's execution of this integrative strategy, I want to address some powerful objections to the project as a whole. If the intentional analysis of human subjectivity is methodologically untenable, then its claim to yield foundational knowledge is empty and vain. Since philosophical behaviorism precludes this type of reflexive investigation, I want openly to face its critical challenge.

D. The Limits of Behaviorism

Disagreements in cognitional theory can be explained partly by the impact of restrictive philosophical programs. The confinement of philosophy to the logical analysis of language encouraged neglect of the subject and the sources of cognitive meaning. Transcendental theories of subjectivity diverted attention from the finite, factual cognitive agent. Philosophical behaviorism, in its various forms, has challenged the legitimacy of intentional analysis. This section is an argument against methodological conventions that have excluded data and evidence of essential relevance to cognitional theory.

The naturalistic tradition in philosophy largely has been united on ontological and methodological principles. Ontologically, naturalists have converged in their denial of extralinguistic abstract entities and immaterial intentional acts. Methodologically, the naturalists have sought to limit legitimate inquiry within the canons of empirical method. The leading principle of scientific method is that all legitimate knowledge claims must be appraised by appeal to an intersubjective evidential base. By making the framework of epistemic confirmation public, the possibility of intelligible argument and mutual agreement is effectively secured. Although many naturalists are divided on the precise relations between philosophy and the factual sciences, they agree that all questions of fact, particular or general, are to be settled by empirical methods.[34] In the domain of fact, empirical science is the measure of what there is.[35]

The important questions of cognitional theory are questions of psychological fact. What are human beings doing, what am I doing, when we pursue knowledge in the practical realm of common sense, in the theoretical realm of mathematics and science, and in the conduct of an authentic philosophy? How are these different ways of knowing, these different realms of cognitive meaning, to be distinguished, related and united? To answer these questions precisely and accurately requires factual analysis of a broad range of cognitional activity. In what forms is that activity accessible for thematic investigation? Here, we come to the crux of the matter. Lonergan argued that the primary though not the exclusive access is through the experiential awareness of intentional subjects. The purpose of intentional analysis is for the subject to proceed from prereflexive cognitive experience to propositional knowledge of the structure of cognition. The knowledge yielded by the reflexive investigation of intentional consciousness is detailed knowledge of cognitional fact. Although the data and evidence of intentional analysis are ineluctably personal, its results are asserted as universally valid. To the skeptical charge that the results of introspection are limited to one's own case, Lonergan answered as Augustine had answered the academic skeptics centuries earlier. When directly engaged in the process of personal appropria-tion, the skeptical critic will exemplify the very cognitive pattern whose universality he openly questions. The ultimate basis of human knowing is not necessity but contingent fact, and the fact is established not prior to one's engagement in knowing but simultaneously with it.[36] The critic, then, must use the contested process of cognition in order to deny its existence or limit its scope. In either case, he involves himself in an inconsistent performance by implicitly relying on the validity of the process whose validity he explicitly refuses to acknowledge.

Behaviorist strategies in cognitional theory have followed a markedly different route. They have restricted their evidential base to observable behavior, primarily linguistic activity, either because they deny the existence of experiential consciousness, or because they despair of developing a verifiable psychological theory for which the field of consciousness provides the primary evidence. The methodological *decision* to confine psychological evidence to observable behavior needs to be distinguished from the methodological *principle* that requires a sensory test for every epistemic claim. The less restrictive decision disregards the data of experiential consciousness for the sake of making psychology an empirical science on a par with the sciences of nature. The more restrictive principle excludes intentional analysis as a source of legitimate knowledge. The effect in either case is to neglect or ignore the intentional subject, who is the operative center of cognitive life.

The validity of the behavioral perspective on cognition is not in question. The observation and analysis of human behavior clearly contributes to our understanding of the history and practice of cognition. At issue, however, is the exclusive validity of that perspective. Does it take sufficient account of the lived experience of the cognitive subject? Does it resort to analogical inference when direct investigation of the subject's performance is possible? Defenders of behaviorism frequently respond that introspection is a doubtful and uncertain enterprise. And, of course, they are right. The modern epistemological tradition, beginning with Descartes, has regularly modeled reflexive analysis on the analogy of ocular vision. According to that analogy, as the subject in sensory perception observes sensible public objects, so in introspection the same subject visually witnesses private episodes in the inner theater of consciousness. Introspection is a matter of looking with an invisible eye at the variety of occurrences and contents in one's privileged interior space. This visual analogy often has been supplemented with the epistemic assertion that introspective intuitions of the contents of consciousness are incorrigible. Although perceptual judgments about the external world are subject to error and revision, introspective awareness of the mind's interiority was alleged to be certain and infallible.

The visual model of introspection and the fiction of incorrigible introspective intuitions clearly gave the intentional analysis of consciousness a bad name. The methodological retreat from consciousness into language and behavior was a prudent reaction to the numerous blunders of the new way of ideas. But sufficient time has elapsed to question the new behavioral orthodoxy. The distinctions rehearsed in the preceding section provide a clear alternative to the Cartesian account of the presuppositions and practice of introspection. The data of consciousness, in Lonergan's theory, are not objects of inner intuition but the subject's prereflexive, experiential awareness of his own intentional operations. Introspection is not a matter of looking at intentional operations but of actively seeking to understand their nature and connection as experienced. Subjects objectify their experiential awareness not by gazing at it, which is impossible, but by applying cognitive operations as intentional to the prior operations as experientially conscious. The attainment of self-knowledge is the result of correctly understanding intentional experience, formulating that understanding in publicly intelligible propositions, and verifying these propositions by appeal to the relevant experiential consciousness. Legitimate claims of privileged access refer to each subject's experiential consciousness of his own psychic life. But such consciousness in itself is not a sufficient condition for knowledge, much less a guarantee of incorrigibility. Epistemic claims based on introspection frequently are mistaken and misleading; behaviorally based claims about the emotional and cognitive life of others are not epistemically inferior to their introspective counterparts. We need to recognize the existence of a generalized empirical method that adopts the behavioral perspective of the observer for knowledge of others and the perspective of intentional analysis for the understanding of oneself.[37] In both cases knowledge is achieved by correctly understanding experience and by reasonably affirming the propositional expression of that understanding. In both instances the possibility of error cannot be eliminated. But the experiential base from which introspection begins is not the observational data relied on by empirical science. If cognitional inquiry is confined to observational evidence in the name of empirical principles, then the evidence of intentional consciousness has been arbitrarily excluded. Unfortunately, philosophical behaviorism supports that confinement and permits that exclusion.

Since discourse about behaviorism is notoriously ambiguous, let us review what I hope are some useful distinctions.

1. *Methodological* behaviorism has a weak form and a strong form.[38] Its weak form centers on the proposal that we restrict the evidential base for psychological theories to publicly observable behavior. Its strong form endorses the principle that all valid epistemic claims are confirmed or confirmable by sensory evidence. Both the proposal and the principle require us to forego the intentional analysis of consciousness.

2. John Dewey's theory was behavioral in both methodology and *substance*.[39] He insisted that all cognitive operations were publicly observable activities guided by directive ideas. In the effort to demystify inquiry and to naturalize Kant's transcendental theory, Dewey brought the entire life of the mind into the domain of sensible appearance.[40]

3. Gilbert Ryle's explicit target in the *Concept of Mind* was Descartes

and the Cartesian tradition.[41] Ryle denied the existence of imperceptible mental episodes and substituted *logical* behaviorism for Descartes's epistemic and ontological dualism. Logical behaviorism is the thesis that all psychological discourse can be translated, without loss of meaning or truth value, into discourse about observable behavior or about dispositions to such behavior.

4. Rorty and Wittgenstein are proponents of *epistemological* and *semantic* behaviorism.[42] They choose to explicate our existing discourse about knowledge and meaning in terms of socially sanctioned linguistic practice. Their therapeutic purpose is to eliminate all philosophical need for invisible psychological episodes and abstract terms of meaning.

5. Sellars was a methodological behaviorist in at least the weak form; but he explicitly rejected substantive, logical, and semantic behaviorism. He affirmed the existence of imperceptible mental acts, and he denied the reducibility of intentional categories to behavioral idioms.[43] Nevertheless, he confined the conceptual and evidential base for cognitional theory to overt behavior. This restriction forced him to take an analogical approach to intentional acts. Although he did not exclude introspection, he severely limited its cognitive role. Introspection, as Sellars understood it, could not be the originating source of a psychological theory. He claimed that whenever we introspect we make a derivative avowal use of preexisiting concepts that others ascribe to us inferentially on the basis of our behavior. Intentional categories, in particular, are construed as functional analogical concepts constructed on the model of semantical discourse about overt speech.[44] Human subjects first learn these concepts in acquiring their native languages and only subsequently learn to apply them noninferentially to themselves. Introspection is Sellars's term for the subject's application of these functional analogical concepts to his own case.

Sellars's strategy is immensely sophisticated, but it raises a series of puzzling questions. Why must the concepts used to characterize mental episodes be analogical? Because they are based on a model of overt linguistic behavior, and the inner episodes of which they are predicated resemble that model only in their common semantical role. Why not investigate intentional episodes directly and secure a nonanalogical understanding of their nature? Because that would require introspection, and introspection is limited to the application of concepts already acquired through previous language learning. Why deny to introspection the capacity to generate new psychological categories? Because that would involve beginning cognitional analysis with the data of consciousness and reaching cognitional theory by a reflexive understanding of these data and their interconnections. But why not proceed in just this way? Because Sellars's theory of psychological concept formation requires that concepts predicable of nonobservable events be formed by analogy from concepts that apply to overt behavior. What is the ultimate basis of that theory? It is based on a more general conception of the structure of theoretical discourse and on a deeper commitment to the principle of psychological nominalism.[45]

The final point, I think, goes to the heart of the matter. Sellars identified intentional acts with episodes of classificatory consciousness. Rather than explain the genesis of intelligible concepts by appeal to prior intentional operations, he reduced all intentional acts to linguistic episodes that presuppose the mastery of a prior conceptual scheme. This made introspection an activity of applying already learned concepts rather than intentionally generating original ones. The concepts available to the introspective subject are the analogically formed categories previously modeled on observable linguistic behavior. Is it reasonable to pursue this methodological strategy in cognitional theory? That depends on two highly problematic assumptions: The first is the truth of psychological nominalism and the second is the adequacy of behavioral methodology in the study of intentional consciousness. If psychological nominalism is based on a limited or mistaken theory of intentional operations and if methodological behaviorism ignores important differences between philosophical and scientific analysis, then Sellars's methodological strategy is not binding for cognitional theorists.

My chief criticism of Sellars is that he ignored the facts of intentional consciousness in the name of methodological behaviorism. An analogical theory of cognition is necessary only if we begin cognitional analysis from the standpoint of the external observer. That starting point is reasonable only if the overt behavior of others is the data most relevant for understanding the structure of human knowing. But I would contend that the data most relevant to the cognitional process are the experientially conscious operations of which it is composed. The subject of those operations can attend to their occurrence, understand their interdependence, formulate that understanding in explanatory concepts, and verify it in his own experience. The deficiencies of analogical reasoning, which must understand one thing on the model of another it partly resembles, can be remedied by intentional analysis in the field of cognition. Analogical approaches to cognitional activity have always tried to understand it on the model of something familiar and obvious. For the spectator theory, knowing was modeled on intuition or immediate perceptual acquaintance; for Dewey, it was modeled on the process of making or building; for Sellars and Rorty, it is modeled on socially sanctioned linguistic episodes. But the factual structure of cognitional process is richer and more complex than any of these behavioral models. Each of them involves omissions or distortions of cognitional structure. They try to understand its nonobservable operational elements by examples drawn from empirical observation. They invariably conflict with one another because each points to an aspect of cognitional activity not reducible to the other's model. Analogical strategies provide a classic case of taking the part for the whole, of identifying what is most obvious about knowing with what knowing obviously is.[46]

Sellars's account of intentional episodes illustrates Rulon Wells's distinction between the failure of a theory because it is a *poor* scientific theory and its failure because it is a *scientific* theory.[47] Wells drew that distinction to support his belief in a profound difference between philosophy and natural science. Contemporary naturalism tends to deny that difference or to minimize it by insisting on the methodological continuity of all valid inquiry. Sellars acknowledged the distinction between science and philosophy, basing it on the discursive irreducibility of factual and metalinguistic predicates. His semantical treatment of intentional categories was designed to satisfy both the requirements of empirical method and his commitment to linguistic pluralism. I consider his analysis of intentional operations to be a failure, not because it is a poor empirical theory but because it is a behaviorally based theory. The decisive evidence for a complete theory of intentionality is not the behavioral evidence demanded by empiricist methodological principles but the intentional operations constituted by experiential consciousness. Methodological behaviorists "may have excuses for barring the data of consciousness, for there exist notable difficulties in determining such data; but the business of the scientist is not to allege difficulties as excuses but to overcome them, and neither objectivity in the sense of verification nor the principle of empiricism can be advanced as reasons for ignoring the data of consciousness. [48]"

As Sellars opposed Quine's call for an extensionalist continuum of discourse, I oppose Sellars's insistence on a continuum of method for the discovery of fact. As disinterested inquirers, we will want to remain open to the entire range of questions that admit a determinate answer. Principles of method are validated by their success in formulating the normative exigencies of intellectual and rational consciousness. Methodological behaviorism is invalid in its strong form because it excludes evidence that is relevant to legitimate questions in cognitional theory. To endorse it in its weak form is to accept two complementary types of psychology. Following Stephan Körner, I call these *behavioral* and *intentional* psychology, respectively.[49] The data of behavioral psychology are drawn from observable activity, its methods are the procedures of natural science, and its discoveries are formulated in an object language that satisfies the metalogical principle of extensionality. Its goal is to develop a causal and explanatory science of human behavior without reference to the facts of consciousness. The field of intentional psychology is the data of experiental consciousness, its method is the reflexive intentional analysis characteristic of cognitional theory in the third stage of meaning, and its discoveries are formulated in factual theories that conform to an intensional logic. Its goal is to develop a comprehensive theory of the intentional subject. Methods should be suited to the resolution of questions and questions to the nature of their subject matter. A method is adequate to a question if it permits the attainment of a satisfactory and rationally defensible answer. The question that defines the task of personal appropriation in the field of cognition is, what am I doing when I am pursuing knowledge? The method best suited to the resolution of that question is the intentional analysis of cognitional process. It is self-defeating for intentional subjects to ignore the disclosures of consciousness when they are bent on appropriating the cognitive dimension of their conscious lives.

E. The Risk of Psychologism

By transcending the restrictive limits of behaviorism, we can secure the legitimacy of intentionality analysis. But the legitimation of a method does not ratify its claim to achieve foundational knowledge. In identifying the foundations of cognition with an operative and recurrent structure of psychological fact, do we not risk lapsing into *psychologism* and ignoring the repeated warnings of our recent philosophical predecssors?[50] The answer to the first question will depend on the meaning of *psychologism*. It is first imperative that we know what psychologism is and why it is necessary for philosophers to avoid it. As for the critics of psychologism, the intention is to preserve their useful insights while avoiding their errors and exaggerations.

The accusation of psychologism charges a thinker with a breach of disciplinary bounds. Traditionally it has been leveled against those who confuse the subject matter, methods, and categories of a philosophical discipline with their equivalents in the science of psychology. Both the transcendental and the logical movements in contemporary thought have pursued this line of attack. Transcendental thinkers, like Kant and Husserl, included cognitional theory within the province of philosophy. They, therefore, recognized a legitimate philosophical concern with subjectivity. But they insisted that the foundations of cognition exist at a level deeper than matters of fact. They assigned the investigation of the finite historical subject to empirical psychology and labeled as *psychologism* any factual analysis of subjectivity that claimed to be philosophical. Logical analysts, like Frege, took a very different tack. They objected to the confusion of cognitive terms of meaning, the senses of linguistic expressions, with the acts and states of the psychological subject. Frege feared psychologism because it threatened the objectivity of meaning and truth. To protect the possibility of science, he postulated an abstract realm of thoughts causally independent of cognitional operations. He effectively segregated the domain of meaning from any causal dependence on subjectivity. This meant that the results of psychological inquiry, whether factual or transcendental, were of no relevance to the logical analysis and reconstruction of the third realm of thoughts. The pioneers in the new way of words, like Wittgenstein and Carnap, followed Frege in excluding psychology from the province of philosophy. At its inception, this tradition restricted philosophy to the logical analysis of scientific discourse. Though he liberalized analytic practice, Sellars supported Carnap's insistence on a sharp distinction between factual and philosophical language. He censured as psychologism the confusion of factual with metalinguistic predicates and actively resisted its presence in the field of semantics and epistemology. For Sellars, none of the central philosophical predicates are factual in character. Matters of fact are the exclusive concern of empirical science.

Quine opposed the Tractarian thesis of a sharp cleavage between philosophy and the factual sciences. When epistemology is naturalized on Quine's projected model, the psychological theories of perception and language learning play a major role it.[51] Quine's objective is not to defend psychology as the foundational level of knowledge but to develop an empirical theory of science by integrating the results of existing scientific theories. Quine explicitly rejected Husserl's belief in an epistemically prior philosophy on which science depends for its legitimation. Since the foundational models Quine opposed are tied to the thesis of logical reductionism, his critical remarks about priority were addressed to the Cartesian picture of foundations, which I also oppose. Moreover, the empirical psychology he admitted into the theory of knowledge is the type of restrictive behavioral psychology unsuited for the task of personal appropriation. The support I receive from Quine is extremely limited.

Dewey's case is more complicated than Quine's. He placed the theory of inquiry at the center of his philosophical project. He insisted that the investigation of cognitional process was more basic than the logical analysis of the propositional products of cognition. But his theory of inquiry was burdened by behavioral prejudices that caused him to neglect important cognitive operations. Dewey's insight that theories of inquiry fail by omission or distortion of essential elements, I think can be applied effectively to his own account. The full reality and functions of the intentional subject are not recognized by the pragmatic analysis of cognition. Dewey and Quine would accept the charge of psychologism but deny its importance. For them, its critical force depended on inherited epistemological distinctions that the naturalization of knowledge was intended to dissolve. Since I accept many of the distinctions they blithely reject and since I oppose their behaviorized naturalism, their posture of enlightened indifference cannot be mine. I shall try to respond to the charge of psychologism by restoring distinctions rather than collapsing them.

The campaign against psychologism should have been directed against the omission of basic distinctions within the matrix of cognitive meaning.[52] Its leading proponents, like Frege and Husserl, did restore some of the neglected distinctions within logical theory, but they also excluded the factual dimension of knowledge from the province of philosophy. This resulted in deficient cognitional theories that failed to do justice to the full complexity of human knowing. There was a conflict, therefore, between the campaign against psychologism as it historically evolved and the objective of full philosophic clarity.

By the close of the nineteenth century, confusions within the British empiricist tradition had turned the theory of knowledge into a swamp. Because essential differences in types of subject matter were overlooked, the boundaries between specific philosophical disciplines had become impossible to define.

1. Because traditional empiricism lacked a clear distinction between intentional and nonintentional entities, it had no objective basis for distinguishing philosophy from natural science.
2. When intentional entities were recognized, the critical differences among the subject, operations, and terms of cognitive meaning were regularly ignored. Without an explicit recognition of these differences, there is no way effectively to distinguish the different kinds and levels of philosophical theory.
3. By failing to distinguish different types of nonintentional entities, the empiricists often identified public objects of perception like the moon with private states of internal consciousness (Fregean ideas), thus raising the specter of solipsism and the loss of epistemic objectivity.
4. Lacking a clear contrast between factual and logical analysis, the empiricists tended to confuse metalinguistic discourse about the terms and expressions of meaning with object-linguistic discourse about the sources and objects of meaning.
5. Lacking the more refined contrast between intentional and nonintentional causal processes, they surrendered all responsibility for causal explanations to empirical science; as a result of this surrender, philosophers who wanted to defend the theoretical validity of their discipline took refuge in semiotics or transcendental analysis.
6. By failing to distinguish the different dimensions of philosophical semiotics, the way of ideas encouraged the restriction of linguistic analysis to logical syntax and hampered the development of an adequate semantical theory. The theory of knowledge has yet to recover fully from this crippling series of omissions and failures.

In order to unravel the web of psychologism, we require acknowledgment of the following distinctions:

1. Philosophy is concerned with those aspects of human cognition that are explicitly intentional in nature; it assigns the nonintentional causes and conditions of knowledge to natural science.[53]

2. The intentional features of cognition can be distinguished and related through the matrix of cognitive meaning. No theory of knowledge can be comprehensive that omits or fails to integrate the different dimensions and elements of that matrix, but the various subdisciplines within philosophy can be distinguished by the specific parts of cognitional structure with which they are concerned.

   a. *Cognitional theory* investigates the core, sources, and acts of cognitive meaning.

   b. *Formal logic* studies the relations of presupposition, implication, and deducibility among formal terms of meaning.

   c. *Epistemology* studies the essential requirements of truth, objectivity, and reasonableness as they apply to full terms of meaning.

   d. *Metaphysics* examines the common intelligible structure of the objects of cognitive meaning.

   e. *Semiotic analysis* provides a syntactical and semantical explication of the expressions of cognitive meaning. The philosophical investigation of knowledge therefore is exceedingly complex. It includes inquiries into psychological fact, exercises in logical analysis and synthesis, and the elucidation of epistemic and semantic categories and relations. Although semiotic, psychological, and logical questions concerning knowledge should be kept distinct from one another, they have equal claim to philosophical legitimacy.

3. Logical analysis is restricted to the internal structure and external relations among terms of meaning; cognitional analysis is concerned with causal relations among sources and acts of meaning; epistemic analysis examines the intentional relations of signification among linguistic expressions and their extralinguistic senses (terms) and referents (objects of meaning). Frege was justified in distinguishing the disciplines of logic and psychology; Sellars also was justified in contrasting the object-linguistic language of cognitional theory with the metalinguistic discourse of semiotics. But they both lacked a rational warrant for excluding the intentional operations of the cognitive subject from the province of authentic philosophy.

4. It is especially critical to distinguish intentional from nonintentional causal episodes within the realm of psychological fact. The causal episodes with specific relevance for the theory of knowledge are the operations of intellectual and rational consciousness that form the central core of cognitional process. Apart from their discovery and acknowledgment, there is no way to understand the intelligent and rational procession of formal and full terms of meaning from

psychological causes. The *intelligibility* of formal terms of meaning and the *reasonableness* of the full terms essentially are derived from the intelligence and rationality of their proximate causal origins.[54] To preserve the semantic and epistemic objectivity of terms of meaning, without causally segregating them from intentional operations as Frege did, it is necessary to distinguish between two types of causal procession within human consciousness. All causal processions are intrinsically *intelligible* but only intentional processions are also *intelligent* and *rational*. The causal procession of an empirically conscious sensation, like a pain or an itch, from physiological or neural stimulation is an instance of nonintelligent causation. By contrast, the procession within cognitional structure of meaningful propositions from acts of direct insight and responsible judgments from acts of reflective insight are special cases of intelligent and rational causation. Philosophy is properly concerned with that region of intentional subjectivity that is intrinsically intelligent and rational. If the intelligent and rational operations of intentional consciousness are the causal ground of the propositional truths and judgments through which the order of being is known, then they have a rightful claim to be called *foundations of knowledge*. And the intentional psychology of cognitional fact, which explores the normative pattern within which these operations occur, also can properly be called a *foundational discipline*. The root cause of psychologism in its manifold variety is the failure to develop an accurate and comprehensive theory of intentionality. The exclusion of intellectual and rational psychology from the practice of philosophy only prolongs that failure.

In the view that I am defending, it is essential to distinguish the intentionality of cognitive operations from the intentionality of terms and expressions of meaning. Formal and full terms of meaning derive their intentionality from the operations that causally ground them; linguistic expressions of meaning derive their intentionality from the terms of meaning that they signify. In and of themselves as physical marks or sounds, linguistic inscriptions are not intrinsically intentional. When we treat them as intentional signs, we tacitly construe them as expressions in a public language capable of appearing in meaningful sentences that can be used to express intelligible propositions. At the source of the intentionality of both language and speech are the prior operations of intentional consciousness on which language ultimately depends.[55]

In urging the distinction between terms of meaning and the linguistic inscriptions that express them, I implicitly accept a further distinction between full acts of judgment and the overt speech acts called assertions. Although these acts are ontologically distinct, there are marked parallels between them. Acts of judgment stand to full terms of meaning as acts of assertion stand to the sentences they explicitly assert. Both types of act are intentional and both make truth claims with universal import about the independent reality to which they refer. The parallels are strict enough to support an analogy of proportion in which the outer word of assertion serves as a model for understanding the inner word of judgment.

Sellars exploited something akin to this parallel in framing his theory of intentional episodes. He argued that the categories of intentionality are the semantic categories originally applicable to overt discourse given analogical extension to imperceptible mental acts. Since semantic predicates are metalinguistic, their application to mental acts requires the conversion of all intentional operations into linguistic episodes. Sellars defended this conversion as the centerpiece in his rational reconstruction of the traditional intentional act-intentional content distinction. How sound is the basic analogy on which he explicitly relied and how comprehensive is the theory of intentionality he was able to construct upon it?

We have recognized an analogy of proportion between the act of judgment and the propositional content it affirms and act of assertion and the sentence it asserts. But this is not the analogy Sellars employed. He modeled his theory of intentionality on language rather than speech (on *langue* rather than *parole*). His analogy is based on the distinction between a sentence type, a particular token of that type, and the propositional role that the token plays within a given linguistic economy. He made the distinction between an abstract linguistic system and its concrete temporal employment equivalent to the distinction between abstract sentence types and concrete sentence tokens. This permitted him to disregard the act of assertion and to conceive of overt discourse as the occurrence of observable sentence tokens tokening inter-linguistic sentence types.[56] Semantic discourse about these sentence tokens classifies them as players of rule-governed propositional roles. When traditional mental acts are reconstructed on this model, acts of judgment are assimilated to sentence tokens in an inner language called *Mentalese* and the propositions they affirm are reduced to the interlinguistic propositional roles those sentence tokens play. The intentional properties predicated of full acts of meaning are reconstructed as metalinguistic properties predicated of the sentences in *Mentalese*. Moreover, Sellars treated the analogy comprehensively, so that all intentional operations are reconceived as linguistic episodes subject to semiotic classification and appraisal.

There are striking asymmetries between Sellars's global model of intentionality and my restricted analogy of proportion. At a first level of approximation, we can clarify the asymmetry by contrasting the complexity of the two models. My model contains four distinguishable elements; Sellars's model appears, initially, to contain three. I recognize two types of intentional act, the judgment and the assertion, and two types of intentional content, the proposition and the sentence. Sellars recognized two kinds of sentence token and one interlinguistic propositional intension common to both of them. But are Sellars's sentence *tokens* really intentional *acts*? He calls them *acts* because they are episodic rather than dispositional in character (*pace* Ryle),[57] and they are called intentional because Sellars extended that property to anything to which the full set of metalinguistic predicates applies. But they are not cognitional intendings constituted by experiential and objective consciousness through which the intentional subject is psychologically open to the universe of being. Strictly speaking, Sellars's sentence tokens, both inner and outer, are intentional *signs* not intentional *acts*. Sellars's theory of intentionality begins by converting all intentional operations into conceptual episodes and ends by making all conceptual episodes linguistic. He recognized the logical products that result from cognitional process but omitted the operations of the intentional subject that are their generative source. From the perspective of my analysis, it is like a performance of *Hamlet* without the prince.

My model contains four distinguishable relations; Sellars's model appears to contain three. I recognize two instances of the relation between an intentional act and its content: that between the act of judgment and the affirmed proposition and the analogous relation between the act of assertion and the asserted sentence. The relation between an intentional act and its content is not reducible to two other types of relation that occur in my model: the causal relation between an antecedent act of judgment and a subsequent act of assertion and the semantical relation between a sentence and the abstract proposition it linguistically expresses. For me, the important parallels are between the outer and the inner intentional acts, their correlative intentional terms or signs, and the analogous intentional relations between the acts and their contents. The *outer word* or sentence parallels the *inner word* or proposition, rather than the intentional operation of judgment, which is paired to the act of assertion. At first view, Sellars appears to recognize two types of relation: the causal relation between sentence tokens in *Mentalese* and their overt counterparts in audible discourse, and the "semantical relation" between the two sentence tokens and their common propositional intension.[58] The parallel elements are the outer and the inner sentence tokens and the parallel relation the "semantic relation" between linguistic expressions and the abstract entities they stand for. Sellars's theory exploited the fact that abstract propositional terms of meaning are the common elements of two distinct kinds of relation: They are the intentional contents of full acts of meaning as well as the semantical intensions expressed by meaningful descriptive sentences. By converting all intentional acts into sentence tokens, he assimilated the act-content relation to the semantical relation of a sentence token to its sense or intension. When intentional acts are reduced to outer or inner words, intentional contents are then reduced to linguistic intensions. If this conversion and reduction are granted, then it follows that intentional categories are irreducibly metalinguistic. In the final stages of Sellars's reconstruction semantical relations also disappear, so that the entire matrix of intentionality becomes internal to the practice of language. For Sellars, like Rorty, there is no intentional *arche* of discourse.

There is a further important difference of scope between Sellars's model and my own. He constructed a general theory of intentional episodes on the analogy of overt discourse. All intentional operations are analogous to observable sentence tokens subject to semantic classification and appraisal. But I limit the analogical relevance of the speech act of assertion to the intentional operation of judgment. The model of behavioral speech acts provides insight into some cognitional operations but, when taken exclusively, it encourages the omission or distortion of others. By reducing mental acts to linguistic episodes Sellars failed to identify the originating source of intentionality and overlooked intentional acts that conspicuously resist his linguistic reduction.

Sellars's theory converts all discourse about the field of intentional reality into metalinguistic discourse. I share his conviction that discourse about the terms and expressions of cognitive meaning is metalinguistic. I also agree that metalinguistic discourse about the logical and the linguistic order is irreducible to object-linguistic discourse about matters of fact. But I explicitly reject his claim that all intentional operations are linguistic episodes and that all reference to their intentionality is through semiotic predicates. Discourse about the intentional sources of cognitive meaning is not metalinguistic. Rather, it is an instance of *intensional* factual discourse used in *intentional* psychology. For Sellars, intentionality is not an intrinsic property of perceptual, intellectual, and rational acts. On his account, items in the causal order of nature become intentional only when they are conventionally designated to play semiotic roles within a language game. All intentionality derives from the metalinguistic rules that regulate the public use of language. Sellars accepted the Tractarian thesis that factual discourse is uniformly extensional; there are no intensional contexts or intentional episodes in *rerum natura*.[59] But, unlike Quine, he preserved the legitimacy of intentional predicates by identifying them with the metalinguistic predicates of semiotics. His support of discursive irreducibility and linguistic pluralism is valuable and welcome; less welcome is his wholesale identification of intentional acts with intentional signs.

In his critique of psychologism, Sellars sharply distinguished factual and philosophical questions. Given his understanding of intentionality this separation was appropriate because the semiotic investigation of truth-vehicles is a logical rather than a factual affair. Starting with the true premise that the subject matter of philosophy is intentional reality, he reached the questionable conclusion that the province of philosophy excludes concern for matters of fact. The troublesome step in his argument was the thesis reducing intentional operations to linguistic events. If this premise is not true, as I have contended, then we are not bound by the argument's conclusion nor by the accusation of psychologism it entails. The terms and expression of cognitive meaning are grounded causally in nonlinguistic cognitional operations. These intentional signs occupy an important but derivative part of the total field of intentional existence. By recognizing other regions of that field, through the matrix of cognitive meaning, we are able to liberalize and differentiate the concept of philosophical analysis. One form of psychologism is the confusion of logical and semiotic analysis with the investigation of psychological fact. The inclusion within philosophy of an intentional cognitional theory is not psychologism but fidelity to philosophy's foundational quest.

Sellars's semantic conception of intentionality displays analytic philosophy in its most inventive and ingenious form. But despite its evident subtlety, it finally is not adequate to the understanding of human intelligence and rationality. It is based on a questionable analogy of limited scope. Although it recognizes philosophy's essential concern with the intentional order, it unduly narrows that order and the disciplines charged with investigating it. The results of that narrowing are critical: the core of cognitive intentionality is never acknowledged; the concept of an intentional operation is severely truncated; important types of cognitional acts are overlooked; and the psychology of human cognition is surrendered to methodological behaviorism. Sellars's version of the new way of words clearly is superior to the way of ideas that it deliberately displaced and to earlier, less flexible, strategies of linguistic analysis. But in its commitment to the priority of language, in the causal and methodological treatment of mind and knowledge, it falls short of the necessary mark.

This discussion of psychologism would be incomplete without more extended attention to Frege. Frege's chief philosophical goal was to preserve the objectivity of meaning and truth.[60] He correctly perceived that science is an intersubjective enterprise that presupposes universal access to the objects and terms of cognitive meaning. If individual scientists are to understand each other's truth claims, then there must be a common stock of thoughts (*Gedanke*) to which all have access, at least in principle. If science is to achieve objective knowledge, then its verified truths must be universally valid, binding for all rational beings, both now and in the future. Frege's inquiry into the conceptual foundations of arithmetic gave him direct exposure to empiricist principles that implicitly negated the objectivity of science. The tendency in classical empiricism to reduce both thoughts and things to impressions and ideas became the focus of his passionate but acute polemics.

Frege began his critique of empiricism by concentration on the elusive notion of an idea. He traced the roots of psychologism back to the absorption of three distinct concepts under one common term. *Idea* (*Vorstellung*) had been used to refer to public perceptual objects, like the moon; to public but nonperceptual concepts, like the concept of the moon; and to private psychological impressions, like Napoleon's image of the moon. He rejected this ambiguous usage and insisted that we restrict the reference of *idea* to the nonintentional conscious states of the psychological subject. Under this restriction it is false to say, as classical empiricists often did, that the immediate objects of human perception are ideas. In fact, the conscious subject never perceives ideas in Frege's restricted sense but merely has them as temporary states of an individual conscious life. What human subjects perceive are spatial and temporal particulars in a common perceptual space. The same moon is the shared visible object for an unlimited range of attentive observers. Moreover, Frege contended astronomers rely on the same concept of the moon when they jointly assert that the planet earth has only one moon. Ideas are private and subjective; they fall within the province of psychology. Perceptual objects and concepts are public and objective; psychology can provide no relevant information about them.

Fearing the assimilation of the logical order of concepts and thoughts to the psychological order of mental acts and ideas,[61] Frege radically segregated the subjective and objective domains of reality. He confined all aspects of human subjectivity within the province of psychology and prohibited their introduction into philosophical issues. He devised basic criteria of objectivity that applied equally to abstract and concrete entities. In doing this, he fashioned a general notion of the objective order that would ensure the universal validity of science. To be objective an entity must be intentionally accessible to all cognitive subjects and causally independent of subjective operations. In devising his theory of objectivity, Frege appeared to rely on the model of perceptual objects. As the moon would exist even if there were no human subjects to perceive it, so abstract concepts and thoughts exist, even if there are no thinkers who actually conceive them. Although Frege denied that the "grasp" of a concept was perceptual, he allowed the model of perception deeply to influence his analysis of objectivity. This led to his belief in the causal independence of the logical order from the intentional operations of the mind. If Frege had conceived of this independence as distributive rather than collective, he could have ensured the intersubjective character of the logical realm without espousing conceptual realism. Although Frege's text is not fully clear on this matter, his belief in the givenness of abstract entities suggests that he was a conceptual realist who granted to concepts the same independence of mind he assigned to the North Sea. If the act of apprehending a thought stands to the thought apprehended as the act of seeing a tree stands to the tree that is perceived, then intentional analysis has no greater relevance to the theory of meaning than the psychology of perception has to forestry. As Frege caustically remarked, a study of the North Sea that focussed on optical questions would strike a real oceanographer as entirely misguided.[62]

The difficulty with Frege's perceptual model of objectivity is that there are fundamental differences between the terms and objects of cognitive meaning; between, for example, propositional truths about the North Sea and the body of European water to which they refer. Frege adverted to these differences with his ontological distinction between abstract and perceptual entities and his linguistic distinction between abstract and concrete singular terms, but he failed to trace them to their source. According to his analysis of objectivity, there is a striking similarity between the *apprehension* of abstract thoughts and the *observation* of concrete objects. Even though the intentional acts differ in kind, each discloses to the subject's awareness a preexistent entity whose being and nature are radically mind-independent. For Frege, the asymmetry between propositions and geographical objects reduces to the difference between public entities that are atemporal, imperceptible, and invariant and ones that are temporal, perceptible, and variable. Since logical entities are alleged to be causally independent of the mind, the method or manner of their discovery is declared irrelevant to the logician's investigation.

I take sharp exception to this analysis and to the analogy on which it is based. Michael Dummett has remarked that Frege had a strong antipathy to idealism.[63] The roots of this antipathy are traceable to Frege's belief that idealism is incompatible with objectivity. But, perhaps, logical idealism is the expression of a partial truth that Frege overlooked, leading him radically to divorce objectivity from the exercise and achievements of the human mind. Frege treated objectivity of any kind as incompatible with causal dependence on the mind; by contrast, epistemic idealists treat all modes of objectivity as essentially mind-dependent. Is it possible that the idealists exaggerate the power of the mind and that Frege sees an incompatibility where none really exists? Can we find a middle path between these opposing extremes?

The objectivity of cognitive terms of meaning, Fregean thoughts, is mind-dependent, for intelligible propositions are the causal results of intelligent acts of understanding. Since these acts are tokens of intersubjective intentional types, the publicity of propositional terms of meaning is preserved for everyone who achieves the requisite level of understanding. Meaningful propositions give logical expression to the intelligible content of intentional and intelligent acts of understanding. The formal acts of meaning that formulate propositions proceed in a lawful, intelligent manner from antecedent acts of insight. Logical terms of meaning are the intelligible products through which the mind gives expression to its tentative understanding of reality. The true foundation of the theory of meaning is not to be located in the philosophy of language but in cognitional theory. Because terms of meaning are distributively but not collectively mind-independent and because the cognitive subject achieves self-transcendence in its authentic acts of understanding and judgment, we can relax Frege's causal criterion without surrendering intersubjectivity and universal truth.

Propositions are true when their truth-conditions are satisfied by the objects to which they refer. The intentional acts of understanding that are generative of propositional terms of meaning are not causally constitutive of the objects the propositions are about. Frege misunderstood the nature of logical entities because he construed their objectivity on the analogy of cognitional objects. Idealists misunderstand the nature of cognitional objects because they construe their objectivity on the analogy of terms of meaning. They both attempt to achieve a general theory of objectivity by treating one aspect of cognitional process as an analogical model for the whole. To obtain the full story that neither of them provides, we need to transcend analogical models of knowing and develop a comprehensive theory of cognitional operations and contents. Intentional analysis will show that the constitutive operations of inquiry are importantly dissimilar and that the terms and objects of cognitive meaning bear very different causal and intentional relations to the human mind.

Why did Frege refuse to consider the possibility that abstract entities, terms of meaning, might be dependent on the mind for their causal origin? Three reasons seem to have prevented this. Given his declared criteria of objectivity, that concession would have compromised the objective standing of logic. In addition, Frege was an epistemic realist who denied that the object of knowledge was constructed or constituted by the process of knowing it. Since he modeled the objectivity of terms of meaning on that of cognitional objects, he ascribed the same ontological independence to thoughts that he did to physical things. Finally, Frege appears to have acknowledged only three types of intentional operation, none of which is causally generative of terms of meaning: the sensory perception of public sensible objects, understanding the thought expressed by an indicative sentence, and affirming or denying the truth value of a proposition. How should this repertoire of intentional acts be augmented for the sake of completeness? Since that is the central topic of section G, now I shall say only that Frege's account suffered from an "oversight of insight."[64] He overlooked the acts of direct and reflective understanding from which formal and full terms of meaning lawfully proceed. These intentional acts are more central to the process of cognition than understanding the sense of a sentence and they markedly resist assimilation to the model of sense perception. However, no one who relinquishes cognitional analysis to avoid the reproach of psychologism is ever likely to discover them.

Not all the critics of psychologism shared Frege's neglect of cognitional theory. Transcendental critics, like Husserl and the neo-Kantians, also wanted to preserve epistemic objectivity but without reliance on Frege's conceptual realism. Although they agreed with Frege that empiricism and naturalism lacked an adequate theory of meaning and truth, they did not subscribe to Frege's realistic ontology and semantics. In an explicit rejection of Frege's methodological principles Husserl made the cognitive subject the center of philosophical inquiry.[65] The best way to understand Husserl's phenomenology is to see it as a radicalized variation on Cartesianism. Husserl shared Descartes's belief in the priority of emancipated subjectivity, but he thought that Descartes had failed to honor his leading principle consistently. In the evolution of Husserl's thought, we can discern the increasing dependence of knowable entities on the constructive operations of the cognitive subject; we can also discern a steady drift toward idealism in the progressive transcendentalizing of the Cartesian ego.[66]

Frege's critical review of Husserl's first book, the *Philosophy of Arithmetic*, alerted him to the dangers of psychologism in logical theory. Husserl attempted to refute psychologism in the opening volume of the *Logical Investigations* by arguing for a major distinction between the ideal order of logic and the causal and temporal order of empirical science. He agreed with Frege that the third realm of *thoughts* differs in principle from the causal order of things and the private realm of subjective ideas. But he rejected Frege's contention that logical entities are wholly independent of intentional acts. Husserl outlined a process of intentional genesis that preserved the objectivity of terms of meaning without conceding their ontological self-sufficiency and independence.

As Husserl's career progressed, his interest shifted from logical and mathematical objects to the subjective operations through which all noematic contents are constituted and eventually known. He identified pure philosophy with the phenomenological investigation of these intentional operations and their correlative intentional contents. The proper task of philosophy was to reconstruct the sequence of intentional operations through which the different species of semantic and epistemic objectivity are given to conscious apprehension. But Husserl diverged from Descartes's rational psychology by insisting that philosophical knowledge could not be factual. For Husserl, philosophy could not be a presuppositionless science unless it identified and bracketed the most pervasive of all *presuppositions*, the natural attitude. Accepting Descartes's assumption that first philosophy must be completely indubitable, he correctly concluded that factual knowledge could not meet this foundational test. Fact is nothing more than verified possibility; it is what is so, not what must be so or could not be otherwise. Husserl thought that to base philosophy, the only truly rigorous science, on a foundation of fact rather than necessity would be to surrender the Cartesian hope for indubitability and to leave theoretical science ultimately ungrounded.

Husserl's foundational strategy resembles Descartes's in attempting to formulate knowledge claims that cannot be coherently doubted. But that strategy is subject to the following limitation. Any epistemic assertion that advances our knowledge of reality can be rationally put into question. The appropriate response to the skeptic is not a series of indubitable assertions but a set of factual judgments that cannot be coherently denied. The effective strategy is to engage a skeptical interlocutor in reflection on the structure of his own inquiry. In this reflexive analysis, the skeptic will encounter basic, factual limiting structures that can be negated only by an incoherent cognitional performance, one that tacitly or explicitly denies a condition of its own possibility. The structure of human cognition is simultaneously factual and foundational. The denial of that structure is not logically inconsistent, for the structure is contingent and clearly might have been otherwise. But the denial of its existence and centrality is performatively inconsistent, since if it is to be intelligent and rational, that denial must exemplify the very pattern of operations it refuses to acknowledge.

Husserl's phenomenology performed the valuable service of directing philosophical attention to the intentional subject and intentional operations. His theory of meaning revealed how the objectivity of logical entities did not preclude their intentional genesis. But in his quest for indubitable foundations of knowledge, he rejected the finite factual subject for the transcendental ego. I do not find the methodological reasons supporting that rejection compelling nor the cognitional theory to which it leads sufficiently nuanced.[67] Although Husserl believed that a factual theory of knowledge could not satisfy the quest for certainty, the specter of psychologism he raised need not frighten us. On the rock of personal appropriation we can shape a balanced theory of objectivity and an answer to the epistemic skeptic more convincing than any Husserl proposed.

The critique of psychologism, begun by Frege and advanced by Husserl and Sellars, was intended to restore the objectivity of meaning and knowledge. This goal was achieved partly by distinguishing intersubjective terms of meaning from psychological episodes and ideas. But it is my belief that the correct relation between epistemic objectivity and intentional subjectivity was never acknowledged. Frege segregated objective truth from its source in cognitive practice; Sellars only partly redressed this omission by emphasizing the linguistic dimensions of inquiry; Husserl brought the operations of the intentional subject to the fore, but his theory of the subject was overly dependent on Descartes and Kant. Legitimate unease about transcendental idealism has kept subsequent naturalistic and analytic philosophers at arms length from the intentional subject. But rather than enhancing their insight into epistemic objectivity, this has actually prevented them from appreciating its full complexity.

F. Transcendental Method

Where other methods aim at meeting the exigencies
and exploiting the opportunities proper to
particular fields, transcendental method is

concerned with meeting the exigencies and
exploiting the opportunities presented by the
human mind itself.[68]

Let us pause a moment to take stock of our progress in this chapter. I began by asserting the critical need in contemporary culture for cognitive integration. The permanent human demand for the unification of knowledge has been intensified by the specialized pluralism and deepened historical consciousness of our time. I then called attention to the project of Bernard Lonergan, who has designed a philosophic strategy to meet the integrative aspirations and requirements of this second stage of modernity. Lonergan believed that a critical contemporary synthesis of knowledge must be preceded by the personal appropriation of the intentional subject. After outlining the presuppositions and procedures of personal appropriation, I confronted two formidable criticisms of this strategy. I defended the legitimacy of intentional analysis against behaviorist objections and defended factual cognitional theory against the charge of psychologism. These defenses, if successful, should free us now to continue the search for the invariant foundations of knowledge.

The guiding idea is that the foundations of cognition are located in the transcultural, transhistorical invariants of intentional subjectivity. We need to distinguish carefully between the existence of these foundations as they operate in experiential consciousness and their objective appropriation through intentional analysis. Through philosophical inquiry we appropriate, or take rational possession of, foundational realities of which we are already experientially aware. We *rely on* these foundations in all our cognitive practice, but we generally fail to acknowledge or attend to them.[69] Prereflexive consciousness naturally is directed away from the subject toward the surrounding world. We begin our cognitive life by exploring the common-sense world into which we are born and only gradually do we extend our inquiry into the intelligibility of nature and the remoteness of history. Only much later, after mastering a body of practical and theoretical knowledge, do we think to question the conditions of its acquisition and validation. In the process of personal appropriation, intentional subjects discover the concrete, experientially conscious conditions of their continuing existences as knowers. These foundational conditions are the source and principle of every cognitive achievement and revision; they are not causal products of cultural advance and development but the prior grounds of their possibility. They exist, generally unacknowledged, at the very center of who we are as human persons.

What are the foundational realities to which I refer? The real principles on which cognition depends are our native endowments of intelligence and reasonableness and the inherent structures of cognitional process.[70] These principles are exercised most fully in the intellectual pattern of experience, but human consciousness is only intermittently governed by strictly intellectual purposes. We enjoy a plurality of desires, interests, and concerns that continuously struggle for our conscious attention and loyalty. The patterns of everyday conscious experience normally are polymorphic rather than uniform; our concern for life and limb, our attachment to beauty and art, our interpersonal engagement with others, our absorption in practical affairs claim the great proportion of our waking awareness. In these different patterns of experience, intelligence and reason are at the service of noncognitive goals. So much so, that Dewey and the pragmatists have denied the existence of any purely cognitive desires. Both personal and historical experience suggest that these pragmatic denials are untrue to the full reality of the intentional subject. "Deep within us all, emergent when the noise of other appetites is stilled, there is a drive to know, to understand, to see why, to discover the reason, to find the cause, to explain."[71] Though few of us make this desire to know the effective center of our lives, it is not absent from any life that can properly be called human. This is the elemental truth to which Aristotle referred in the opening passage of his *Metaphysics*: "All men by *nature* (*physei*) desire to know."[72]

Both Plato and Aristotle recognized the desire to know as the origin or principle (*arche*) of philosophy. But the eros of mind is operative whenever human beings inquire not just in philosophical reflection. It is the exigent source of wonder (*thauma*) that the Greeks explicitly recognized and the spirit of rational criticism raised to prominence by Descartes and the Enlightenment. Exploratory questions of intelligence and the habit of regular critical reflection testify to its relentless demands, but they cannot exhaust them. The human desire to know, by nature, is unrestricted and disinterested. It seeks knowledge without limit and for its own sake. Because other competing desires often dominate my conscious experience, I very rarely satisfy its insistent demands. But whenever human consciousness is governed by the eros and exigence of the mind, it follows an intellectual pattern that has a determinate normative structure. The unrestricted, disinterested desire to know is the core or ground of all cognitive meaning because it underpins, energizes, and constantly renews the cognitive process through which we arrive at meaning and truth.

Because the desire to know naturally is unrestricted, it will not be satisfied until we know everything about everything. Although the aspiration to knowledge is comprehensive, every actual epistemic contribution is the answer to a specific and limited set of questions. The exploratory questions with which human inquiry begins are the intellect's distinctive response to the world we immediately perceive. These questions become articulate and determinate only when the child has learned a language, but the native spirit of inquiry antecedes that acquisition. The eros of mind is operative in human consciousness before it becomes articulate and literate; once the human subject is able to speak and write, it is the inexhaustible source of all further original questioning. Language clearly is necessary to make effective questioning possible and communicable, but it is our native intelligence, enriched by the mastery of language, that makes questions relevant, important, and profound. Though prior to all linguistic articulation and specific questioning the desire to know is not prior to experiential consciousness. This does not mean that the cognitive subject must explicitly advert to the desire or openly acknowledge it, but it does mean that the subject's intelligence and reasonableness, his innate curiosity and critical spirit are constituted by consciousness as his normal circulatory states are not. As the sensitively conscious subject desires food, warmth, and shelter, so the intellectually conscious subject wants understanding and intelligibility, and the rationally conscious subject wants sufficient evidence and truth. In each case, the desire, the wanting, is experientially conscious, even though the different levels of desire are distinguished by their objects and by the pattern of operations through which they are satisfied.

Lonergan names the unrestricted human desire to know *the transcendental notion of being*.[73] The desire to know is transcendental in both the scholastic and Kantian senses of that term. As a comprehensive, conscious, intelligent, intending of reality, it is not confined to any particular genus of inquiry or to any specialized field of investigation. It underpins inquiry in all of its modalities and serves as the core of all cognitive terms of meaning at which inquiry arrives. It therefore satisfies the scholastic concept of the transcendental as that which pervades all categories of being and discourse. But the desire to know also meets the Kantian transcendental requirements by serving as an underlying universal condition that makes possible human knowledge of objects.[74] The pure desire to know, as a transcendental notion, is an unrestricted intentional intending of an equally unrestricted object. The transcendental concept of being is a second-order conceptualization of the unrestricted object intended by the eros of mind. From within the intellectual pattern of experience, being is first intended and later conceptualized as the intentional object of the unlimited desire to know. What we seek to know through the eros of mind is being; what we do know whenever we satisfy that desire is being. The first foundational invariant of intentional subjectivity is the unrestricted desire of human intelligence to know being. The personal appropriation of this desire is effectively balanced by the recognition of our polymorphic consciousness. A critical subject must be able to distinguish the eros of mind from other desires and the intellectual from the other patterns of experience. When philosophical judgments about knowledge, objectivity and reality are made it is imperative that the philosopher make them under the guidance of that eros and subject to the norms of that pattern.

The second foundational invariant in the subject is the dynamic pattern of recurrent and related operations, in which the pure desire to know normatively unfolds. This pattern consists in experientially conscious intentional operations linked to each other by relations of presupposition and complementarity. Through intentional analysis, we learn to identify the different cognitive operations in that pattern and the dynamic relations that bind them into a patterned unity. Cognitional process is a formally dynamic, self-assembling structure that begins at the level of sensitive experience, is carried forward by the intellect's desire for intelligible relatedness and unity, and climaxes in the judgments of reason on the truth value of full terms of meaning. Each successive level of the process is marked by a different quality of intentional consciousness and by different types of intentional operations. More advanced levels of cognitional structure presuppose and complement the acts and contents of preceding levels. Without the substratum of empirical consciousness, there is nothing for inquiry to question and investigate; without the exploratory thought elicited by questioning, there are no meaningful discoveries; and without discoveries, there are no explicitly formulated hypotheses to examine and appraise for adequacy and truth.

There are, then, three sequential levels on which the human quest for knowledge unfolds. It begins in sensory or imaginative experience, in the empirical awareness of the world. The contents of perceptual consciousness to which the subject attends provide the original field for intellectual scrutiny. The human response to perceptual awareness varies widely within the different patterns of experience, but in the intellectual pattern of consciousness it arouses the active desire to understand what perception discloses. The native orientation of the human intellect is to seek the intelligibility of whatever it encounters. The anticipation of a determinate type of intelligibility, rooted in one's earlier training and education, leads to the framing of particular questions and the active search for their answers. Intentional subjects progress from empirical to intellectual consciousness as they actively aspire to understand, articulate that aspiration in a set of linked and related questions, and intelligently seek their coherent resolution.

At the second level of cognitional process, human thinking is guided by specific heuristic anticipations. The very form of the questions that guide inquiry reveals that intelligence in its active operations always seeks a specific type of intelligibility.[75] Exploratory thinking finds a partial resolution in moments of discovery when the subject discerns a relevant pattern of intelligibility that appears to satisfy the orienting set of questions. The content of intellectual discovery is formulated hypothetically and provisionally in a formal term of meaning. Meaningful propositions are the answers framed by intelligence to its own determinate questions about the nature and relatedness of the objects of experience.

Even if intellect is momentarily satisfied with the discovery and conceptualization of apprehended intelligibility, human rational consciousness is not. Our critical reason demands that the putative answer be true or the closest approximation to truth of which we are presently capable. The human quest for knowledge reaches a decisive level when our formal terms of meaning are faced with the normative exigence of rational consciousness. Before we can responsibly affirm the truth of our tentative answer, we must be convinced that the evidence is sufficient to justify the assent. The dominant feature of rational consciousness is its spirit of critical reflection. However exciting the alleged discovery, however clear its resultant articulation, reason insists on detachment. We hesitate to embrace an answer as true until we have assembled sufficient evidence to show that its truth-conditions are satisfied in the relevant domain of experience. The terminal act in the complex process of cognition is the act of judgment. In judgment, we freely and responsibly commit ourselves to the truth of our answers; we implicitly declare that they have met the normative standards of rational objectivity, and that, therefore, they are binding on all rational beings. Even as we acknowledge our finitude, fallibility, and historical rootedness, we claim for our judgments the property of self-transcendence. We claim that by satisfying the immanent norms of intelligence and reason, we can achieve a knowledge of reality with universal validity. *Transcendental method* is Lonergan's name for this normative pattern of recurrent and related operations that begins in experience, rises to the level of understanding and conception, and terminates in judgment.[76] The critical moment in Lonergan's philosophical strategy is the personal appropriation of transcendental method as the normative structure of the intellectual pattern of experience. This is the water shed to which foundational analysis leads and from which cognitive integration flows.

The structure of human cognition is a dynamic pattern composed of dissimilar but coalescing intentional acts. The continuing dynamism of the process is supplied by the native *eros* and *exigence* of the human mind. The thirst for knowledge drives the process of inquiry relentlessly forward; until the demand for objectivity and truth are met, the mind is denied the satisfaction of even provisional closure. But such closure as the mind attains through knowledge is always limited and partial. Because the desire to know is unrestricted, the more we know the more our operative desire is heightened. The taste of truth only deepens our hunger for it. Although we have spoken of a transcendental *method* of cognition, this does not mean that there are rules for discovery or verification or that the synthesis of knowledge is a matter of algorithmic routine. Transcendental method is a framework for collaborative creativity; it is a common ground, universally shared by the human investigators in every specialized field and discipline. As the normative pattern for understanding the immanent intelligibility of experience, it is not specified by any particular field or subject matter, nor confined to any particular genus or category of inquiry.[78] But by suitable additions and adaptions it can be specified to any field of investigation. Transcendental method is the invariant common core of the methods of the specialized disciplines. It leaves them free to develop their particular determinations of its universal structure and to frame their own categorial frameworks. It is a unified foundational invariant that explicitly anticipates linguistic pluralism, categorial development, heuristic innovation, and methodological variability. It provides a foundational core of unity, continuity, and identity for a culture of autonomous practices profoundly committed to specialization, originality, and change.

Although the intentional operations constitutive of transcendental method are functionally complementary, they are qualitatively dissimilar. This explains why analogical theories of cognition have failed uniformly. The sensory operations of empirical consciousness do not resemble formal acts of meaning, any more than these acts resemble the operation of reflective insight. Moreover, the dynamic relations linking the successive operations into a unified cognitive whole also are qualitatively different. The desire for unrestricted intelligibility is as different from the detached demand for sufficient evidence as the task of the investigating detective is from that of the jury charged with the judgment of guilt or innocence. Classical theories of knowledge emphasized the quest for discovery and intelligibility, while the moderns since Descartes have concentrated on the issue of evidential justification and truth. Taken in exclusion from one another, both approaches are deficient and incomplete. The intellectual consciousness that culminates in formal terms of meaning needs to be *completed* by critical reflection; rational consciousness with its explicit concern for objectivity and truth *presupposes* the prior understanding of experience, the intentional and causal source of the terms of meaning it is asked to appraise. The contexts of discovery and justification are complementary aspects or moments in the unified process of cognition. When detached from the comprehensive whole to which they belong, they each tend to be assigned an exaggerated place in the cognitive matrix.

Another critical feature of transcendental method is its effective grouping of nonlogical and logical operations.[79] In the preceding chapter, I cited Hamilton's metaphor of the tunnel and the arch. Hamilton believed that the progress of developing knowledge required antecedent movements of thought that were then consolidated by complementary developments of language. I endorsed this belief and noted its negative implications for theories of intentionality that limited intentional acts to linguistic episodes. I criticized Sellars, Rorty, and Wittgenstein for failing to explain the source(s) of linguistic originality and change. They acknowledge and emphasize the advance of the arch of language but are unable to offer an intentional account of how the unexplored portion of the tunnel is excavated. The nonlogical, nonlinguistic operations of perception, heuristic anticipation, exploratory thinking, direct insight, critical reflection, marshalling of experiential evidence, and reflective understanding keep knowledge permanently open to development and revision. The logical and linguistic operations of describing phenomena, raising and answering questions, deducing the suppositions and implications of hypotheses, and articulating full terms of meaning consolidate and stabilize existing achievement. To be born into a mature linguistic community or to join an ongoing historical practice is to enter the tunnel of knowledge at the point of its most recent arch. Through effective education, we acritically appropriate the practical and theoretical achievements of our predecessors. As we mature, we become more critical of our cultural inheritance, even though we continue to rely upon it for guidance. The developing intentional subject is invariably at the center of an ongoing interior quarrel between language and experience. The activity of thinking consists primarily in two complementary operations: the assimilation of new experience to available understanding and categories and the adaptation of our habits of understanding and discourse to the disclosures of conflicting experience.[80] The point to insist upon is that both of these modes of thinking are marked by intelligence and rationality. To limit human rationality to its logical operations or human intentionality to linguistic episodes is to neglect the probing, inarticulate preconceptual explorations of the mind that, in each instance, have given rise to the discoveries that are consolidated by the next arch of meaning.

G. The Centrality of Insight

To grasp it [insight] in its conditions, its working,
and its results is to confer a basic yet startling unity
on the whole field of human inquiry.[81]

We are exploring a comprehensive philosophy that takes its stand on the personal appropriation of the dynamic structure of cognitional activity. It is a philosophy based on psychological facts that can be discovered and verified in the subject's intentional experience. At the risk of repetition, I again want to distinguish the recurrent operation of cognitional process in human beings from their intentional analysis of that operation. The unity of the intentional subject and the normative pattern of intentional operations are given in conscious experience prior to cognitional analysis; "intentional inquiry and discovery are needed not to effect the synthesis of a manifold that, as given, is unrelated, but to analyze a functional and functioning unity."[82] The task of cognitional investigation is to identify and distinguish the different operations within transcendental method and to discover the dynamic relations that bind them into a complex cognitive whole. The fruit of successful analysis is a personally appropriated theory of cognition, whose basic terms and relations refer to the immanent, recurrently operative pattern in the theorist's consciousness. Through personal appropriation intentional subjects begin to understand what they are actually doing in the pursuit of knowledge.

Cognitional analysis reveals three interdependent levels of intentional operations. The central operation in this complex normative pattern is an intentional act called *insight*. Two basic kinds of insight are required for human cognition: direct and reflective. Direct insights are the pivotal operations on the second level of cognitional process; reflective insights play a similarly critical role on the third level of rational consciousness. Although insights of both kinds occur frequently, their existence and importance normally are overlooked by cognitional theorists. Lonergan believed that this omission, this oversight of insight, is profoundly significant for two reasons: First, because an adequate and comprehensive cognitional theory is the centerpiece of a critical philosophical strategy; and second, because the acts of direct and reflective understanding are the central operations within the framework of transcendental method. To grasp them in their conditions, working, and results is to uncover the basic unity of human inquiry and knowledge. Lonergan's most important text, *Insight, A Study of Human Understanding*, provides an elaborate defense of these important and largely unfamiliar claims. In the remainder of this chapter, I hope to provide an intelligible outline of his strategic argument. My proximate aim is to help secure for his work the wider philosophical audience it deserves. The more remote intention is to reorient the practice of philosophy in this time of cultural transition and uncertainty.

　　The strategy of *Insight* unfolds in three stages.[83] Lonergan begins by establishing the fact and nature of the act of understanding. At this initial stage of exposition, insights are identified as psychological events that occur in the course of human inquiry within the different realms of cognitive meaning. After examining their interdependence with and distinction from the other cognitive operations, he proceeded to explore the philosophical implications of insight. These implications prove to be far-reaching, extending from cognitional theory into epistemology and metaphysics. Finally, the dialectical importance of *insights* is emphasized. They provide the key to a critical philosophy of philosophies that effectively distinguishes the merits and limitations of opposing philosophical theories. The pattern of textual argument advances from the operations constitutive of knowing, through the achievement of objective knowledge to the nature and coherence of the reality known. Having secured the foundational base and its legitimate expansion into correlative philosophic disciplines, Lonergan doubled back to assess contrasting accounts of the same terrain. Lonergan's cognitionally based philosophy is intended to be comprehensive, methodical, and critical. It seeks to address the full range of disputed questions concerning knowledge, objectivity, and being and to provide an effective procedure for resolving intractable philosophical disputes. This ambitious theoretical enterprise rests on a foundation of psychological fact that awaits discovery and appropriation by the mature and reflective thinker. Let us now examine that foundation and the acts of insight that are said to constitute its operating center.

　　What is it for a human being to understand? Our immediate response to this question is likely to be vague and imprecise. To remedy this imprecision we must begin to focus on the determinate manner in which our intelligence operates and develops. To understand thoroughly what it is to understand is the goal of personal appropriation. The first fact to be acknowledged is the complexity of human knowing. Opponents of the spectator theory of knowledge are justified in rejecting the confrontational model of cognition. We do not come to understand a new field of experience by staring or looking at it. The development of understanding is a gradual discursive process rather than an ecstatic intuitive event. We enhance our understanding of a field of inquiry by asking and answering questions about it. The shared activity of interrogative dialogue, first portrayed philosophically in the Socratic-Platonic philosophical dramas, provides a richer image of the cognitive context than any empiricist model of direct intuition. But even discursive models of cognition are inadequate if they fail to acknowledge the nonlinguistic desires and operations on which both questions and answers depend. The emphasis on interactive linguistic behavior, favored by Rorty and the later Wittgenstein, is valuable because it corrects the historic tendency to identify knowing with some form or variety of looking. But it needs to be supplemented by a complete account of the nonlinguistic intentional operations that the meaningful use of language presupposes.

The central cognitive act that both empiricists and linguistic behaviorists tend to overlook is the act of insight. The human act of understanding is not intuitive in nature. Rather, it grasps in simplifying schematic images intelligible possibilities that may or may not prove relevant to an understanding of the data of experience.[84] As the preceding description indicates, insights do not occur in an intentional vacuum. They are intellectually conscious events at the second level of cognitional process, which presuppose prior levels of intentional operation. The immediate antecedent of insight is the activity of thoughtful inquiry that frames the questions and shapes the schematic images to which insight responds. Insight momentarily breaks the tension of inquiry by discerning a possible solution to the problem or question in which the investigating subject is absorbed. But exploratory inquiry is not without its own presuppositions. As investigative questioning and thinking are prior to understanding, so the data of experience are prior to the onset of questioning. It is the mark of active intelligence that it seeks to understand the content of its experience. Because many regions of our experience are not immediately intelligible to us, we raise specific questions about them in the hope of comprehending the reality they have partially disclosed. The operating presence of our native intelligence is manifest at every phase of this patterned procedure. Because we are intelligent, we seek to understand experience, anticipate the kind of understanding we may attain, frame particular questions in the light of that anticipation, and play with schematic models or images of potential relevance to the intelligibility that is sought. Direct insights, then, do not occur haphazardly or at random. They result from thinking through an exploratory question for intelligence that was prompted by antecedent perceptions, images, or memories. Nor are insights automatic or subject to explicit rules. Until they occur, the answer to the absorbing question eludes us, increasing the tension of our intelligent search. But what precisely happens when they do occur? Insight is a preconceptual event that consciously unifies and organizes the data of experience the subject is investigating. In the act of understanding, the cognitive subject either grasps an *intelligible unity* within that data or grasps a pattern of *intelligible relations* among its various elements. The intentional content that is grasped is a function of the selected data, the precision of the exploratory question, and the subject's own effort, intelligence, and cognitive background. Direct insights are the preconceptual acts of understanding that transport the subject from the perplexing question to its possible solution. They occur in every field of inquiry, both theoretical and practical, in which human intelligence is engaged.

Before we examine the manner in which insights cluster and coalesce, it is important to highlight their distinctive intentional content. What direct insights apprehend is either an *intelligible unity* within individual data or a *correlative pattern* of relatedness within a range of experienced elements. Insights grasp concrete patterns of intelligibility within the manifold of concrete experience. They apprehend intelligible forms that exist within the sensible, the imaginable, the remembered, or the experientially given.[85] Although their intentional content is concrete, it also is universal. They grasp a universal intelligibility immanent within the content of experience. In so doing they serve as a pivot or mediator between the concreteness of sensory experience and the abstractness of conceptual formulation. The concrete intelligible content grasped by insight receives its abstract expression in the logical order of concepts and propositions. It is essential to distinguish the abstract, logical propositional content that is the product and effect of the act of understanding from the preconceptual intelligible content of insight. In order to say what it is we understand, we must use abstract universals, but the immanent content of the act of understanding is a concrete universal, an intelligible form.[86] The immanent intelligibility of the concrete particular case gives the mind access to the formulated general principle.

A single insight taken in isolation is of limited cognitive significance. The key to the development of human understanding is the achievement of a cumulative succession of insights. Because direct insights pass into the habitual texture of the mind, human beings are capable of learning.[87] Until we understand the experience we are exploring, we are perplexed by the absorbing or tantalizing problem; but once we have effectively understood, what had been perplexing becomes routine. In the act of understanding, we cross an asymmetrical heuristic gap. We cannot undo, even by an act of deliberate volition, the fruit of our earlier intellectual development. The more we have understood the more capable we become at understanding; unhappily the inverse of this principle is also true. Learning is a self-correcting process through which we try to master a field of investigation. In this process earlier insights are qualified, complemented, and corrected by their successors. Intellectual mastery is achieved only when we command a cumulative cluster of insights that allow us to systematize our knowledge of a determinate field of experience. An axiomatic system of definitions, postulates, and theorems is a provisional logical context of terms of meaning that articulates the present state of our understanding. Given the dynamic process of scientific inquiry, these categorial systematizations often are historically unstable. Deeper reorganizing insights may lead to a higher intellectual viewpoint allowing us to treat earlier theories as special cases of more general principles. Contemporary empirical science anticipates a continuing succession of these logical systems, each phrased in a theoretically adjusted vocabulary. For this reason Rorty was fully justified in resisting the absolutization of normal scientific discourse. But his behavioral account of linguistic change totally neglects the reorienting insights that make these conceptual transformations intelligible. What appears from the logical point of view as a discontinuous instance of conceptual change is understood methodologically as the attainment of a higher intellectual viewpoint within the framework of a unifying heuristic structure. The advantage of the methodological perspective over that of both logic and behaviorism is that it preserves the historic continuity of scientific inquiry while providing an intelligent account of the process of conceptual change. This allows us to retain a normative vision of theoretical science as the cooperative historical search for explanatory understanding.

Close attention to the development of understanding makes us sensitive to the horizons within which inquiry and insight occur. The questions we ask in the interrogation of experience reflect the kind of intelligibility we seek and expect to find. Depending on our orienting desires and heuristic purposes, we may ask significantly different questions of the same set of experiential data.[88] In thinking out the answer to a question for which we lack an adequate response, we rely on the construction of schemas, models, or images. We attempt to combine in a surveyable working model the range of information we consider relevant to the solution of the problem. Judgments of relevance also reflect the existing horizon of our thinking, our operative beliefs, values, presuppositions, and orienting concerns. The deeper our present understanding of a problem context, the more penetrating are our determinations of relevance, and the more suggestive are our heuristic models. But the inverse is also true. If we have cumulatively misunderstood experience in the past, we are vulnerable to blind spots, to prejudicial anticipations that block the path to discovery and comprehension. No human being enters the process of inquiry in a condition of cognitive neutrality. Our antecedent personal achievements and failures of understanding as well as those of our cultural community profoundly influence the direction and content of our thought. This explains why learning is a protracted self-correcting process and why the frequency of insight is dependent on antecedent conditions of abstraction and the suitability of our heuristic anticipations. Even before we actually understand, we use our active intelligence to prepare the ground for understanding. Objective abstraction,[89] the intelligent elimination by the mind of the irrelevant because it is understood to be irrelevant, is operative in the heuristic anticipation of intelligibility, in the framing of questions for intelligence, in the design of a schematic model, in the operations of selection and emphasis, and in the detection and organization of clues.

What does direct insight add to experience, questioning, and exploratory thought? The act of direct understanding is the intellectual apprehension of the anticipated pattern of intelligibility within the model or schema fashioned by the imagination under the guidance of objective abstraction. Insight is the apprehension of an intelligible form or structure that unifies or organizes the contents of experience. Before the insight occurs we may have the requisite experience, the focusing questions, the thoughtful analysis and exploration, but we lack the act of understanding required for a satisfactory answer. Insight is the intelligent cause and intentional ground of propositional conceptualization. It is the effective intelligent mediator between the questions that elicit and guide inquiry and the answers provisionally offered to these questions. The answers offered in response to inquiry emerge simultaneously with the relevant acts of understanding, but they are numerically and specifically distinct from these acts that serve as their intelligent ground. Conceptual formulations express the intelligible content grasped by insight together with what is essential to its apprehension in the schematically organized materials that are understood.

The heart of Lonergan's cognitional theory is his insistence on the distinction and yet lawful interrelation between the grounding acts of understanding and the derivative acts of resultant conceptualization. *Propositions, formal terms of meaning, inner words, logical truth-vehicles*—these are simply different expressions for the provisional answers offered by the intellect to its own questions about the data of experience.[90] These answers, when they are relevant and apposite to the questions guiding inquiry, proceed intelligently and consciously from the intellect in act. The propositional inner word is a conceptual or logical expression of what is understood by the inquiring subject preconceptually. The proposition consolidates or stabilizes, renders articulate and therefore subject to critical reflection, what is apprehended in the nonlinguistic intentional operation of insight. The formal term of meaning is the lawful, conscious intelligible *product* produced by the act of insight into the appropriate heuristic image. Just as there is no insight without experience and exploratory inquiry, so there is no apt and meaningful answer without a prior development of understanding. The more penetrating the development of understanding, the more numerous and internally connected are the propositions in which that development finds expression. When the anticipated answers are not forthcoming, we reasonably may infer that the required understanding has not occurred. *Tene rem et verba sequentur*. It is in the very nature of the human mind to express its intellectual development conceptually. But to go beyond changing concepts and propositions to their intelligent source and causal ground is to recover the direct insights on which they essentially depend.

The process of human cognition is not complete with the formulation of a tentative answer on the basis of a direct insight, however. As the second level of transcendental method presupposes the antecedent contents of experience, so its third and culminating level presupposes the availability of formal terms of meaning. Because meaningful propositions are tentative, provisional answers to questions for intelligence, we submit them to an appraisal of truth value. To determine whether a given answer or set of answers is true is the central purpose of the critical reflection characteristic of rational consciousness. There are an unlimited number of questions which the intentional subject may address to experience, but there is only one basic question of reflection: Is it *true* that the formulated proposition(s) correctly and comprehensively answer(s) the original question(s) about this determinate field of experience? The explicitly formulated question of intelligence and the heuristic context out of which it arises set the standard of relevance for critical reflection. As exploratory thinking is the development of the mind toward the occurrence of direct insights, so reflective thinking is its purposeful movement toward the attainment of reflective insight. The function of reflective thought is to determine the truth conditions of formal terms of meaning and to assemble the evidence required for a judgment of their truth value. A formal term of meaning is true if its truth conditions are satisfied by the appropriate array of evidence; it is known to be true if the intentional subject's reflective understanding apprehends that those conditions are satisfied. Inversely, if the relevant evidence is incompatible with the articulated truth conditions, then the proposition is false, and known to be false when the evidence assembled is so apprehended. The process of critical reflection is often unable to amass sufficient evidence to determine whether the truth conditions of a proposition are satisfied. The more penetrating and comprehensive an insight, the more complex are the truth conditions of its propositional expression and the more difficult it is to determine their truth value.

Reflective inquiry is a pivotal return from the abstract propositional synthesis produced by developing insight to its concrete sources in sense and direct intelligence. It is a rational pivot from the abstract logical order back toward concrete experience. The truth conditions of the formulated proposition are understood abstractly, in an act of nonintuitive intellectual apprehension. But the evidence that bears on the satisfaction of these truth conditions ultimately is concrete. The process of reflective inquiry, of propositional verification, originates in the logical order, the order of presupposition and deductive implication, but it culminates finally in the order of concrete experience. We take exception, then, to theories of rational justification that portray reflective inquiry as an exclusively logical affair. The intentional operations constitutive of verification are not confined within the world of propositions nor is the range of potentially relevant evidence exclusively propositional. Without slighting the central role of logical inference in the activity of rational consciousness, we want to emphasize the experiential evidence that so often is neglected in today's epistemic theories.[91] Just as acts of direct insight grasp a potential intelligibility in the schematic models prepared by objective abstraction, so acts of reflective insight grasp a grounded or ungrounded intelligibility in the accumulated evidence assembled by reflective inquiry.[92] As in the earlier stage of intellectual consciousness, objective abstraction intelligently eliminates the irrelevant because it is understood to be irrelevant; critical reason marshals and organizes evidence, both propositional and experiential, in the light of its grasp of the proposition's truth conditions.

There is an immanent operative standard of reason that the human being uses in appraising propositional claims to truth: Is the problematic proposition an instance of the virtually unconditioned; that is, are its truth conditions satisfied in the field of potentially relevant evidence? The entire process of critical reflection points toward this determination. A proposition is virtually unconditioned if it has antecedent conditions and those conditions are in fact fulfilled. Reflective acts of understanding meet the question for reflection by grasping the link between the conditioned proposition and its truth conditions and by determining whether those conditions obtain within the field of experience.[93]

The act of reflective insight is a conscious rational apprehension of the sufficiency or insufficiency of the marshaled evidence to ground the proposition's truth. The proximate criterion of truth is reason's normative demand for a truth-vehicle that is virtually unconditioned. The remote criterion of truth is the yet more exigent demand that reflective insights be invulnerable, that they be immune to revision in the light of further reflection, experience, and intellectual development. An act of insight is invulnerable only if there are no further relevant questions bearing on the issue it is intended to resolve. This determination can be made only over time by objective abstraction in the self-correcting process of mastering a domain of inquiry. It is only through the further questions generated by the process of learning that new insights will occur to modify or revise the originally satisfactory answer.[94]

How do we determine when there are further questions that bear on a cognitive issue? This depends in part on the horizon of inquiry and its internal standards of relevance. Common sense and theoretical science, for example, operate with strikingly different criteria of inquiry. But there are no recipes or rules in any cognitive domain for producing appropriate questions, any more than there are rules of discovery or confirmation. To demand a decision procedure for relevant questions is to demand more than human ingenuity can supply. The norms of intelligent questioning are immanent within the unrestricted human desire to know. It is the disinterested surrender to that desire by individual subjects that concretely determines whether further questions will arise and what they will be. The norms of responsible judgment cannot be separated from the concrete human beings who apply them in practice. But we can be counseled to avoid two extremes that threaten our capacity to judge well. The fact that I, as a single individual, cannot think of further questions is no guarantee that there are none. No adequate account of cognitive objectivity can avoid referring to an intentional subject who is alert, disinterested, familiar with the concrete situation, and intellectually at home in it. If I do not possess these properties, then my poverty of questions establishes nothing of cognitive importance. The other extreme that vitiates responsible judgment is unwarranted indecision. To demand the impossibility of further questions before we assent to a proposition's truth is to demand too much. Since the knowledge that scientists, philosophers, and persons of common sense seek is factual knowledge, it is the factual absence of further relevant questions that bears on the insight's invulnerability. It is only further factual inquiry by informed and disinterested subjects that can determine whether significant questions have been overlooked.

The rigor of the remote criterion of truth, its demand for invulnerable insights, has prompted skeptics to charge that an objective judgment of fact is beyond human capacity. But Lonergan insisted that the dynamic structure of his own cognitional activity confronts the skeptic with a basic limiting pattern he cannot evade. The appropriate strategy is to engage the skeptic who refuses to make judgments of fact in the process of personal appropriation. In the course of investigating the operations of his own cognitive structure, the skeptic is involved in a second instantiation of that structure. If his inquiry is to be intelligent and rational, the skeptic must appeal to experience, pursue inquiry, make discoveries, formulate them provisionally, submit the provisional formulation to reflection, assemble the appropriate evidence, grasp its sufficiency or insufficiency for a determination of truth, and reach a reasonable judgment in the light of that grasp. The evidence for a psychological judgment of cognitional fact is to be found in the skeptic's own epistemic reflection. Now, an affirmation of that structure would silence unrestricted skepticism, and a denial of it would be incoherent with the operative conditions of reasonable negation. The skeptic's only refuge in the face of his own foundational reality is to refuse the invitation to self-knowledge. But can this refusal be made in good faith? The traditional dignity and strength of the skeptic has been a readiness to ask the critical questions of others. The skeptic cannot reasonably refuse to address these questions simply because they threaten his entrenched position. The point of this self-reflexive exercise is not chiefly to joust with professional skeptics, but to establish that reasonable judgments of fact are generally possible and in the specific case of personal appropriation rationally unavoidable. The goal of cognition in its culminating rational stage is to reach factual judgments of this kind.

As direct insight issues consciously and intelligently in formal terms of meaning, so reflective insight issues consciously and reasonably in propositional judgments of truth or falsity. The act of rational judgment is the act of positing or assenting to the proposed propositional synthesis as true. It is unreasonable to grasp the accumulated evidence as sufficient for the truth of the proposition and yet to refuse assent to its truth. As long as the assembled evidence is insufficient, as long as further relevant questions are to be raised, as long as the proximate and remote criteria are unsatisfied, the subject rationally may withhold assent from a formal term of meaning. But once those criteria are satisfied, to refuse assent is to be unreasonable, even foolish; it is to refrain from acknowledging fact, verified possibility, what is actually the case, whether I want it to be so or not. Judgment adds the "yes" of affirmation or the "no" of denial to the propositional terms of meaning causally grounded in direct insight. In the act of judgment, the intentional subject advances from supposition and hypothesis to personal commitment. Cognitional process is a cumulative, complex, many-leveled structure of functionally complementary operations. The act of judgment is the final incremental moment in that normative structure, which progresses from the originating level of experience through the intellectual level of understanding experience to the rational level of verification of that formulated understanding. Through assent to true propositions that are grasped in reflective insight as virtually unconditioned, the human person brings one circuit of the cycle of cognition to a close.

The conclusions to which we have been brought in this section may be summarized by stating[95]

1. There exist two types of insight: direct and reflective;
2. They arise in response to inquiry, to questions for intelligence or critical reflection;
3. They grasp either intelligible patterns immanent in experience or the sufficiency of evidence required for reasonable judgment;
4. They are the causal ground and intentional origin of the intentional acts of conceptualization and judgment;
5. These logical operations proceed from insights, not on some obscure analogy of the emergence of terminal states at the end of material processes, but as conscious expressions of the intellect in act;

6. The center of human cognitional analysis should be held not by the logical products of intelligence, such as concepts or propositions, but by the underlying acts of insight from which they causally derive;

7. The basic cognitional structure of experience, understanding, and judgment is a matter of psychological fact that awaits personal appropriation by the cognitional theorist;

8. The oversight of insight rooted in methodological scruples or conceptualist prejudices[96] leaves the theory of cognition without its critical center.

Before we turn to the different cognitive contexts in which direct and reflective insights occur, I want to express a terminological caveat. Since the term *insight* is not Lonergan's private property, his theory of understanding can be clarified by stating explicitly what insights are not. They are not operations of sense, imagination, or, memory. These acts occur at the first level of empirical consciousness, whereas insights arise only on the second and third levels of intelligence and reason. They are not logical or linguistic operations like describing phenomena, raising and answering questions, deducing the suppositions and implications of hypotheses, formulating theories, or articulating judgments. Insights presuppose and complement logical operations but they are themselves preconceptual in nature. There are no observable models for insights; they are fundamentally different from the traditional acts of fabrication, speech, and perception that have repeatedly served as the analogical base for classical and modern philosophies of mind. Explicit denial of the existence of insights has usually confused them with a fictitious species of intentional act; namely, intellectual or rational intuitions. When Sellars, for example, attacked as epistemologism the thesis that terms of meaning are immediately given to the mind, he was rejecting an errant phenomenological theory, but he was not referring to insights. There is no evidence that intentional intellectual intuitions of abstract terms of meaning actually occur, but the acts of intentional understanding from which concepts and propositions causally proceed unmistakably do. To pass beyond thinking of insights as intuitions or linguistic episodes of any kind is to surrender the demand for an analogical model of human intelligence and to accept the human mind and its diverse range of intentional operations and contents for what they are. Once you understand what it is to understand, you cannot fail to discover the fact of direct and reflective insight nor the normative pattern of operations to which it belongs. Expand that initial understanding until it embraces the different contexts of human inquiry, the different realms of cognitive meaning, and you will achieve the foundational base for a comprehensive and critical philosophy.

H. Realms of Meaning and Heuristic Structures

In the two preceding sections, I have treated cognitional process at the highest possible level of generality. I have been outlining a transcendental method that is the common core and ground of all specialized methods of inquiry. This method is intended to be comprehensive and universal; it is not specified by any particular field or subject of investigation, but by suitable additions it can be adapted to any investigatory context.[97] Nevertheless, it remains true that only the particular case gives access to the general pattern. The dynamic structure of transcendental method comes to light only after the actual development of determinate fields of knowledge. In the order of introductory exposition, transcendental method may be prior to all of its specialized applications in distinct realms of meaning; but in the order of occurrence and discovery, particular departments of knowledge, restricted to a limited viewpoint and field, claim priority and precedence. An objectified method is the fruit of reflection on prior intentional performance. Until this moment, I have outlined the development of understanding in abstraction from specific domains of inquiry. Let us turn now from the universal pattern to the specialized applications that mark the development and differentiation of intentional consciousness.

Because human consciousness is polymorphic rather than uniform, the same human being is the subject of contrasting eroses and exigencies. This plurality of desires, aspirations, and regulative norms grounds different patterns of intentional experience. The flow of purposive consciousness within any pattern is ordered toward the attainment of its determinate goal. As human beings mature, their intellectual development follows the evolutionary law of specialization and differentiation. This principle applies with particular force to the theoretical and practical pursuit of knowledge. As the cognitive quest increasingly becomes differentiated, it creates a plurality of distinct realms of meaning. Each of these realms is a specialized application of the universal matrix of cognitive meaning. It has its own cognitive aspirations, intentional viewpoint, field of investigation, mode of understanding, standards of relevance, conceptual vocabulary, style of transmission, and sustaining community. To master a realm of meaning is to become intellectually and linguistically at home in a form of life unintelligible to those who dwell outside its boundaries. Viewed from the linguistic perspective, a realm of meaning is a family of distinct but similar language games. But viewed from the perspective of intentional analysis, it is a specialized differentiation of intentional consciousness within a particular pattern of experience. I welcome the insights into human diversity arising from these different traditions but reject the methodological canon that confines philosophic evidence to linguistic behavior. I contend that there is an experientially conscious intentional ground deeper than discourse on which the variety of linguistic practices rests. The apprehension of this ground lets us understand the sources of linguistic plurality as well as the deeper pattern of unity that underlies them. The fact of linguistic difference is no longer merely a brute given but the intelligible consequence of a prior intentional variation. To illustrate the complementarity of linguistic and intentional analyses of meaning, let us explore two contrasting realms of intelligibility in which these different heuristic strategies are at work.

Practical common sense and theoretical science are distinct realms of cognitive meaning.[98] Although both are genuine forms of intellectual development, they are rooted in different conscious aspirations and demands. In each context development depends on inquiry, the accumulation of insights, and the collaborative transmission of discoveries; each is an authentic example of the normative pattern of transcendental method. But the practical pursuit of knowledge within the horizon of common sense differs significantly from the systematic quest for understanding characteristic of theoretical science. Implicitly, we recognize the contrasts between these horizons of inquiry but rarely make the effort to objectify them. Our purpose in this section is to draw an extended contrast between the practical and the theoretical realms of meaning in the hope of clarifying their basic differences and underlying unity.

Common sense is the most universal manifestation of human intelligence but the most difficult to objectify. It is a spontaneous, communal development of understanding that occurs outside the context of methodical canons, logical norms, or technical language. While the content of common sense is historically and culturally variable, its mode of apprehension and style of discourse are common and invariant. Common sense aspires to cognitive mastery of the concrete and particular, of the familiar world of persons and things as they are experienced by us and as they are relevant to our practical interests and concerns. Since it has no theoretical inclinations, the questions and answers of common sense are bounded by the interests and preoccupations of daily human living. Its canons of relevance restrict further questions to those that make an immediately palpable difference to particular situations in our personal or communal life. Its cognitive objects are known, without reliance on scientific method, through the self-correcting process of spontaneous learning.

The theoretical realm of meaning is genetically posterior to the emergence of common sense. It is entered through the intellectual pattern of experience, the region of purposive conscious life dominated by the unrestricted desire to know. In contrast to the practical realm of meaning that antecedes it in time and familiarity, the theoretical realm results from the collective human aspiration to universally valid knowledge. Theoretical science aspires to cognitive mastery not of the concrete and particular but of the abstract and the universal. It abstracts systematically from the individuality of the concrete individual instance and from the particularity of times and places. It pursues universally verified principles and laws that are valid in any of a specified set or series of instances. These laws are given exhaustive expression in a technical language regulated by rigorous logical norms.

Empirical science is the most vivid historical example we have of the essential dynamism of human intelligence. The most relevant aspect under which to envisage the mind engaged in science is not truth as in Aristotle, nor certitude as in Descartes, nor deduction as in the Euclidean ideal of the rationalists, nor perceptual experience as in epistemic empiricism, nor synthetic a priori judgment as in Kant, nor eidetic intuition as in phenomenology, nor prediction and control as in Dewey and the pragmatists. The decisive goal of the modern scientific quest is understanding, insight, the grasp of immanent explanatory intelligibility verifiable in empirical instances. Taken collectively, the empirical sciences constitute the comprehensive human quest for explanatory understanding.[99] Because scientists seek increased understanding, they raise questions and revert to problems. Because understanding grasps intelligibility in discontinuous empirical data, scientists observe, measure, count, and experiment. Because understanding conceptualizes what it grasps, scientists formulate hypotheses. Because the apprehended intelligibility is not necessary but only possible, these hypotheses need verification. Because such possibilities abstract from the material conditions of space and time, the mathematical expression of scientific laws proves invariant under transformation of coordinates. Because relevant data may be overlooked, even verified hypotheses are subject to later revision. Yet, because every discovery, every revision, and every theoretical breakthrough will result from a recurrence of the same cognitional process, the invariance of empirical science is the invariance of method. Scientific certitude regards not the changing content of particular theories but the permanent structure of method. Empirical science, then, rests on two distinct grounds: as *insight* grasping intelligibility, it is science; as *verification* selecting the possibilities that in fact are realized, it is empirical.

Though common sense and theoretical science generally investigate the same range of objects, they envisage their objects in radically different ways. Common sense considers reality from the intentional standpoint of practically oriented sense perception. It examines particular things in their descriptive relations to us as active perceivers and agents embedded in a matrix of making and doing. The horizon of inquiry accessible from this standpoint is a limited, imaginable domain of spatiotemporal particulars. At a given time and place, the field of common sense is parceled out individually into overlapping domains of fact, with each domain corresponding to a common set of practical interests and concerns. The intelligible content of common sense is unalterably relative, varying from one historical period and cultural region to the next.

Theoretical science investigates its objects not in their descriptive relations to sensory perceivers but in their explanatory relations to one another. The systematic exigence of theory not only raises questions common sense cannot answer but demands a context for its answers that common sense cannot supply or comprehend. That context is a comprehensive, universal nonimaginable domain of things, not as they appear to sensory perception but as they exist in their intelligible relations with one another. While objects in the domain of theory can be ascended to from common sense starting points, they properly are known not by this ascent but by their internal relations and the lawful functions they satisfy in their continuing interaction.

Common sense and science not only operate within different horizons of inquiry, but they also create separate universes of discourse. Common sense discourse is a species of interpersonal communication conducted in ordinary language. It often relies on elliptical utterances supplemented by nonverbal bodily commentary. Common-sense communication is a work of art that defies strict logical rules. It involves no technical terms introduced through implicit definition and, therefore, does not require the formal mode of speech. As Wittgenstein insisted in the *Philosophical Investigations*, the meanings of its terms are given by their use within an evolving language game, and its generalizations are practical guidelines not intended as premises for logical deduction. Wittgenstein wisely resisted the attempt to impose systematic logical norms on the language of common sense. In so doing, he corrected the procrustean urge so characteristic of the *Tractatus*; but despite his sensitive treatment of common sense discourse, it remains doubtful whether his later philosophy provides an adequate account of theoretical language and meaning.

The expressions of theoretical science are a set of explanatory conjugates introduced into a technical language by a formal mode of speech, and implicitly defined through empirically verified explanatory relations.[100] The logical norms of science promote an ideal of complete articulation, coherence, and rigor. This ideal leads to the organization of scientific language within a systematic logical structure. From the perspective of classical consciousness, the logically ordered results of science are viewed as a permanent epistemic achievement. From the historical standpoint, these logical systemizations are treated as provisional and subject to indefinite revision. They provide a clear, coherent, and rigorous expression of the existing level of scientific understanding within the specialized empirical disciplines.

Strikingly different linguistic communities correspond to the different realms of meaning. To become an affiliated member of a particular community is to master its cognitive aspirations, traditions, beliefs, methods, language, norms, and logical structures. Mutual incomprehension is the inevitable result when the legitimate expectations of one realm are uncritically transposed into the governance of another. Because the regulative purposes of common sense are not set by the unrestricted desire to know, its horizon of inquiry does not advance from description to explanation; its terms of meaning are not subject to the strict requirements of formal logic; its standards of objectivity are practical rather than systematic, incorporating a different concept of further relevant questions and a different notion of invulnerable insights; and its linguistic expressions are drawn from the resources of ordinary language without reliance on the formal mode of speech. The task of a critical philosophy is to correct misplaced heuristic requirements by objectifying the different realms of meaning and tracing them to their source in contrasting exigencies of the intentional subject. Though the realms of common sense and theory are conceptually distinct, in practice they partly interpenetrate and partly merge, both in the mind of the individual and in the different strata of society. This interpenetration has ambiguous philosophical results, as the dialectical analysis of Chapter 8 will reveal.

If the preceding account is correct, then common sense and theoretical science are distinct realms of cognitive meaning. However, their numerous significant differences do not entail intellectual incompatibility. They both are specialized applications of a single transcendental method. Taken together, they provide exhaustive coverage of every aspect of sensible data, for they are complementary in their modes of objective abstraction. Theoretical science prescinds from precisely those aspects of the experiential data to which common sense conscientiously attends. In fact, the complementarity is pervasive, with common sense mastering particular cases and refraining from universal claims and theoretical science formulating universal principles and laws on which concrete cases converge on from which they diverge nonsystematically. An extended analysis of their interrelations would show that they are complementary in their specialized methods and results as well as in their intentional standpoints. Therefore, we are confronted with a permanent duality of cognitive procedures and universes of discourse. But the question remains, How they are to be integrated within the single consciousness of the individual person? There is no simple ordering pattern to which we can appeal. Whereas common sense is prior in the genetic and pedagogical order, theoretical science is prior in the order of causal explanation. The descriptive relations that concern common sense actually are special cases of the more general explanatory relations of things to one another. Many contemporary philosophers have argued that theoretical science is simply a refinement of common sense; whereas others have insisted on their intractable opposition and conflict.[101] We want to distinguish our account of their differences from both of these views. Common sense and theoretical science are importantly similar in that they both instantiate the basic structures of cognitional process, but they do so in manners that are irreducibly different. These differences, however, complement rather than contradict one another, thus releasing us from the alleged need to choose irrevocably between them. They are complementary developments of one and the same human mind, a mind that eventually is driven by its own need for unity to work out their distinctions and relations in detail. It is just this properly philosophic task that we have been conducting in outline here.

As human intelligence develops, both historically in human communities and existentially in the individual person, it advances from unity to multiplicity, from the undifferentiated state of the child to the complex cognitive consciousness of the adult. In a mature individual or culture, cognitive pluralism is the rule rather than the exception. The most significant plurality within the context of theoretical science itself is its development of contrasting heuristic structures. In the transition from a logical to a methodological analysis of science, philosophy shifts its focus from conceptual frameworks to these critical heuristic patterns. But what precisely is a heuristic structure?[102] In the process of inquiry, human intelligence anticipates the act of understanding for which it strives. The content of that anticipated act can be designated as an unknown, and its discernible properties used as clues to assist the desired discovery. We can determine in advance the general properties of answers by fixing the type of questions and insights from which they are expected to proceed. A heuristic structure, then, is defined by a set of functional relations between experiential data, determinate anticipations of intelligibility, and exploratory questions, insights, and answers of a specific type. Let me clarify this very general description by two classical examples.

In the early Platonic dialogues, Socrates repeatedly asked a certain kind of question. What is piety? What is justice? We can generalize his question in the form, What is x?, where the values of x are particular moral virtues. Although Socrates rarely answered his own questions explicitly, he did work out their distinctive heuristic structure. The appropriate answer to a Socratic question would be an intensional definition. We know what x is when we can state the set of properties common to all xs and only to xs. Even when we lack a specific answer to the question, What is x?, however, we know the conditions a good answer must satisfy once we have grasped the Socratic model of dialectical inquiry. Socrates usually did not teach his interlocutors answers to Socratic questions but he did try to lead them to see the essential properties of a good answer to a question of that sort. In fact, it appears that this insight rather than the myth of *anamnesis*, was his deepest response to Meno's dilemma of inquiry.[103]

In his introduction to the *Physics* and the *Metaphysics*, Aristotle outlined the basic structure of classical scientific inquiry.[104] The goal of science, as he described it, is to advance from experiential awareness of a substance to knowledge of its causes, from knowing *that X* is so to knowing *why X* is so. There are four causes that are assignable to every natural object and artifact; the material, formal, efficient, and final. Aristotle intended that the causal matrix combine the heuristic insights of Plato and the Pythagoreans into forms with those of the naturalistic tradition into matter; taken collectively his predecessors had anticipated three of the four kinds of intelligible causes. Aristotle's four-part model of causal analysis objectifies the heuristic structure proper to his classical theory of science. By itself, the causal matrix is not part of any particular theoretical discipline; rather, it outlines the general pattern to which all the natural sciences are expected to conform.

The development of inquiry since the Greeks has generated types of question that neither Plato nor Aristotle anticipated. The most revolutionary moments in that development have been the emergence of new concepts of explanatory intelligibility. Within science, the deepest sort of paradigm shift is a change in our notion of what it is to understand a familiar range of phenomena. In the course of modern empirical science, four distinct heuristic structures have gradually appeared on the scene, each based on the anticipation of a novel kind of intelligible relation. These different heuristic structures can be defined by linking a specific form of question with a specific sort of heuristic anticipation.[105]

1. The classical method of Kepler, Galileo, and Newton in the science of mechanics is based on the anticipation of a constant lawful system in nature to be discovered concretely in the measurements of the appropriate perceptual field. Classical heuristic structure is defined by the question; What is the constant functional correlation between the measurable aspects of the data in this experiential domain?

2. The genetic method, first raised to prominence by Darwin in his evolutionary biology, is based on the anticipation of an intelligibly related sequence of systems to be discovered in an evolving subject matter. Genetic heuristic structure is defined by two related questions; What is the series of functions successively realized within the relevant empirical data? What is the operating higher-order function that intelligibly connects the different successive functions in that series?

3. The statistical method, used to increasing effect in both the natural and the social sciences today, is based on the anticipation that the data in a given field will not conform to a classical system. Statistical heuristic structure is defined by the question; What is the ideal frequency of occurrences to occasions for well-defined classes of events from which actually observed frequencies diverge non-systematically?

4. Dialectical method is the appropriate heuristic strategy for a science of humankind and human affairs that is meant to be simultaneously empirical and critical. It is based on the anticipation that the

relations between the successive states of changing human systems and structures will not be directly intelligible. As applied to the individual human being, it assumes our incapacity for sustained emotional, intellectual, and moral development. Dialectical heuristic structure is defined by the question; What are the concrete principles whose linked interaction accounts for both the achieved intelligibility and the failures in intelligibility in the transition between successive human schemes of recurrence.

This compact unifying scheme of Lonergan's correlates the different types of empirical methods, the questions that implicitly define them, and the heuristic anticipations on which these questions are based. Since "empirical data must either conform or not conform to system, and successive systems must either be related or not related in a directly intelligible manner...the methods taken together are relevant to any field of data; they do not dictate what the data must be; they are able to cope with data no matter what they may prove to be."[106] In addition to objectifying these different empirical heuristic structures, Lonergan has also established their internal complementarity as forms of scientific inquiry. Each structure is a specialized application of the invariant pattern of scientific method. Each shares a starting point in perceptual experience and a common base in the field of intersubjective observation. The irreducible heuristic pluralism emerges with the anticipation of different kinds of intelligibility to be discovered within the field of experience. To classical expectations of invariant systems correspond mathematical functions, correlating the measurable aspects of a recurrent phenomenon; to statistical expectations of divergence from a classical system correspond ideal frequencies or probabilities for well-defined classes of events; to genetic expectations of an ongoing series of systems belong higher-order explanatory species that successfully integrate otherwise coincidental aggregates in lower-order manifolds; to dialectical expectations of human development and decline belong a linked interaction between normative intelligence as a source of development and obstructive bias as a cause of decline. Substantive answers to determinate empirical questions, of course, are the responsibility of first-order investigators in the fields of science and common sense and not of the reflective methodologist. But the philosopher, by reflecting on the diversity of empirical method, can articulate its distinct forms, establish their mutual compatibility, and limn the critical principles by which answers within each form are to be appraised.

Cognitive pluralism has its deepest ground in the intentional sources of the different realms of meaning and in the complementary heuristic structures that differentiate the scientific method. These are the prior foundations to which we must appeal when we undertake the integration of cognitive discourse. Because full terms of meaning are embedded within the framework of unifying heuristic structures, we can trace the polydimensional pattern of cognitive discourse to the antecedent heuristic pluralism. Logical analysis finds its limit at the level of heuristic difference, for there is no logical transition from one universe of discourse to another. The continuity of transcendental method is preserved *between* different heuristic structures, but logical continuity is only preserved *within* a given structure at a given period in its history. In fact, the identity of an enduring heuristic structure over time forms the unifying principle in a series of successive theoretical explanations.[107] This allows us to compare the explanatory power of different answers to the same set of questions and to map their logical connections. But heuristic pluralism subverts the logician's attempt to impose a single universe of discourse on the domain of knowledge. I applaud the integrative aspiration that prompted Carnap's search for a unified language of science, but I do not endorse that particular strategy. The need for integration can be satisfied by less draconian measures, which fully respect the heuristic and discursive materials to be integrated.

Sellars accepted the principle of logical continuity within factual discourse but he rejected its uniform application to human language. This decision led him to treat scientific and common-sense discourse as rivals and to relegate intentional language to the metalinguistic level.[108] His treatment of factual language rests on the thesis of extensionality and ignores cognitional process. Our approach rests on intentional analysis and rejects the uniform imposition of the principle of extensionality as an arbitrary constraint. By recognizing the existence of complementary realms of meaning, we avoid opposing common-sense to scientific theory, and we refuse the dubious choices erected on that opposition. The descriptive predicates of common-sense discourse occur in answers to common-sense questions. They are used to express the properties of things as they are sensibly perceived by practical subjects. At the most elementary level, they include *color as seen, sound as heard*, and *extension and duration as directly experienced*. The explanatory predicates of science are used to express the properties of things as they are defined implicitly by empirically verified explanatory relations. They include *color as defined by relations between light waves, sound as defined by verified equations in acoustical theory*, and *extension and duration as defined by the geometry used in stating the verified equations of physics*. Since these different sets of predicates are used in stating the answers to different but complementary questions within distinct realms of meaning, they themselves are intellectually compatible. But once we overlook the origin of propositional answers within the horizon of heuristic anticipations, questions, and insights, it is easy to assume that the two accounts of sensible properties are in conflict. Yet, if we make this assumption, we are faced with all the dilemmas to which Eddington's two tables give rise. We are confronted with the unpalatable choice between an instrumentalism that undervalues explanatory scientific theory and a scientific realism that insists the sensible colors we perceive are not real but merely appearance. To escape from this dilemma we must go behind propositional claims to their source in insights and questions. We must acknowledge that heuristic structures are philosophically more fundamental than the discourse they contain and that propositional conflict occurs only within a common heuristic structure.[109]

Sellars continually has opposed the procrustean urge within logical empiricism. Yet his account of factual discourse is marred by the sort of arbitrary constraint against which he successfully campaigned. The appropriate base for a critical integration of discourse is a nuanced cognitional theory connecting the multiple discursive products of cognition with their sources in distinct intentional procedures. In the project of cognitive integration within the context of historical consciousness the key to achieving continuity without rigidity is the shift from logic to method.

I. Critical Realism: Epistemic Objectivity and the Knowledge of Being

Any philosophy, whether actual or possible, will
rest on the dynamic structure of cognitional activity
either as correctly conceived or as distorted by
oversights and mistaken orientations.[110]

The aim of philosophy is the integrated unfolding of the unrestricted desire to know.[111] This relentless desire is at the core of all theoretical inquiry, and it prefigures the goal of unified knowledge that philosophy actively seeks. As human intelligence develops in the individual person and in the community of inquiry, the diversity of knowledge dramatically increases and the task of integration becomes more difficult. Philosophic strategies of synthesis adopted in an earlier stage of meaning no longer appear promising or plausible.

The present context of philosophy is marked by an unprecedented linguistic and cultural pluralism. The empirical sciences have distinguished themselves from common sense and been emancipated from philosophical authority. They have created new heuristic strategies for the understanding of experience, which in principle are intended to cover all of the observable world. Historical consciousness has become culturally pervasive; science no longer is conceived as a permanent achievement but as an ongoing process of collaborative inquiry whose fundamental unity is methodological. Disciplinary autonomy, theoretical pluralism, historical development, and increasing specialization—these are the realities of our time that make the integrative project seem nearly impossible. The relentless modern intellectual development that commenced in the Renaissance and came to full flower in the Scientific and Historical Revolutions has created the present philosophical crisis. The need for cognitive unity has never been greater, but to many responsible thinkers the aspiration to satisfy it now seems vain and illusory. They believe that we must learn to live, culturally and personally, without intellectual connection and unity.

If the invariance and unity to which philosophy aspires precluded multiplicity and change or if the quest for integration were inconsistent with the fact of historicity, then the contemporary critics of philosophy surely would be right. But my thesis has been that these oppositions are false; that intentional unity is the ground of multiplicity, foundational invariance is the source of change, and epistemic historicity is the reason why integration is necessary. What is needed, then, is not the abandonment of traditional philosophy but the emergence of a philosophic strategy suited to our historical context. What philosophy requires most at the present time, is a critical core of reflective thinkers, fully aware of the achievements and limitations of the past; fully alert to the realities, needs and opportunities of the present. The work of Bernard Lonergan, I believe, is a good example of such indispensable thought. It contains a nuanced philosophical strategy around which a gathering center might build. Lonergan's guiding idea was to tackle the problem of unprecedented intellectual development by going to its source in the intentional subject. Like Socrates and Augustine before him, he made the subject's self-knowledge the basic ground on which to resolve philosophic controversy.[112] Although schooled in the Aristotelian and Thomistic tradition, he broke with his scholastic predecessors on the question of integrative strategy. He shifted the starting point of philosophic analysis from the objects and terms of cognitive meaning to the intentional subject and that subject's cognitive operations. Intentional analysis thus replaced metaphysical and logical analysis at the center of philosophical practice. The result was a new architectural design, with cognitional theory located at the base of operations, providing the foundation for the expanding theoretical structure. With this major shift in orientation, logic, epistemology, and metaphysics lose their strategic priority. Although they retain a place within the house of intellect, they no longer are assigned the central position.

Lonergan's cognitionally based philosophy is meant to be comprehensive in two distinct respects.[113] It is designed to accommodate both heuristic and categorial developments in the realms of science and common sense. Transcendental method is sufficiently flexible that it can integrate both present and future forms of cognitive pluralism. It also is comprehensive in its bearing on disputed philosophical issues. Cognitional theory is meant to provide a secure base for the ordered expansion of philosophy into the questions of epistemology and metaphysics. With the insights gained through personal appropriation, we are equipped to defend a critical epistemic realism that applies to all realms of cognitive meaning. In the final section of this chapter, I shall sketch the argument for epistemic realism and in Chapter VIII develop the counter arguments needed to refute its philosophical rivals.

The complexity of human knowing involves a parallel complexity in the related notions of epistemic objectivity and being.[114] By grasping the structure of our knowing, we are empowered to understand the epistemic properties of terms of meaning and the metaphysical features of cognitive objects. The key factors in this extended parallel among knowing, knowledge, and the known are the three levels of intentionally conscious operations. For the sake of simplicity, I shall designate them as *experience* (level 1), *understanding* (level 2), and *judgment* (level 3). In cognitional theory, I focused on direct and reflective insights as the pivotal operations on the second and third levels of cognitive process. In that context, I emphasized the importance of insight as a constitutive operation in the process of *knowing*. But in epistemology, the emphasis shifts to the role of insights in the constitution of *knowledge*. Formal and full terms of meaning claim center stage and the already explored sources of meaning recede into the background of attention. A formal term of meaning is a proposition or set of propositions formulated tentatively by the subject as the answer to a question for intelligence. A full term of meaning is a true proposition affirmed in response to a question for critical reflection. The true propositions that increment the domain of knowledge are rationally verified judgments of fact. The central question in epistemology complements the earlier discoveries of cognitional theory. What conditions make possible a true and reasonable judgment of fact? Four distinct but related conditions would appear to be necessary:

1. Normative rational standards of judgment that are satisfied at the level of critical reflection. Concretely, this means that the content of the prospective judgment is grasped by the subject as virtually unconditioned in an act of reflective insight (level 3);

2. The reflective grasp of a proposition as rationally grounded presupposes a level of intelligent activity that posits systematic unities and relations with some independence of a field of fulfilling conditions but with reference to such a field (the intelligent formation of explanatory hypotheses, level 2);

3. The positing of intelligible unities and relations that can be grasped as unconditioned presupposes a prior experiential field containing what can become fulfilling conditions (the field of evidence for the indirect confirmation of theory, level 1),

4. The coordination of these conditions for a judgment of fact requires a single intentional subject whose cognitive performance unifies the different cognitive operations, determines that the operative norms

are satisfied, and affirms or denies the terms of meaning that result (the unity of intentional consciousness).

Cognitional theory and epistemological reflection reach corresponding conclusions, although they follow an inverse pattern in their process of discovery.[115]

The task of epistemology is to advance from the conditions of the possibility of full terms of meaning to a clarification and explanation of their properties. Objectivity and truth are the most important epistemic properties of rationally affirmed propositions. There are three related aspects of epistemic objectivity corresponding to the three levels of intentional consciousness. Full terms of meaning are instances of objective knowledge, if they meet the demand of rational consciousness for sufficient evidence (the absolute aspect), if they meet the demand of intelligent consciousness for no further relevant questions (the normative aspect), and if they secure in experiential consciousness the range of fulfilling conditions demanded by a rigorous reflective judgment (the empirical aspect). The explanatory grounds of the objectivity of knowledge are the normative operations of the intentional subject occurring under the sway of the unrestricted desire to know. Semantic and epistemic objectivity, then, are not antithetical to subjectivity as Frege contended, but the legitimate fruit of authentic, self-transcending subjective intentionality. By satisfying the operative norms at each level of intentional consciousness, the intentional subject produces a public piece of propositional knowledge with universal validity. This knowledge takes the form of a virtually unconditioned judgment that claims the assent of every rationally conscious person. In this conjunction of semantic publicity, universal validity, and virtually unconditioned rationality, we find the core features of epistemic objectivity.

The functionally operative demand for objectivity and truth plays a decisive role in the process of human inquiry. But this demand, although immanent in our conscious intentional activity, is originally inarticulate. We have an inherent desire to understand experience correctly, but initially we are unclear by what norms correct understanding is to be measured. Cognitional analysis articulates the operative norms of intellectual and rational consciousness and fixes their contributions to the attainment of legitimate knowledge. Epistemology complements cognitional theory by establishing that the desire for objective knowledge is fulfilled when the subject complies with these norms in actual epistemic practice.

The ordered expansion of philosophy from its base in a personally appropriated cognitional theory does not stop with epistemology. Having grasped the intentional structure of our knowing and the required conditions of objective knowledge, we inevitably turn to the nature of the known. The question that explicitly confronts us by now should be well defined: What do we know when we assent to objectively true terms of meaning? The immediate answer to this question is straightforward but insufficiently clear. What we know when we know objectively are the objects of cognitive meaning. The sense of the term *object* in this context is drawn from the three levels of intentional consciousness. Cognitive objects, *pace* Kant, are not the contents of perceptual intuitions. Rather, they are what we *intend* when we ask exploratory questions of intelligence and what we *know* when these questions are answered objectively.[116] But our original answer, even under this restriction, still requires clarification; for what is the ontological status of these cognitive objects known through full terms of meaning? We find the clue to a satisfactory reply in the ancient scholastic adage: Truth is the medium in which being, or reality, is known. What we know through assent to objectively true terms of meaning is being or reality. Being is what the questions of intelligence intend and what the answers of reflection make known.

Since the notion of being is notoriously confused, this second, supposedly clearer answer, only raises a further clarifying question, What does it mean for something to exist, to be real? What is the sense or meaning of the interchangeable terms *being* or *reality*? These questions, which lead into the center of classical metaphysics, require me to introduce an explicit critical caution. At least two opposing notions of being appear to be operating on the different levels of the philosopher's intentional consciousness. The first, which is drawn from extroverted empirical consciousness, pictures being as the already, out, there, now real. Being, on this view, is the opaque and independent other that stands over and against the conscious subject, either as a potential object of direct intuition or as an operating constraint on thoughts and actions. This notion of being served as the uncritical source of the Kantian *ding-an-sich*, the mind-independent reality that transcends human knowledge but that somehow makes an indirect contribution to the constitution of the phenomenal world. I shall treat this notion of being as explicitly precritical and deliberately contrast it with the operative notion of being within the intellectual pattern of experience. Earlier, I defined the critical concepts of objects and objectivity with reference to the principles of cognitional theory: now I shall take the same tack with being. Empirical consciousness is oriented toward being as an object of possible perception. But for intellectual consciousness, being is the unrestricted objective of the human desire to know. What we desire to know whenever we intellectually and rationally seek knowledge is being. On this intellectual account of the contested metaphysical notion, being is the distant goal, not of empirical perception but of intelligent search and rational reflection; being is what exploratory questions intend and verified answers reveal

This preliminary definition of being is a definition of the second order. It does not tell us explicitly what being is, but it defines being heuristically as the unrestricted goal of the cognitive quest. We can fix the notion of being more precisely through a series of heuristic definitions corresponding to our foundational principles. With reference to human cognitional process, being can be defined as whatever is grasped intelligently and affirmed reasonably by the intentional subject. With reference to our epistemological theory, being can be defined as whatever would be known through the totality of true and objective judgments. Since this totality corresponds to the complete set of correct answers to the entire range of intelligent questions, I am postulating a limit notion beyond finite human attainment. The human person simply cannot understand being in its entirety. We can grasp, however, the functionally operative notion of being within our own process of cognition and articulate its meaning with increasing heuristic precision.

The real principles on which metaphysics depends are the foundational principles of philosophy: the polymorphic human subject, the pure desire to know, and generalized empirical method. Prior to the unfolding of these principles, historically and existentially, the condition of metaphysics is latent or potential; as they unfold, but before they are known and appropriated, metaphysics is problematic and internally divided; when the human subject appropriates the structure of knowing and works out its philosophical implications, metaphysics finally can become explicit.[117] Explicit metaphysics takes its stand on the known structure of our knowing: If the human subject is in the intellectual pattern of experience and is knowing an object within the domain of proportionate being,[118] then that knowing will have an invariant structure and the being that the subject knows will have a structure isomorphic with the pattern of knowing. In cognitional process, three levels of intentional acts coalesce to form a single instance of knowing. In the structure of being, three levels of intended intentional correlates coalesce into a single known. The pattern of relations between the intentional acts is isomorphic with the pattern of relations between their intended contents. As higher-level cognitional acts presuppose and complete their operational antecedents, so do their correlative intentional contents presuppose and complete theirs. As being is defined heuristically in terms of the unrestricted desire to know, so the metaphysical elements constitutive of being are defined with reference to the appropriate intentional acts in which that desire unfolds. Human knowing is a compound of experience, understanding, and judgment; the known object is a proportionate compound of potency, form, and act. Potency corresponds to the content of intentional experience; form to the content of intellectual grasp; and act to what reason demands from the intelligible content of intellect. The intentional isomorphism between the epistemic subject and object pole, between the structure of knowing and the structure of the known, is the basis for an explicit metaphysics.

Proportionate being consists of cognitive objects whose complete range of aspects are accounted for by the six metaphysical elements. Existing things are individual by virtue of their central potency, unified and intelligible by their central form, and existent by their central act. They are capable of being distinguished from and related to other beings by virtue of their conjugate potencies, are intelligibly distinguished and related by their conjugate forms, and become actually distinct terms of verified relations by virtue of their conjugate acts.[119] A metaphysical analysis of the structure of cognitive being is not an explanation of the categorial features of any particular object of knowledge. Rather, it provides a virtual and formal account of what empirical investigation shall discover substantially and in detail.[120]

The second goal of explicit metaphysics is to integrate the multiple objects of explanatory knowledge. All of these objects are known through specific forms of factual inquiry. The universe of proportionate being is composed of entities that can be investigated through the methods of common sense, explanatory science, and philosophy. The metaphysician argues from the complementarity of these distinct methods of knowing to the complementarity of the objects, properties, and relations known through them. This is done at a structural level by integrating the multiple heuristic structures affirmed in cognitional theory; this is done concretely by unifying the results of the pluralistic modes of inquiry. The different realms of cognitive meaning supply the epistemic materials for metaphysics to integrate; metaphysics, itself, supplies the basic integrating structure. A reciprocal interdependence is at work. Without prior factual investigation of being, metaphysics has no heuristic structures or explanatory contents with which to work. Without metaphysics, the specialized modes of factual inquiry generate a manifold of cognitive objects without order, relation, or discernible unity. New developments in the theoretical realm of meaning at the heuristic or explanatory level demand a new metaphysical integration. When metaphysics is conceived as the department of human knowledge that unifies all the other epistemic departments, it becomes factual, progressive, and methodical; factual, because it is grounded in the operative structure of all human cognition and dependent for its materials on the factual judgments supplied by the sciences and common sense; progressive, because it must respond and remain open to novel cognitional developments in the different spheres of inquiry; methodical, because its presuppositions, objectives, and evidential standards are made fully explicit by the reflective metaphysical investigator.

In his analysis of *Metaphysics as Science*, Lonergan summarized these methodical principles with impressive economy.[121] We can divide the field of possible knowledge of proportionate being into knowledge of things as related to us and knowledge of things as related to one another. We can divide the latter field into science that explains and metaphysics that anticipates the general structure of proportionate being as explained. We can divide metaphysical anticipations into grounded assertions that possess a factual premise in the utilized structure of our knowing and empty assertions that lack such a premise. We can divide grounded assertions into coherent positions that are based on the correct cognitional theory and invite development and into incoherent positions that are based on incorrect cognitional theories and invite reversal.

Lonergan's conception of metahysics satisfies the native human demand for the whole in knowledge without suffering from the illusion that is the whole of knowledge. It meets the integrative aspiration of philosophy without infringing on the hard-won autonomy of science and common-sense. It allows us to preserve metaphysics, traditionally the most contested of all philosophical disciplines, as a factually based science with strictly imposed limits and effective criteria for adjudicating differences. A factual and critical metaphysics of this kind is not a theoretical luxury. It provides a needed, critical clarification of the ambiguous notion of being, and it rests on a developed understanding of the manner in which being is actually known. It ends the isolation between the different scientific disciplines and bridges the gap that logic cannot close between the different realms of cognitive meaning. Finally, it reveals the structure of the universe proportionate to our intellect, which in our finite ways we all actively struggle to understand.

Epistemic realism is critical when it rests on a fully developed account of the matrix of cognitive meaning. Neither naive realism, which rests on the spectator theory of knowing, nor representational realism, which rests on a copy theory of truth, provides such an account. Their conspicuous failure has led, since Kant, to a movement away from realism and toward some version of critical idealism, pragmatism, or relativism. The critics of realism have raised persuasive arguments against epistemic immediacy and the copy theory, but they have not provided a satisfactory alternative. In the concluding chapter of this book, I shall try to defend critical realism against both Kantian and post-Kantian criticism. I shall try to explain and apply the basic principles of Lonergan's dialectical analysis and to show their relevance for both cultural and philosophical conflict.

8

Philosophical and Cultural Conflict

*All our predecessors render us the double
service of hitting off the truth for us or of
missing the mark and so of challenging us to get
to the root of the matter ourselves.*[1]

*In an intellectual age there can be no active
interest which puts aside all hope for a vision of
the harmony of truth. To acquiesce in discrep-
ancy is destructive of candor and of moral
cleanliness. It belongs to the self-respect of
intellect to pursue every tangle of thought to its
final unravelment....A clash of doctrines is
not a disaster; it is an opportunity.*[2]

A. A History of Conflict

Western philosophy has been marked by deep intellectual conflict since its
origin in ancient Greece. The fragments of Xenophanes and Heraclitus, the
eristic paradoxes of Zeno, and the dialectical criticism conducted by Plato and
Aristotle bear witness to its intensity and range. The competing schools of the
Hellenistic era were followed in the medieval period by the rival traditions of
realism and nominalism. Nor did philosophical strife diminish in the modern
age. The epistemological clash between relationalists and empiricists was
temporarily checked by Kant's transcendental criticism, but the Kantian

project soon generated its own adversaries and critics. In the twentieth century, the polemical spirit has only intensified. The deflationary thrust of logical positivism finds its answering counterpart in contemporary deconstructive strategies that seek to subvert the ruling assumptions of the historic philosophical disciplines.

The fact of conflict is not peculiar to philosophy, of course. Passionate divisions and revolutions figure prominently in the history of art and science as well. But the great scientific and artistic upheavals have been unified into common traditions that successfully incorporate the controversies of their past. Despite its history of conflict, science has achieved a unified tradition differentiated by distinct and cooperative disciplines. Philosophy, by contrast, has a history of opposing traditions whose assessment of the past is primarily divisive. The tradition of science has an epistemic authority for practicing scientists that no philosophical tradition can rival. Practicing philosophers tend to agree on a list of the major figures in their history but not in the assessment of their intellectual contributions. There is no greater source of philosophical conflict than the understanding and evaluation of their common past.

The divisions of the past remain active in the tensions of the present. They help to explain why philosophers cannot reach agreement on a common field and method of inquiry, a shared set of categories and beliefs, and even on a cluster of essential questions. According to Alasdair MacIntyre, the arguments of philosophers cannot be resolved rationally because they are framed in incommensurable vocabularies and proceed from premises that enjoy only partisan support.[3] Even when philosophers agree on the language they use, there is often a critical ambiguity in the meanings assigned to the same terms by opposing traditions. Philosophical debates are intensified rather than resolved by concurrent appeals to rationality, objectivity, knowledge, and truth.

If conflict has been constant in philosophical history, the response of philosophers to it has been strikingly variable. In the ancient world, it was customary to review and assess the opinions of one's predecessors. Aristotle regularly began his philosophical lectures with a dialectical survey of the *endoxa*.[4] The spirit of his surveys is communicated in the epigraph of this chapter; our predecessors do us intellectual service whether they hit the truth or miss the mark. It is exceedingly difficult to encompass the truth as a whole, and partial accounts challenge us both to complete their deficiencies and identify their sources of error. Aristotle's holistic, reconciliatory approach later was adopted by Leibniz, who argued that philosophers tend to be right in what they affirm and wrong in what they exclude or omit. Both Leibniz and Aristotle see philosophical conflict as natural, given the comprehensive complexity of the truth to which philosophy aspires. Their critical tolerance generally was not shared by the great modern thinkers. Given the Cartesian commitment to the quest for certainty and the enlightenment ideal of continuous intellectual progress, it is not surprising that the moderns experienced unresolved philosophical conflict as a scandal. Thus, we find in modernity a series of methodological revolutions designed to put philosophy on the sure path of science. We also find a growing tendency to equate rationality with logical inference, with the adoption of an algorithmic method for ensuring philosophical consensus. In the concerted effort to model philosophy on the science of mathematics, emphasis shifted from the epistemic performance of the philosophical subject to the discovery of an impersonal decision procedure.

The failure to find an algorithmic method for philosophy eventually resulted in skepticism and suspicion about its epistemic claims. This skepticism took a variety of forms ranging from the tolerant humanism of Montaigne and Hume to the critical unmasking of Nietzsche and Rorty. It also led to Kant's critique of reason and his effort to establish the scope and limits of philosophical knowledge on a basis of principle. Beginning with Kant, there was a recurrent effort to limit what philosophers can know and meaningfully say. Kant, himself, sought to bring traditional metaphysics to an end; Wittgenstein attempted to eliminate distinctively philosophical propositions and theories; the logical positivists dismissed theology, metaphysics, and ethics as cognitively meaningless; and Rorty, as noted, called for the destruction of foundational epistemology. All of these initiatives were radical in that they sought to dissolve rather than to solve traditional problems. In their most severe forms, they prefigure the possibility of a postphilosophical culture, in which the disappearance of philosophical conflict will coincide with the disappearance of philosophy itself.

In Rorty's case an ulterior motive is behind the emphasis on philosophical disagreement. He wants to emancipate the secular culture of the Enlightenment from its dependence on Cartesian and Kantian ideas of reason. By showing that philosophy has never been a rigorous science, he hopes to discredit the cultural functions it has claimed for itself in the modern era. According to Rorty, modern philosophy attempted to fill the cultural space left vacant by the decline of the Christian church. It presented itself as the judge or authoritative critic of the diverse cultural practices that slowly gained maturity in the course of the Enlightenment. Philosophy's right to this magisterial office is intensely problematic if it cannot bring order and unity into its own ranks. Loss of patience with philosophy's pretensions has led many modern thinkers to believe that science might fill the gap that religion and philosophy left vacant. But Rorty's explicit hope is that no practice will emerge as the ultimate critic and judge of our culture. Just as we have developed a secular moral life without reliance on religion, so we can learn to conduct our common cultural life without philosophy. Philosophy can then abandon its aspiration to rigorous and authoritative science and become a creative and hermeneutic voice in the conversation of humankind.[5]

Faced with controversy about the theoretical power of reason, Kant argued that two extreme positions were to be avoided: dogmatism and skepticism. Perhaps, there is a comparable dichotomy to oppose in the responses to philosophical conflict. At one extreme is the search for an algorithmic method to eliminate philosophical disagreement. At the other there is the attempt to subvert and terminate philosophy because of its inability to resolve internal opposition. Kant maintained that the alternative to both skepticism and dogmatism was a critical examination of the faculty of reason. Drawing on the dialectical practice of Aristotle and the critical strategy of Kant, let us adopt a comparably balanced approach to the problem of philosophical conflict. Following Lonergan, I shall speak of a dialectical criticism of philosophical theories.[6] This strategy is dialectical in the Aristotelian sense that it seeks to review the major philosophical oppositions, to order them by similarity and difference, and to trace them to their sources in fundamental insights and oversights. It is critical in the Kantian sense that it seeks to resolve conflict through a sustained reflection on the powers and operations of the intentional subject. Only after a reflective appropriation of the subject is it possible to evaluate philosophical differences in a manner that is neither dogmatic nor skeptical. The goal of dialectical criticism is not the elimination of philosophical conflict, but the achievement of a critical center from which to judge the merits and limitations of the opposing philosophical traditions. If that judgement is to be responsible and compelling, it must proceed from a foundation of principle. In the sphere of dialectical criticism, as in the sphere of cognitive integration, comprehensive self-knowledge should serve as the required foundation.

It is a mark of historic continuity that self-knowledge remains the center of the philosophical enterprise. It is the indispensable condition for critically appropriating the complexity of the philosophical past. But its importance extends beyond the boundaries of philosophy. For as human beings we belong to culture and history that have their own ambiguous inheritance. If we are to discern effectively the merits and limitations of that inheritance, if our precritical belonging to culture is eventually to become mature and responsible, then we need a ground within ourselves for distinguishing the genuine from the inauthentic. This is an exceedingly difficult judgement to make, and self-knowledge is not sufficient for its occurrence. But I want to suggest that it is a necessary condition for critically belonging to any tradition, whether philosophical or cultural. In human life self-knowledge serves as the basis for sustained self-transcendence; it is a requirement of wisdom.

B. Dialectical Principles and Strategy

When philosophers can find no way to adjudicate their differences, they appear limited to opinions and incapable of knowledge. Yet, ever since Plato, it is the very opposite condition to which they have aspired.[7] The depth of the present crisis in philosophy is indicated by the fact that metaphysics and epistemology, two of the most important philosophical disciplines, are under severe attack. Not only are their basic terms and principles being challenged, but their very coherence as theoretical enterprises is in question. Traditional metaphysics has never recovered fully from Kant's critique. And if Rorty is successful, foundational epistemology may have a similar future. Although Kant's criticism of metaphysics was based on transcendental principles, the pragmatic rejection of epistemology is a more eclectic affair; yet, in large measure it rests on the perceived failure of traditional theories of knowledge. This failure has led many post-Kantian philosophers to reject epistemic realism and, in Rorty's case, to reject the historical problematic to which a realistic epistemology belonged.

Since I believe that neither realism nor epistemology should be abandoned, I need to defend their validity against an array of powerful critics. Let me begin by proposing a first interpretive principle. The critique of epistemic realism, in both its naive and representational forms, derives its power from a more fundamental challenge to the spectator theory of knowing.[8] The strength of the argument against realism has its source in the rejection of epistemic intuitions and the copy theory of truth. Despite their internal differences, idealists, pragmatists, linguistic relativists, and proponents of autonomous grammar are agreed in what they oppose. Insofar as traditional realism depended on an essentially intuitive cognitional theory, it has lost its base of support. This has left realism defenseless, a precarious condition for a philosophical theory under fire. It has also left believers in realism with an urgent question: Is it possible to develop a critical defense of realism on the basis of a nonintuitive theory of knowledge? Epistemic realism needs to offer a reasoned account of the object of human cognition. A critical epistemic realist will base that account on an antecedent theory of the cognitive subject and that subject's normative pattern of knowing.

Let me propose a more general dialectical principle about the sources of philosophical conflict. Because of the structure of intentionality, every coherent notion of objectivity is inseparable from a correlative notion of the epistemic subject. Blunty stated, defensible accounts of knowledge and the known presuppose a more fundamental account of human knowing. To cite three examples that illustrate this dialectical principle; naive realism is based on the spectator theory of knowing; critical idealism is based on the constructive theory of mind; pragmatic relativism is based on an antecedent linguistic conceptualism. In each case, because the underlying cognitional theory is flawed, the epistemolgical derivative is indefensible. A full critical position requires an explicit and adequate account of the entire intentional matrix. Neither the critics of realism nor its intuitive defenders speak from such a position.

In fact, there is an ironic overlap between the governing assumptions of the naive realist and those of his Kantian critics. Reduced to its essentials, naive realism is based on three intersecting philosophical concepts: the concepts of knowing, being, and the object of knowledge. For the naive realist, knowing is primarily intuitive, being is the already out there now real, and the primary object of knowledge is being as immediately intuited by the knower.[9] Kant broke with naive realism only in its first and third assumptions. For Kant, intuition is necessary but insufficient for knowing, being is the already out there now real, and the object of knowledge is limited to phenomenal appearance. The epistemic object is an object of sensory intuition, but human intuitions are confined to phenomena and never reach being itself. The naive realist's concept of being is equivalent to the Kantian notion of the thing in itself. Whereas the naive realist held that we can know the thing in itself by directly intuiting it, Kant explicitly denied this claim. Kant correctly insisted that the naive realist's conception of knowledge, both of the epistemic subject and its object, is severely flawed. The critical realist agrees but carries the objection one important step further. An explicit and adequate account of human knowledge is not to be found in Kant either. The central concepts in traditional epistemology need to be fundamentally reconceived.

In the spirit of these preliminary remarks, let me now outline the comprehensive dialectical strategy first created by Lonergan in *Insight*.[10] The purpose of this strategy is to bring basic philosophical conflicts to light, to trace them to their originating source, and to resolve them in a nonarbitrary manner.

The core of philosophical conflict is the polymorphic complexity of the intentional subject. Intentional consciousness is a many-leveled, highly differentiated dynamic structure. That structure exists and is recurrently operative in every philosopher; yet because intentional awareness is naturally directed toward objects, it regularly goes unthematized by those who instantiate it. Only through a reflexive effort of intentional analysis does the philosopher bring his own intentional operations under scrutiny. Only through a slow and gradual process of personal appropriation does he bring his intentional complexity to the level of self-knowledge. The philosopher's lack of adequate self-knowledge is the root cause of philosophical error. However extensive his knowledge of other disciplines, the philosopher's standpoint remains precritical if he has not come to terms with his own intentional polymorphism.

The full range of disputed questions in philosophical semantics, epistemology, and metaphysics are traceable to truncated or distorted accounts of intentional subjectivity. Because of the defects in these accounts, many of the basic philosophical terms—*being, knowledge, objectivity, truth,* and *rationality*—are in a state of semantic disorder. Even when philosophers adopt the same vocabulary, their use of it will continue to be divisive as long as the full complexity of the subject is neglected or treated by oversimplified analogies.[11] The stubborn and misleading myths about human knowledge all have a partial basis in intentional fact. There is an aspect of intuition, constructive formation, and discursive conversation to cognitional process. But the prevailing cognitional theories all take some aspect of cognitional structure and generalize it to represent the whole. As a result of distorting or reducing the subjective pole of cognition, they proceed to do the same to the epistemic object and the terms of meaning through which it is known. Over the past two centuries, this process has led first to a rejection of metaphysics, then to a critique of epistemology and ethics; it threatens to conclude with a wholesale elimination of the philosophical tradition.

What is the dialectical alternative? To trace the opposing philosophical traditions to their source in mistaken cognitional theories. To see philosophical conflict itself not as an historical aberration but as the intelligible result of a basic and largely inadvertent polymorphic fact. Philosophical error is the result of incomplete intellectual development in philosophers themselves. As the complexity of human knowledge has increased dramatically, the full complexity of the knower has become proportionately harder to understand. This partly explains the intensity of the present crisis. As the importance of self-knowledge has risen, unfortunately so has its difficulty. Faced with a bewildering array of opposing philosophical traditions and lacking critical grounds with which to appraise them, it has seemed more authentic simply to hope for an end to the whole affair. Rather than arbitrarily selecting an indefensible opinion, why not keep silent or talk about something else.

C. Cognitional Theory—Positions and Counter Positions

From the philosophical perspective, the personal appropriation of cognitional structure is not an end in itself. An understanding of the process of cognition leads to a concern for the intentional terms of meaning it produces and for the epistemic objects to which those terms refer. Philosophical inquiry proceeds from a theory of cognitional operations to a critical account of objectivity, truth, knowledge, and the known. The operative dependence of terms and objects of cognitive meaning on antecedent desires and operations is recognized in this investigative order. At the source of all conceptual and epistemic development are the concrete, factual, cognitional tendencies in the existential subject. Their causal priority in the intentional matrix explains why the new architecture of philosophy places cognitional theory at the foundation of semantics, epistemology, and metaphysics. It also explains Lonergan's dialectical strategy, which traces epistemological and metaphysical disagreements to their roots in cognitional theory. "Just as every statement in theoretical science can be shown to imply statements regarding sensible fact, so every statement in philosophy (epistemology) and metaphysics can be shown to imply statements regarding cognitional fact."[12]

The implications of this principle are momentous, for it proposes a method of critical philosophical verification. By transposing contested philosophical statements to their origins in cognitional activity, it underwrites an effective distinction between philosophical positions and counterpositions.[13] Philosophical positions can be divided into the *basic* propositions that constitute the correct cognitional theory and the *expanded* propositions that explicate their semantic, epistemic, and metaphysical implications. The counterpositions also are divisible into a *base* of mistaken cognitional theories and a parallel *expansion* into the correlative philosophical disciplines. Because the positions are consistent with the process of their discovery and verification, they invite intelligent and reasonable development. Because the counterpositions are inconsistent with the cognitional performance needed to confirm them, they invite reversal when confronted with cognitional fact. Both sets of statements have their experiential ground in the polymorphic complexity of the intentional subject.[14] But the positions are the result of the normative application of the intellectual pattern of experience to itself. In their case the affirmed theory is concordant with the cognitional performance that serves as its intentional ground. In the case of the counterpositions, there is a performative inconsistency between the proposed account of human cognition and the experienced reality of cognitional process. But that inconsistency remains implicit until the philosopher brings his cognitional performance to the level of self-knowledge. Without that cognitive appropriation the philosopher has not attained the full critical position required by an effective dialectical strategy.

There are striking parallels and contrasts between cognitional theory and the theories of empirical science. In each case the process of inquiry proceeds from experience through understanding and conceptualization to empirically verified judgments. But cognitional theory, unlike its scientific counterparts, is inherently self-referential. The intentional content of the theory refers to the cognitional performance through which it was discovered and confirmed. Because philosophical theories are self-referential, counterpositions are subject to the test of performative consistency. Mistaken philosophical theories often may be logically inconsistent, but their deeper incoherence is with the intentional activity of grasping them intelligently and affirming them reasonably. They explicitly contradict the operative conditions of their own possibility. Because cognitional theory uses the invariant structure of cognitional process to investigate itself, its verification has singular properties. In the ordinary case of empirical verification, "the scientific hypothesis is the antecedent, its implications are the consequent, and the confirming evidence corresponds directly only to the consequent."[15] This explains why scientific verification is inherently indirect and subject to revision in the light of additional evidence. But in the case of cognitional theory, the confirming evidence for both antecedent and consequent are given in intentional experience. In the typical scientific instance, hypothetical revision involves a change in the theory but not in the objects to which the theory refers. However, the revision of a confirmed cognitional theory would involve a change in the factual structure of human cognition itself. Because that structure is ontologically contingent, its transformation cannot be excluded logically. What can be excluded is any coherent theory of knowledge that performatively relies on that structure to deny or revise a true account of its nature.

It is time to proceed from an exposition of dialectical strategy to its concrete application in cognitional theory. What is the basic philosophical position on which a critical epistemology and metaphysics rests? Cognitional theory is an account of the dynamic intentional process through which human knowledge is achieved. It refers explicitly to *human* knowing and not to the modes of cognition proper to animals or to the divine. Animal cognition appears to be essentially intuitive, but human knowing is a complex discursive process of asking and answering questions. Although questions and answers are formulated at the level of observable speech, their underlying intentional sources are not behaviorally evident. A comprehensive cognitional theory must trace discursive intentional practice to the deeper prelinguistic principles on which it depends. The core of cognitional process, the originating source of the intellectual pattern of experience, is the unrestricted human desire to know.[16] This desire is a distinctively intellectual *eros*, whose scope of intending is inherently without limit. Although the cognitive achievement of human persons is always finite, they remain epistemically restless because their cognitive aspirations are unbounded. The first foundational invariant of human cognition is this disinterested intellectual desire to know.

Although human beings possess neither innate knowledge nor innate ideas, they do have a natural tendency toward knowing. Cognitional process is the normative unfolding of that tendency toward its unrestricted objective under the impetus of intellectual desire. Human knowing is a formally dynamic structured whole of intentional operations.[17] It is not some single activity but a complex dynamic pattern whose constitutive elements are intentional acts. These acts are not related by similarity but by functional complementarity. Successive cognitional operations presuppose and complement their intentional antecedents. Because cognitional elements do not resemble each other, the traditional reliance on analogy in cognitional theory has been a source of continuing error. Whether the primary analogue has been an intuitive, constructive, or discursive operation, the result has been a truncation or distortion of cognitional process as a whole. This explains why we need to study each cognitional operation in itself and in its functional relation to the other elements in the unified structure of knowing. The epistemic burden of cognitional theory is to make the transition from that structure as experienced to the same structure as objectively known.[18]

The process of human cognition unfolds on three distinct intentional levels. Each level is defined by its characteristic operations and operators. Like the intentional operations they contain, these levels are not linked by similarity but by functional interdependence. The succession of levels is achieved intentionally by the emergence of a new type of question. Questions for intelligence effect the transition from empirical to intellectual consciousness; questions for reflection, the transition from intellectual to rational consciousness; and questions for practical deliberation, the transition from objective knowing to authentic living.[19]

The level of empirical awareness constitutes the rudimentary beginning of human cognition. Lonergan speaks of this level as the level of *experience* in a technical sense of that familiar term. By *experience* he refers to the infrastructure of human knowing that is presupposed by the practice of inquiry.[20] The level of experience is a level of intentional givenness, of *data*. These data are the intentional contents of acts of sensation, imagination, and memory. In the normal case, empirical awareness does not occur in an intentional vacuum. Human sensations become perceptions when they occur, as they almost invariably do, in a context of desires, interests, and anticipations that are completed by images, memories, and emotional responses.[21] These complementary contextual associations vary from one pattern of experience to another; they also vary within the intellectual pattern of experience depending on the heuristic anticipations of the human inquirer. In recognizing this basic stratum of intentional givenness Lonergan's theory is empirical without being empiricist. Experiential awareness is a necessary but not a sufficient condition for human knowledge. It serves as the functional ground on which the operations of intellectual consciousness emerge. The three defining operations of intellectual consciousness each presuppose a prior level of empirical presentations. The questions for intelligence that initiate inquiry presuppose a field of experience to be investigated; the acts of direct understanding that emerge in response to thoughtful questioning apprehend intelligibility in the sensibly or imaginably given; the hypotheses and theories that articulate the intentional content of insight abstract from all aspects of the given that are not essential to the occurrence of understanding.

The operations of empirical awareness are intentional occurrences at the level of sensibility. They differ markedly from the acts of intellectual and rational consciousness that perfect and complete them. The *eros* of mind responds to the empirical given with a specific heuristic anticipation; guided by that anticipation, the subject formulates an exploratory question for intelligence; investigative thinking then fashions schematic heuristic images in the light of experience, antecedent belief, and the exploratory question. Thinking at the intellectual level is an active search by the subject for the understanding it insistently desires. Acts of direct insight respond to inquiry by grasping a potentially relevant intelligible form in the appropriate schematic images; acts of conceptual formulation express the intelligible content apprehended by direct understanding. These formulations of intelligence are its provisional responses to the originating questions that give inquiry its focus. Human intellectual development clearly requires an active interplay of intentional operators and integrators.[22] At the second level of cognitional process, the exploratory questions function as operators and the tentative answers as provisional integrators. Second-level integrators characteristically are provisional because further inquiry, understanding, and conception can require their refutation or revision.

The native *eros* of mind is the dynamism driving intellectual consciousness. Its intentional counterpart at the level of rational consciousness is the human *exigence* for reasonableness and truth. The unrestricted desire to know energizes the subject's active pursuit of understanding; the critical norms of human rationality require the formulations of understanding to satisfy the criteria of truth. At the third level of cognitional process, the exigent norms of rationality are the intentional operators; the culminating judgments of fact that satisfy those norms are the decisive integrators in the patterned structure of human cognition. Like its antecedents, rational consciousness is defined by a sequential array of intentional operations: the rational subject demands that the formulations of intelligence are true and adequate to the field of experience to which they refer; to ensure compliance with this demand all provisional answers are submitted to the test of critical reflection; although questions for intelligence vary with contrasting heuristic anticipations, the question of critical reason always is the same: Does the formulated answer to the exploratory question satisfy the requirements of truth? As investigative thinking frames schematic images to assist direct understanding, so reflective thinking marshals the relevant evidence that bears on the assessment of truth value. The decisive operation of rationality is the act of reflective insight that apprehends the assembled evidence as sufficient or insufficient to answer the question for reflection. Acts of direct insight are the *intelligent cause* of meaningful answers to questions for intelligence. Acts of reflective insights are the *rational cause* of the judgments of truth or falsity in which the process of cognition reaches its term.[23]

In Lonergan's study of the different realms of cognitive meaning, practical, theoretical, and methodological, he shows how this same pattern of knowing is recurrently actualized. Although these realms vary in their intentional standpoint, heuristic orientation, and norms of verification, they enjoy a marked analogical resemblance in the process through which they achieve knowledge. This deep epistemic similarity permits the development of a comprehensive cognitional theory that treats the methods of the empirical sciences as special cases of this universal pattern.[24] Lest the reference to method be misleading, it again should be made clear that the method of epistemic discovery and verification is not a set of rules to be followed automatically but a framework of collaborative creativity.[25] Generalized empirical method is not an algorithmic procedure but a normative pattern of operations that in the long run is epistemically efficacious.

To affirm the position in cognitional theory is to recognize explicitly the desires, operations, norms, and patterns characteristic of human knowing; it is to affirm the three levels of intentional consciousness with their functionally complementary cognitional operations. Having achieved a firm and articulate grasp of the basic position, the various counterpositions are much easier to identify and understand. The counterpositions invariably take some part of cognitional structure for the whole. Either they eliminate the unrestricted desire to know, as in pragmatism, or the norms of human rationality, as in relativism, or they misconstrue the operations and levels of intentional consciousness. The result is a distortion or truncation of the complex dynamic structure just articulated. These inadequate cognitional theories derive their plausibility from certain recurrent analogies that dominate the history of the discipline. The various metaphors of confrontation, mirroring, construction, and conversation all reflect some aspect of the whole they claim to represent.

Our dialectical narrative of the counterpositions begins with the spectator theory of knowing, the traditional base of support for naive realism. The experiential ground of the spectator theory is the human capacity for vision. Human beings regularly orient themselves in the world on the basis of looking and seeing. The experience of vision is so pervasive and familiar that it easily serves as a model for all intentional operations. This leads to the claim that intentional operations are essentially intuitive, that they are either acts of vision or analogical counterparts of it. In these intuitive operations the intentional subject is immediately confronted with a sensible given. Human intuitions, unlike those of God, are said to be receptive rather than creative. By receiving the given immediately in intuition the subject knows the object with which it is directly acquainted. When this object is identified with the already out there now real, we have the convergence of the spectator theory with naive realism. For the naive realist, human knowledge of reality is achieved through the immediate intuition of being. This account of human cognition has the great and lasting attraction of simplicity. It confines human knowing to the level of empirical consciousness and entirely avoids the complex operations of intelligence and rationality. But its simplicity is extremely deceptive, for the spectator theory confuses what is most obvious about knowing with what knowing obviously is.[26]

Before we completely abandon cognitional empiricism it is important to recognize some historical variations on the spectator theme. We can take cognitional operations to be essentially intuitive without confining them to the sensory order. If we elevate receptive intuitions to the higher cognitional levels, we promote a theory of intellectual and rational intuitions. These postulated intentional acts resemble sensory vision in their immediacy and receptivity, but they have fundamentally different intentional contents. Intellectual intuitions are assigned an intelligible or conceptual content; rational intuitions are said to be immediate perceptions of truth. I agree with Kant and Sellars in their rejection of these postulated mental acts. As human beings, we do not enjoy an intellectual intuition of the logical order nor a rational intuition of the truth. We do have intentional access to concepts and judgments, but it is not through acts of intuition. It is imperative, therefore, that we not confuse direct and reflective insights with intellectual and rational intuitions. Direct insights are the intensional *cause* of concepts and propositions; reflective insights are the rational *ground* of judgments of truth.

The epistemic immediacy of the spectator theory was directly challenged by representational realism. Representationalists like Descartes preserved the earlier emphasis on intuition but they reconceived its intentional content as mind-dependent ideas. Epistemically, the most important of these ideas are truth bearers that are alleged to correspond with the mind-independent sources of their truth value. In both rationalist and empiricist versions of representationalism, truth was conceived as a mirroring or copying relationship between a true idea in the mind and the extramental original to which it referred. But if truth is a relation of intuitive similarity between an intentional representation and its referent, then knowledge of truth requires a synoptic intuition capable of comparing the copy with its original. By the strictures of representationalism such a super-intuition is impossible, since the objects of intuition have been limited to the immanent contents of the mind. Therefore, human knowledge is either restricted to the subject's immanent ideas (solipsism) or self-authenticating intuitions must occur that certify correspondence without the required comparison (Cartesianism). The epistemological upshot of these critical reflections was twofold: a general rejection of representational realism in its mentalistic version and a growing suspicion of the correspondence theory of truth. This suspicion is warranted if correspondence is treated as intuitive similarity between terms of meaning and the epistemic objects they signify. The super-intuition needed to substantiate the copy theory of truth does not exist. Recognition of this fact requires defenders of correspondence to abandon a resemblance theory of truth and explore more carefully the nonintuitive operations of intellectual and rational consciousness on which the knowledge of truth depends.

An influential strategy in modern cognitional theory has been to supplement intuition with the operations of logical inference. This strategy assumes that the nonintuitive operations involved in cognition are essentially logical. In Spinoza's *Ethics* we find a pure case of logical rationalism. Intuitive reason is charged with discovering the axioms and principles of demonstrative science. Once the foundations of knowledge are intuitively certified, their logical implications can be deduced through demonstrative inference. Spinoza made explicit his reliance on the Euclidean ideal of self-evident axioms and deductively certain conclusions. But this ideal lost its compelling exemplar with the discovery of non-Euclidean geometries and the general acknowledgment that postulate sets lack the intuitive certification once claimed for them. Logical rationalism was inseparably tied to the classical theory of science. When both mathematics and the empirical disciplines abandoned that theory, the plausibility of rationalism had been severely undercut. But the ideal of linking intuition with logic did not disappear.

Logical empiricism attempted the same combination in a suitably altered mode. It replaced rational intuitions with empirical perceptions and deductive logic with inductive. Rather than constructing knowledge from the top down, it attempted to build it from the bottom up. The axioms of rationalism were replaced by protocol or observations sentences and the deductive principles of inference by canons of induction. This empiricist version of foundational epistemology eventually was subverted from within. Quine's critique of the dogmas of empiricism, Sellars's challenge to the myth of the given, and Hansen's insistence on the theory-ladenness of observation all supported a picture of holistic interdependence at variance with the intuitive model.[27] But there is a deeper problem for logical empiricism than that of epistemic holism. If empirical perceptions are of concrete sensory particulars by what intentional operations do we arrive at abstract concepts and propositions? Logical operations presuppose the availability of truth-bearing sentences or terms of meaning and cannot be used to create them. There is no empirical or logical path from the order of perception to the order of truth. What is lacking in both versions of logical intuitionism is any recognition of the role of insight. Direct insights mediate the transition from concrete perceptions to abstract concepts and reflective insights mediate the relations between logical propositions and concrete reality. Empirical intuitions and logical operations are limited parts of a much larger cognitional whole.

The various theories of intuitive cognition all rest at some level on the model of *receptive* vision, on the givenness of intentional content to the subject's immediate awareness. Under the influence of modern mathematics, this ideal of intellectual receptivity was explicitly challenged and a new model of the *constructive* mind was actively advanced. Traditional theories of mathematical knowledge had emphasized the intellectual vision of abstract entities. Pure geometrical shapes and ideal arithmetic proportions were thought to exist and be knowable in independence of their empirical instantiations. As a result of Descartes's analytic geometry, a new conception of the mathematical mind emerged. According to this new concept, the mind no longer perceived a pregiven shape or numerical pattern, but it constructed geometrical objects in accordance with algebraic equations. These equations served as rules of constructive formation that allowed the mind to produce the objects of its own inquiry. The metaphor of the constructive intellect was not limited to the sphere of mathematics. Vico argued for the superior epistemic value of historical inquiry because in the study of history the mind confronted objects and events of its own making.[28] As Blumenberg has argued persuasively, the diminished confidence in a pregiven order of nature or creation led to the perceived need for humanly constructed order. "The zero point of the disappearance of natural order and the point of departure for the rational construction of order are identical."[29] By the eighteenth century, the image of the productive mind had become a commonplace. Kant raised this image to the level of explicit theory in his critique of theoretical reason. Drawing on Vico's principle, he asserted that we humans can only know what we have first made after a plan of our own. Kant's insistence on the autonomous power of the mind was not a declaration of creation *ex nihilo*. The transcendental understanding depends for its matter on the receptive faculty of sensibility. But it imposes its own lawful order and unity on the unprocessed sensible material it receives. Like the ancient philosophers, Kant made intelligible form the basis of epistemic comprehension, but he no longer thought of form as an object of intellectual vision or abstractive reception. The lawfully patterned relations that constitute the objects of experience as intelligible are the direct result of the mind's transcendental synthesis. The transcendental subject creates the objects of empirical knowledge by first producing the intelligible forms through which they are known.

In the ensuing paragraphs, I want to sketch briefly the transcendental account of cognition on which Kant's critical idealism depends. At the outset, it is important to recognize the strategy Kant followed in arriving at his theory of knowledge. He began with the question of whether and how scientific knowledge is possible. Because Kant accepted the classical theory of science, he required scientific judgments to provide true, certain knowledge of causal necessity. Kant set the standards for universally valid knowledge at a rigorous level as his concentration on synthetic a priori judgments makes clear. The initial question thus is transformed into its more technical equivalent of whether and how synthetic judgments a priori are possible. Traditional theories of knowledge had required the true judgment to conform to the epistemic object. But Kant, following the inspiration of Copernicus, proposed a reversal of perspective. Why not make the object of knowledge conform to the conditions of the epistemic judgment? This would explain better how a priori knowledge of existential objects could occur, thus blunting Hume's scepticism about the validity of physical science. Kant's Copernican reversal had the effect of further complicating the question with which he began. If the new perspective were adopted, then the transcendental conditions of the knowledge of objects also would serve as necessary conditions of the objects of knowledge. In Kantian epistemology, the a priori conditions of knowledge are identical with those of the known.

But, where are the underlying *conditions* of this two-part *conditioned* to be found? Kant reinforced his Copernican strategy by locating the conditions of epistemic objectivity in the transcendental subject. Thus, he made the objects of knowledge and the judgments by which they are known conform to the a priori requirements of an impersonal, formally postulated ego. Kant's transcendental subject is not a concrete human inquirer intelligently asking and rationally answering questions, nor is it the temporally and causally conditioned empirical ego disclosed through the introspective deliverances of inner sense. The transcendental ego is a formal condition postulated by Kant to ensure the unity of knowledge by guaranteeing that all epistemic representations belong to one apperceptive consciousness. Even while Kant brought the epistemic subject into technical prominence, he made only minimal concessions to its reality and to its array of intentional operations.[30] These restrictions become clearer when we consider Kant's mode of access to transcendental subjectivity. Lonergan based cognitional theory on an intentional analysis by the subject of the experientially conscious operations involved in his own practice of cognition. But the Kantian context does not allow for this approach, since it reduces experiential consciousness to the introspective awareness of temporally successive representations by the empirical subject. Since, for Kant, these subjective representations are themselves objects of experience, they belong by definition to the conditioned and cannot serve as its conditioning ground. There is, I believe, a two-part deficiency in Kant's method of understanding subjectivity. He lacked an appreciation of the experiential consciousness that is concomitant and correlative to intentional awareness of objects; and he tended to obscure the critical distinction between intentional acts and intentional signs, with the result that epistemic faculties are differentiated not by operations but by types of representation. For these two reasons, his account of epistemic subjectivity must be based on a transcendental inference from the objects and judgments of science to their postulated grounds in an inaccessible ego, whose resources and functioning are a matter of hypothetical speculation. Although Kant's hypothetical account of the subject is admittedly ingenious, it has serious substantive limitations that are directly traceable to these original methodological flaws.

Kant's transcendental psychology is his theory of the process by which the field of scientific cognition is constituted. The theory is original in its attempt to combine epistemic elements that are normally separated or opposed: receptive intuition, formal logical inference, constructive intellectual synthesis, and the immanent sources of speculative reasoning. Kant assigned to the transcendental subject three distinct epistemic faculties: sensibility, understanding, and reason. This assignment paralleled Lonergan's division of intentional consciousness into the three levels of cognitional operations. The Kantian faculties are not differentiated by intentional acts, however, but by specific types of epistemic representation with their specific modes of cognitive functioning. These representations are further differentiated in accordance with three criteria: genetic origin, significative character, and constitutive or regulative epistemic use. Pure representations are innate possessions of the subject and conditions of the possibility of experience. Empirical representations, by contrast, are acquired by the subject through a psychological process that originates in sensory experience. Pure and empirical representations are distinguished by reference to their genetic origin. The contrast between intuitions and concepts, however, is based on a difference of significative character. Intuitions are representations of particular objects, whereas concepts by their very nature are universal. Concepts have only a mediated relation to particulars that depends on their antecedent relation to intuitions. The pure intuitions of sensibility and the pure concepts of understanding are representations with objective validity because they constitute the objects of scientific knowledge. In this respect they differ from the pure ideas of reason, whose epistemic function is exclusively regulative in nature. The intuitions of sensibility, the categories of understanding and the ideas of reason are classified by Kant as *representations* because of their intrinsic intentionality and their ontological dependence on transcendental subjectivity. Both they and the epistemic objects and judgments they condition have being only for mind.

The task of Kant's transcendental deduction is to show how the interplay of the faculties and their respective representations constitute the objects and judgments of scientific knowledge. By this exhibition, the objective validity of mathematics and physics is demonstrated. At the same time, the epistemic limits of pure reason also are made known. Since the ideas of reason lack the complementary relation to intuition enjoyed by the categories, they are incapable of constituting an epistemic object. Transcendental psychology thus establishes both the scope and the limits of our cognitive powers and provides the basis for a critical judgment on the mode of reality of the epistemic object.

The starting point of Kant's explicit cognitional theory is his account of sensibility. Sensibility is the faculty of receptivity and givenness. That which is given to sensibility, its immediate content, Kant called *empirical intuitions*. Although his terminology is not always consistent, Kant generally used *empirical intuition* to refer to the sensibly given content for which the cognitive subject cannot take responsibility. Kantian intuitions, then, are intentional contents rather than intentional acts. Their reception by the transcendental subject initiates the process of human cognition. Against the claims of the spectator theory, Kant insisted that the immediate awareness of the sensibly given is not sufficient for human knowledge. Kant both followed and departed from Hume in this respect. Like Hume, he treated the immediate given of sensibility as discrete and disconnected. But he insisted that the field of perceptual awareness invariably exhibits an aesthetic and categorial order that Hume was unable to account for. This insistence required Kant to explain how the unprocessed sensible given is transformed into the structured field of perceptual experience. Kant appealed to two distinct levels of pure representation in his explanatory account. Space and time, the pure *forms* of sensible intuition, provide part of the perceptual structure, but sensibility by itself is unable to ensure what objective experience requires. Without concepts, intuitions, even pure intuitions, are blind. A distinct but complementary faculty is demanded to produce the intelligible order characteristic of the field of cognition.

Kant called the complementary faculty *understanding*, or *the faculty of spontaneity*. In opposition to the rationalists and to certain classical theories of intellect, he insisted on the nonreceptive, nonintuitive character of understanding. For Kant, this is a constructive, synthetic, and form-generating faculty. Understanding does not intuit forms or abstract them from the sensible given; rather, it produces them and imposes them upon the intuitions of sense. This process of constructive synthesis does not occur haphazardly or at random. The pure categories of understanding are universal and invariant rules that regulate the ordering and unification of the unprocessed material received by sensibility.[31] Because the understanding invariably synthesizes the discrete impressions of sense, the field of perceptual experience, whether actual or possible, has its own categorial structure. Thus, for Kant, the intuitions of sensibility need to be differentiated from the objects of perceptual experience, because the latter have an intelligible order that the former intrinsically lack. The objects of experience depend on empirical intuitions but cannot be reduced to them. To use a traditional metaphor, intuitions provide the *matter* of perceptual objects but not their correlative *forms*. Kant follows Aristotle in distinguishing but refusing to separate the material and formal aspects of his epistemic objects. At the level of perceptual experience, matter and form are invariably connected, even though they find their origin in different representations and at different levels of subjectivity.

Since the interdependence of form and matter is reciprocal, it is not surprising to find an essential epistemic correlation between concepts and intuitions. Concepts without intuitions are as empty as forms without matter. Although neither concepts nor intuitions have objective validity in isolation, it is critical to distinguish the precise contribution each makes to the constitution of objects. According to Kant, the intuitions of sensibility are the only epistemic representations in immediate relation to the objects of knowledge.[32] Those objects are spatiotemporal particulars that stand over and against the empirical subjects who perceive and judge them.

If intuitions are in immediate relation to epistemic objects, the same cannot be said of the representations of understanding. Pure concepts are related to objects only through the mediating intuitions they lawfully synthesize. These concepts possess objective validity through this synthesizing process on which the constitution of objects depends. There is a problematic tendency in Kant to equate epistemic objects with objects of perceptual experience. This tendency obscures the critical difference that Kant recognized between perceptions and judgments. At his best, Kant was clear that human knowledge consists of judgments and not perceptions alone. In many respects, Kant treated judgments as analogous to concepts. Both are logical representations at the level of understanding that secure objective validity through their relation to intuitions. Where concepts constitute objects by synthesizing their constitutive elements, judgments represent the intelligibility of objects through an intuitively validated connection between the referents of their subjects and predicates. True judgments share with the objects they represent a synthesized structure traceable to the same laws of constructive understanding. Understanding is assigned the double function of synthesizing intuitions into epistemic objects and, with the aid of intuition, synthesizing concepts into the judgments by which these objects are known.

What is the ontological status of the object made known through true judgments? Since that object is a nexus of intuitions, and intuitions, by definition, are appearances to sensibility of an unknowable *ding-an-sich*, human knowledge is confined to the sphere of appearance. The epistemic value of human judgments is no greater than that of their confirming intuitions, and intuitions are irreparably phenomenal. Why, then, are we subject to the transcendental illusion that through science we can know reality as it is in itself? In Kant's analysis the object of knowledge is essentially conditioned by the representations of the transcendental subject; its very being is constituted by their collaborative interaction in the cognitive process. But the third epistemic faculty, the faculty of reason, is not satisfied with a subjectively conditioned epistemic object. To the receptivity of sense and the spontaneity of intellect, reason adds an unrelenting demand for *unconditioned* principles of unity. Such principles cannot be found at the level of phenomenal appearance, because that level is intrinsically conditioned. Nor can they be found at the transcendental level of intuitions and concepts, for the transcendental representations are not *objects* of knowledge but conditions of their possibility. What reason demands is an object of knowledge that transcends the field of sensible experience. Kant calls such an entity a *noumenal object* to contrast it with the phenomenal objects of perception and their underlying transcendental conditions.

The ideas of pure reason identified by Kant are the ideas of God, the soul, and the world as a unified totality of objects. These ideas represent unconditioned principles of unity that reason invariably desires to experience and comprehend. But they also symbolize reason's more general demand for a transphenomenal object of knowledge. For Kant, there is no error in reason's wanting to know objects that transcend the domain of appearance; that is its natural disposition as a cognitive faculty. The transcendental illusion of reason is its unjustified claim to achieve such knowledge, since that claim violates two of Kant's most basic epistemological principles: The only conceivable epistemic objects are immediately related to intuitions, and the only intuitions available to humans are sensitive in nature. Unconditioned, noumenal "objects" transcend our epistemic range because we lack the intellectual and rational intuitions required to know them. Nor is it possible to reach them by a transcendental or causal inference from the objects of experience. Causal relations, by definition, are restricted to the phenomenal realm, and transcendental inference cannot reach beyond subjective representations to their originating ground or referent. The pure ideas of reason, then, lack objective validity because they lack the requisite tie to empirical intuition; and reason's demand for the unconditioned has a purely regulative function in the practice of legitimate science. This explains the continuing attracting as well as the epistemic failure of speculative metaphysics. The ideas of reason provide the basis for a speculative exercise that never can be brought to epistemic fulfillment. Kant's transcendental dialectic critically disciplines reason by forcing it to recognize intrinsic limits that it constitutionally seeks to go beyond. In this respect, epistemic realism and transcendent metaphysics are akin, for they both ask of theoretical reason what, according to Kant, it never can deliver.

The pivotal faculty in Kant's theory of objectivity is sensibility, the faculty of intuition. The reliance on intuition is central to his critique of speculative reason and to his dissent from realism. To appreciate its importance, we have only to consider the following Kantian claims: Every possible object of knowledge must be immediately related to sensible intuition. Because sensibility is confined to phenomena, human knowledge has a parallel limitation. Because sensible intuitions lack intelligible order, the synthetic functions of understanding are required to unite and connect them. The judgments of understanding must be confirmed by intuition if they are to have objective validity. Because the ideas of reason lack intuitive correlates, they are denied epistemic objectivity. The judgments of traditional metaphysics are classified as irredeemably speculative because they lack intuitive confirmation.

When the *subject* pole in Kant's cognitional theory is so heavily dependent on intuition, the restriction of the *object* pole to the field of sensible objects is not surprising. And when sensible objects are thematized as appearances, the dependence of critical idealism on the prior account of subjectivity becomes apparent. To transcend Kant's theory of objects and objectivity, then, we need to challenge his transcendental account of the epistemic subject, and in particular, the pivotal role he assigns to intuition.

Kant's epistemic subject is a postulated formal ego, the locus of intentional *representations* and their constructive interplay. To this transcendental postulate, we oppose the concrete human inquirer, the center and source of functionally complementary intentional *operations*. The focal operations of cognition are not intuitions but the raising of intelligent questions and the affirmation and defense of rational answers. The intentional analysis of questioning forces us to conceive of cognitional operations, not on the analogy of sense but in distinctively intellectual and rational terms.[33] The result is a radically different conception of the epistemic subject and object. When the *subject* is conceived as a center of questioning, then the *object* becomes the unknown that the question intends, an unknown that becomes known more fully as answers to questions become more comprehensive and determinate.[34]

The shift from intuition to questioning reflects a deeper shift from empirical to intellectual and rational consciousness as the basis for a critical theory of objectivity. The core of these higher levels of consciousness is not intuition but the unrestricted desire to know; and the object of that intentional desire is not sensible phenomena but reality itself. Kant's theory of the object is marked by a vestigial empiricism.[35] The Kantian object is that which stands against the intuitive and perceptive subject. We can know phenomenal objects because we sensibly perceive them; we cannot know the transphenomenal because we lack intellectual and rational intuitions of noumena. Within the Kantian framework, the only way to transcend idealism is to postulate nonempirical intuitions of being. A more trenchant and critical approach is to challenge Kant's basic correlation between intuitive subjectivity and objects, and to replace it with the deeper correlation between intentional questioning and the universe of being. The epistemic activity immediately related to being, and to objects, is not sensory intuition but intellectual questioning; all other cognitional operations are related to being as specific ways of answering questions.[36] The intention of being in questioning bears no resemblance to the operations of sensitive consciousness, just as epistemic objectivity differs radically from extroversion to the sensibly immediate.

This attempt to revise Kant's epistemic context does not preclude similarities between positions and counterpositions. Like Kant, I recognize three levels of intentional subjectivity. For him, these were psychological faculties marked by distinct kinds of representation; for us they correspond to different sets of cognitional operations and contents. Where Kant made sensibility the pivotal epistemic faculty, I treat empirical consciousness as the rudimentary level of human cognition. Empirical consciousness refers to the intentional operations of sensation, imagination, and memory. The intentional contents of these acts are not empirical representations of an unknowable noumenon, but simply the intentionally given data of sense and experiential consciousness.[37] Kant made sensibility intentional by treating its contents as representations of noumena. But the basic intentionality of empirical consciousness lies not in its *contents* but in its *operations*. Empirical consciousness is the subject's awareness of the sensibly and experientially given.

The critics of the spectator theory are justified in refusing to equate empirical consciousness with knowledge. Intentional operations at this basic level are necessary but not sufficient for human cognition. They serve as the functional ground on which the decisive intellectual and rational operations arise. Four connected operations define intellectual consciousness; each has its source in the subject's desire to understand the empirically given. The first intellectual operation, questioning, presupposes a field of experience to be investigated. The second operation, objective abstraction, intelligently orders that field with a view to answering the question at hand. When objective abstraction is fruitful, human intelligence apprehends a potentially relevant unity or pattern of relations in the given of sense and imagination. The act of conception formulates the intelligible content of that apprehension as well as the empirical conditions required for its occurrence. In one sense, Kant clearly was right. The operations of intellectual consciousness are not intuitive in nature. Questioning, exploratory thinking, understanding and conceiving differ fundamentally from the operations of empirical consciousness. But in another sense he was deeply wrong, for he conflated these four irreducible intentional acts into functions of constructive synthesis. In Kant's theory, what links the data of sense to the concepts and propositions of intellect are unconscious, rule-governed constitutive operations. In the theory I defend empirical data are linked to formal terms of meaning by intelligent inquiry and gradually developing understanding.[38] For Kant, the transcendental interplay of intuitions and concepts is sufficient to produce epistemic objects and judgments. But the actual result of experience, inquiry, understanding, and conception is not the achievement of knowledge but the provisional formulation of answers to questions.

The deepest differences between Kant's theory and ours arise at the level of rational consciousness. He assigned to reason a purely regulative role in the practice of cognition, and he treated its demand for the unconditioned as the source of the transcendental illusion. Kant located judgments at the level of understanding and their validating intuitions at the level of sensibility. For both these reasons, he failed to develop an adequate account of rational consciousness and reflective inquiry. The cumulative result of the operations of empirical and intellectual consciousness is the articulation of formal terms of meaning. But the native exigence of rational consciousness demands that these intelligible answers be adequate and true. This demand initiates the process of reflective inquiry, verification, and judgment. Kant treated the verification of propositions as essentially intuitive, but again this is to take a part of the process for the whole. Reflective verification requires grasping the truth conditions of formal terms of meaning and assembling the relevant evidence to determine whether they are satisfied. There is an empirical aspect to verification, but the process is not primarily intuitive. In the standard case, there is a cumulative convergence of direct and indirect evidence toward the normative ideal of the virtually unconditioned.[39] Reflective inquiry proceeds from provisional formulation to rational grasp of the unconditioned; and that grasp or its absence leads to the affirmation or denial of full terms of meaning.

The coalescing operations of cognitional process reach their culmination in the rational *act* of judgment. In Kant's idiom, *judgments* refer to the logical synthesis of concepts at the level of understanding. Kantian ampliative judgments are a synthesis of representations validated by immediate intuitions. Once more, he treated as intentional signs what we identify as intentional acts. Judgment is not an intellectual synthesis of logical signs, but the rational positing or rejection of a synthesis already reached at the level of intellect.[40] Before the culminating *act* of judgment, the synthetic element is already present in the propositional formulation of the content of insight. But the direct insights that yield formal terms of meaning need to be confirmed by reflective insights that grasp these terms of meaning as virtually unconditioned, that is as a *conditioned* whose *conditions* in fact are fulfilled.[41] Kant treated reason's demand for the unconditioned as a merely regulative ideal and not as a constitutive component of judgment. But the existential judgments that amplify human knowledge are validated judgments of fact. Being as fact is reached empirically only by first reaching the virtually unconditioned in judgment; true judgment is the appropriate medium through which mind-independent being is known. The universe of being intended in questioning is a universe of factual existents and occurrences. These are the real objects of knowledge made known through the affirmation of virtually unconditioned answers to the questions of intelligence first raised about the data of experience. In the attainment of human knowledge, all three levels of subjectivity make a basic and indispensable contribution. Once the Kantian model of objectivity as extroversion to the intuitively given is challenged, then it is only through the rational grasp of the unconditioned that the validity of human knowing can be established.[42]

I have given considerable attention to Kant's cognitional theory because it is the counterposition of greatest importance in the modern critique of realism. I have tried to show how Kant neglected or distorted critical aspects of epistemic subjectivity and failed to acknowledge the full range of cognitional operations. Among the noteworthy omissions in Kant's account of knowing are the acts of direct and reflective insight. The oversight of insight is not unique to Kant but is a common counterposition in cognitional theory. There are many reasons for this oversight, but one of the most significant is methodological. In the study of the human subject, Kantians begin with an analysis of *judgments*, the intelligible *products* of the mind; linguistic analysis begins with the publicly observable *expressions* of the mind in symbols and discourse. Both approaches fail to go behind logical and linguistic entities to their intentional source in mental acts. To avoid this failure, Lonergan emphasized the intentional analysis of experientially conscious operations. His cognitional theory is a form of intellectualism that affirms both levels of insight and establishes their causal relation to the full array of intentional signs.[43]

What does it mean to be an intellectualist in cognitional theory? It is to hold that logical concepts, propositions, and judgments depend for their existence on acts of understanding; that they emerge as the immanent intentional term of intelligent and rational inquiry; that they emerge in concordance with the acts of insight that are their prior causal ground; that they express the intelligible content of what has been actively understood; and that the more perfect the act of understanding, the more numerous are the propositions in which its content finds expression.[44] For the intellectualist, concepts and judgments are the term and product of an intelligent and rational process. They are the answers offered by human subjects to their emerging questions about experience. It is in the nature of the human intellect to express its discoveries in intentional signs. The most important signs of cognitive meaning are the truth-bearing propositions affirmed in the act of judgment. Their epistemic function is to provide true answers to the exploratory questions that guide the process of inquiry. The core of intellectualism is its contention that these logical propositions and the sentences that express them are the *intelligible* product of acts of understanding that are not only intentional but *intelligent*.

Historically, the major rival to this philosophical theory has been conceptualism. The conceptualist strongly affirms concepts and propositions, and intentional signs generally, but neglects their source in direct and reflective insights. For the conceptualist, human understanding is preceded by the formation and acquisition of concepts. Because the possession of concepts is treated as the defining condition of rationality, the process by which they are generated and revised is not understood to be intelligent and rational.[45] Thus, in Kant, for example, pure concepts precede the exercise of understanding and cannot be explained by reference to it. Kant and the post-Kantian critics of realism generally endorsed some version of conceptualism, although there is room for great diversity within this common rubric. Kant is a particularly good example of a transcendental conceptualist. He treated the pure categories and principles of understanding as invariant and universal representations that could not be traced to any prior intentional source. They are the transcendental principles on which human knowledge depends, but are not themselves the results of cognitive inquiry. As noted in Chapter VI, the linguistic post-Kantians significantly modified Kant's transcendental approach. They replaced the transcendental ego with the historically evolving language community and substituted variable linguistic roles for his a priori subjective representations. Despite these important revisions, they continued to embrace conceptualism, as Wittgenstein's insistence on the autonomy of grammar and Sellars's rejection of an *arche* beyond discourse make clear. These linguistic conceptualists recognize the vital epistemic role of intentional signs, but they lack an adequate account of their discovery and verification.

What the conceptualist fails to appreciate are the triple functions of insight at the level of intellectual and rational consciousness: Direct insight gives intellectual consciousness its inner coherence by *responding* to questions for intelligence, *grasping* in simplified schematic images intelligible possibilities and *expressing* the intelligible content of that grasp in formal terms of meaning. Reflective insight performs a similar function at the level of rational consciousness by *responding* to reflective inquiry, *grasping* formal terms of meaning as virtually unconditioned and *expressing* the significance of that grasp in the affirmation of reasonable judgments.[46] Direct insights are the basis for a theory of intellectual discovery; reflective insights are the basis for a theory of rational verification. Because intellect discovers intelligible possibilities in empirical presentations, its conceptual formulations are provisional. Because reason insists on actuality and truth, it verifies or disconfirms the possibilities proposed by intellect. Direct insight provides the pivot between concrete experience and abstract propositions; reflective insight links abstract intentional signs to the concrete universe of being. Without direct insight, there is no way to understand the intentional genesis of terms of meaning; without reflective insight, it remains a mystery how these terms of meaning mediate our knowledge of the real.

The limitations of conceptualism are traceable directly to its neglect of insight.[47] The first example of these limits is the problem of conceptual change. Taken by themselves and in isolation from insights, concepts are abstract, immobile, and invariant. This is how they remain in Kant's transcendental theory, where the categories and principles are conceived as innate and a priori. Kant's historically minded successors restored variability to concepts but were unable to explain their development, refinement, and revision. Left to themselves concepts do not change; but they are changed by the minds that form them through the self-correcting process of learning. When they are divorced from that process, concepts are not only immobile but excessively abstract. Kant recognized this abstractness when he insisted that concepts without intuitions are empty. For Kant, the only way to link the logical with the existential order is through the mediation of empirical intuitions. But his solution overlooks the deeper connection between the concrete and the abstract established by acts of insight. Direct insights grasp universal intelligible forms in the concrete data of experience and therefore unite at the level of intellect what Kant bifurcated between sensibility and understanding. Reflective insights validate the objective reference of abstract propositions by displaying them as instances of the virtually unconditioned. Kant's conceptualist theory of objectivity rests on the occurrence of empirical intuitions; its intellectualist counterpart emphasizes intellectual and rational insights that serve as the intentional bond linking experience to understanding and understanding to judgment. The deficiencies of conceptualism, therefore, are threefold: In cognitional theory, it offers a truncated account of the intentional subject; in epistemology, it is unable to account for the origin and objective validity of propositional terms of meaning; in metaphysics, it misconceives the objects of knowledge to which those terms of meaning refer.

Contemporary linguistic theories of cognition trace their origin to Kant by way of Wittgenstein. Like Kant, their proponents begin by rejecting the myth of epistemic immediacy. To the many versions of the spectator theory, they oppose an account in which intentional signs play a critical mediating role. Although often distancing themselves from Kant's critical idealism, they share his refusal to reduce propositional knowledge to an immediate, intuitive confrontation with the given. The influence of Wittgenstein is evident in the reconception of the mediating signs. Inheritors of the linguistic turn have substituted publicly observable sentences for the private ideas of Descartes and the abstract logical judgments of Kant. Since they conceive of epistemic practice as a communal activity, they emphasize the publicly shared language in which it is conducted. In the early stages of the linguistic turn, Carnap defined epistemology as the logical analysis of the language of science. But in the intervening period, syntactical analysis has been incorporated into a comprehensive theory of speech acts, and the range of acceptable epistemic discourse has been enlarged. What logic had treated simply as truth-bearing propositions, the theory of inquiry views as answers given to questions. A new metaphor of intentional activity has replaced the older models of confrontation, correspondence, and construction. Intentional episodes now are conceived as irreducibly linguistic, and epistemic practice is pictured as a disciplined discursive exchange between members in a common language game. Philosophers like Sellars who were inspired by the early Wittgenstein continued to emphasize the syntactical and semantical dimensions of epistemic language; whereas others like Rorty who draw their cues from Dewey's pragmatism stress the instrumental and functional uses of discourse. Both wings of analytical thought agree that human cognition is an essentially linguistic affair.

The great merit of this analysis is its emphasis on the speech acts that are fundamental to cognition: recording observations, describing problems, asking questions, offering provisional answers, defending, refuting or confirming the hypotheses that the community of inquiry takes seriously. Its major limitations flow directly from the oversights of conceptualism. The linguistic account of cognition fails to identify the continuing source of intelligent questions in the unrestricted desire to know. It fails to acknowledge the origin of meaningful answers in objective abstraction and direct insight. Finally, although it highlights the importance of rational verification, it offers a partial account of this highly complex process. I welcome numerous aspects of the twentieth-century's concentration on language, and I accept its indispensable role in the practice of human cognition. But I have deep objections to certain tendencies in this highly ramified movement. It is a mistake to reduce intentional operations to linguistic episodes as Sellars did. It is a related mistake to accept a purely dispositional account of human understanding in terms of acquired linguistic competence. For their true significance to be appreciated, logical and linguistic signs need to be situated within a comprehensive theory of intentionality centered on insight. Within the whole of cognitional process, there is a functional complementarity between linguistic and nonlinguistic operations, with language consolidating the development that inquiry and insight have made possible. *Nous* and *logos*, *intellectus* and *verbum*, mind and language need to be understood in their complex and fully determinate interdependence. In my opinion, neither Wittgenstein, Sellars, Quine, nor Rorty has achieved the comprehensive account of intentionality that we require. Their very different theories all suffer from the limitations of conceptualism. The result is a strong tendency toward intralinguistic immanence in the treatment of linguistic reference or an avoidance of the problems of intentional reference altogether. Frege's insight that linguistic reference is mediated by sense needs to be supplemented by the deeper intellectualist understanding of sense that even Frege failed to achieve. Because the object of reference has numerous intelligible aspects, it can be referred to by an indefinite number of true descriptions. The heralded fear of linguistic reductionism, the fear that we must embrace one of these descriptions or vocabularies to the exclusion of others, really is misplaced. Its source is a failure to appreciate that descriptions and explanations are answers to questions, that questions arise within different realms of meaning and heuristic structures, and that discursive pluralism is the faithful response of cognition to the multifaceted intelligibility of being.

Human language is a resource of extraordinary power, and its semantic functions are by no means limited to the expression of propositional knowledge. But renewed attention to the noncognitive uses of language, important as they are, does not justify the misconstrual of epistemic discourse. The pragmatic, behavioral account of knowledge proposed by Rorty is an example of such misconception. Rorty's account draws its power from his justified critique of the metaphors of confrontation and correspondence. However, the pragmatic metaphor of coping with which he replaced them is hardly a satisfactory substitute. The goal of human inquiry is the deeper understanding of experience. The great contribution of cognitional theory to philosophy is that it tries to explain in precise detail just how such understanding is achieved.

D. A Defense of Critical Realism

A critical and comprehensive cognitional theory has far-reaching philosophical implications. Both the positions and the counterpositions in epistemology and metaphysics find their factual ground in this antecedent analysis of knowing. A defensible epistemic realism must establish that human knowing involves an intentional self-transcendence; and to do that, it must first discover what human knowing actually is.[48] The focus of cognitional theory is on knowing as intentional activity. As noted, this theory thematizes the epistemic subject, that subject's unrestricted desire to know, and the normative pattern of intentional operations in which that desire recurrently unfolds. Epistemology complements cognitional theory by examining the propositional terms of meaning that result from this pattern of activity. It seeks to clarify and explain objectivity and truth, the most important epistemic properties of terms of meaning. Because propositions and the sentences that express them are intentional, epistemology needs to be completed by metaphysics, which analyzes the objects of knowledge to which these intentional signs refer. When they are assembled in this cumulative order, cognitional theory, epistemology, and metaphysics form a comprehensive account of cognition that advances from knowing through knowledge to the nature of the known.

Philosophical conflict is pervasive because it is extremely difficult to achieve a fully critical position on these three interwoven themes. There is a deep tendency to be naive or unreflective in our explicit account of the practice of cognition. This tendency is traceable to the polymorphism of human consciousness. Not only are there three different levels of intentional consciousness, but intentional operations occur within fundamentally disparate patterns of experience. Corresponding to these different patterns and levels of the subject are incommensurable notions of being, knowledge, objectivity, and objects. These patterns and notions exist in philosophers with the same frequency as in other adults. The objective of personal appropriation is not to eliminate their occurrence but to restrict their influence on philosophical theories. The critical philosopher must be able to differentiate these existential patterns and notions and to confine theoretical judgements to the intellectual pattern of experience.[49] Without this strict discipline, there will be an unavoidable ambiguity in the central terms of philosophic discourse; for these terms vary in meaning, depending on the pattern of experience or the level of consciousness in which they are used. This systematic ambiguity is a fundamental cause of the division of philosophical theories into positions and counterpositions. The positions are based on a fully critical account of being, knowledge, and intentional subjectivity; the counterpositions, by contrast, base their denial of realism on an uncritical treatment of objectivity and a truncated conception of the intentional subject.

Throughout the history of philosophy, there has been a recurrence of vestigial empiricism in the treatment of knowledge. Prereflective accounts of cognition tend to emphasize empirical consciousness to the exclusion or reduction of the intellectual and rational levels. This results in a kind of picture thinking that substitutes images or metaphors for a detailed account of cognitional operations. The most notable instance of such precritical picture thinking is the counterposition I have called naive realism.[50] The *metaphysics* of naive realism is based on a prereflective notion of being and its *epistemology* on a precritical conception of knowledge. The naive realist pictures being as the object of empirical and biological extroversion.[51] Being is the already-out-there-now-real that stands against the empirical subject in his biological orientation to the data of experience. Each term in this description is significant, both for what it emphasizes and for what it omits. *Already* indicates that being is prior to the intentional activities of raising questions and pursuing answers. *Out* signifies the extroversion of empirical consciousness from the percipient body to its surrounding environment. *There* suggests the orientation of spatial sense organs to spatially localized objects. *Now* correlates the time of the empirical observer with the time of the sensibly observable. *Real*, from the biological perspective, distinguishes sensible appearances that satisfy bodily drives from those that do not.[52] Although this operative notion of the real is extremely primitive, it is not without experiential grounds. Human beings, after all, are animals; and they share with the animals this sensory orientation to the objects in their immediate environment. At the same time, this rudimentary empirical notion of reality is unaffected by the eros of intellectual consciousness and the critical exigence of human rationality. It is a notion of being developed outside of the intellectual pattern of experience and without recognition of its internal complexity.

To this empirical notion of being, naive realism adds a fragmentary conception of knowledge. The underlying picture is that of a subject directly confronting the immediately given. The epistemic subject is depicted as essentially intuitive; the object of knowledge is identified with the immediate content of that subject's receptive intuition; epistemic objectivity supposedly is achieved through veridical intuitions in which the subject sees only what is actually there now. This spectatorial conception of knowledge merges with naive realism when the intuited object is equated with the already-out-there-now-real. Their historic alliance is challenged later by representational theories of perception that insert a veil of sensible appearances between the percipient subject and "objective reality". But even representational theorists preserve the intuitive metaphor by contrasting "the God's eye view" of being with our restricted mode of human perception.[53]

The modern critique of realism begins with this rejection of epistemic immediacy. Following Descartes and Galileo, the moderns adopted a new and more complex criterion of knowledge. They abandoned the inherited picture of naive realism because they no longer accepted its account of sense perception. According to the new physics, the immediate objects of perception are mind-dependent appearances or ideas. The ancient trust in intuition was rejected as naive once its sensible contents were taken to conceal the underlying reality of nature. Modern critical thinking proceeded from the premise that sensible appearance and reality have parted company. The new goal of scientific knowledge is to penetrate the veil of appearances that separates humans from the invisible universe of being. Since we are denied immediate epistemic access to reality, we must learn to know it through the mediation of intentional signs. Galileo and Descartes retained the notion of being as the already-out-there-now-real just as they kept being itself as the intended object of scientific inquiry. But they insisted that human subjects can know being only through the mediation of truth-bearing ideas. Their incomplete break with naive realism is responsible for the morass of modern epistemology. For on Cartesian premises, it seems impossible to know whether ideas in the mind resemble the extramental objects they are alleged to represent. Although Descartes had intended to increase epistemic certainty, the enduring legacy of his revolution was the expansion of philosophical skepticism.

The enterprise of modern epistemology is dependent on the framework of mediating ideas. That framework attempts to combine a semicritical theory of epistemic mediation with a precritical notion of being. In Descartes's representational realism, mediation is not viewed as an obstacle to epistemic correspondence. But the skeptical critics of Descartes saw no way to confirm an intuitive resemblance between Cartesian ideas and their extramental referents. To preserve the objectivity of science against skeptical doubt, Kant felt compelled to abandon epistemic realism. He radically reconceived objectivity and truth as complex relations within the field of representations alone. In his limiting concept of the thing-in-itself, the old notion of being survived though it is no longer available for human cognition. It is neither possible nor necessary to go beyond mediating representations to a transcendent object. Kant limited the horizon of attainable knowledge to sensible phenomena and their constitutive transcendental conditions.

Epistemic realism made a brief recovery at the inception of the linguistic turn. Both Frege and Wittgenstein rejected ideas as the appropriate epistemic mediators. Linguistic expressions and the thoughts they convey become the new bridge between the knower and the known. The metaphor of correspondence is detached from mental representations and reassigned to linguistic or logical entities. In the *Tractatus*, language is linked to the extralinguistic in two distinct ways: It is both a constituent *in* the world and a sign *of* its objects and states of affairs. Truth-bearing language is a picture of extralinguistic reality. The transcendental logic of the *Tractatus* presumes an isomorphic correspondence between language and being. As we have seen, this discursive identity of structure is distinct from the problematic intuitive similarity espoused by Descartes; but it is no less open to criticism. In his later philosophy, Wittgenstein abandons the imagery of semantic correspondence altogether. He rejects the relational theory of meaning and encourages us to think of language in a radically new way. Linguistic signs no longer are compared to semantic representations but to tools or pieces in an historically evolving game.

Wittgenstein's later philosophy is sensitive to history and to linguistic pluralism, as the shift from logic to grammar makes clear. Kant used transcendental epistemology to critique traditional metaphysics; the later Wittgenstein used grammar to subvert both of these philosophical projects. His emphasis on the autonomy of socially conditioned grammars opened the way for Quine's ontological relativism; his rejection of semantic and epistemic realism was the inspiration for Rorty's behavioral pragmatics. Prelinguistic epistemology had struggled with the tension between intuitive immediacy and eidetic mediation. The symbol of this struggle was the clash between confrontation and correspondence as images of knowledge. Sellars's rejection of the myth of the given was a direct assault on the ideal of intuitive immediacy. By converting all intentional acts into linguistic episodes, he made human knowledge an exclusively discursive affair. Sellars preserved the semantical rubrics of truth and reference, but he construed them in nonrelational terms. Although Sellars himself was not an epistemic relativist, Rorty used his principle of the ubiquity of language against the scientific realism to which Sellars was committed.

Richard Rorty's pragmatism brings this dialectical narrative of epistemology to its therapeutic climax. Rorty completely rejected the epistemic metaphors of confrontation and correspondence as well as the intuitions and semantic representations to which they gave rise. He made a frontal attack on every version of the intentional relation between language and the extralinguistic. This attack included mirror imagery, isomorphism, and the entire framework of intentional reference. Rorty is prepared to drop the already-out-there-now-real as a world well lost.[54] He realizes, as most of his predecessors did not, that the modern concept of mediated knowledge is incompatible with the naive realist's notion of being. He therefore keeps mediated knowledge as an exclusively linguistic exchange and abandons the idea of an extralinguistic reality to which language must be semantically faithful. The concepts of truth, knowledge, and objectivity are retained but they have lost their intentional import. Rorty gives us truth without extralinguistic sources of truth value and knowledge without intentional relations between knower and known. Objectivity becomes a matter of compliance with the conventions of the operative language game and science is reduced to a strategy for coping with the surrounding environment. Although I find Rorty's pragmatic alternative exceptionally bleak, I am impressed by his critical insights. If we are to avoid the skepticism endemic to modern epistemology, we need to break completely with the precritical notions of naive realism. To Rorty's credit, he is fully prepared to do this; but his projected substitutes are a long way from what we presently need.

An epistemological narrative that begins with the spectator theory and ends with pragmatic behaviorism leaves realism on the defensive. But the truly compelling aspect of the preceding narrative is its moral: Modern epistemology is the result of an unwieldy mixture of critical and precritical notions. A credible defense of realism must begin with a fully critical notion of knowledge and being. This is why Lonergan's dialectical strategy begins with an explicit and detailed conception of human knowledge. His leading idea is quite simple: No philosophical account of knowledge is critical if it takes a part of cognitional process for the whole. Each of the three levels of intentional consciousness makes an essential contribution to cognition. The spectator theory limits knowledge to the level of empirical awareness and effectively neglects the operations of intellect and reason. The eidetic and linguistic theories of mediation go beyond the level of intuition, but they truncate or distort the nonintuitive aspects of inquiry. None of them adequately recognizes the *eros* of intellectual consciousness or the *exigence* of human rationality.

The critical operations in human knowing are the raising of intelligent questions and the giving and defending of reasonable answers. Because these operations are intentional, they orient the inquiring subject toward the unknown; because all intelligent questions have their source in the unrestricted desire to know, they seek to make known a part of its limitless objective. But what is the objective that intellectual desire intends and inquisitive questioning explores? What is the object of the subject's *full* epistemic intentionality? In philosophy, this is the critical question, par excellence. For naive realism and for most of its epistemological critics, being is the already-out-there-now-real. But for critical realism, with its emphasis on intellectual and rational consciousness, being is the objective of the unrestricted desire to know; being is what is intended in intelligent questions and partially known through true and objective answers.[55] It is not enough for philosophers to break with empiricism in their conceptions of knowledge; it is just as important to reject the notion of being that arises from empirical extroversion. Whether being, as empirically conceived, is immediately accessible to intuition or veiled behind appearances, it is invariably pictured as an object of vision, actual or potential, human or divine. Semicritical references to "the God's eye view" make the key point clear. Being is the already-out-there-now that some intuitive subject can directly examine even if we humans cannot. Given this precritical notion of being and the recognition of epistemic mediation, it is not surprising that realism is suspect. For the mediating representations all stand between the subject and the already-out-there-now preventing the immediate encounter that intuitive knowledge would require. A critical reconception of the epistemic subject needs to be extended to its intended object. Taken as the object of human knowledge, being is not the content of an immediate intuition but the reality intended in questioning that becomes known through the act of true judgment. Every notion of being depends on an implicit reference to intentional subjectivity. When the concept of the intentional subject is not sufficiently critical, the account of the epistemic object invariably follows suit.

The standard modern objections to the spectator theory all rest on a semicritical notion of mediation. By this I mean that they emphasize intentional signs to the neglect of intentional operations. Whether the mediating representations are psychological, logical, or linguistic, their most important intentional relations are left obscure. I refer particularly to their intentional source in direct insights and their validated reference to being in reflective verification. All of the mediated counterpositions we have examined are instances of conceptualism. They contain a strong affirmation of terms of meaning, a universal omission of insight, and a predictable inability to explain the origin and referent of intentional signs.

To understand how human inquiry achieves knowledge of being, we need to address the concept of objectivity. What does it mean for human knowing to be objective? How is that objectivity achieved? The notion of objectivity, like the antecedent notions of being and knowledge, is often thematized in an uncritical manner. There is a repeated tendency for empirical awareness to dominate, as in the naive realist's concept of veridical intuitions or the Kantian notion of intuitively validated judgments. The critical account of epistemic objectivity rests on a thorough understanding of cognitional structure. The originating intentional drive that calls forth and unites cognitional operations is the unrestricted desire to know.[56] That desire by its very nature consciously, intelligently, and rationally goes beyond the limits of the inquiring subject. It drives the subject successively from one level of intentional contents to another; from data to intelligibility, from intelligibility to truth, from truth to being, and from being toward the whole of what exists. While the achievement of human inquiry is always finite and partial, its underlying aim is all-inclusive. The eros of mind is not limited by any principle of subjective immanence for its comprehensive goal is reality itself. To achieve that goal human knowing must transcend whatever is dependent on or conditioned by subjectivity; it must reach terms of meaning that are semantically public, universally valid, and virtually unconditioned.

The objectivity of human knowing consists in the intentional self-transcendence of the subject. This self-transcendence is not accomplished by any single cognitional operation. Epistemic objectivity is not some simple property of terms of meaning but a compound of quite different properties, each related to a different level of intentional consciousness.[57] Since the full pattern of cognitional process is required to achieve objectivity, each level of that process makes a distinct contribution to its nature. There is an *empirical* aspect to objectivity in the givenness of data and experiential evidence; there is a *normative* aspect to objectivity in the complete surrender of inquiry to the exigent demands of intellect and reason; there is an *absolute* aspect to objectivity in the reflective grasp of the virtually unconditioned.[58] Withdraw any of these complementary aspects and the attainment of objectivity is vitiated. The objectivity of human knowing rests on an unrestricted intellectual intention (the *eros* of mind) and an unconditioned epistemic result (the achievement of full terms of meaning.)[59]

The self-transcending process of cognition culminates in the *act* of judgment. If critical realism finally is to be intelligible, the character of human judgment must be understood precisely. Judgment is an operation of rational consciousness whose intentional content is a full term of propositional meaning. What does human reason require if the act of judgment is to be truly responsible? The operative exigence of reason can be stated clearly: The epistemic subject must apprehend the content of the judgment as virtually unconditioned. Rational consciousness complements the prior levels of cognition by putting formal terms of meaning to the test. The intelligible possibilities grasped by intellect are formulated conceptually in meaningful propositions. Reason demands to know whether those possibilities are actualized, whether the propositions that objectify them are true. The native spirit of human rationality is one of critical reflection. After specifying the truth-conditions of formal terms of meaning, critical reason shifts its concern to their satisfaction. Reflective inquiry marshalls the evidence that bears on the question of the proposition's truth. When the relevant evidence is assembled, reflective insight determines whether the truth- conditions of the proposition are fulfilled. From the reflective grasp of the proposition as virtually unconditioned, the act of judgment proceeds rationally.[60] To affirm the proposition in advance of that grasp is premature; to withhold assent in its wake is to be foolish. The *normative exigence* of rational judgment is identical with the proximate *criterion* of truth. When the content of the judgment is grasped as virtually unconditioned, then the act of judgment is true.

The content of a reasonable judgment is a full term of meaning. This content, as a *de facto* unconditioned, is independent of the judging subject who verifies and affirms it. Rational consciousness issues in a product, in a term of cognitive meaning, that is objective and self-transcendent. Because propositional truth is detachable from the process that discovers and verifies it, it has the publicity and communicability that Frege required.[61] Both formal and full terms of meaning are accessible, in principle, to every epistemic investigator. But they are not given to reason as semiintuitive objects of perception; rather, they are, generated by the intentional subject through direct and reflective acts of insight.

The act of understanding that rationally grounds judgment is conditioned by antecedent operations and beliefs. Every judgment belongs to a larger context of judgments that qualify, refine, and complete its limited content. Significant judgments are like insights; they never occur in isolation. They need to coalesce to form a meaningful context of learning. Because of this interdependence the proximate criterion of truth needs to be reinforced by a stricter normative requirement. Reasonable judgments not only must satisfy the rational demand for the unconditioned, but they must occur within a context of learning that is governed by the pure desire to know. The process of inquiry is authentic only when that desire is given full sway. Only its unrestricted drive can yield the questions, insights, and revisionary challenges needed to give judgment its balance and proportion. Because of our finitude and fallibility, and because the process of learning is self-correcting, antecedent judgments regularly are modified in the course of further inquiry. But that fact is no cause for skepticism, for the process of meaningful epistemic revision is identical with the cognitional structure we have repeatedly thematized. Through the same normative pattern of intentional operations, we correct mistaken judgments and produce those that are enduring and true.

What, then, is truth? Truth is a property immanent within rationally conscious acts of judgment.[62] Ontologically and formally it resides only in the subject, but intentionally its content is independent of the persons who affirm it.[63] Because the responsible act of judgment is an instance of subjective self-transcendence, the intentional content of judgment is objective. When the act of judgment is rational, the subject goes beyond what he thinks, feels, believes, and hopes to what is in fact so. Only the unconditioned content of judgment can ground the objectivity of truth. It is a famous adage of scholastic epistemology that truth is the medium in which being is known. The only properly human way to know reality is by rationally assenting to the true propositions that signify it. The full term of meaning has a complex intentional character. It is simultaneously the intentional content of a rational act of judgment and an intentional sign of a mind-independent reality. By affirming the truth of a judgment's content, the subject thereby affirms the actuality of what that content signifies. It is in this sense that truth is a relation of correspondence between knowing and being. When the act of judgment is true, its content corresponds to what is the case. And this correspondence is known to obtain not by an intuitive comparison of terms and objects of meaning, of copies and originals, of intuitive representations and surveyable objects, but only by the reflective grasp of the judgment's content as virtually unconditioned. The virtually unconditioned is the cognitional counterpart of what metaphysics refers to as *contingent being*.[64] The factual existents and occurrences that we know through true judgment do not depend for their being on the cognitional process through which they are discovered and verified. They are de facto conditioneds, whose particular conditions are understood to be fulfilled. Epistemic objectivity and truth are the fruit of an authentic and normative subjective achievement. As human beings, we can respond to the demands of our native intelligence and rationality and, by meeting them, achieve a limited knowledge of the real.

What are the implications of this analysis for theoretical science? What does it imply about the truth value of scientific theories and the reality of theoretical constructs? Since the nineteenth century, closer study of the history of science has yielded a more realistic understanding of its character. We have thematized this revision by contrasting the classical and historical theories of science.[65] The classical theory required scientific judgements to be certain and true, but its historical replacement has relaxed these rigorous criteria. Scientific theories are no longer canonized as true; instead, they are treated as the best explanations available in the light of the relevant data and evidence. This reconception coincides with our own epistemological analysis, for the positive content of these theories does not meet the requirement of the virtually unconditioned.[66] Scientific verification is no longer to be confused with demonstrative proof. By the very nature of verification, the hypotheses it tests are subject to revision and change: and the higher we rise in the theoretical structure, the greater is the possibility of change.[67] Measured by classical standards, such theoretical revisions are deeply anomalous, for apodictic knowledge is not subject to rational correction. But in fact the revisions of inherited theories have been occasions of scientific triumph. This is because the hypotheses of science are not expressions of verified knowledge; they are critically controlled beliefs that are aimed at an ever-closer convergence to truth.[68]

Epistemic realism maintains that the object of knowledge is independent of the process by which it is known. Precritical versions of realism tried to explain this independence by stressing epistemic receptivity. If the act of cognition were an instance of immediate perception and its intentional content a preexistent reality, then realism could be established without any need for critical argument. But this naive assurance did not survive the modern emphasis on epistemic mediation. The moderns reconceived the process and object of cognition but unreflectively retained the precritical notion of being. In the wake of Kant, they made the object of knowledge dependent on cognitional process and thus separated it irrevocably from the thing-in-itself. As they saw it, epistemic mediation was a permanent obstacle to the knowledge of being. Their rejection of realism seems to rest on the following inference. Human knowledge must be immediate—that is, intuitive—for realism to be true, since only an intuitive cognition could reach the already-out-there-now-real. However, human knowledge is not immediate but essentially discursive in nature. Therefore, realism in all of its traditional forms, is mistaken and must be replaced by an alternative account of the epistemic object.

The weak point in this argument is its premise that knowledge by acquaintance is the basis of realism. Although naive realism rests on that assumption, critical realism explicitly disavows it and presents a radically different account of cognitional process. Once the full intentionality of the subject is recognized, the naive conceptions of objectivity and being no longer can be sustained. But the conceptualist critics of realism fail to achieve this comprehensive view of intentionality; they therefore misconceive the epistemic significance of mediation. Properly understood, epistemic mediation is not an obstacle to knowledge of reality but the very condition of its achievement.

For these complex thematic and historical reasons, Lonergan based epistemic realism on a critical account of cognitional process. Although that process originates in empirical immediacy, it is constituted by a succession of intellectual and rational mediations of the given. The animating source of these intentional mediations is the unrestricted desire to know. This intellectual *eros* by its intentionality intends an unlimited object, namely, being. But intending being is one thing, and knowing it objectively is another. To proceed from aspiration to achievement, the spirit of inquiry summons forth the mediating operations of questioning, thinking, understanding, and conceiving. The result of this intellectual mediation is a provisional term of meaning. The exigence of reason demands that this term of meaning be objective and true. This critical exigence, in its turn, summons forth the mediating operations of rational consciousness: reflective questioning, the assembling of evidence, grasp of the virtually unconditioned, and the self-transcending act of judgment. The discursive term of meaning affirmed in the judgment is not a barrier between the cognitive subject and object. On the contrary, it is the human being's explicit way of knowing the object that it first intends in questioning. That object becomes known only through the subject's affirming what is true. Epistemic objects are intended in questioning; although never exhaustively understood, they become better known as our answers to questions become fuller and more accurate.[69]

Still, the decisive metaphysical question remains to be answered: What is the ontological character of this epistemic object that the process of cognition makes known? The critical realist's reply is unqualified. What the *desire* to know intends, what the *exigence* of reason demands, what cognitional *operations* disclose, and what *full terms of meaning* signify is one and the same, namely, being. Should the critic of realism reply, "but how do you know that the object of knowledge is real?" the appropriate response is clear. What is the relevant philosophical sense of the term *real* and what is the rational criterion by which determinations of reality are measured? Every operative notion of being is traceable to some level of intentional consciousness and to some prevailing pattern of experience. To think of being as the already-out-there-now is to objectify the implicit notion of reality at the level of empirical consciousness. The major reason for our extended attention to the intentional *subject* has been to disclose the partiality of that level and the precritical meanings it assigns to philosophical terms. To give these terms their critical meaning, I have insisted on thematizing the full reality of the human inquirer. The implicit notion of being at the level of intellectual and rational consciousness is that being is the object of intentional desire, the goal of unrestricted inquiry, the referent of rational judgment. The philosophically relevant sense and criterion of being are given critically by objectifying the whole of cognitional process. Conversely, they are given uncritically by objectifying only a limited part or aspect of that process. The critical sense of being is that it is the object of intellectual grasp and reasonable affirmation; and only through such grasp and affirmation can the content of being be concretely determined and specified.

Pace Kant, cognitive operations do not exercise a constitutive effect upon their object; they simply reveal epistemically what that object already is.[70] However, it is possible to identify three aspects of that object corresponding to the three levels of cognitional process. Since the central operations at each level are intentional, we are able to define their appropriate contents heuristically. To the operations of empirical consciousness corresponds the potency of the epistemic object; to the act of insight corresponds its intelligible form; and to the grasp of the unconditioned corresponds the actualization of its being. There is an isomorphism at the core of human cognition, but it is not where Kant and Wittgenstein located it. They postulated an isomorphism between the terms and objects of cognitive meaning, between intentional signs and the epistemic entities they signified. But the isomorphism that actually obtains is between intentional operations and their correlative metaphysical contents. Intentional experience is the experience of ontological potency; intentional understanding is the apprehension of intelligible form; intentional judgment is the affirmation of existential act. Just as experience, understanding, and judgment coalesce to form one cycle of knowing, so potency, form, and act coalesce to form one instance of the known. Because human knowing is the knowing of being, their correlative structures are isomorphic. This very basic isomorphism allows the epistemic realist to proceed from a generalized account of human cognition to an equally generalized account of the reality cognition intends.[71] To work out both of these accounts in their full detail is beyond the scope and purpose of this chapter. My more limited intention is to sketch the basic argument for epistemic realism and to show

how a critically structured metaphysics finds its ground in an equally critical cognitional theory.

E. The Critical Appropriation of Tradition

The contemporary crisis in philosophy has arisen at a turning point in the history of modernity. In the course of the nineteenth century, a new understanding of rationality, science, and culture began to emerge. The heuristic emphasis of human studies shifted from constancy to change, from the abstract and essential to the historically concrete. As the awareness of cultural pluralism deepened and as the empirical and formal sciences asserted their autonomy, the quest for certainty gradually lost its hold on Western intellectual life. Nothing indicates more clearly the weakening of Cartesian influence than the new attention to human historicity and sociality. Despite a general rejection of Hegel's absolute idealism, his concept of objective spirit played a major role in the theoretical viewpoint that began to gain ascendancy.

The center of Cartesian philosophy had been the disembodied and disembedded rational self, the solitary ego. In the nineteenth century, the theoretical focus shifted to the supraindividual social communities within which human beings are born and develop. These communities are constituted by common meanings and values that are not the work of single individuals nor even of single generations.[72] On the whole, personal development occurs through the individual's participation in the prior achievement of his antecedents. Most of what we do and say consists in using the resources of a culture we have inherited.[73] But the dynamic of historical development is not limited to the lives of individual persons. Cultural, political, and economic communities also develop and decline as the common meanings that give them identity come into being and pass away. The nineteenth century's heightened sensitivity to history eventually affected all of the great cultural practices, including science. As philosophers of science became more familiar with its history, they no longer could maintain the classical account of its nature.

The dominant ideals of the Enlightenment did not survive this transition in their original form. The purified reason of Descartes and Kant is inconsistent with the historically mediated subjectivity described by Hegel. The ideal of apodictic science is at variance with the actual practice of the theoretical community. The normative model of culture founded upon adherence to rational method is explicitly contrasted with alternative ways of ordering communal life. These thematic revisions reach their climax in the general critique of foundational epistemology. Once the quest for certainty is abandoned, philosophical guarantees of scientific rigor lose their point. Postmodern critics like Rorty derive their impetus from the philosophical theories and projects that they opposed. Rorty directed his severest criticism against a certain view of philosophy's cultural function. A long tradition traceable to Plato grants philosophy disciplinary authority over other cultural practices. Because the philosopher returns from the sunlight into the civic cave with a directive knowledge his fellow citizens lack, he is authorized to be their judge and ruler. The traditional Platonic images of the philosopher as critic and teacher presume his possession of a politically relevant higher knowledge. The philosopher's mastery of this wisdom and the continuing civic need for it provide the justification that authority inherently requires. Legitimate authority presupposes an inequality of knowledge and responsibility between the governor and the governed. Without this epistemic inequality the philosopher's claim to authority would be null and void.

The second stage of the Enlightenment is permeated by the spirit of suspicion. The masters of suspicion—Marx, Nietzsche, and Freud—find common cause in their critique of traditional philosophy.[74] Their deconstructive descendants like Rorty intensify this criticism, particularly in its cultural applications. Philosophy's demand for cultural authority is depicted as a mask that conceals a hidden will to domination and control. The allegedly superior knowledge invoked to justify its cultural claims does not exist. A critical study of philosophy's past reveals a history of opposing traditions with no capacity for consensus or unity. All legitimate authority depends on a cooperative transfer of power from the past to the present.[75] This transfer makes the achievements of the past available to the present in the continuation of their common work. But if philosophical history is marked by elevated rhetoric and meager achievement and its present and past are rent by division, then philosophy lacks both power and authority.

Of course, scepticism about philosophical knowledge is hardly new. The tradition is filled with philosophers turning against the theoretical results of their predecessors and proposing new methods to ensure rational agreement and progress. But the deconstructive critics carry this adversarial challenge to a more basic level. They seek to problematize the theoretical problems and epistemic aspirations that give philosophical inquiry its meaning. When the idiom of critical discourse shifted from "mistaken theories" to "*meaningless propositions and questions*," the legitimacy of philosophy itself was finally at stake. During the last two hundred years, repeated attempts have been made to delegitimatize theology, metaphysics, epistemology, and ethics by uncovering the dubious principles on which they are alleged to depend. The spirit of suspicion first released by Descartes has been turned against its original champions. Descartes had wanted to emancipate secular reason from the authority of the church and the university. The purpose of this liberation was to establish purified reason and rigorous science at the foundation of modern culture. But Rorty's intention is far more radical. He views all forms of cultural authority as inherently despotic. The therapeutic function he assigns to philosophy is to subvert their putative legitimacy, not to sanction it by indefensible arguments.

Rorty has often insisted that our judgment of philosophy is dependent on our reading of its history. Explicit scepticism about philosophy's cultural function originates in an even deeper scepticism about the philosophical tradition itself. In Rorty's view, *Philosophy* has historically aspired to a form of directive knowledge that is simply not attainable.[76] In aiming at a cultural position above or beneath ordinary discursive practices, it has forfeited the important mediating function it might have performed. What liberal culture needs is not a governor or judge but a hermeneutic mediator between its normal and abnormal discourses. Unless philosophy is willing to assume this more modest office, it will remain on the margins of contemporary culture. Rorty explicitly invokes the guidance of Gadamer in the transition from epistemology to hermeneutics. But Gadamer's understanding of the effects of history suggests a different way of approaching these difficult issues.[77] Gadamer has emphasized that precritical belonging is our fundamental relation to history. We belong to the world and its intersecting communities and practices long before we can objectify and criticize them. Through this belonging, we participate in their traditions, in the resources they transmit from the past. Our concrete development as persons has two interwoven dimensions. We develop from below through adherence to the normative patterns of cognition and action. Sustaining this process of personal achievement is a massive contribution from above. Through the many forms of cultural education, we share in the beliefs and aspirations of the world into which we are born. These two modes of development are tightly interdependent. Without the available contribution of the past, it is impossible to get beyond prehistory. Without authentic personal involvement, it is impossible to appropriate what tradition has effectively transmitted. In the uncertain process of human development, existential responsibility and historical belonging are distinct but reciprocally connected dimensions.

Traditions accelerate our personal development by focusing our aspirations, providing measures for our performance, and deepening our awareness of human possibility. On the basis of continuing education, we slowly learn to think for ourselves, to make our own decisions, and to extend our freedom and responsibility.[78] As MacIntyre and Gadamer have emphasized, living traditions are not static and homogeneous. They are centers of conflict and opposition as well as agreement. Internal criticism, renewal, and change are as vital to their continuance as conservation of the past. *Vetera novis augere et perficere*.[79] The purpose of tradition is to augment and perfect the old with the new. In this process, authentic traditions open themselves and their adherents to the strange and unfamiliar, to the aspects of experience they previously had neglected or misconceived. Because we belong simultaneously to several traditions, we find it difficult to coordinate their divergent emphases and viewpoints. Through reading, travel, and open conversations with friends and strangers, we are confronted with pluralism and the limitations of our original inheritance. With the awareness of pluralism, a certain loss of innocence ensues. We recognize that not only ourselves but the multiple traditions to which we belong are finite and fallible, that, to use Heidegger's idiom, they disclose and conceal at the same time.

Whitehead drew an important distinction between the beliefs that we hold and the manner in which we hold them.[80] A parallel distinction can be applied to the members of an historic tradition. Specific virtues are needed to preserve the proper balance between conservation and openness. Frequently, the adherents of a tradition become rigid and exclusionary. Fearing the unfamiliar and alien,they reject it; troubled by the refractory and dissonant, they seek its reduction to comfortable and conventional forms. Extended over time, this process deprives a tradition of life. Because all of their carriers are mortal, traditions must be authentically transmitted and renewed, if they are not to become prisons of the spirit. Even the richest traditions are finite and thus unable to meet the full depths of human aspiration. As a result, we alternately dwell in and break out of the fiduciary frameworks to which we belong.[81]

After the initial period of acceptance and transmission there is no fixed pattern of response, by an individual or a community, to its inherited traditions. At different periods in history, certain characteristic patterns have emerged, although they usually provoked a dissenting response in succeeding generations. Thomas Aquinas, for example, granted provisional authority to Aristotle's metaphysics even as he subordinated it to the higher authority of the scriptural tradition. But Thomas's attempt to synthesize the Hellenic and Hebraic cultures was not sustained in the late Middle Ages. The early moderns, like Bacon and Descartes, encouraged a radical rejection of Aristotle in order to establish philosophy on a foundation of alternative principles. Centuries later Nietzsche excelled in creating subversive genealogies that reversed the self-understanding of traditional moral theories. Under the spell of these deliberate reversals, it is difficult to maintain an innocent relation to the tradition he rebelled against. Nietzsche's influence is apparent in the various deconstructive movements that have sought to problematize the philosophical tradition as a whole. In recent years, their excessive suspicion has aroused a countermovement, symbolized by Gadamer and MacIntyre, that seeks to restore the notion of tradition to its original dignity.

I accept Gadamer's insight that belonging is a constitutive feature of human existence. The real question is not *whether* we shall belong to a tradition but in *what manner* we shall belong. Can we achieve a dialectic of belonging and distance, which preserves the riches of tradition but keeps us sensitive to its limits?[82] In the case of our complex philosophical inheritance, Lonergan recommended a strategy of critical appropriation, of patiently distinguishing the achievements and limitations of our predecessors. To this end he developed the dialectical strategy of position and counterposition. I have just applied this strategy to the problem of epistemic realism in order to test its power and validity. The deeper purpose of this exercise was to rehabilitate epistemology and metaphysics as legitimate theoretical endeavors. But the execution of dialectical strategy is not in the least automatic. It presupposes the attainment of the full critical position by the thinker who performs it. Naive or partial attempts at critical appropriation only compound the problem they are meant to address. Every established tradition has its limitations and weaknesses. The cure for these liabilities is not to undo the tradition but to undo its inauthenticity.[83] How does the finite individual distinguish the authentic from the inauthentic in the great philosophical and cultural traditions? The relevant philosophical criterion is the test of performative consistency. Philosophical positions invite development when they are intelligently grasped and reasonably affirmed. The counterpositions, by contrast, invite reversal because they deny or ignore the conditions of their own possibility.

Religious, political, and cultural traditions are appraised by appealing to their sources and their outcomes. At the root of all authentic developments are the *eros* and *exigence* of the human spirit. Their faithful observance promotes excellence and justice in personal and communal life. But that observance sets a norm from which actual practice regularly diverges. Fidelity to the precepts of the spirit repeatedly is compromised by the manifold forms of bias that obstruct authentic performance.[84] Actual human living is a dialectical mixture of authenticity and inauthenticity, the result of a complex interplay between the acceptance and refusal of self-transcendence. Our acknowledgment of the real and our pursuit of the good constantly are frustrated by bias and self-love. In general, we are disposed to conceal these sources of disorder or to rationalize them away. But our strategies of concealment cannot escape the eventual verdict of history. The fruit of authenticity is sustained development and reciprocal influence; the fruit of its antithesis is isolation, breakdown, and decline. In critically evaluating a tradition, we are not limited to a judgment of its intentional sources. Ultimately, it is by their enduring fruits that we know and appraise them.

Over a century of reflection on human historicity has altered our conception of reason and transformed our theory of science. It has emphasized the inevitability as well as the dangers of communal association. It has disrupted traditional patterns of philosophical practice and made the future of philosophy a matter of intense debate. If this heightened historical consciousness is to be fully responsible, its exercise must be both empirical and critical. As a form of empirical reflection, it must do justice to the facticity and concreteness of human existence. As a critical activity, it must learn to appraise historical change, to distinguish human development from decline. A critical appraisal of change must not be narrowly partisan. Neither the old nor the new, neither the individual nor the community has a monopoly on virtue or vice. The threat of inauthenticity applies to everything human. There is the danger of minor inauthenticity when we fail to honor the demands of our sustaining traditions. There is the greater danger of major inauthenticity when an enduring tradition violates the immanent norms of the human spirit.[85]

A just and critical appraisal of human practice requires wisdom on the part of the appraiser. The appropriate intellectual virtue is called *phronesis* or *practical insight*. *Phronesis* does not consist in the application of abstract principles to concrete situations. Practical reflection evaluates action as the outcome of concrete dialectical principles and as the causal origin of foreseeable consequences. An immanent law of historical sanctions applies to human conduct. When the norms of the human spirit are violated, when self-transcendence is repeatedly refused, the resultant disorder in personal and communal life bears eloquent witness. In this respect, the history of philosophy is no different from the history of every other human practice. Order and disorder, positions, and counterpositions, development and decline are mixed together in a tangled web. By patiently distinguishing the different strands in the web and tracing them to their intentional origins, we grow to appreciate the great complexity of the human spirit. The counterpositions in philosophy result from confusing a part of intentional consciousness with the whole. The more dangerous counterpositions of history absolutize limited and partial goods and deny or destroy the greater human good of which they are a part.

Critical appropriation attempts to bridge the divide between the hermeneutics of recollection and the hermeneutics of suspicion.[86] Both of these orientations are legitimate, for every tradition contains elements worthy of retrieval and others unfit for transmission. But it is important to be critical about the posture of criticism itself. Hermeneutic suspicion is an ambiguous interpretive outlook, even though it has become a dominant stance in our intellectual culture. It is possible to grant allegiance to a tradition that is inauthentic; but it is equally possible to be alienated from what is genuine and good. The evaluative interpretation of a tradition is conditioned by the personal horizon of the interpreter.[87] But that horizon is as subject to inauthenticity as the tradition against which it is directed. In assessing a radical critic like Nietzsche or Rorty, it is important to ask; How just are the genealogical narratives that they create as weapons of criticism? How valid are the critical principles underlying their deconstructive activity? The point of this reminder is not to endorse a conservative outlook on our uneven inheritance. Enduring theoretical traditions are subject to significant limitations. They can fail to transmit important aspects of the past; they can refuse to acknowledge what is original and unprecedented; they can shape a conceptual grid that distorts or truncates important and recurrent experiences; they can forget or ignore the most basic and important questions.[88] The tradition of epistemic realism is a case in point. The critics of realism were right in their emphasis on epistemic mediation and their rejection of the spectator theory; but they were wrong to confine their philosophical opponents to the horizon of intuitive immediacy.

MacIntyre has recently reminded us that special virtues are required for effective interaction with tradition.[89] His own appropriation of Aristotle's practical philosophy is a good example of such virtues at work. MacIntyre locates his moral theory squarely within the Aristotelian tradition. He adopted Aristotle's principle of internal teleology and his careful interweaving of ethical and political categories. At the same time, MacIntyre sought to modify the comprehensive framework within which the virtues are situated. He challenged Aristotle's lack of historical sensitivity, his unduly optimistic analysis of tragedy, and his confinement of the virtues to their home in the classical polis.[90] There is a parallel structure to Lonergan's appropriation of Aristotle's theoretical position. Lonergan's cognitional theory draws freely on Aristotle's rational psychology. Like Aristotle, he highlighted the human desire to know, the interplay of sensibility and intellect, the central importance of insight into phantasm, and the immanent intelligibility of the sensible. Despite these deep agreements he also faulted Aristotle for his lack of historical consciousness. This attention to history led Lonergan to reject Aristotle's classical theory of science, his cosmology of causal necessity, and his rigid separation of theory and practice. Both MacIntyre and Lonergan appropriated the Aristotelian tradition critically by preserving its enduring achievements and transcending its most serious limitations.

These notable modifications of Aristotle stand in sharp contrast to the early modern rejections of his philosophy. By a peculiar irony, Aristotle's modern critics preserved what was weakest in his philosophy, the classical theory of science, and abandoned what was most worthy of preservation, his epistemic realism and his virtue-centered political and moral theory. The excesses of modernity should make us cautious about postmodern appeals for a radical break with tradition. In the first place, such ruptures tend to be exaggerated, as Etienne Gilson amply demonstrated in the case of Descartes. But apart from radical hyperbole, I have a deeper concern that complementary polarities will be treated as antithetical. I welcome the postmodern emphasis on history, sociality, language, and symbolism but am uneasy with its tendency to one sidedness. The renewed awareness of *nomos* should not lead to the denial of *physis*. For this reason I have concentrated on our native intelligence and reasonableness, centered discussion around intentional consciousness, and emphasized the importance of cognitive meaning.

I am in full accord with the recent judgment of Paul Ricoeur: "Nothing is more necessary today than to renounce the arrogance of critique and to carry out with patience the endless work of distancing and renewing our historical substance."[91] Patience and humility are needed to make a mature transition from the first stage of the Enlightenment to the second. The example of our celebrated antecedents is sobering, for these qualities were notably lacking at the inception of modernity. Will late modernity simply repeat the extravagance of its origin? It does not have to be so. What we most need in our time is a critical center of collaborating thinkers who are able to understand and appreciate the old and the new.[92] It appears that we stand at a decisive historical juncture in which development and decline are occurring simultaneously. The dynamic development of modernity is the product of unprecedented specialization. The hard won autonomy of science and culture has encouraged a dispersion of spiritual energy. The arts and the sciences have been transformed by this liberation, but the integrative practices like politics and philosophy have suffered. The human price paid for our centrifugal development is a loss of coherence and unity. To be sure, meaningful coherence cannot be restored easily. When the center does not hold, the risk of procrustean integrative strategies is great. In the quest for unity, we shall continue to see reductionist attempts to deal with the new and unfamiliar. But the forms of integration appropriate to our age cannot be reductionist. In the human context, unity without multiplicity always will be tyranny. What we need and must cultivate is sufficient maturity to be both comprehensive and coherent. Theoretical specialization does not abolish complementarity, and the multiplication of differences is consistent with a deeper and yet unrealized concord.[93]

F. The Love of Wisdom

According to legend, the term *philosopher* owes its origin to Pythagoras. The life of this ancient Greek is shrouded in mystery, and this legend may be apocryphal. Still, it seems fitting that we should have a new name for the participants in a new form of fellowship. The earliest philosophers were those who joined together in their love and search for wisdom. Their common activity was erotic and communal at the same time. As Plato taught us, it was erotic because it originated in the recognition of a deep human need. Human beings love and long for the wisdom that they find themselves without. But the pursuit of wisdom, though it has its share of solitude, draws those who undertake it into friendship. Although no one, in principle, is excluded from this association, there are never many who make the love of wisdom the effective center of their lives. Although the desire to know is natural to humans, it competes with a plethora of other desires for human allegiance and devotion.

From the beginning, there has been uncertainty about the relation between knowledge and wisdom. There are many forms of knowledge that do not make us wise. Yet, the desire for wisdom seems to be a desire for knowledge of some kind. According to Aristotle, the knowledge of the wise man is both basic and comprehensive. It is a knowledge of the first principles that apply to all of being. Aristotle called this knowledge *sophia* and made it the special concern of metaphysics. Those who follow in the tradition of Aristotle retain his concern for foundations and comprehensiveness, even when they revise his integrative strategy. We have located the foundational principles of philosophy in the intentional subject. The native *eros* and *exigence* of the human spirit are the true principles of cognitive and moral development. These are not static, logical foundations confining inquiry with an a priori conceptual scheme. Rather, they are methodological principles whose normative unfolding accounts for epistemic innovation and revision. The development of the human spirit throughout history has produced an increasingly differentiated set of epistemic outcomes. There are multiple functions of intentional meaning, numerous heuristic structures, and irreducibly different universes of discourse. The human desire to integrate these diverse achievements remains in force, but the task of integration never has been more difficult. Small wonder that reference to wisdom, even the love of wisdom, has become so rare.

There is a justified fear in contemporary philosophy that integration will be achieved only through procrustean methods. This has led to incessant reminders of our finitude, our fallibility, and our historicity. As a check against philosophical hubris these reminders are welcome; but the love of wisdom needs tempering rather than repression. Lonergan's great contribution to philosophy in this century has been to devise a strategy of epistemic integration that is deeply sensitive to cognitive pluralism and change. But the integration he envisaged is neither an escape from nor a surrender to the power of time and history.

"Professing themselves to be wise, they became fools."[94] The great temptation of philosophers is to become sophists, to forget the difference between loving wisdom and having it. I do not think it is an accident that many of the ancient sophists were also sceptics. The wisdom the sophists claimed to possess was a truncated version of what their antecedents and successors actively longed for. Philosophical scepticism tends to become a negative wisdom that limits our sense of human possibility. In opposition to the sceptics—ancient, modern, and contemporary—philosophy should take its stand on the capacity of the human being for self-transcendence. Objective knowing, authentic living, and cultural maturity and openness are within the range of human achievement. Sophisticated ideologies that tell us otherwise are counsels of despair. The great cultural function of philosophy in our time is to elevate the human faculties not to complete their prostration.[95]

Notes

Preface

1. Richard Rorty, "Overcoming the Tradition: Heidegger and Dewey," in *Heidegger and Modern Philosophy,* ed. Michael Murray (New Haven, Conn.: Yale University Press, 1978), p. 243.

2. Bernard Lonergan, *A Third Collection* (New York: Paulist Press, 1985), p. 8.

3. Harold Rosenberg, *The Tradition of the New* (New York: Horizon Press, 1959).

4. The dialectical narrative I have crafted does not claim to be exhaustive. I have concentrated on those thinkers who sought to define a new relation between philosophy and the empirical and formal sciences. At the heart of the narrative is a common concern for scientific autonomy and for the philosophical implications of human historicity. I recognize the importance of a very different critical approach to the philosophical tradition that begins in Nietzsche and proceeds through Heidegger and Derrida. My silence on this alternative deconstructive strategy does not imply an indifference to its challenge.

I. The Crisis of Philosophy

1. Wilfrid Sellars, *Essays in Philosophy and Its History* (Boston: D. Reidel Publishing Co., 1974), p. 4.

2. Bernard Lonergan, *Insight: A Study in Human Understanding* [1957] (New York: Philosophical Library, 1970), p. 527.

3. Rene Descartes, *The Principles of Philosophy,* in *The Philosophical Works of Descartes,* vol. 1, trans. E.S. Haldane and G.R.T. Ross (Cambridge: Cambridge Univ. Press, 1972), p. 211.

4. The medieval respect for Aristotle is vividly reflected in Thomas Aquinas's frequent references to him as *The Philosopher* and in Dante's historic phrase *'Il maestro di color che sanno,'* the master of them that known.

5. Francis Bacon, *Novum Organon,* ed. T. Fowler (Oxford: 1889), p. 209.

6. See Alexander Koyre, *From the Closed World to the Infinite Universe*

(New York: Harper and Bros., 1958) and Alfred North Whitehead, *Science and the Modern World* (New York: Macmillan, 1925). The note of bewildered alarm is memorably struck by John Donne:

> ...new Philosophy calls all in doubt,
> The Element of fire is quite put out;
> The Sun is lost, and th'earth, and no mans wit
> Can well direct him where to looke for it.
> And freely men confesse that this world's spent,
> When in the Planets and the Firmament
> They seeke so many new; then see that this
> Is crumbled out againe to his Atomies.
> 'Tis all in peeces, all cohaerence gone;
> All just supply, and all Relation.

John Donne, *Anatomy of the World,* First Anniversary [1611] ed., Nonesuch Press, p. 202.

7. In designing this list, I have drawn on the semantical and epistemological insights of Gottlob Frege, Wilfrid Sellars, and Bernard Lonergan. Lonergan's analysis of cognitive meaning in *Method in Theology* (New York: Herder and Herder, 1973), pp. 76-99, is the source of the most important categories; i.e., heuristic structure, realms, and stages of meaning.

8. Lonergan, *Insight,* pp. 173-81.

9. Aristotle, *Physics,* Book 1, 184a 16-20, in *The Basic Works of Aristotle,* ed. Richard McKeon (New York: Random House, 1941), p. 218.

10. I am indebted to Bernard Lonergan for many aspects of this distinction; I have drawn in particular on four essays from *A Second Collection* (Philadelphia: Westminster Press, 1974): "The Transition from a Classicist World-View to Historical-Mindedness," "Theology in Its New Context," "The Absence of God in Modern Culture," and "Theology and Man's Future."

11. Aristotle, *Posterior Analytics,* Book 2, Chapter 19, *The Basic Works of Aristotle,* pp. 184-86.

12. Evert W. Beth, *The Foundations of Mathematics* [1965] (New York: Harper and Row, 1966), pp. 38-48.

13. All those respected and cultivated persons who, having acquired their notions of science from reading, and not from research, have the idea that science means knowledge, while the truth is, it is a misnomer applied to the pursuit of those who are devoured by a desire to find things out." Charles S. Peirce, *Collected Papers of Charles S. Peirce* (Cambridge, Mass.: Harvard Univ. Press, 1931), 1.3-14.

14. See Whitehead, *Science and the Modern World,* p. 168. "Consider this contrast: when Darwin or Einstein proclaim theories which modify our ideas it is a triumph for science. We do not go about saying that there is another defeat for science, because its old ideas have been abandoned. We know that another step of scientific insight has been gained."

15. B. Lonergan, *Collection,* ed. Frederick Crowe (New York: Herder and Herder, 1967), pp. 259-60.

16. The preceding analysis of meaning as well as the matrix that follows offer a compressed formulation of central principles in Lonergan's cognitional theory.

They rely heavily on the argument developed in *Insight* and *Method in Theology*, pp. 73-99. A more expansive account and defense will be given in Chapters VII and VIII.

17. Lonergan, *Insight*, pp. 348-59; Aristotle, *Metaphysics* Book 1, 980a 23.

18. Lonergan, *Method*, pp. 4-25.

19. "Its [insight's] function in cognitional activity is so central that to grasp it in its conditions, its working and its results, is to confer a basic yet startling unity on the whole field of human inquiry and human opinion." Lonergan, *Insight*, p. x. Lonergan had discovered the decisive importance of insight *(intelligere)* while reconstructing Aquinas' theory of the inner word. See *Verbum: Word and Idea in Aquinas* (Notre Dame, Ind.: University of Notre Dame Press, 1967).

20. L. Wittgenstein, *Philosophical Investigations*, trans. G.E.M. Anscombe (New York: Macmillan, 1953), p. 8: "to imagine a language means to imagine a form of life."

21. This concept of science is fully developed in Michael Polanyi's *Personal Knowledge* (Chicago: University of Chicago Press, 1958) and in Marjorie Grene's *The Knower and the Known* (New York: Basic Books, 1966).

22. As Chapters V and VII will show, the most profound philosophers of our time continue to see the project of integration as the central purpose of philosophy. But disagreement remains over the level at which the deepest integration should occur. For Sellars, the integration of the different strands of human discourse is primary; for Lonergan it is the integration of the different patterns of intentional experience. Contrasting analyses of the nature of intentionality prove to be at the heart of the divergent strategies.

23. Lonergan, *Method*, pp. 114-15.

24. Lonergan, *ibid.*, p. 25. "Very precisely, it [transcendental method] is a heightening of consciousness that brings to light our conscious and intentional operations and thereby leads to the answers to three basic questions—What am I doing when I am knowing? Why is doing that knowing? What do I know when I do it? The first answer is a cognitional theory. The second is an epistemology. The third is a metaphysics."

25. See Michael Dummett, *Frege: Philosophy of Language* (New York: Harper and Row, 1973), and Chapters II, VI and VII.

26. This condensed account of Kant's philosophy of mathematics is based on the Transcendental Aesthetic of *The Critique of Pure Reason*, trans. N. K. Smith (New York: St. Martin's Press, 1961), pp. 65-91, and *Prolegomena to any Future Metaphysics*, trans. W. Beck (Library of Liberal Arts: Indianapolis, Indiana, 1950).

27. Kant, *Critique of Pure Reason*, p. 53.

28. See Bertrand Russell, "Logical Atomism," in *Logical Positivism*, ed. A. J. Ayer (New York: The Free Press, 1959), p. 32.

29. Beth, *Foundations*, pp. 55-56.

30. See Peter Strawson, *Introduction to Logical Theory* (London: Methuen, 1952).

31. George Boole, *The Mathematical Analysis of Logic*, cited by Beth, *Foundations*, p. 60.

32. E. Schroder, *Vorlesungen uber der Algebra der Logik* (Exakte Logik). Leipzig 1:1890, 11/1:1891, 111:1895, 11/2:1905.

33. Evert W. Beth and Jean Piaget, *Mathematical Epistemology and Psychology* (Dordrecht, Holland: D. Reidel Publishing Co., 1966), pp. 137-38.

34. G. Frege, *Begriffschrift, eine der arithmetischen machgebildete Formelsprache des reinen Denkens.* Halle: 1879.

35. Plato introduced the form of the Good in the sixth book of the Republic; Aristotle's argument for the existence and nature of God as the first cause and principle of being occurs in Book Lambda of the *Metaphysics.*

36. Descartes's *Discourse on Method* and *Meditations on First Philosophy* both reveal how the quest for epistemic certainty requires foundational principles and prescribes the standards they must satisfy.

37. See L. Wittgenstein, *On Certainty,* trans. D. Paul and G. E. M. Anscombe (New York: Harper and Row, 1972); W. Sellars, "Empiricism and the Philosophy of Mind," in *Science, Perception and Reality* (London: Routledge Kegan Paul, 1962); Richard Rorty, *Philosophy and the Mirror of Nature* (Princeton: Princeton University Press, 1979). See also Chapter VI.

38. This will be a major thesis of Chapter VII.

39. See Aristotle's remarks on psychological method in Book 1, Chapter 1 of *De Anima,* where the order of investigation is the inverse of the explanatory order.

40. Cited by Hermann Weyl, *Philosophy of Mathematics and Natural Science* (New York: Atheneum, 1963), p. 33.

41. G. Frege, *The Foundations of Arithmetic,* Trans. J. L. Austin (Oxford: Blackwell, 1953).

42. Edmund Husserl, *Philosophy as Rigorous Science* (1911), trans. Quentin Lauer in *Phenomenology and the Crisis of Philosophy* (New York: Harper and Row, 1965), p. 82.

43. The first precept of the simplified method stated in the *Discourse* reads: "to accept nothing as true which I did not clearly recognize to be so: that is to say, carefully to avoid precipitation and prejudice in judgments, and to accept in them nothing more than what was presented to my mind so clearly and distinctly that I could have no occasion to doubt it." The more radical exercise of Cartesian doubt is practiced in the first meditation.

44. Naturalistic opposition to these dualisms has persisted for the past hundred years. A contemporary version is well represented in this passage from Quine: "my position is a naturalistic one; I see philosophy not as an *a priori* propaedeutical groundwork for science, but as continuous with science. I see philosophy and science in the same boat. . . . There is no external vantage point, no first philosophy." W. V. Quine, "Natural Kinds," *Ontological Relativity and Other Essays* (New York: Columbia University Press, 1969), pp. 126-27.

45. Psychophysics was connected most closely with the experimental interests of G. Fechner.

46. Both the phenomenological and the linguistic movements in twentieth-century philosophy sharply criticize the confusion of ideas with concepts and thoughts. See Chapters II-VII.

47. Both Brentano and Husserl insisted that authentic philosophy be "strictly scientific." They approved the motivating intention of philosophical naturalism, but rejected its attempt to naturalize intentional consciousness. See Chapter III.

48. E. Husserl, *Phenomenology and the Crisis of Philosophy*, p. 76.

49. A psychological theory is empirical if its discovery and confirmation depend on an intersubjective base of perceptual evidence. Empiricistic psychology has its point of departure in phenomenalism. The contrast is between a methodology based on observable behavior and one based on epistemically private ideas.

50. David Hume, *An Inquiry Concerning Human Understanding:* Section II "Of the Origin of Ideas." (Indianapolis, Indiana: Library of Liberal Arts, 1955).

51. E. Husserl, *Prolegomena to Pure Logic, Logical Investigations*, vol. 1, trans. J. N. Findlay (London: Routledge and Kegan Paul, 1970), pp. 225-40.

52. See Chapter III for Husserl's account of the epistemic foundation of pure logic.

53. Husserl's opposition to the "naturalization of consciousness" is threefold: He opposes the reduction of logical entities to ideas, the conduct of phenomenology within the natural attitude, and the attempt to physicalize intentional acts.

54. G. Frege, "The Thought: A Logical Inquiry," trans. A. M. Quinton and Marcelle Quinton in *Philosophical Logic*, ed. P. F. Strawson (London: Oxford Univ. Press, 1967), p. 35.

55. Ibid., pp. 17-18.

56. Ibid., pp. 19-20.

II. The Primacy of Logic—A Case Study in Foundational Inquiry

1. Rulon Wells, "Is Frege's Concept of Function Valid?" *Journal of Philosophy* 60 (1963): 720; hereafter cited as "Frege's Concept of Function."

2. Gottlob Frege, *Translations from the Philosophical Writings of Gottlob Frege*, ed. P. Geach and M. Black (Oxford: Blackwell, 1952), p. 104; hereafter cited as *Translations*.

3. Frege, "The Thought: A Logical Inquiry," trans. A. M. Quinton and Marcelle Quinton in *Philosophical Logic*, ed. P. F. Strawson (London: Oxford University Press, 1967), p. 20; hereafter cited as "The Thought."

4. Frege titled his constructed notation the *Begriffschrift;* it was "a formalized language of pure thought modelled upon the Language of Arithmetic." For a contemporary translation, see *Conceptual Notation and Related Articles*, trans. T. W. Bynum (New York: Oxford University Press, 1972).

5. Frege, "The Thought," p. 26.

6. G. Frege, *The Basic Laws of Arithmetic*, trans. and ed. Montgomery Furth (Berkeley and Los Angeles: University of California Press, 1964), p. 13; hereafter cited as *Basic Laws*.

7. Ibid., p. 10.

8. Frege, *Translations*, p. 161.

9. John Stuart Mill, *A System of Logic* (London: 1893); Immanuel Kant, *Critique of Pure Reason, Collected Works*, ed. Hartenstein, vol. 3; E. Heine, "Die

Elemente der Function Lehre," *Journal für die reine und angewandte Mathematik,* 74 (1872): 172-84; J. Thomae, *Elemente Veranderlichen, 2 ed. (Halle A. S.: 1898).*

10. *Frege attempted to execute this project in Grundgesetze der Arithmetik, begriffschriftlich abegeleitet* (Jena: Verlag Herman Pohle, vol. 1, 1893; vol. 2, 1903). The edited English edition is cited earlier as *The Basic Laws of Arithmetic.*

11. Frege, *Basic Laws,* p. 12.

12. Ibid., p. 15.

13. Reference is to B. E. Erdmann, *Logik,* I (Halle a.S.: Max Niemeyer, 1892), pp. 272-75.

14. Frege, *Basic Laws,* p. 14.

15. Ibid., p. 13.

16. Christian Thiel, *Sense and Reference in Frege's Logic* (Dordrecht, Holland: D. Reidel, 1968), p. 23.

17. Frege, *Basic Laws,* p. 15.

18. G. Frege, *The Foundations of Arithmetic,* trans. J. L. Austin (Oxford: Blackwell, 1959), p. x; hereafter cited as *Foundations.*

19. Ibid., p. 37. "I shall myself, to avoid confusion, use 'idea' only in the subjective sense. It is because Kant associated both meanings with the word that his doctrine assumed such a very subjective idealist complexion, and his true view was made difficult to discover. The distinction here drawn stands or falls with that between psychology and logic. If only these themselves were to be kept always rigidly distinct.!"

20. Ibid., p. 105.

21. David Hume, *An Enquiry Concerning Human Understanding* (Section 27, "Of the Origin of Ideas"). (Indianapolis, Indiana: Library of Liberal Arts, 1955).

22. Michael Dummett's excellent writings on Frege make explicit the distinction between Frege's semantical realism based on truth conditions and an alternative approach to meaning deriving from the later Wittgenstein in which knowledge-conditions are prominent. See his *Frege: Philosophy of Language* (New York: Harper and Row, 1973).

23. Frege, *Foundations,* pp. 69, 116.

24. Ibid., p. 70.

25. Ibid., pp. 71-72.

26. Ibid., p. 116.

27. Frege, *Basic Laws,* p. iv.

28. Frege, *Translations,* p. 50.

29. In his philosophy of language, Frege drew a firm distinction between the sense and reference of a linguistic expression. He also clearly distinguished names from predicates and connected this contrast with the ontological division between objects and functions. He explicitly stated that the names that *refer* to objects also *express* a sense ontologically distinct from their referent. But he is less clear whether the sense-reference distinction applies in the same manner to predicates and, if it does, whether functions are the references of predicates or their senses. The interpretation I have followed is that predicates refer to functions on the model of names referring to objects. But, see note 32.

30. First-level concepts take only objects as arguments; second-level concepts take first-level concepts as arguments. Frege, *Translations,* pp. 50-51.

31. Ibid., p. 47.

32. Ibid., p. 54. Since thoughts are the *senses* of indicative sentences, it might be argued that functions as essential constituents of thoughts are the senses and not the references of predicate expressions.

33. Thiel, *Sense and Reference in Frege's Logic*, p. 23.

34. Frege carefully distinguished among (1) an object *falling under* a concept, (2) the *subordination* of a specific concept to a more inclusive generic concept at the same logical level, and (3) the *subsumption* of a first-level concept within a second-level concept.

35. Frege, *Translations*, p. 22.

36. "All numbers must be numbers of something: there are no such things as numbers in the abstract." Mill, *A System of Logic*, vol. 2, p. 6, n. 2. "Every numeral *denotes* physical phenomena and connotes a physical property. . . belonging to the agglomeration of things which we call by the name." Mill, ibid., vol. 3, p. 24, n. 5, cited in Thiel, *Sense and Reference in Frege's Logic*, pp. 26-27.

37. Frege, *Translations*, p. 22; *Basic Laws*, p. 16.

38. Frege contrasted the property belonging to the number 1 of being the result of multiplying itself by itself with the properties of (1) the numeral *1*. No "microscopical or chemical investigation, however far it was carried out, could ever detect this property in the possession of the innocent character that we call a figure one." Frege, *Translations*, p. 22; (2) "since the number one, being the same for everybody, stands apart from everyone in the same way, it can no more be researched by making psychological observations than can the moon. Whatever ideas there may be of the number one in individual souls, they are still to be as carefully distinguished from the number one, as ideas of the moon are to be distinguished from the moon itself." Frege, *Basic Laws*, p. 16; (3) numbers are objects, sensible properties are concepts, no concept is an object.

39. Frege, *Foundations*, p. 34.

40. Frege, *Translations*, p. 46.

41. Frege distinguished carefully between the *semantical relation* that connects indicative sentences with the thoughts they express and the *intentional relation* of grasping or understanding through which a person understands those same thoughts. He construed thoughts as objective abstract entities: they are as causally independent of language as they are of mind. In Chapter V, we will see how Wilfrid Sellars assimilates the contents of intentional acts to Fregean senses and those acts themselves to linguistic episodes. After reducing intentional relations to semantical relations, Sellars proceeded to reconstruct semantical idioms in such a way as to eliminate semantical and intentional relations altogether.

42. Frege, "The Thought," p. 34.

43. Rulon Wells, "Frege's Ontology," *Review of Metaphysics* 4 (1951): pp. 537-73.

44. Ibid., p. 563. Wells offered a schematized version of Frege's ontology. The categories of entities exceed the expectations of common sense. All entities: A. Objects (1) ordinary denotations; (a) truth-values, (b) ranges, (c) function-correlates, (d) places, moments, time spans, (e) ideas, (f) other objects. B. Functions (1) functions all of whose values are truth-values (a) with one argument-concepts, (b) with two arguments-relations, (2) functions not all of whose values are truth-

values (a) with one argument, (b) with more than one argument. Ibid., p. 542.

45. Frege, *Basic Laws*, p. 17.

46. Implicit in Frege's philosophical stance is an unshakeable confidence in science's capacity to achieve objective truth.

47. Frege, *Basic Laws*, p. 23.

48. Ibid., p. 23.

49. Frege, *Foundations*, p. 34.

50. Ibid., p. 115.

51. Wells, "Frege's Concept of Function," p. 720.

52. Ibid., p. 720.

53. Frege, *Basic Laws*, p. 7.

54. Wells, "Frege's Ontology," p. 563.

55. Wells, "Frege's Concept of Function," p. 720.

56. Ibid., p. 729.

57. Frege, *Basic Laws*, p. 2.

58. Frege, *Translations*, pp. 48-51; *Foundations*, pp. 102-104.

59. Evert W. Beth, *The Foundations of Mathematics* (New York: Harper and row, 1966), pp. 31-32.

60. J. M. Bochenski, *The Methods of Contemporary Thought* (New York: Harper and Row, 1968), pp. 70-71.

61. Wells, "Frege's Concept of Function," p. 730.

62. Frege, *Translations*, pp. 185-86.

63. Ibid., p. 186.

64. The philosophical issues raised by the Skolem paradox include the nature and scope of mathematical knowledge, criteria of ontological reduction, and finitary versus nonfinitary interpretations of arithmetic.

65. Frege, *Foundations*, p. 22.

III. The Genesis of Husserl's Phenomenology
—From Descriptive Psychology to
Transcendental Idealism

1. The most important neo-Kantians, like Cohen and Cassirer, divided epistemology into two complementary disciplines: transcendental logic and transcendental psychology. They distinguished the first from formal or propositional logic and the second from the psychology of the empirical ego. It was Kant himself who carefully distinguished transcendental and empirical methods of inquiry.

2. The project of laying foundations for science originates with Descartes' *Discourse on Method*. Husserl makes this Cartesian program the central objective of his philosophical practice. There is no agreement in contemporary epistemology as to whether science needs a philosophical foundation or what form such a foundation should take. See Chapter I, Section E.

3. For Husserl's use of *naive* see *Philosophy as Rigorous Science*, reprinted

in *Phenomenology and the Crisis of Philosophy*, trans. Q. Lauer (New York: Harper and Row, 1965), p. 85.

4. Edmund Husserl, *The Idea of Phenomenology*, trans. William Alston and George Nakhnikian (the Hague: Martinus Nijhoff, 1964), pp. 13-17.

5. "In modern philosophy and thought, doubt occupies much the same central position as that occupied for all the centuries before by the Greek *thaumazein*, the wonder of everything that is as it is." Hannah Arendt, *The Human Condition* (Garden City, N.Y.: Doubleday Anchor Books, 1959), p. 249.

6. Edmund Husserl, *Logical Investigations*, vol. 1, trans. J. N. Findlay (New York: The Humanities Press, 1970), p. 42.

7. Aron Gurwitsch, *Studies in Phenomenology and Psychology* (Evanston, Ill.: Northwestern University Press, 1960), p. 68. Both Gurwitsch and Joseph Kockelmans, in *Edmund Husserl's Phenomenological Psychology* (Pittsburgh: Duquesne University Press, 1967), are effective in tracing the evolution of Husserl's phenomenology from its origins in psychology.

8. Valuable biographical material on Husserl is available in A. Osborn, The Philosophy of Edmund Husserl (New York: Gartland Press, 1949); H. Spiegelberg, *The Phenomenological Movement*, vol. 1 (The Hague: Martinus Nijhoff, 1960); M. Farber, *The Foundation of Phenomenology* (Cambridge, Mass.: Harvard University Press, 1943).

9. Cf. Kockelmans, *Edmund Husserl's Phenomenological Psychology*, pp. 53-59.

10. Cf. ibid., 65-71; Spiegelberg, *The Phenomenological Movement*, pp. 35-44.

11. Kockelmans, ibid., pp. 71-73; Spiegelberg, ibid., pp. 55-56.

12. Spiegelberg, ibid., p. 28.

13. *Philosophy as Rigorous Science* has as its central theme the contrast between philosophy and the positive sciences. Husserl's thesis is that the normative demands of reason are unsatisfied until a scientific philosophy has been achieved.

14. *Philosophie der Arithmetik: Psychologische und Logische Untersuchungen*, Erster Band (Halle a. S.: Pfeffer, 1891).

15. *Zeitschrift für Philosophie und Philosophische Kritik* 103 (1894), pp. 313-32. Excerpts from Frege's review appear in *Translations*.

16. Frege, ibid., p. 317. Cited in Thiel, *Sense and Reference in Frege's Logic*, p. 25.

17. *Logical Investigations*, vol. 1, p. 42.

18. *Logische Untersuchungen*, 2 vols. (Halle a. S.: Max Niemeyer, vol. 1, 1900; vol. 2, 1901). References in the text apply to the Findlay translation cited in note 2.

19. Critique of psychologism as a thesis in the philosophy of logic *(Investigations*, vol. 1, pp. 90-210). Second, the critique of psychologism as a "perversion of the pure meaning of philosophy" is a recurrent theme of *Ideas*, trans. W. R. B. Gibson (New York: Collier Books, 1962) vol. I, p. 10.

20. Husserl, *Investigations*, vol. 1, p. 56.

21. Ibid., pp. 90-91.

22. Ibid., pp. 92-95.

23. Ibid., pp. 98-110.

24. Ibid., p. 136.

25. Ibid., p. 144.

26. The more sophisticated empiricists of this century have forged a nonpsychologistic philosophy of logic without embracing Platonist or Idealist conclusions. See Chapter V, Section D.

27. Husserl, *Investigations,* vol. 1, p. 170.

28. Ibid., p. 175.

29. Ibid., pp. 185-86.

30. Noetic acts "present" their noematic content to the intentional subject. For a critical view of Husserl's general concept of presentation, see Section E.

31. Husserl, *Investigations,* vol. 1, p. 195.

32. Husserl acknowledged the close connection between his concept of logic as the theory of science and Bolzano's *Wissenschaftslehre. Investigations,* vol. 1, pp. 222-24.

33. Ibid., p. 232.

34. Ibid., vol. 2, p. 4, examines the concepts of *Unsinn* and *Widersinn,* the core concepts in pure logical grammar and the formal theory of validity. The concepts of truth and evidence are explored in ibid., p. 6, Chapter 5. A schematic account of these fields of pure logic is presented in Husserl, *Formal and Transcendental Logic,* trans. Dorion Cairns (The Hague: Martinus Nijhoff, 1969), pp. 49-55.

35. Y. Bar Hillel criticizes Husserl's appeal to the realm of meaning in his theory of logic. "Husserl's Conception of a Pure Logical Grammar," *Philosophy and Phenomenological Research* 17 (1957): 362-69. For a spirited defense of Husserl, cf. J. N. Mohanty's *Edmund Husserl's Theory of Meaning* (The Hague: Martinus Nijhoff, 1969).

36. "Husserl's meaning categories turn out to be nothing else than the objective counterparts of the grammatical categories regarded as standard for his time for Indo-European languages...the actual reference is to grammatical categories. The detour through the realm of meanings is at best superfluous." Bar Hillel, ibid., p. 365. Findlay responds, "The logical laws of formation govern our symbols only because they govern the meanings which inform those symbols." Translator's introduction, *Logical Investigations,* vol. 1, p. 23.

37. *Investigations,* vol. 2, pp. 269-335.

38. Volume 2 of the *Investigations* contains eidetic rather than factual judgments. Factual theories are based on inductive methods of inquiry; eidetic analyses depend on the method of imaginative free variation. Husserl claims that eidetic conclusions are a priori, whereas empirical generalizations are never more than probable.

39. Gilbert Harman provides a useful stratification in "Three Levels of Meaning," *Journal of Philosophy* 65 (1968).

40. For Husserl causes and effects are temporal occurrences in the real order, whereas the senses constituted by meaning-bestowing acts are items in the logical or ideal order. Acts of constitution are instances of intentional genesis that originate propositional contents. These contents are themselves intentional. For a detailed account, see Chapter VII.

41. Not all objects of reference must be real. In the science of logic, reference is to ideal entities.

42. *Investigations,* vol. 2, p. 287.

43. P. Thevenaz, *What Is Phenomenology?* (Chicago: Quadrangle Books, 1962), p. 41.

44. Cf. Gilbert Ryle, "Phenomenology," *Proceedings of the Aristotelean Society,* Supp. Vol. (1932): 75-81; Ryle, "Are There Propositions?" *Proceedings of the Aristotelean Society* (1929-30): 93-94.

45. Husserl, "Propositions," pp. 93-94.

46. Husserl, *Investigations,* vol. 2, p. 5, Chapters 2 and 3.

47. Husserl, *Ideas,* pp. 75-76.

48. "It is true that prior to judgment there are other components in knowledge but it is not true that the other components of knowledge prior to judgment are complete as knowledge" Bernard Lonergan, *Insight: A Study in Human Understanding* [1957], 3d ed. (New York: Philosophical Library, 1970), p. 489. For a recent defense of nonepistemic seeing, see F. Dretske, *Seeing and Knowing* (London: Routledge and Kegan Paul, 1969), Chapter 2. A full account of variations on the verb *to see* would require a distinction between seeing, seeing *as,* and seeing *that.* Seeing occurs at the level of empirical consciousness; seeing *as* takes place at the level of intellectual consciousness (it is a form of understanding); and seeing *that* is a form of rational consciousness, a mode of judgment.

49. For a compact account of the distinct but related levels of intentional consciousness, see Bernard Lonergan's *The Subject* (Milwaukee: Marquette University Press, 1968).

50. Husserl, *Idea of Phenomenology,* p. 45.

51. Examples:

Type of Noematic Content	Type of Noetic Act
Perceptual object	Sensory intuition
Material essence	General eidetic intuition
Categorial sense	Categorial intuition

Qualitatively different noetic acts may have an identical noematic content; for example, the same propositional content may be understood, doubted, affirmed, and denied.

52. For a critique of Husserl as an intellectual empiricist, cf. Lonergan, *Insight,* p. 415.

53. Cf. B. Lonergan, *Collection: Papers by B. Lonergan,* ed. F. E. Crowe (New York: Herder and Herder, 1967), pp. 175-78.

54. Rene Descartes, *The Philosophical Works of Descartes,* vol. 1, trans. E. S. Haldane and G. R. T. Ross (Cambridge: Cambridge University Press, 1972), pp. 7, 92.

55. Arthur Danto, *Analytical Philosophy of Knowledge* (Cambridge: Cambridge University Press, 1968), p. 159.

56. To know that p, m must not only experience the referent of p as satisfying p's truth-conditions, but m must also grasp the sufficiency of the evidence for the truth of p. See Chapter VII, for a theory of reflective insight and *Insight,* p. 489.

57. See Chapters V, VII and VIII.

58. Edmund Husserl, *The Crisis of European Sciences and Transcendental*

Phenomenology, trans. David Carr (Evanston, Ill.: Northwestern University Press, 1970), p. 193.

59. Ibid., p. 68.

60. Ibid., pp. 68-70.

61. Ibid., p. 204.

62. Husserl, *The Idea of Phenomenology* (The Hague: Martinus Nijhoff, 1964), p. 20.

63. Ibid., p. 21. Philosophical naturalists like Hume and Rorty adamantly rejected this Husserlian principle, see Chapter VI; and W. V. Quine, "Epistemology Naturalized," *Ontological Relativity and Other Essays* (New York: Columbia University Press, 1969), pp. 69-90; Richard Rorty, "Cartesian Epistemology and Changes in Ontology," in *Contemporary American Philosophy,* ed. John E. Smith (New York: Humanities Press, 1970), pp. 273-292.

64. Husserl, *The Crisis of European Sciences,* (Evanston, Illinois: Northwestern University Press, 1970) pp. 65-120. The following paragraphs summarize Husserl's extended account of this significant historical transformation.

65. Husserl, *Ideas,* p. 19.

66. Ibid., p. 10. The transcendental standpoint articulated in the *Ideas* is brought to bear on logical issues in *Formal and Transcendental Logic,* trans. Dorion Cairns (The Hague: Martinus Nijhoff, 1969).

67. Husserl, *The Crisis of European Sciences,* pp. 135-52.

68. Ibid., p. 151.

69. Ibid., pp. 114-16.

70. Ibid., pp. 203-208.

71. Suzanne Bachelard, *A Study of Husserl's Formal and Transcendental Logic* (Evanston, Ill.: Northwestern University Press, 1968), p. xix.

IV. Wittgenstein's Linguistic Turns

1. Ludwig Wittgenstein, *Notebooks* 1914-1916 (New York: Harper, 1961), p. 79. In this chapter, references to Wittgenstein's *Notebooks* (NB), *Tractatus* (TR), *Philosophical Investigations* (PI) and *Remarks on the Foundations of Mathematics* (RFM) will be given directly in the text.

2. L. Wittgenstein, *Tractatus Logico-Philosophicus,* trans. from 1st German ed. D. F. Pears and B. F. McGuinness [1921] (London: Routledge and Kegan Paul, 1961).

3. The phrase *the linguistic turn* is borrowed from Gustav Bergmann, *Logic and Reality* (Madison: University of Wisconsin Press, 1964), p. 226. Cf. Richard Rorty, *The Linguistic Turn* (Chicago: University of Chicago Press, 1967).

4. This schematic outline coordinates passages that occur independently in the *Tractatus.*

5. Wittgenstein, *Notebooks,* p. 93.

6. Bertrand Russell, *Our Knowledge of the External World* (London: Allen and Unwin, 1949), pp. 42-69; hereafter cited as *Our Knowledge.*

7. Ibid., p. 67.

8. Ibid., p. 53.

9. This assumption—common to Russell, Wittgenstein, and Sellars—is the linguistic version of the "like is known by like" doctrine of classical metaphysics.

10. B. Russell, *Our Knowledge*, p. 63.

11. B. Russell, "On Denoting" and "The Philosophy of Logical Atomism," *Logic and Knowledge* (New York: Macmillan, 1964), pp. 39-56; 228-40.

12. B. Russell, *Our Knowledge*, Chapters 3 and 4.

13. B. Russell, "The Philosophy of Logical Atomism," *Logic and Knowledge*, pp. 175-283; and *Mysticism and Logic*, Chapters 6 and 8 (Garden City, N.Y.: Anchor Books, 1957).

14. James Griffin, *Wittgenstein's Logical Atomism* (Oxford: Clarendon Press, 1964); and G. E. M. Anscombe, *An Introduction to Wittgenstein's Tractatus* (London: Hutchinson, 1963).

15. This requirement is derived from Frege. "Never ask for the meaning of a word in isolation but only in the context of a proposition." *Foundations*, p. x.

16. For an original use of the Tractarian concepts of picturing and signifying, cf. Wilfrid Sellars, *Science, Perception and Reality* (New York: Humanities Press, 1963), pp. 50-59, Chapters 6 and 7; also Sellars, *Science and Metaphysics* (London: Routledge and Kegan Paul, 1968), Chapters 4 and 5. Sellars argued that picturing is properly understood as a factual relation between sign-designs and the circumstances of their use. *Signifying* is a semantical term used in classificatory metalinguistic discourse. See Chapter 5, Section D.

17. For an insightful view of Wittgenstein's Tractarian theory of language, see Arthur Danto, *Analytical Philosophy of Knowledge* (Cambridge: Cambridge University Press, 1968), Chapter 10.

18. Post-Tractarian linguistic philosophy has divided over the thesis of extensionality. Quine attempted to regiment all semantically appraisable discourse within an extensionalist continuum. Sellars accepted the thesis of extensionality for factual sentences but rejected it for metalinguistic discourse. See Chapter VI, for the two wings of contemporary linguistic naturalism.

19. TR 5.4 makes it clear that these negative remarks are aimed at Frege's ontology and the semantical theses that support it.

20. Erik Stenius highlighted the parallels between Kant's aims and methods in the *Critique* and those of Wittgenstein in the *Tractatus*. After the linguistic turn, the *Critique of Pure Reason* becomes a *Critique of Pure Language*. E. Stenius, *Wittgenstein's Tractatus: A Critical Exposition of Its Main Lines of Thought* (Oxford: Blackwell, 1960).

21. Max Black, *A Companion to Wittgenstein's Tractatus* (Ithaca, N.Y.: Cornell University Press, 1964), p. 319.

22. In the *Remarks* and the *Investigations* logical propositions are stripped of this shadow of aboutness. They lose their ontological significance.

23. The philosophy of logic embedded in the *Tractatus* is not based on psychology or on an empirical study of language. To understand the propositions of logic, insight into the essential nature of the proposition is required. No form of empirical inquiry can yield essential insight. The shift from thought-processes to sign-language represents the linguistic turn, the turn from ideas to words.

24. Wittgenstein's dilemma resembles that of Neo-Kantians like Cassirer. Neither can say what he wants to say in a language whose resources limit significant assertion to factual claims.

25. L. Wittgenstein, *Briefe an Ludwig Von Ficker* (Salzburg: Otto Muller Verlag, 1969), pp. 35-36. Quoted in English translation in Paul Engelman, *Letters from Ludwig Wittgenstein with a Memoir* (Oxford: Basil Blackwell, 1967), pp. 143-44.

26. Allan Janik and Stephen Toulmin, *Wittgenstein's Vienna* (New York: Simon and Schuster, 1973); William W. Bartley III, *Wittgenstein* (London, Quartet Books Limited, 1974).

27. Engelman, *Letters from Ludwig Wittgenstein with a Memoir*, p. 143.

28. Ibid., p. 144.

29. L. Wittgenstein, *Philosophical Investigations,* trans. G. E. M. Ancombe [1953] (New York: Macmillan Publishing Co., 1965), p. 23.

30. L. Wittgenstein, *Remarks on the Foundations of Mathematics* (Cambridge, Mass.: MIT Press, 1967). For a persuasive argument that, despite its disclaimers, the *Philosophical Investigations* is categorically committed to theses about language and the mind, see Everett W. Hall, *Philosophical Systems* (Chicago: University of Chicago Press, 1960), pp. 60-68.

31. The answer of the *Tractatus:* by virtue of an ineffable identity of structure that must be uncovered by philosophical inquiry.

32. "My whole task consists in explaining the nature of the proposition...in giving the nature of all facts whose picture the proposition is." Wittgenstein, *Notebooks,* p. 39.

33. In the *Tractatus* clarification is necessary because the essence of language is concealed. The purpose of clarification in the *Philosophical Investigations* is to convince us that nothing of importance is hidden. For the parallels with Dewey, see Chapter VI, Section D.

34. For a parallel criticism, cf. Gilbert Ryle, "Theory of Meaning," in *The Importance of Language,* ed. Max Black (Englewood Cliffs, N.J.: Prentice-Hall, 1962), p. 167.

35. "When linguistic expressions have the same role or function they have the same sense.... Meanings are not things, not even very queer things.... The meaning of an expression is not an entity denoted by it but a style of operation performed with it." Ibid., 161-67.

36. According to Wittgenstein, we are more likely to be deceived by the verbal form of mathematical propositions than by the verbal form of most other propositions. *Remarks on the Foundations of Mathematics,* IV, p. 25.

37. The *Tractatus* limited meaningful sentences to descriptions of possible states of affairs.

38. Robert Fogelin, "Wittgenstein and Intuitionism," *American Philosophical Quarterly,* 5 (1968): 267.

39. Ibid.

40. Paul Bernays, "Comments on Ludwig Wittgenstein's *Remarks on the Foundations of Mathematics,"* in *Philosophy of Mathematics,* ed. P. Benacerraf and H. Putnam (Englewood Cliffs, N.J.: Prentice-Hall, 1964), p. 528.

41. R. Fogelin, "Wittgenstein and Institutionism," p. 270.

42. Bernays, "Comments on Ludwig Wittgensteins *Remarks on the Foundations of Mathematics.*"

43. Michael Dummett, "Wittgenstein's Philosophy of Mathematics," in *Philosophy of Mathematics,* p. 503. Cf. Wittgenstein, *Remarks,* III, 44; II, 73, 75.

44. "In using a mathematical expression we are not simply uttering a rule, we are stating that something is a rule. . . . Mathematical expressions are modal assertions, for example, "it is a rule that p rather than imperatives." Fogelin, "Wittgenstein and Institutionism," p. 268.

45. Ibid., p. 272.

46. Dummett, "Wittgenstein's Philosophy of Mathematics,' pp. 503-504.

47. L. Wittgenstein, Blue Book (New York: Harper Torch books, 1958), p. 41.

48. Richard Rorty has drawn attention to the multiple rhetorical devices at work in the *Philosophical Investigations.* Wittgenstein was not trying to refute philosophy by argument. He refused to play the game by the old rules. Rorty, "Keeping Philosophy Pure," *The Yale Review,* LXV (1976) pp. 336-56.

49. Cf. Rorty, *The Linguistic Turn,* p. 33. For an answer to Rorty, see Chapter VI, Section F, and Chapter VIII.

V. The New Way of Words

1. Wittgenstein, *Tractatus,* 4.111.

2. "The attempt to draw a clear distinction between philosophy and the empirical sciences can almost be taken as the defining trait of the analytic movement in contemporary thought." W. Sellars, "Pure pragmatics and Epistemology," *Philosophy of Science* 14 (1947): 181.

3. Rudolf Carnap, *The Logical Syntax of Language* (Paterson, N.J.: Littlefield Adams, 1959), pp. 282-83; hereafter cited in the text as *LSL.*

4. It is important to distinguish, as Carnap often did not, between formalism as a substantive thesis and formalism as a methodological strategy. Substantive formalism identifies the subject matter of logic with uninterpreted inscriptions; methodological formalism permits abstraction from the semantic dimension of signs at the calculation level of syntax. Hilbert, whose metamathematical program provides the model for Carnap's enterprise, is guilty of the same ambiguity.

5. For purposes of calculation, logical syntax can disregard the sense of the expressions in a calculus. But the expressions themselves require a sense if they are to be expressions in a language. An uninterpreted calculus is not a language.

6. Rudolf Carnap, *Philosophy and Logical Syntax* (London: Kegan Paul, 1935), p. 9; hereafter cited in the text as *PLS.*

7. Carnap develops this argument in "The Elimination of Metaphysics through the Logical Analysis of Language," *Logical Positivism,* ed. A. J. Ayer (New York: The Free Press, 1959), pp. 60-81.

8. A complete account of the relations between object and metalanguages requires a threefold distinction between (1) object-linguistic sentences, (2) metalinguistic rules, and (3) metalinguistic statements that attribute syntactical properties to the object-linguistic sentences in the light of the rules. See Section C of this chapter.

9. Charles Morris, *Foundations of the Theory of Signs, International Encyclopedia of Unified Science, Vol. I, No. 2.*

10. Ibid., p. 14.

11. Ibid., p. 48.

12. Many analytic philosophers are dissatisfied with Carnap's principle of tolerance. "The thesis that logical properties vary with linguistic rules loses its plausibility once it is admitted that logical relations hold primarily between propositions not sentences." A. Pap, *Semantics and Necessary Truth* (New Haven, Conn.: Yale University Press, 1958), p. 413. Pap contends that logical properties are absolute modal properties that belong to extralinguistic propositions.

13. R. Carnap, *Meaning and Necessity: A Study in Semantics and Modal Logic* (Chicago: University of Chicago Press, 1947).

14. Cf. W. V. Quine, "Two Dogmas of Empiricism," *From a Logical Point of View* (New York: Harper and Row, 1963), pp. 37-42.

15. Beth and Piaget, *Mathematical Epistemology and Psychology,* p. xviii.

16. Carnap later rejected the purely syntactical analysis of meaning of *The Logical Syntax of Language.* He credited Tarski with having convinced him that the formal method of syntax must be complemented by semantical rules no less exact than those of syntax. See Carnap, *Introduction to Semantics,* (Cambridge, Mass.: Harvard University Press, 1942), where the concepts of truth and designation are introduced as irreducibly semantical concepts. Carnap's mature semantical theory is found in *Meaning and Necessity.*

17. W. Sellars, "Realism and the New Way of Words" (RNWW), in *Readings in Philosophical Analysis,* ed. H. Feigl and W. Sellars (New York: Appleton Crofts, 1949); "Epistemology and the New Way of Words" (ENWW), *Journal of Philosophy,* no. 44 (1947); and "Pure Pragmatics and Epistemology" (PPE), *Philosophy of Science,* no. 14 (1947); hereafter references to RNWW, ENWW, and PPE will be given in the text.

18. A schematic outline of Sellars's distinctions in the philosophy of language:

Three Senses of "Language"	Three Disciplines
Language as norm or type	Pure semioitic
Language as behavioral fact	Empirical linguistics
Language as behavioral fact qua token of language as type	Applied semiotic

19. Cf. W. Sellars, *Science and Metaphysics* (London: Routledge and Kegan Paul, 1968), pp. 60-151.

20. Ibid., pp. 65-66.

21. See W. Sellars, *Philosophical Perspectives* (Springfield, Ill.: Charles C. Thomas, 1967), Chapter 9; and *Science and Metaphysics,* Chapters 3 and 4.

22. Sameness of metalinguistic rule is interlinguistic sameness of type not intralinguistic sameness of token. If German and English are treated as two exemplifications of the same conceptual framework, then they share a common set of metalinguistic rules. Sameness of type at the metalinguistic level can be analyzed on the model of object-linguistic synonymy.

23. In addition to the works already cited, see Sellars, *Science, Perception and Reality* (New York: Humanities Press, 1963) Chapters 2-7, 10, and 11.

24. Ibid., pp. 109-18.

25. *Science and Metaphysics*, pp. 60-115.

26. *Science, Perception and Reality*, p. 40.

27. W. Sellars, "Intentionality and the Mental," *Minnesota Studies in the Philosophy of Science*, vol. 2 (Minneapolis: University of Minnesota Press, 1958), p. 507.

28. Ibid., p. 508.

29. Cf. "Empiricism and the Philosophy of Mind," *Science, Perception and Reality*, pp. 177-78. For a detailed contrast of classical and semantical philosophies of mind, see the Chisholm-Sellars correspondence in "Intentionality and the Mental." Chisholm stated his version of the "classical" position in six theses: (1) thoughts are intentional, they are about something; (2) linguistic entities are also intentional; (3) nothing else is intentional; (4) thoughts would be intentional even if there were no linguistic entities; (5) but if there were no thoughts linguistic entities would not be intentional; and (6) thoughts are a source of intentionality, nothing else would be intentional if thoughts were not (p. 533).

30. The literal formulation of theses 1-14 appears in "Intentionality and the Mental," pp. 521-22. My version of the semantic theory of intentionality is a synoptic reconstruction based on the full extent of Sellars's work.

31. W. Sellars, "Language as Thought and as Communication," *Philosophy and Phenomenological Research* 29 (1969): 525-26.

32. Sellars, *Intentionality and the Mental,"* pp. 533-36.

33. *Science and Metaphysics*, p. 151.

34. *Science, Perception and Reality*, pp. 38-39.

35. Ibid., p. 40.

36. R. Rorty, *The Linguistic Turn*, p. 3.

37. See *Science and Metaphysics*, pp. 73-77, for the important distinction between rules of action and rules of criticism.

38. Throughout his career, Sellars relied on a regulist strategy to preserve nominalist theses while avoiding the temptations of reductionism. He was as ardent a linguistic pluralist as he was an ontological naturalist.

VI. The End of Epistemology

1. John Dewey, *The Quest for Certainty* [1929] (New York: Capricorn Books, 1960), p. 6.

2. Alexis de Tocqueville, *Democracy in America* [1840] (New York: Vintage Books, 1960); vol. 2, p. 331.

3. This common note is struck by such diverse thinkers as Michael Polanyi, Richard Bernstein, Stanley Cavell, Hubert Dreyfuss, Alasdair MacIntyre, and Bernard Lonergan.

4. Richard Rorty, *The Linguistic Turn,* pp. 1-39.

5. Rorty, "Overcoming the Tradition," p. 243.

6. Rorty, *The Linguistic Turn,* p. 33.

7. Richard Rorty, *Philosophy and the Mirror of Nature.*

8. Rorty, "Cartesian Epistemology and Changes in Ontology," in *Contemporary American Philosophy,* ed. J. E. Smith (London: Allen and Unwin Ltd., 1970), p. 275.

9. Rorty, "Overcoming the Tradition," p. 242 and throughout *Philosophy and the Mirror of Nature.*

10. Rorty, *The Linguistic Turn,* p. 39.

11. Wittgenstein, *Remarks on the Foundations of Mathematics,* V, 12.

12. Rorty, "Dewey's Metaphysics," in *New Studies in the Philosophy of John Dewey,* ed. Steven Cahn (Hanover, N.H.: University Press of New England, 1977), p. 62.

13. L. Wittgenstein, *On Certainty,* p. 47.

14. Dewey's conjectures about Plato are offered at a high level of generality. There is limited reference to texts or specific passages in the dialogues. But given Socrates' ethical objections to traditional poetry and theology in the *Republic,* this particular conjecture lacks initial plausibility.

15. Dewey's general line on Plato as a cultural conservative is highly questionable. To take just three counterexamples, consider the three waves of Paradox in the *Republic,* the Socratic discourse on love *(eros)* in the *Symposium,* and the reassessment of Athenian political heroes in the *Meno* and the *Gorgias.*

16. Dewey emphasized the *chorismos* (separation) between the order of time and eternity. But he failed to balance the account with Platonic references to participation *(methexis).* In the *Timaeus,* time is described as the moving image of eternity, the visible expression of an invisible reality.

17. One can use the divided line in Book 6 of the *Republic* to map Plato's major epistemic and ontological distinctions and to chart the journey of the soul from the cave to the sky of ideas.

18. The political typology in Book 8 of the *Republic* reflects decreasing levels of psychic harmony in the rulers of the successive regimes.

19. John Dewey, *Reconstruction in Philosophy* [1920] (Boston: Beacon Press, 1948), p. 112.

20. Dewey, *The Quest for Certainty,* p. 44.

21. Dewey, *Reconstruction in Philosophy,* p. 117.

22. This principle is intimated in the *Meno* and made explicit in the discussion of *Republic* 6.

23. Rorty, *The Linguistic Turn,* p. 37.

24. The Socratic identification of knowledge with virtue makes the charge of exclusivity very doubtful. The Aristotelian distinction between the theoretical and practical intellect is not clearly present in the dialogues and is hard to reconcile with the notion of the philosopher-ruler.

25. The opening passages of the first book of the *Metaphysics* outline the

succession of epistemic states recognized by Aristotle and articulate the grounds on which he distinguished them.

26. Rorty, *Philosophy and the Mirror of Nature*, p. 42.

27. Both Plato and Aristotle recognized the soul, *psyche*, as the principle of life and *nous* (intellect) as the principle of knowledge. As biological life ties the soul to the body, so the life of the mind provides an experience of disengagement from embodied conditions.

28. It should also be noted that an invisible likeness of form between knower and known cannot be easily assimilated to the mirror image of a sensible object. Platonic and Aristotelian images shaped for essentially conversational and pedagogical purposes should not be treated as explicit epistemological doctrines. Dewey and Rorty are vulnerable to this criticism. Since they were less interested in Aristotelian doctrine and Platonic theory than in the collective effect of particular images on the historical tradition, they might dismiss it as irrelevant to their restricted purpose.

29. "I do not know when knowledge will become naturalized in the life of society," Dewey, *The Quest for Certainty*, p. 298.

30. For Aristotle, the act of understanding apprehends the intelligible form in the sensible image. Bodily operations are required to produce the sensible image, but the operation of intellect is independent of bodily organs. Matter serves Aristotle as a principle of limitation. Since the power of understanding is essentially unrestricted, by implication, it is immaterial.

31. Book 6 of the *Nicomachean Ethics*, where Aristotle distinguished the virtues of the speculative and practical intellect.

32. Aristotle remarked, in the *Ethics*, that politics would be the best human activity if humans were the highest beings in existence. Since God is superior to humankind, however, the excellence of activities should be judged by reference to the divine life.

33. In the *De Anima* Aristotle reviewed the opinions of his predecessors on the nature of the soul. He sought to disentangle the different senses of the principle that "like is known by like." Neither the materialists nor the Platonists drew the correct conclusions from the principle of cognitive likeness.

34. It is striking that in the *De Anima*, where Aristotle offered his basic analysis of cognitive psychology, the metaphysical categories of potency, form, and act are presupposed. In the *Posterior Analytics*, where he outlined his theory of scientific knowledge, there is only passing reference to cognitional structure. The primary emphasis is on the logical requirements of scientific discourse.

35. There are at least four perspectives from which Aristotle examined the fact of knowledge: psychological, logical, metaphysical, and ethical. There are valuable and interesting treatments of knowledge in the *De Anima*, the *Posterior Analytics*, the *Metaphysics*, and the *Ethics*, but in no text or section of a particular text does Aristotle integrate the results of these relatively autonomous investigations.

36. In Book X of the *Ethics* Aristotle makes his strongest defense of the *Bios Theoretikos* and his strongest claims for a kinship of nature between human and divine.

37. Aristotle's principle of functional complementarity makes higher acti-

vities causally dependent on lower ones. Thus we eat and reproduce in order to live but we live in order to live well. Living well consists in the exercise of the virtues, moral and intellectual. The attainment and practice of intellectual virtue presupposes an emotional life ordered by reason. The whole of human nature must be well ordered if the highest human activities are to be enjoyed.

38. In her remarkable work, the *Human Condition,* Hannah Arendt explored the political significance of questioning common sense and devaluing the world of sensible appearance. Her concern was with the world alienation that resulted from Galilean Science, pp. 225-68.

39. One of Rorty's central objectives is to break this yoke—to preserve enlightenment practices but without the philosophical apologies first offered in their support.

40. Dewey, *Reconstruction in Philosophy,* p. 70.

41. Descartes drew heavily on Augustine's Christian neo-Platonism in shaping his theory of cognition. The debt is substantial but not acknowledged explicitly.

42. The classical distinction is between intellect and sensibility as psychic powers; the Cartesian distinction is between mind and body as separate substances. Although the classical distinction has metaphysical import, its implications are not Cartesian.

43. Descartes's principle appears to be that mediation is the source of potential error. The mind cannot be mistaken about anything it immediately experiences if it restricts its judgment to what experience discloses directly.

44. I borrow the phrase from Wilfrid Sellars.

45. A representation is privileged if it satisfies the first law of Cartesian method—"to accept in judgment nothing more than what was presented to my mind so clearly and distinctly that I could have no occasion to doubt it."

46. Dewey, *The Influence of Darwin on Philosophy* (New York: Henry Holt and Company, 1910), p. 97.

47. Kant appeared to say that transcendental psychology could know what reason *does* but not what it *is.* We can discover the constitutive functions of reason but not its noumenal reality. Sellars appropriated this Kantian stance and naturalized it while framing his own philosophy of mind.

48. *Transcendent* metaphysics aspires to knowledge of things in themselves, particularly of God and the human soul. *Transcendental* metaphysics investigates the conditions of the possibility of a priori knowledge of objects. Kant's contention was that transcendental discoveries prove the impossibility of transcendent knowledge.

49. Like Wittgenstein in the *Tractatus,* Kant could reasonably say that the *point* of his work was to perform an ethical deed.

50. Kant, *Critique of Pure Reason,* p. 93.

51. Kant restored the classical distinction between intellect and sensibility, but he confined receptivity and intuition to the faculty of sense. He then reconceived the theoretical intellect on the model of the fabricating mind.

52. On this issue, Kant's position was the opposite of Frege's. Frege based the ontological status of thoughts on the model of perceptual objects. Kant based the ontological status of perceptual objects on the model of propositions or

judgments. Frege's view leads to conceptual realism, Kant's view leads to transcendental idealism.

53. Kant retained Aristotle's *nous poietikos* but abandoned his *nous pathetikos.* When the receptivity of intellect is transferred to sense, we are left with a mind that literally is able to make all things.

54. Dewey, *The Influence of Darwin,* pp. 64, 97-98.

55. Ibid., p. 210.

56. Dewey, *Reconstruction in Philosophy,* p. 134.

57. Rorty was uneasy with Dewey's attempt to replace older dualistic ontologies with a new metaphysics of experience. He distinguished two divergent strands in Dewey's criticism. The first strand undermines traditional distinctions through cultural or historical investigations of their origin; the second strand substitutes a new metaphysical vocabulary for the universal categories of the tradition. Rorty believed that Dewey effectively pursued the first strategy but that he should have abandoned the second. See "Dewey's Metaphysics" in *New Studies in the Philosophy of John Dewey.*

58. Dewey, *The Quest for Certainty,* p. 251.

59. Ibid., Chapters 5 and 6; Dewey, *Logic: The Theory of Inquiry* (New York: Henry Holt, 1938), pp. 101-19.

60. Israel Scheffler, *The Conditions of Knowledge* (Glenview, Ill.: Scott Foresman, 1965). p. 4.

61. "They learned that reason has insight only into that which it produces after a plan of its own." Kant, *Critique of Pure Reason,* p. 20.

62. Dewey, *Logic,* p. 514.

63. Dewey, *The Quest for Certainty,* p. 22.

64. John Dewey, "From Absolutism to Experimentalism," in *On Experience, Nature, and Freedom,* ed. Richard Bernstein (New York: Bobbs-Merrill, 1960), p. 18.

65. W. V. Quine, "Two Dogmas of Empiricism," *From a Logical Point of View,* p. 46.

66. R. Carnap, "Empiricism, Semantics and Ontology," in *Meaning and Necessity,* pp. 205-21.

67. Quine, *From a Logical Point of View,* pp. 20-46; cf. *The Ways of Paradox* (New York: Random House, 1966) and *Word and Object* (Cambridge, Mass.: MIT Press, 1966).

68. Quine, *Point of View,* pp. 36-42.

69. Ibid., p. 42. Quine applauded Frege for broadening the scope of semantical analysis from the word to the sentence. But he contended that this extension was insufficient. The entire web of belief is the working unit of logical theory.

70. Ibid., p. 41. Quine acknowledged his reliance on Pierre Duhem for the thesis of linguistic holism. But, in fact, Duhem's position is more restrictive than Quine's and should not be identified with it. See Pierre Duhem, *La Theorie Physique: son objet et sa structure* [*The Aim and Structure of Physical Theory*] (New York: Atheneum, 1962) (Paris, 1906).

71. Quine, *Ways of Paradox,* p. 134.

72. Quine, *Word and Object,* pp. 270-76. For application of semantic ascent

to the philosophy of logic, see Quine, *The Philosophy of Logic* (Englewood Cliffs, N.J.: Prentice-Hall, 1970), pp. 10-14.

73. Quine, *Philosophy of Logic*, pp. 10-13.

74. Quine, *Ontological Relativity* (New York: Columbia University Press, 1969), p. 74.

75. Ibid., pp. 126-27.

76. Quine, *Word and Object*, pp. 274-75.

77. Quine, *Ontological Relativity*, p. 26.

78. "A psychology is behavioristic in the broad sense, if although it permits itself the use of the full range of psychological concepts belonging to the manifest framework, it always confirms hypotheses about psychological events in terms of behavioral criteria. . . . Behaviorism, thus construed, is simply good sense." Sellars, *Science, Perception and Reality*, p. 22.

79. Quine, *Ontological Relativity*, pp. 83-90. Quine wavered in his treatment of epistemic evidence. Should the empirical evidence for a theory be identified with neural stimulation of the sense organs, perceptual awareness of sensible objects and their properties, or with the observation sentences of the relevant linguistic community.

80. "It is possible to be interested in a phenomenon in a variety of ways. But we talk about it as we do about the pieces of chess when we are stating the rules of the game, not describing their physical properties." Wittgenstein, *Philosophical Investigations*, p. 108.

81. Wittgenstein, *On Certainty*, # 471. Textual references to *On Certainty* hereafter will be cited after the relevant passage as *OC*.

82. I borrow the distinction from Michael Polanyi's *Personal Knowledge*.

83. Stanley Cavell's *The Claims of Reason* (Oxford: Clarendon Press, 1979) emphasizes the significance of this point for the project of traditional skepticism. Cavell sees a profound unity between the later Wittgenstein and Heidegger in their approach to this issue.

84. Rorty, "Cartesian Epistemology and Changes in Ontology," p. 283.

85. Ibid., p. 282.

86. Rorty, *Philosophy and the Mirror of Nature*, p. 174.

87. For the contrast between Socratic and Sophistic *paideia* (the Greek equivalent of Gadamer's *Bildung* and Rorty's edification), it is useful to reexamine the agonal struggle between Socrates and Protagoras in Plato's dialogue the *Protagoras*.

88. I refer here to critical rather than naive realism. For the limitations in Rorty's treatment of realism, see reflection "Afterthoughts," the next section, 4.

89. Rorty, *Philosophy and the Mirror of Nature*, p. 337.

90. Sellars, *Science, Perception and Reality*, p. 169; Rorty, *The Mirror of Nature*, p. 389.

91. Rorty, "The World Well Lost," *Journal of Philosophy*, 69 (1972), 661.

92. Rorty's division of conversation into normal and abnormal discourse is a generalized adaptation of Kuhn's distinction between normal and revolutionary science.

93. Rorty, *The Mirror of Nature*, p. 12.

94. Sellars, *Science, Perception and Reality,* p. 196; Rorty, *The Mirror of Nature,* p. 390.

95. Rorty, *The Mirror of Nature,* p. 341.

96. Ibid., p. 357.

97. *Edification* was Rorty's translation of Gadamer's term *Bildung.* It referred to the self-transformation accomplished by participating in the conversation of humankind.

98. Chapter VII examines Lonergan's vision of the meaningful practice of philosophy in the third stage of cognitive meaning.

99. For the concept of passing over and passing back as a response to existential and historical pluralism, see the work of John Dunne, *A Search for God in Time and Memory; the Way of all the Earth.*

100. Pierre Duhem, *The Aim and Structure of Physical Theory,* p. 313.

101. See Arthur Danto, *Analytical Philosophy of Knowledge* pp. 231-65.

102. Duhem, *The Aim and Structure of Physical Theory,* p. 314.

103. Quoted by Rulon Wells in "Comprehension and Expression" in *Studies in Thought and Language,* ed. J. L. Cowan (Tucson; University of Arizona Press, 1970), p. 37.

104. Bernard Lonergan, *Insight,* p. 308.

VII. The Need for Cognitive Integration

1. Bernard Lonergan, *Insight: A Study in Human Understanding,* p. 424.

2. Blaise Pascal, *Pensées (New York: Modern Library, 1941), 870, p. 308. Translated by W. F. Trotter.*

3. For a brilliant study of the impact of philosophical ideas on Western civilization, see Alfred North Whitehead, *Adventures of Ideas* (New York: Macmillan Company, 1923).

4. My underestanding of Lonergan's project is based on a careful reading of the following texts: *Verbum: Word and Idea in Aquinas; Insight: A Study in Human Understanding; Collection; Method in Theology; A Second Collection.*

5. For a penetrating account of this theoretical shift and its disruptive effect on the philosophical tradition, see Hannah Arendt, *Between Past and Future* (New York: Viking Press, 1968), especially Chapters 1 and 2.

6. See "The Transition from a Classicist World-View to Historical Mindedness" and "Theology in Its New Context" in *A Second Collection.*

7. A more detailed account of this heuristic reversal was given in Chapter 1, Section B, "From Classical to Historical Consciousness."

8. Despite their epistemological differences, philosophers of science like Michael Polanyi, Marjorie Grene, Thomas Kuhn, and Imre Lakatos are agreed on this point.

9. The arguments for and against critical realism are given in Section I of this chapter and elaborated in Chapter 8.

NOTES

10. Aristotle drew a clear distinction between the order of discovery and the order of systematic exposition. He treated metaphysics as first philosophy even though it was the last theoretical discipline to be developed. Metaphysics was first in two senses: It studied the first causes and principles of all things; its fundamental categories of potency, form, and act were presupposed in the systematic formulation of every other science.

11. David Hume, *A Treatise of Human Nature* [1739], ed. L. A. Selby-Bigge (Oxford: Clarendon Press, 1967), p. xix.

12. For a compact critique of Hume's psychology, see Chapter 1, Section G.

13. Frege's concept of foundational inquiry is expounded in Chapter 2 of this text.

14. Husserl's development from descriptive psychology to transcendental idealism is traced in Chapter III.

15. Sellars, Quine, and Rorty are good examples of this second wave of philosophical naturalism.

16. Rorty's principle of *methodological nominalism* makes language the vehicle for investigating conceptual issues; Sellars's principle of *methodological behaviorism* restricts the science of psychology to an intersubjective evidential base based on observation.

17. Lonergan, *Method*, p. 94.

18. The finite, intentional subject has the embodiedness lacking in the Cartesian self and the embeddedness lacking in Kant's transcendental ego.

19. The problems with the Kantian transcendental subject are not overcome even in historically sensitive accounts from Neo-Kantians like Ernst Cassirer.

20. Lonergan, *Insight*, pp. 181-89.

21. Lonergan, *Method*, p. 4.

22. Lonergan, *Insight*, p. 429.

23. Brentano introduced the scholastic concept of intentionality into the modern philosophy of mind. See *Psychology from an Empirical Standpoint* (New York: Humanities Press, 1973). For a naturalistic modification of Brentano's principle, see Sellars's treatment of intentionality outlined in Chapter V.

24. Lonergan, *Method*, p. 8.

25. Lonergan, *Collection*, p. 226.

26. Lonergan, *Insight*, pp. 320-28.

27. Lonergan, *Collection*, p. 227.

28. Lonergan, *Method*, p. 14.

29. Ibid., pp. 125 and 261.

30. Thomas Aquinas, *Summa Contra Gentiles* 2, c-76, section 17, cited in Lonergan, *Collection*, p. 183.

31. Lonergan, *Insight*, p. xxiii.

32. Ibid., pp. 181-89. For the critical significance of the patterns of experience in dialectical analysis, see Section I and Chapter 8.

33. A parallel process is involved in emotional and cognitional self-appropriation, see *Second Collection*, p. 269.

34. Quine made this conviction explicit in his essay "Epistemology Naturalized." But the theme is common to the many naturalistic thinkers who derive their naturalism from Dewey.

35. In the dimension of describing and explaining the world, science is the measure of all things, of what is that it is, and of what is not that it is not." W. Sellars, *Science, Perception and Reality*, p. 173.

36. Lonergan, *Insight*, p. 332.

37. Ibid., pp. 72 and 243.

38. Sellars, *Science, Perception and Reality*, p. 186.

39. John Dewey, *Logic*.

40. Dewey believed that the life of the mind occurred entirely within the space of appearances. For a diametrically opposing view, see Hannah Arendt, *The Life of the Mind, Thinking* (New York: Harcourt, Brace Jovanovich, 1977).

41. Gilbert Ryle, *The Concept of Mind* (London: Hutchinson's University Library, 1949).

42. Richard Rorty, *Philosophy and the Mirror of Nature*, p. 174. Wittgenstein's semantic behaviorism is on continual display in *The Philosophical Investigations*.

43. Sellars framed his analysis of intentionality as an explicit alternative to the opposing accounts of Descartes and Ryle.

44. Sellars, *Science and Metaphysics*, pp. 71-77, see Chapter V, Sections D and E.

45. Sellars, *Science, Perception and Reality*, p. 160.

46. Lonergan, *Insight*, p. 416.

47. Rulon Wells, "Thought and Expression," in *Studies in Thought and Language*, ed. J. L. Cowan (Tucson: University of Arizona Press, 1970), p. 62.

48. Lonergan, *Insight*, pp. 235-36.

49. Stephan Körner, *Experience and Theory: An Essay in the Philosophy of Science* (London: Routledge and Kegan Paul, 1966), pp. 198-212.

50. See the successive critiques of psychologism in the first six chapters of this work.

51. See W. V. Quine, "Epistemology Naturalized," pp. 69-90.

52. See Chapter I, pp. 15-28.

53. The nineteenth century effort to "naturalize consciousness" neglected the distinction between intentional and nonintentional causes of cognition. See Chapter I, Sections F and G.

54. Lonergan, *Verbum*, pp. 141-42.

55. Lonergan, *Insight*, pp. 553-58; and *Method*, pp. 254-55.

56. For Sellars's concept of talking out loud, see *Science and Metaphysics*, pp. 71-77.

57. Sellars accepted Ryle's behavioral starting point in the philosophy of mind; but he rejected Ryle's opposition to imperceptible mental acts that cause shifting linguistic dispositions. See Chapter V.

58. Sellars denied that there are any actual semantical relations. His reconstruction of semantical discourse converted propositional contents into interlinguistic conceptual roles. He transformed the reference of "inner words" from propositions to inner-speech episodes that play those conceptual roles. He retained logical realism within the framework of methodological, psychological, and ontological nominalism.

59. Four essays from *Science, Perception and Reality* develop the implica-

tions of the thesis of extensionality for the philosophy of mind: "Philosophy and the Scientific Image of Man"; "Being and Being Known"; "Empiricism and the Philosophy of Mind"; and "Truth and Correspondence." Sellars contrasted the factual relation of *picturing* with the semantical matrix of *signifying* in the course of integrating *The Tractatus* with the *Philosophical Investigations.*

60. See Chapter II, Sections C and D.

61. Gottlob Frege, *The Foundations of Arithmetic,* p. xe.

62. This principle formed the basis of his general critique of psychologism; it provided the specific focus of his objection to Husserl's *Philosophy of Arithmetic.* See Chapter III, Section B.

63. See Michael Dummett, *Frege: Philosophy of Language.*

64. Lonergan, *Insight,* p. xi.

65. Without reducing the logical to the psychological order, Husserl insisted that the ideal propositional meanings are dependent on intentional operations, that semantic objectivity is derivative from intentional subjectivity.

66. See Chapter III, Section F.

67. For a critique of Husserl's cognitional theory, see Chapter III, Section E.

68. Lonergan, *Method,* p. 14.

69. For the distinction between *relying on* and *attending to,* see Michael Polanyi, *The Tacit Dimension* (Garden City, N.Y.: Doubleday Books, 1966).

70. Lonergan, *Insight,* p. 308.

71. Ibid., p. 4.

72. Aristotle, *Metaphysics,* Book I, 980a23.

73. Lonergan, *Insight,* pp. 348-59.

74. Lonergan, *Method,* pp. 13-14.

75. See Lonergan's remarks on heuristic assumptions and heuristic concepts, *Insight,* pp. 36-38, 63, 541-42.

76. Lonergan, *Method,* p. 4.

77. For a succinct account of the properties and functions of transcendental method, see *Method,* pp. 3-25. For a more detailed and elaborate account, see *Insight,* Part II, "Insight as Knowledge."

78. In this respect it conforms to the scholastic sense of the *transcendental;* but the reference now is beyond transcendence of the grammatical categories. With the shift from logic to method, the transcendence of particular regional fields of inquiry and specific disciplines also is intended. See *Method,* pp. 11-13.

79. Lonergan, *Method,* p. 6.

80. See Michael Polanyi, *Personal Knowledge,* for the complementary distinction between *dwelling in* and *breaking out* of a framework of inherited concepts.

81. Lonergan, *Insight,* p. ix.

82. Lonergan, *Method,* p. 17; *Insight,* pp. 319-32.

83. Lonergan, *Insight,* pp. xii-xiii.

84. Lonergan, *Second Collection,* p. 268.

85. For the concept of a generalized empirical method applicable to both sensible data and the experiential data of prereflexive consciousness, see *Insight,* pp. 72 and 243.

86. For the Thomist origin of the distinction between the intelligible form and the abstract universal concept, between the *species quae* and the *species in qua,* see Lonergan, *Verbum: Word and Idea in Aquinas.*

87. Lonergan, *Insight,* p. 6.

88. For the complementarity of common sense and theoretical inquiry, see *Insight,* pp. 173-81; for the complementarity of theoretical heuristic anticipations, see *Insight,* p. 485. For the complementarity of the four realms of meaning, see *Method,* pp. 81-85.

89. For the critical differences among objective, formative, and apprenhensive abstraction, see *Verbum,* pp. 140-81. Also, see the concept of enriching abstraction in *Insight,* pp. 25-32.

90. Lonergan used one formulation rather than another depending on the context of analysis and the intended audience for whom the distinction was emphasized.

90. In particular, see the remarks on *experiential objectivity* in *Insight,* pp. 381-83.

92. For a comprehensive treatment of reflective understanding, see *Insight,* pp. 279-316; for the general form of reflective insight, pp. 280-81.

93. Ibid.

94. Ibid., pp. 284-87.

95. This summary is an attempt to consolidate Lonergan's discoveries in cognitional theory. For his own parallel formulation of Aquinas' cognitional discoveries, see *Verbum,* pp. 141-42.

96. For a critique of conceptualism—the recognition of abstract concepts but the neglect of their intentional source in insights, see *Verbum,* pp. 142-89 and *The Subject,* pp. 8-12.

97. For its applications to mathematics, theoretical science, common sense, and philosophy, see *Insight.* For its extension into theological methodology, see *Method.*

98. *Insight,* pp. 173-81; *Method,* pp. 81-96.

99. *Insight,* pp. 484-85; *Collection,* "The Isomorphism of Thomist and Scientific Thought," pp. 142-51.

100. *Insight,* pp. 79-83.

101. Quine, Dewey, Rorty, and the pragmatic tradition generally, emphasized the continuity between common sense and explanatory science; Sellars, following the line adopted by Descartes and Galileo, argued for an irreconcilable tension between the manifest and the scientific images of man and nature.

102. For an introduction to the notions of heuristic anticipation and heuristic structures, see *Insight,* pp. 32-46.

103. Although Socrates does not provide Meno with an intensional definition of *virtue, arete,* he does explain to him the properties required of any good intensional definition: It must apply to *all* objects that fall under the concept in question and it must apply *only* to those objects.

104. See *Metaphysics,* Book 1, Chapter 1; and *Physics,* Book 1, Chapter 1.

105. *Insight,* p. 485, summarizes the results of five earlier chapters: Chapters 2, 4, 7, 14, and 15.

106. Ibid.

107. See Patrick Heelan, "The Logic of Framework Transpositions," in *Language, Truth and Meaning,* ed. P. McShane, (Notre Dame, Indiana: University of Notre Dame Press, 1972) pp. 99-111; also see *Insight,* p. 737.

108. For the contrast between descriptive and explanatory categories, see Sellars, *Science, Perception and Reality,* pp. 26-28; for the contrast between the extensional nature of factual discourse and the intensional nature of metalinguistic discourse, see *Science and Metaphysics,* Chapters 3, 4, and 5.

109. See Heelan, "The Logic of Framework Transpositions."

110. *Insight,* p. 530.

111. For the elaboration of this principle and its use in philosophical criticism, see ibid., Chapter 14, "The Method of Metaphysics."

112. See ibid., pp. xx-xxi; 319-47.

113. Ibid., p. xii-xiii.

114. Ibid., Chapters 12 and 13; "Cognitional Structure," *Collection,* pp. 221-39.

115. *Insight,* pp. 336-39.

116. Lonergan, *Second Collection,* pp. 121 and 249.

117. *Insight,* p. 391.

118. The technical metaphysical term for what we know through the cognitional cycle of experience, understanding, and judgment is *proportionate being.*

119. *Insight,* pp. 431-37.

120. Ibid., p. 508.

121. Ibid., pp. 524-25.

VIII. Philosophical and Cultural Conflict

1. Lonergan based his approach to philosophical conflict on the dialectical practice of Aristotle and Aquinas. Bernard Lonergan, *Verbum: Word and Idea in Aquinas,* p. 38.

2. Alfred North Whitehead, *Science and the Modern World* (New York: Macmillan, 1925), p. 258.

3. Alasdair MacIntyre, *After Virtue* (Notre Dame, Ind.: University of Notre Dame Press, 1981), pp. 8-11.

4. For examples of this expository and pedagogical strategy, see Aristotle's *Physics, De Anima, Metaphysics,* and *Ethics.*

5. For a more detailed and expansive account of Rorty's project, see Chapter VI, Section H, "From Epistemology to Hermeneutics."

6. Lonergan developed the concept of dialectical criticism in *Insight,* pp. 242-44 and applied it to specific philosophical theories later in the same text, pp. 385-430.

7. In both the *Meno* and the *Republic,* Socrates draws a fundamental distinction between opinion *(doxa)* and knowledge *(episteme).*

8. Rorty, *The Linguistic Turn,* p. 39.

9. Lonergan, *Insight, pp. 250-54.*

10. Ibid., pp. 385-90.

11. Lonergan, *Collection,* p. 224; and *Second Collection,* pp. 73-75.

12. *Insight,* p. xii.

13. Ibid., pp. 387-90.

14. Ibid., pp. 385-87.

15. Unpublished notes of B. Lonergan.

16. *Insight,* pp. 348-52.

17. *Collection,* pp. 222-24.

18. *A Second Collection,* p. 172.

19. Ibid., pp. 79-81.

20. Ibid., p. 220; *A Third Collection,* p. 57.

21. *Insight,* pp. 73-74.

22. Ibid., pp. 467-73.

23. For a more detailed account of the parallels between direct and reflective insight, see Chapter VII, Section G.

24. Lonergan, *Method,* p. 316.

25. Ibid., p. xi.

26. *Insight,* p. 416.

27. See Chapter VI, Section F.

28. In *The Human Condition,* Hannah Arendt shows to what extent the concept of *homo faber* dominated the early modern conception of knowledge.

29. Hans Blumenberg, *The Legitimacy of the Modern Age* (Cambridge, Mass.: MIT Press, 1983), p. 220.

30. Lonergan, *Second Collection,* p. 70.

31. For the purpose of expository simplicity, I have not drawn the necessary distinctions between the pure categories and principles of the understanding and the transcendental schemata.

32. Kant, *Critique of Pure Reason,* A, 19; B, 33. For Lonergan's critique of Kant's excessive reliance on *Anschauung,* see *Collection,* p. 208.

33. Lonergan, *Collection,* p. 216.

34. *Second Collection,* p. 123.

35. *Insight,* p. 414.

36. *Second Collection,* pp. 78-79.

37. *Method,* p. 263.

38. *Second Collection,* p. 31.

39. Ibid., pp. 124-25.

40. *Insight,* p. 366.

41. Ibid., pp. 280-83.

42. Ibid., p. 414.

43. Lonergan elaborated the distinction between intellectualism and conceptualism in *Verbum,* pp. 151-56, 184-89.

44. Ibid., pp. 9-10.

45. Ibid., p. 26.

46. *Second Collection,* pp. 74-75.

47. Ibid.; and *Verbum,* pp. 210-13.

48. *Second Collection*, p. 76; *Method*, pp. 35-38.

49. *Insight*, p. 268.

50. Ibid., pp. 250-54.

51. Ibid., p. 385.

52. Ibid., p. 251; *Second Collection*, p. 219.

53. The concept of the "God's eye view" plays an important contrastive role in the epistemologies of Descartes and Kant and in the Kantian-inspired internal realism of Hilary Putnam.

54. Rorty, *Consequences of Pragmatism*, (Minneapolis, Minn.: University of Minnesota Press, 1982), pp. 3-18.

55. *Second Collection*, p. 123.

56. *Collection*, p. 228.

57. Ibid., p. 229.

58. Ibid., p. 230.

59. Ibid.; *Insight*, pp. 375-84.

60. *Insight*, pp. 274-81, 323-32, 549.

61. See Chapter II, Sections F and G; *Insight*, pp. 549-50.

62. *Insight*, p. 707.

63. *Second Collection*, p. 70.

64. *Collection*, pp. 160-61; *Insight*, pp. 500-502.

65. See Chapter I, Section B.

66. *Insight*, pp. 299-304.

67. Ibid., pp. 334-35.

68. "But if empirical science is no more than probable, still it truly is probable. If it does not attain definitive truth, still it converges upon truth. This convergence, this increasing approximation, is what is meant by the familiar phrase, the advance of science." *Insight*, p. 303.

69. *Second Collection*, p. 123.

70. *Collection*, p. 176.

71. *Insight*, pp. 431-37.

72. *Collection*, p. 245.

73. *Second Collection*, p. 233.

74. *Masters of suspicion* is Ricoeur's description of Marx, Nietzsche, and Freud. See *Freud and Philosophy: An Essay on Interpretation* (New Haven, Conn.: Yale University Press, 1970).

75. Lonergan, *Third Collection*, p. 6.

76. For Rorty's distinction between philosophy and *Philosophy*, see the introductory essay in *Consequences of Pragmatism*.

77. Hans-Georg Gadamer, *Truth and Method* (London: Sheed and Ward, 1975), pp. 232-74.

78. Lonergan, *Third Collection*, p. 156.

79. Lonergan invoked this Latin motto of Pope Leo XIII to characterize his theoretical and cultural project. *Verbum*, p. 220; *Insight*, p. 747.

80. The distinction appears in Whitehead's *Adventures of Ideas* (New York: Macmillan, 1933), but I have been unable to find the precise citation.

81. This is Michael Polanyi's way of referring to our complex involvement in

the scientific, cultural and religious frameworks to which we belong. Michael Polanyi, *Personal Knowledge,* pp. 195-202.

82. Paul Ricoeur sketched a model of this dialectic in his essay on Gadamer and Habermas, "Hermeneutics and Critique of Ideology." The essay is reprinted in *Paul Ricoeur, Hermeneutics and the Human Sciences,* ed. John Thompson (New York: Cambridge University Press, 1981), pp. 63-101.

83. Lonergan, *Third Collection,* p. 122.

84. For a survey of the most obstructive forms of human bias, see *Insight,* pp. 217-42.

85. Lonergan, *Collection,* p. 246.

86. The distinction belongs to Ricoeur. It is one way of expressing the contrast between the Romantic and the Enlightenment approaches to tradition.

87. Lonergan, *Third Collection,* p. 196.

88. In the critical essays in *Between Past and Future,* Hannah Arendt charged that our tradition of political thought has failed us in all of these ways.

89. MacIntyre, *After Virtue,* p. 207.

90. Ibid., pp. 137-53.

91. *Paul Ricoeur, Hermeneutics and the Human Sciences,* p. 246.

92. Lonergan, *Collection,* p. 167.

93. *Second Collection,* p. 29.

94. St. Paul, Epistle to the Romans, 1:23.

95. Alexis de Tocqueville, *Democracy in America* [1840] (New York: Vintage Books, 1960), vol. 2, p. 93.

Name Index

Subject Index